THE INTERNATIONAL CIVIL SERVICE

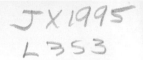
THE INTERNATIONAL CIVIL SERVICE

ITS ORIGINS, ITS NATURE, ITS EVOLUTION

by

GEORGES LANGROD

Preface by

PAUL GUGGENHEIM

*Professor at the Faculty of Law of Geneva University and
at the Graduate Institute of International Studies, Geneva
President of the World Federation
of United Nations Associations*

A. W. SYTHOFF – LEYDEN
OCEANA PUBLICATIONS, INC. – DOBBS FERRY, N.Y.
1963

Original title:
LA FONCTION PUBLIQUE INTERNATIONALE
Translated by F. G. Berthoud

On the wrapper:
United Nations Headquarters Building
(Courtesy of the United Nations)

LIBRARY OF CONGRESS
CATALOG CARD NUMBER: 63-22349

PREFACE

As President of the World Federation of United Nations Associations, I have been asked to introduce to the reader Mr. Georges Langrod's work on the international civil service. In responding to this request, I shall not attempt to discuss the technical aspect of the book, since no such introduction is necessary. Its high qualities are self-evident, as indeed we should expect from the well-known competence of its distinguished author. Any such commentary on my part being therefore superfluous, I shall confine myself to a few general observations which occured to my mind as I read this important monograph.

A study of the evolution of the international civil service shows that its role is still expanding, although its growth goes almost unnoticed by the general public and although there are no apparent changes in the legal status of international officials. It is hard to discern the underlying causes of this expansion. It is certainly based on the invariable and permanent elements which Mr. Langrod has strikingly described in his final chapter. The international organization has shown itself indispensable as a centre for contacts, negotiations and compromise between divergent interests; and the permanent officials with specialized knowledge of certain questions, and with experience of multilateral diplomacy, are better equipped for certain international work than are the traditional diplomats. This is what Mr. Langrod has felicitously called the "institutionalization" of international co-operation. The international civil service has grown, not only in size and complexity, but in fundamental unity, and the result is a remarkable *esprit de corps*.

But, as Professor Langrod points out, this metamorphosis of public service in the international organizations is not without its drawbacks. These are of two kinds. The first resides in the usual difficulty encountered by every bureaucracy and technocracy: professionalization naturally brings with it a state of mind which is easily satisfied with technical efficiency and shuns the new responsibilities imposed by the expansion of the international organization. Secondly, as a further consequence of the same unadventurous spirit, the administration submits to the control of those with power in the international world, accepting interference too meekly, even though that interference is sometimes due not to the constant and permanent forces of contemporary history, but to the action of certain governments.

Mr. Langrod is right, therefore, to insist on the decisive part played by the head of the international administration. His personal authority not only inspires and directs the action of his subordinates, but also imposes itself on governments. It is he who stands for the institution in the eyes of the world, who must give it a sense of mission and yet must keep its activities within the bounds of its constitution. His action is not only administrative, but political. Mr. Langrod was therefore right to give us a portrait of some of these great chiefs, contrasting, for instance, the accomplished diplomat, Sir Eric Drummond, with the fighting social reformer, Albert Thomas.

In times of crisis, it is the chief's personality which gives the international organization its unity and its distinctive character, independently of the States of which it is composed, and which, too often, would like to reduce it to a "clearing house" without responsibility of its own. Of course, the chief may, and often does, seek advice from knowledgeable colleagues, who are also in touch with their home countries and so are able to keep him informed of world political currents. But it is not by accepting collective responsibility that a man like Dag Hammarskjöld could have carried so many enterprises through to success.

I hope that this book, the product of wide research and deep knowledge, for which we are indebted to Mr. Langrod, will contribute to a fuller understanding of the machinery and needs of the international organization, whose sphere of action is growing every day, and whose future is assured only if it develops according to its own rules and in its proper environment.

February 1963 PAUL GUGGENHEIM

EXPLANATORY NOTE

The idea of producing a book dealing with the origins, the nature and the evolution of the international civil service first arose at the end of November 1960, during a conversation between Dag Hammarskjöld and the present writer.

Despite the abundance of the literature on this subject, to say nothing of the official documentation, particularly since the time when the creation of the League of Nations and the International Labour Office began to interest specialists on international law and political science, no up-to-date work giving a comprehensive survey of the new phenomena constituted by the international administration and the international civil service has yet made its appearance.

Accordingly, the World Federation of United Nations Associations at Geneva, true to one of its aims—namely, "to promote research, information and education about the principles, activities and potentialities of the United Nations" ª—decided to publish under its auspices a book which, without claiming to deal with the subject in all its details, nevertheless endeavours to bring out its main outlines and essential problems.

In carrying out this project, the Federation had the benefit of the assistance of Mr. John D. Rockefeller III of New York, who for a short time (in the summer of 1928) was a member of the Secretariat of the League of Nations. It is thanks to this initial encouragement that the Federation has been able to undertake the publication of the present work.

Professor Georges Langrod, Director of Research at the Centre national de la Recherche scientifique in Paris, agreed to undertake the planning and writing of the present work. Miss Krystina Marek, research assistant at the Graduate Institute of International Studies at Geneva, gave him valuable help in checking the numerous sources of information. The Federation is extremely grateful to the author and his assistant for the care with which they have performed their task, which, owing to the complexity of the subject, called for particularly detailed research and a constant comparison of theory and practice.

(a) Constitution of WFUNA (article 1 (a), paragraph 6).

The Federation, although the initiator of this work, leaves full responsibility for its contents to the author, who has accepted this responsibility.

A. Pelt

Secretary-General of the
World Federation of United
Nations Associations

TABLE OF CONTENTS

Part III: Its Evolution

Part IV: Final Considerations

SOME TERMINOLOGICAL OBSERVATIONS
BY THE AUTHOR

ADMINISTRATION[a]

The term "Administration" is very difficult to define, since it is currently used in a number of different ways, not only by theorists, but in the practice of the various state systems and of the international organizations. These differences lead to unfortunate semantic confusion. We must therefore give the reader, as briefly as possible, an idea of the sense in which the term is used in the present work.

I

Theorists generally use the term "Administration" in a functional sense to designate a specific type of activity. According to this common usage, it refers to a certain form of public action—namely, the conduct of affairs to be performed for a social purpose, by particular means. It therefore contains two elements: the *aim* pursued (satisfaction of a social need); and the *means* (employment by a public body of a group of persons—public officials—and of material—public property).

But the same term is also frequently used in an organic sense to designate collectively the *staff* who "administer" and who form for that purpose an organization. Here the term no longer refers to a type of action, but to a human group or institution entrusted with a given task.

The term being habitually employed in relation to the State and its subsidiaries, the "administrators" are contrasted on the one hand with the other public authorities (legislature, judicature) and on the other hand with the private individuals who benefit from the "administrative" services. Thus, in the State we find other public activities side by side with administrative action, which, of course, is not the only method of performing public tasks, and other branches of governmental authority; the symmetry between these branches and the Administration constitutes the *differentia specifica*. Lastly, the

---

(a) We refer here to *public* administration only, even if the explanatory adjective is omitted, as frequently happens in common usage. The difference of meaning compared with private administration (management of affairs) is sometimes indicated by the use of a capital initial in the first case. The use of the plural ("administrations") refers to administrative organs in general, even if they consist of a number of separate institutions and are highly specialized.

activity of private persons—"administrees"—remains separate, though it may be parallel, and may have the same object although the methods may be different (authoritarian procedures).[a]

II

In practical usage the difficulties are perhaps still greater, not so much for purely linguistic reasons as because of the specific characteristics of the different state systems and administrative régimes.

(a) Thus in the United States of America—and under its influence in several other countries—the term "Administration" is chiefly used to designate the President in the exercise of his *executive* power (or simply the Executive: "Executive branch of government"). For example, the expression "Roosevelt Administration" refers to a particular Chief Executive and to the branch of "government" of which he was the head. This is therefore an organic use of the term. It also refers to the period or term during which he held office.

But this use is not exclusive. In the U.S.A., the term "administration" is also sometimes applied to the branches of the Federal Administration as a whole, thus distinguishing the Federal Administration from the other federal authorities and from the administrations of the states of the Union. Moreover, certain units of the Federal Administration use the word "Administration" in their titles, and it is then synonymous with "bureau" or "office." Examples are the P.W.A. (Public Works Administration), the W.P.A. (Works Progress Administration), or, among the outside agencies, the Veterans' Administration set up in 1930. Similarly we find subdivisions of the federal "ministerial" departments called by this name—for example, in the Department of Agriculture, the Agricultural Research Administration, the Farm Credit Administration, the Production Marketing Administration. Further, the federal institution which deals with bilateral technical and financial assistance to developing countries was called the "International Cooperation Administration." The various meanings of this term in the U.S.A. must be borne in mind in order to avoid terminological confusion.

(b) In Great Britain[b] the term "Administration" generally designates a sector of public action which must be distinguished from the judiciary and the legislative[c] or more specifically a function exer-

(a) In the United States of America for example, the term "public administration" is used to designate a branch of scientific research (synonym of "science of administration" or "administrative science").

(b) The term "United Kingdom" is used in official texts, but we have usually employed the term Great Britain in the present work.

(c) Thus S. A. de Smith (*Judicial Review of Administrative Action*, London, 1959, p. 31) writes: "the term 'administrative' is capable of bearing a wide range of meanings, some of which are remote from the problems raised by the classification of statutory functions. In such phrases as 'administrative law', 'administrative

cised by public agents assuming responsibilities of authority and supervision. Thus, according to the British terminology, there can be no question of identifying the "administrative" and the "executive." In the British Civil Service the highest category of officials is described as the "administrative grade" while officials of medium rank are of "executive grade." There is therefore here a marked difference between the British and the United States terminology. The former is used in several state systems which follow the British model.

(c) In France the term "Administration" is used as much in the functional as in the organic sense. The "Executive" being one of the three great branches of state power, administration in the sense of action is not the sole task of the Executive (which has several others, particularly the maintenance of constitutional relations between the Government and Parliament),[a] but no other branch of authority is in theory responsible for administration. The duties of the *public services* are to keep order (police) and to provide public facilities.

III

For over a century there has been talk of an "*international* administration," and there is a whole literature on the subject. But the exact signification of the term in the theory and practice of international organizations remains very confused, and here again it is used in different senses.

Thus, the Preparatory Commission of the United Nations, meeting in London in 1945, used the terms "Administration" and "executive" without indicating their respective meanings and, in particular, without defining the word "Administration."

In the United Nations family there is a tendency, when approaching the problem "*from outside*," to identify the whole "Secretariat" with the "Administration." This is particularly the case in the relations between each organization and the members of its staff (for example, in connection with the staff union, or in disputes between officials and the organization). This derives from the use of the term accepted in the United States of America.

But in approaching the same problem "*from within*"—i.e., in relation to the organization's structure and internal set-up, it is usual to confine the term "Administration"—conceived not in an organic, but in a functional sense—to a part of the Secretariat. Here, "administration" refers to the activities of the Office of Personnel (i.e., questions concerning the staff of the Secretariat, including outlying units) and the Office of the Controller (i.e., all financial questions). In other

tribunal' and 'judicial review of administrative action, it refers to broad areas of governmental activity in which the repositories of power may exercise every class of statutory function. We need not dwell upon these usages...."
(a) Cf. for example G. Vedel, *Droit administratif* (2nd edition, Paris, 1961, p. 17 ff.)

cases this functional notion takes on an organic aspect: thus the Staff Committee negotiates with the "Administration" on salaries—that is to say with one or both of the two departments mentioned above. At the same time, these two offices of the U.N. Secretariat, and the similar departments in the specialized agencies, tend to regard themselves as responsible for "administration," the rest of the staff and all the other units in the Secretariat being regarded as "users" of their services. This idea is reflected both in the reports of the Secretariat and in the Advisory Committee on Administrative and Budgetary Questions and the Fifth Committee of the General Assembly.

The international organizations, unlike the national administrations, have no *government* placed outside and above the "administration" and they have no private *users* (at least in theory).[a] That is self-evident, since the representative organs of the international organizations express their majority collective opinions in the form of resolutions, which in most cases are only recommendations to the governments of the Member States. The Secretariat's role is then simply to transmit the resolutions to the proper quarter without having to apply them. In an association of States, there is neither a "government" nor persons "governed," and the idea of "users," in the usual sense of the term, does not arise.

Nevertheless, the representative organs may adopt resolutions which relate to the internal life of the organization and which then assume the character of semi-legislative rules. The head of the Secretariat may also be entrusted with measures to be taken outside the organization (preparation and supervision of a plebiscite, international use of military contingents)—subject, of course, to the condition that the States are ready to accept them. In this case, various special devices are used which to some extent fill the "authority vacuum," and enable the Secretariat to carry out its "operational" tasks. In certain specialized agencies small governing bodies—within the framework of the "Assembly system" in general international use—act as intermediaries between the periodical conferences of government representatives and the "executives" in the Secretariat. It should also be noted that in the "general" international organizations, the head of the secretariat tends to function as a sort of embryonic "executive."

There are exceptional cases where persons "administered" by the international organization are outside that organization—for example,

---

(a) There are other differences which we need not go into here. Suffice it to say that the "Assembly" is not a legislative authority in the true sense of the term, since it has no power to conclude treaties—which replace "laws" in the international sphere and since its members do not possess any individual authority, but are simply representatives of the governments of the States Members carrying out the instructions they have received.

in the case of narcotics control by the U.N. and epidemics control by W.H.O. Here the organizations are in contact with private "administrees" comparable to the users of national public services.

In spite of these exceptions, we may ask ourselves whether it is possible to speak of an international "Administration."

IV

An affirmative reply may be given for the following reasons: first, there is absolute identity of purpose between the international and the national administrations. Both exist to satisfy collective needs of a social character, recognized as imperatively demanding the intervention of public organs. National and international needs differ, but that does not matter; an administration, by definition, exists to satisfy *any need* which may arise in society and which is of sufficient public interest to justify public action.

Secondly, as regards method, the situation is similar. In both cases, an organized body of men and materials must be used in order to release the social energy necessary to fulfil a public need. Both national and international administrations consist of career officials connected with one another by vertical and horizontal links. They are a unit, capable of acting in co-ordination, subject to uniform and independent control and subordinate to the policy-making authorities. Any public administration is permanent machinery with a co-ordinating function and acting according to a specific scale of values. Continuity, impartiality and anonymity are essential, as also are vigour and discipline within the hierarchy. Though the relationship between "public authority" and private initiative is not the same in an international as in a national administration, the fact remains that in both cases we are concerned with public services, comparable with one another.

We therefore approach the international secretariat as an "administrative undertaking" in conformity with the western model of the national civil service, which is considered as a triumph of civilization and as characteristic of the "administrative period" of cultural development.[a] Clearly the international administration will usually employ techniques and procedures similar to those of any other public administration. Occasionally we meet an "administrative phenomenon" which combines all the factors which we have mentioned. Occasionally the same general (universally applicable) rules apply, particularly as regards personnel, internal communications and outside relations.

We can adopt a narrow point of view and accentuate the administrative character of "supporting services" (personnel, finance)— known in the United States as auxiliary services—and consider that

(a) A. Siegfried, *Technique et culture dans la civilisation moderne* (Paris, 1948, p. 17).

the other services which directly carry out the organization's programme are primarily *users* or beneficiaries of the former; in other words, are "administered." This interpretation corresponds best to the present stage of evolution of the international secretariats. On the other hand, we can follow the Bruce report of 1939 *(ut infra)* and take the broader view of an administration, by including in it all public services without differentiating between "administrator" and "administered."

It is in this last sense that the United Nations experts, reporting in 1962 on public administration in the United Nations and specialized agencies, observe:

> The total public administration of a country is not just the equivalent of the sum of all its parts. It is the common trunk which sustains and nourishes the many branches which are the individual disciplines. It provides the structural and procedural framework to bring forth, energize and harmonize the entire network of special services which the modern State needs in the implementation of the decade of development. The same applies in the international world, and an intensified activity in the public administration field requires a growing co-operation of all the agencies which comprise the United Nations family.[a]

It is in this sense (but without forgetting the other possible meanings) that the author uses the term in this work (cf. in particular chapter 3). International administration is not an end in itself, but a series of methods; it is not governed by empirical improvisation, but by basic principles which are part of "administrative science"; it is not a new achievement, but an adjustment of old, well-known conceptions, built on experience, to the sphere of international co-operation. These are the conditions on which its "institutionalization" depends.

EXECUTIVE [b]

This word is not to be found in the constitutions and regulations of the international organizations, although it appeared in certain preparatory texts. It is sometimes used as meaning "executor," sometimes as a synonym for "Administration" as distinct from policy-making organs.

We propose to employ the term "executor" to denote a person who performs a task, usually in the material sense. We reserve the term "Executive" to refer to "the executive power," according to the habitual usage of countries where there is a separation of powers, particularly the United States of America.

(a) Doc. E/3630 of 7 May 1962, paragraph 241 (cf. also resolution 796 (XXX) of the Economic and Social Council).
(b) To be compared with the explanation of the term "Administration."

INTERNATIONAL CIVIL SERVANT

This applies to the members of the staff of an international secretariat, whether permanent or temporary (as opposed to consultants with limited duties).

GENERAL INTERNATIONAL ORGANIZATION

This expression [a] relates to a multipurpose international organization of an essentially political character, as opposed to specialized organizations of a mainly technical character. Thus, in the United Nations family the U.N. is an example of the first term, W.H.O. or the U.P.U. of the second. The category to which UNESCO belongs is a matter of doubt, despite its legal status as a specialized agency. Its multiple aims put it in the first category, its non-political character in the second. Generally speaking, the first category includes the "major organizations," the second the "small" or "medium-sized" ones.

SECRETARIAT [b]

In view of the origins of the use of this term in international organizations (cf. below, chapter 1, p. 34), we use it in the sense of the "Administration" of the organization concerned.

SECRETARY-GENERAL

This refers to the head of the "secretariat," whatever the official title used in the international organization concerned ("Secretary-General" or "Director-General").

(a) Cf. declaration by the Big Four at Moscow on 30 October 1943.
(b) To be compared with the explanation of the term "Administration."

LIST OF ABBREVIATIONS

ACC	Administrative Committee on Co-ordination
ADI	Hague Academy of International Law
CERN	European Organization for Nuclear Research
ECOSOC	Economic and Social Council
ECSC	European Coal and Steel Community
FAO	Food and Agriculture Organization of the United Nations
FBI	Federal Bureau of Investigation (U.S.A.)
FICSA	Federation of International Civil Servants' Associations
GATT	General Agreement on Tariffs and Trade
IAEA	International Atomic Energy Agency
ICAO	International Civil Aviation Organization
ICEM	Intergovernmental Committee for European Migration
ICJ	International Court of Justice
ICSAB	International Civil Service Advisory Board
IIA	International Institute of Agriculture
ILO	International Labour Organisation (Office)
IMCO	Inter-governmental Maritime Consultative Organization
IRO	International Refugee Organization
L. of N.	League of Nations
NGO	Non-Governmental Organization
O & M	Organization and Methods
OAS	Organization of American States
ONUC	United Nations Organization in the Congo
OPEX	Programme for the Provision of Operational, Executive and Administrative Personnel
PASO	Pan-American Sanitary Organization
PCIJ	Permanent Court of International Justice
POSDCORB	Planning, organization, staff, direction, co-ordination, reports, budget.
SUNFED	Special United Nations Fund for Economic Development
TAA	Technical Assistance Administration of the United Nations
TAB	Technical Assistance Board
TAC	Technical Assistance Committee
UN	United Nations

UNEF	United Nations Emergency Force
UNESCO	United Nations Educational, Scientific and Cultural Organization
UNICEF	United Nations Children's Fund
UNKRA	United Nations Korean Reconstruction Agency
UNPWA	United Nations Relief and Works Agency for Palestine Refugees in the Near East
UNRRA	United Nations Relief and Rehabilitation Administration
UNTSO	United Nations Supervision Organization in Palestine
UPU	Universal Postal Union
USSR	Union of Soviet Socialist Republics
WFUNA	World Federation of United Nations Associations
WHO	World Health Organization
WMO	World Meteorological Organization

INTRODUCTION

The object of this work is to introduce the perceptive reader to the world of the universal international organizations considered from the administrative angle. We propose more particularly to describe, briefly, but as completely as possible, the genesis, the nature and the evolution of the *international civil service*.

Despite its comparative youth, this phenomenon has given rise to an abundant literature in every language: different aspects of the problem (legal position, recruitment and its methods, geographical distribution of posts, duration and legal basis of appointments, privileges and immunities, training and improvement, morale of officials, etc.) have been analysed in detail. But what seems to be lacking is an over-all view aimed at clarifying and defining the conception of the *international administration* to which the idea of the international civil service is closely linked. The administrative aspect of international co-operation tends to be overshadowed by the diplomatic and ideological struggles which occupy the forefront of the international scene and apparently monopolize it. Consequently, the scope of international administrative action is underestimated, though it plays an ever larger part in international relations today. "It modifies international relations in depth, and in the long run will perhaps have a greater effect than any other form of action."[a] The institutional reinforcement and quantitative growth of the international organizations—whether universal or regional, permanent or temporary, general or specialized—in relation to the aggravation of their responsibilities on the economic, social, cultural, communications and transport, public health and other planes—make them real public services on a large scale and embracing the whole world. Their importance is still growing *pari passu* with the interdependence of the modern world. The work thus accomplished, or in process of accomplishment, cannot be neglected by anyone wishing to understand the true tendencies of our epoch.

Though achievements in this sphere far exceed the boldest anticipations, ideas seem to have lagged behind. Surprising though it is, "in looking at this impressive network of (international) organizations... it is impossible to fail to detect a certain poverty of concep-

(a) M. Virally, *L'O.N.U. d'hier à demain*, (Paris, 1961, p. 12).

tion," says Clive Parry.[a] Analogies are sought in state institutions; out-of-date ideas are repeated; and there is an unfortunate lack of firmly established guiding lines. Thus, practical institutional development is ahead of the development of thought: man finds himself intellectually at sea in the face of phenomena which correspond to genuine needs and are already in practical effect, but fit in ill with traditional mental habits. Even a global ideological vision of international co-operation and of the indispensable solidarity of the peoples of the world is not sufficient *in itself* to enable the methods of action and the resources available to be apprehended. Hence, misunderstandings and repeated crises behind which, independently of the events which directly provoke them, we always find the same principal cause—the absence of a definite conception which is generally understood. Man, who claims to be master of his own destiny and believes that he has succeeded in domesticating nature, who has split the atom and is launching into the conquest of space, continues to be ignorant of the very foundations of international life: he cannot see the wood for the trees. The complications continually created by rivalry and competition between States, the need to resort to temporary expedients to mitigate destructive and centrifugal forces, make it difficult to obtain a comprehensive view and prevent the establishment of a genuine body of logical and constructive doctrine. That is the reason for the constant paradoxes and repeated contradictions which would merely seem absurd if one did not know how irrational are the forces which govern our social relations.

"A visitor from Mars might be greatly impressed by the degree of Earthman control over nature—on the assumption of course that Martians had not equalled our scientific achievements. But if he were a rational human being, he would be greatly puzzled by the inadequacy of our political and social institutions and concepts for dealing with the problems which have been created by our scientific advances. If we think in terms of our knowledge of the earth, the extent to which we are technically capable of developing its resources to meet human needs, the facility and speed with which people can travel and communicate with each other, and the number of our common concerns, Wendell Willkie's *One World* makes a great deal of sense. It seems to describe quite accurately the fact of human involvement and the limits of the common concerns of mankind. But if we look at the political and social arrangements under which people live together and seek to deal with their common affairs, "One World" ceases to be a reality and becomes a myth, or at best a goal to be realized in the distant future."[b]

We must therefore draw the rational conclusions from the obvious unity of the human family. A realistic theory of international administration is particularly important in order to place the international

(a) "The International Public Corporation", in *The Public Corporation. A Comparative Symposium*, (W. Friedmann, publisher, Toronto, 1954, p. 537).
(b) L. M. Goodrich, *The United Nations*, (London, 1960, p. 1).

civil servant in his true context and thus to facilitate an understanding of the "great change" which he foreshadows and personifies. In a divided world and in relation to an institution whose justification, principles and methods are continually being challenged, an approach *sine ira et studio* is clearly essential. But we do not propose here to describe the details systematically or to be content with legal or other formalism. The author intends to draw the reader's attention to the historic origins of the international administration—born of the pressure of events, gradually institutionalized and endowed with a competent staff. In the course of a process of organic growth, the successive stages of which will be observed, the staff, at first "borrowed," temporary and enjoying no particular status, has become stabilized, has increased in numbers and has constituted a new *human category* which must be analysed owing to its originality in relation to the past and to the permanent role which it is bound to play on the international scene. In the eyes of a superficial and uninformed observer, he may and often does appear as a paradoxical and hybrid creation, a strange creature half national, half international, and ill adapted to the contemporary reality of inter-State relations.

> Inter-State relations are expressed in and through certain activities, activities of persons whom I shall call symbolic, the diplomat and the soldier. Two men, and only two, act, no longer as ordinary members of their community, but as its representatives. The ambassador in the exercise of his functions *is* the political unit in whose name he speaks; the soldier on the field of battle *is* the political unit in whose name he kills his fellow man.... The ambassador and the soldier embody and symbolize the international relations which, between States, are simply diplomacy and war.[a]

Nevertheless, in this "theatre of nations", on the stage where in theory there is room only for these "representatives" of States, a third person has appeared who by definition is neither a protagonist nor a referee, who, by virtue of constitutional provisions in force, "represents" no one, who thus occupies a special place without precedent in history. He must work in the common interest, rising above all particularism, but respecting the values which each people contributes to humanity. Neither a diplomat nor a soldier, but the personification of world solidarity, the international civil servant, if he is indeed impartial, occupies a strategic position of the highest importance in a pluralist world whose mentality is governed by, and tends towards, force. He symbolizes the breach with the methods of the past, and by his very existence opposes anarchy between nations, since his function is to introduce elements of order and stability among them. Called upon to some extent to play the diplomatic game (particularly that of "preventive diplomacy"), his contribution is to provide the adminis-

(a) R. Aron, *Paix et guerre entre les nations*, (Paris, 1962, pp. 17-18).

trative factor, characterized by continuity, and putting the permanent administration of common affairs at the service of the peace and security of all.

It is hardly surprising that with his universal objectives and his trans-national view of a united world, the protagonist of a persistently sought universalism seems in conflict with reality. The idea of a system freed from traditional ties, inasmuch as its creators and appliers place themselves intellectually on the plane of the general interest, is familiar from the works of many thinkers who have propounded and defended it in the course of centuries. But this notion was only a theory, both mystical and mythical. When theory becomes reality, the basis of thought must be adjusted if we are to acquire a true and clear vision of the present and the future. The product of reason in pursuit of a purpose—as Max Weber would say—the international civil service is the outcome of many compromises illustrated by its growth and necessary in order to adapt the work of creation to the shifting political forces which surround it. Hence, concessions, hesitations, setbacks, contradictions of all kinds. Hence, too, what appear to be insurmountable difficulties in achieving a homogeneous system. It is all the more important to raise the discussion to the level of principles in order to realize how far the tendency to accept compromise may go. While compromise is always admissible in secondary matters—relating to structure, organization, instruments, technique, etc.—it must never be allowed in matters of principle, lest the whole edifice be destroyed. Thus it has been said that there can be no compromise between partiality and impartiality; and this has been proved despite arguments, doubts and the mistrust even of enlightened opinion. As the British representative, Philip Noel-Baker, said at the twenty-first session of the Assembly of the League of Nations at Geneva in April 1946:

> ...I remember how one night in the Hotel Crillon Hymans expressed his doubts and fears. "I understand the Assembly," he said; "that is like the Conference at The Hague. I understand the Council; it is like the Concert of the Powers. But the Secretariat? How can men and women of forty different nations work together beneath a single roof? It will be not only a Tower of Babel, but a Bedlam too."
> ...Well, the Secretariat did it;...I am as proud of our British Civil Service as any man could be, but I can say with truth that in none of our departments did I find a higher standard of technical efficiency, a higher level of personal and official probity, a greater industry and devotion to their cause, than I found in the Secretariat as I knew it then....[a]

And, since that date, an enormous network of international administrations has grown up throughout the world and a gigantic task has been accomplished. Despite all defects due to "childhood ailments",

(a) Records of the Twenty-first Session of the Assembly of the League of Nations, April 1946, (League of Nations, *Official Journal, Special Supplement No. 194*).

to the novelty of the enterprise or to situations arising from basic and fatal compromises, the international civil service has developed quantitatively and qualitatively, has proved its potentialities and has justified its existence in the modern world. At the same time, its possibilities have become clearly apparent to all those who are able to see and to foresee:

> International organization is still in its infancy, the developments of the last generation are merely the precursors of more effective forms of international organization on a far more ambitious scale, and the law now being evolved by the rapid accumulation of precedent must therefore be sufficiently solid to support a more imposing superstructure than we can yet visualize. . . .[a]

In order to reach the essence of a phenomenon of such importance and such actuality, we therefore propose not to be content with appearances and not to accept current stereotypes. The only way to do this is to abandon the fragmentary approach and to present the international civil service from the angle of its growth. It may be hoped that a description of this dynamic evolution will help to correct the mistaken or superficial ideas which are entertained here and there with regard to international administrative action. Without writing a history of the subject, it is necessary to situate different individual problems within the general framework. This should make it possible to distinguish a pattern of events and tendencies, to give a rough diagnosis of the various ills from which the international administration suffers. At the same time, as certain authors have already proposed,[b] the phenomenon must be studied in the context of "administrative science", in order to emphasize the *administrative aspect* of international organization. In spite of the uneven development of this branch of social science in our time, it will thus be possible— thanks to a limited plan of work and to the choice of specific criteria— to avoid the traditional breaking up of the subject according to the various branches of specialized knowledge. As frequently happens when the subject of an analysis straddles more than one kind of research—in this case the field of international relations and that of administrative action proper—it is liable to be neglected because specialists in the two fields fail to give it the full attention which it deserves. At best, each approaches it from his own point of view,

(a) C. W. Jenks, *The Proper Law of International Organizations*, (London 1962, p. XXXVII).
(b) e. g. E. F. Ranshofen-Wertheimer, "*The International Secretariat. A Great Experiment in International Administration*, (Washington, 1945, p. 7 ff.); D. C. Stone, "Administrative Achievement in World Organization" in *Perspectives on a Troubled Decade: Science, Philosophy and Religion, 1939-1949. A. Symposium*, (New York, 1950, p. 425); E. Giraud, "Le Secrétariat des institutions internationales", (*Recueil des cours A. D. I.*, 1951, II, p. 373 ff.); T.C. Young, *International Civil Service: Principles and Problems*, (Brussels, 1958, pp. 16 and 231).

sometimes in a haphazard manner, and the already complicated picture is thus liable to be distorted.

It is not the author's ambition—nor is he able—to undertake here a complete analysis of this complex problem. He takes the liberty of referring the reader to his previous studies in which various aspects of the same problem have been discussed more exhaustively. He confines himself here to the oecumenical international organizations (those aiming at universality), and among them gives preference to those of general competence (non-specialized) and with multiple aims (League of Nations, United Nations). Only for purposes of comparison—particularly important in social science, in which opportunities for experiment are few—does he discuss the International Labour Office, the senior of the major specialized agencies and now a member of the United Nations family. At the same time, the author confines himself to the problems of the international civil service which he considers most important and characteristic. If he may be reproached with having made an arbitrary choice of topics, that is easily explained by the limited scope of the present work and by practical considerations. His object is to explain to the reader the questions which provoke the most misunderstandings and controversies, and to examine them from different angles, at the same time sketching the history of the various crises and their solutions. Obviously this does not mean that other questions or other international organizations do not deserve a full analysis, particularly the organizations not belonging to the United Nations family, or connected with the regional movement, which will inevitably influence all the international administrative structures in the long run. The author hopes that subsequent works, including his own, will supplement the considerations set forth in this book, by going into the details of the respective problems and enlarging and expanding the discussion.

The reader's attention is drawn to the urgency of bringing some semantic order to this subject, in which the drawbacks of a muddled or incorrect terminology are great. Some problems having been deliberately dealt with in the chronological account of the evolution of the international organizations, a subject index has been added at the end of the book to facilitate research. A few terminological problems of particular importance are dealt with for the reader's benefit on page 13. Lastly, the author draws the reader's attention to the bibliography (page 329).

It is the author's agreeable duty to thank all those who have been kind enough to suggest that he should write this book, to help him with their support and advice and to arrange for the appearance of this work in two languages simultaneously.

In the first place his thanks go to Professor Paul GUGGENHEIM and

Dr. Adrian PELT, respectively President and Secretary-General of the World Federation of United Nations Associations. Having realized the necessity of such a work, they spontaneously asked the author to write it and did all in their power to assist him in his task. The author thanks them very sincerely for their advice and help, which has been particularly valuable owing to their wide international experience. Dr. PELT has also been good enough to undertake to read the manuscript, and the author is extremely grateful for his valuable comments and the help of all kinds received during the preparation of the work. He wishes to make it clear, however, that he is solely responsible for its contents.

He also wishes to thank numerous specialists in the international organizations who have been good enough to help him by providing information on various individual points and by giving him valuable advice, based on their experience.

In this connection, the author wishes to express his special gratitude to Mr. BREYCHA-VAUTHIER, Librarian of the European Office of the United Nations at Geneva.

He also thanks Miss Krystyna MAREK, Research Assistant at the Graduate Institute of International Studies at Geneva, for her valuable help.

Lastly, the author wishes to say how greatly he is obliged to the staff of the Secretariat of the Federation, who undertook the typing of the French and English manuscripts and checked innumerable references.

Paris, February 1963   G. L.

The alphabetical references in the text refer the reader to footnotes. The references in the text bearing serial numbers refer the reader to notes given at the end of the chapter.

CHAPTER I

THE ANTECEDENTS

The phenomenon of international organization as we know it today did not appear suddenly in modern times. It is a stage—an important one, but by no means final or definitive—in a long historical process, characterized throughout the centuries (and even millennia) by the persistent search for equilibrium between States and by endeavours to secure a durable organization of this equilibrium. Thus, alliances—essentially temporary attempts at inter-State co-operation, directed in most cases against a common adversary—or "concerts"—more stable forms of continuous alliance and of concerted co-operation but not yet institutionalized in any way—were organized in particular geographical areas with certain common objectives.

A special technique of international relations has gradually developed in connection with numerous "associationist" experiments—conferences of plenipotentiaries, "peace" or other congresses, meetings between heads of States, etc. Did not Confucius in chapter 7 of the *Li-ki* say that "the perfect system of the law of nations is to constitute an international association [composed] of delegates chosen amongst the most virtuous and most capable citizens [in order] to apply international good faith and ensure the reign of concord between States"?[1] This idea of a "Great Union" is repeated by a whole series of thinkers in the course of history. As to practical achievements, we can trace the origins of such forms of collective inter-State action back to the most ancient times: regional agreements in the Middle East (Assyria-Babylon-Egypt) dating from some time between the middle of the second millennium and the middle of the first millennium before Christ; "amphictyons"—leagues of cities based on equality between partners in ancient Greece; the Etruscan "lucomons"; it would be easy to find comparable phenomena in other parts of the world at all times: political understanding, economic interdependence, cultural affinity, the determination to carry out certain undertakings by common agreement, have always promoted the formation of confederations or federations of States, unions of free cities, etc. Examples are the *Hanseatic League*, which in the thirteenth and fifteenth centuries constituted a very important commercial union (some writers speak of it as a "commercial State"—*Handelsstaat*), or the German customs union of 1854, formed by eighteen States with a population of twenty-three million inhabitants. By collaborating with one another and acting as a unit, small States have tried to escape from isolation, to gain strength through co-operation. By ensuring peace in a given geographical area, at least for a limited period, these forms of restricted international co-operation have also dealt with the consequences of economic and technical progress. The most obvious example is in communications—that of river transport and particularly navigation on international rivers. The European Commission of the Danube at the Congress of Paris in 1856 was referred to as a "river State"; in those days, whenever a public service embraced several countries, it was attached to a fictitious "State", for it was still impossible to imagine such a service as an *extra*-State service. In this way emphasis was placed on the external character of the régime established in relation to the riparian countries.

Thus, as in modern times States have freed themselves from autarky of every kind, so the old forms of cohesion have become richer, more complex and more differentiated and it has become necessary to devise systems to deal with the international situation. As international exchanges of all kinds continually multiplied and intensified, the instruments of political agreement became inadequate. Diverse procedures of economic, social and cultural internationalization became more and more essential and were perseveringly sought. Thus, in the common interest, embryonic public services appeared, becoming more elaborate as international relations developed.

The formation of the initial framework

The main lines of this process are well known; but we shall recall briefly the stages by which international public administration grew up. During the period when *alliances* were the dominant feature of international co-operation, discussions took place intermittently at conferences which were either sporadic or periodical; but it became necessary to avoid *gaps* between successive meetings, to ensure continuity of contacts and to prevent a long interruption from destroying the advantages gained by co-operation. Thus it was that the *secretariats* of international meetings began to play a role which went beyond mere office technique. These units, originally designed only to provide the internal services of the meeting concerned (minutes and records of meetings, organization of premises, distribution of documents, translation, material organization of debates) extended their ephemeral existence beyond the discussions themselves, though retaining their temporary character. They increasingly provided a sort of liaison not only between the different meetings of one session, but also between two or more successive sessions, thus exerting an executive and preparatory action. Composed of officials appointed for the purpose by the organizers of the meeting, in practice by the host State, these units were gradually enriched by the addition of the nationals of other countries. Their composition tended more and more to be of mixed nationality, the inviting State continuing to assume responsibility for the material and technical organization of the meeting. But there was a trend towards close co-operation within the "secretariat" between the nationals of the different States participating in the meeting, the "host" State retaining the numerical preponderance for reasons of convenience. As the process of evolution went on— helped by work in common and the division of labour—the secretariat of large international meetings became a microcosm of the meeting itself, although its duties were limited to predominantly material questions with little or no bearing on diplomacy. Thus the second Hague Conference of 1907 had a secretariat of about twenty-five members appointed by the participating States; although this organ was regarded as *a priori* temporary and subordinate, its importance (both quantitative and qualitative) and the effectiveness of its role should not be underestimated.

The international unions and their offices

The second half of the nineteenth century saw the appearance of stable institutions marking a new stage in the evolution described above—namely, the "international unions," which constitute a new phenomenon of the greatest importance. Certain writers on international law even refer to the nineteenth century as "the century of international unions." Created on the international plane by treaties between States, the unions also remained wide open to non-member States, since their purpose was the benefit of all. They may be regarded as the direct predecessors of the international organizations of today. Identified by certain authors[2] with "organized treaties," the unions were remarkable for their solidity, a breach of the inter-State agreement on which they were based being a difficult matter. The stability of the unions effectively resisted international tensions and even war.[3] Several of them lasted until the present day in spite of all the upheavals which have occurred since their foundation. In the course of the last century they have also shown an ability to bring their structures and methods up to date and to adapt them to new requirements.

These international bodies had specific functions related to a particular sphere of *social* relations such as those which belong to a branch of the public administration within the State. At that time there was no question of political action proper or of multiple competences exceeding the narrow limits of the special branch in question. It was exclusively a matter of common undertakings in spheres increasingly open to international traffic, and notably in the following:

Transport and communications (river, maritime, land, later air)—e.g., the Universal Postal Union at Berne (founded in 1874), the International Telecommunication Union (founded in Paris in 1865 for the telegraphic service, and at Berlin in 1906 for the radio-telegraphic service, amalgamated in 1932 with headquarters at Geneva);

Cultural problems—e.g., the International Union for the Protection of Industrial Property at Berne (founded in 1883) and the International Union for the Protection of Literary and Artistic Works at Berne (founded in 1886). The offices of these two unions were later combined and have since been called United International Bureaux for the Protection of Industrial, Literary and Artistic Work, with headquarters at Geneva;

Customs problems; several forms of international co-operation in customs are well known; (e.g., the International Union for the Publication of Customs Tariffs at Brussels, founded in 1890);

Public health (International Health Councils; the International Health Office founded in 1907 in Paris);

Agriculture—e.g., the International Institute of Agriculture at Rome (founded in 1905);

Protection of labour—e.g., the International Labour Bureau (of a semi-private character) at Basle (founded in 1901).

The fact that this form of international action (involving embryonic public services) has proved increasingly effective, precisely in those spheres considered traditionally as *administrative*, proves that these branches lend themselves particularly well to organized international action. "It is in the sphere of administration in the widest sense that the first and most considerable developments of international organization have taken place" ... "the unions constituted, particularly in the field of transport and international communications, the closest society of States which existed before the creation of the League of Nations."[a] This led certain authors[4] to doubt the *practical* possibility of any future extension of international organization in "extra-administrative" spheres, that is to say outside the sphere of social interests. Nevertheless, international action was not long in extending its scope, and even in transcending the strict limits of specialization, by co-ordinating piecemeal administrative action and embracing developing zones of international co-operation of a regional character. Thus the Pan American Union at Washington, founded in 1890 for economic purposes, has proved a standing example of a "union" with multiple aims and on a continental scale. Moreover, it was on the model of the international unions that in the twentieth century, universal organizations of a politico-administrative character were formed with predominantly political aims.

(a) A. Rapisardi-Mirabelli, "Théorie générale des unions internationales", (*Recueil des cours A.D.I.*, 1925, II, p. 351).

The unions did not undertake any direct administrative action, being content to co-ordinate and protect certain social functions of an international nature. It was in this that they differed from the "international commissions" (e.g., river commissions), which were closed organizations of States responsible for taking important decisions and administering certain installations or certain parts of national territories. Thus the unions came to constitute a model of indirect administration, parallel to the national administrations, but never replacing them. The continuity inherent in any administrative action was soon found to be essential to the unions if they were to act effectively in their own predominantly technical sphere; it was a condition of the success of the inter-State undertakings concerned, and formed a particularly important element in the methods of international co-operation, marking the passage from the *sporadic* to the *permanent*.

But progress was empirical without any pre-established plan, and measures had to be improvised to meet the urgent necessities of international life as they arose. Since the problem was not approached as a whole, it was inevitable that these scattered experiments should have been very timid and haphazard. The theoretical framework did not emerge until later. A whole literature sprang up dealing with the problems of the unions (frequently described by the authors as "administrative unions") to describe their principal or even their sole character and purpose, and authors such as Kazansky, Lorenz von Stein and Martens,[5] by drawing the logical conclusions from this evolution, forecast the scope and future of international administration. Thus, despite differences of terminology and attribution, and despite the organic nature of each body concerned, the unions came to be considered as a *phenomenon* constituting an important and definite stage in the history of international relations. This unity of conception was the more important as it was necessary to differentiate the "unions" from the international associations of a private character ("international non-governmental organizations"), which developed much earlier than any modern "union" of States; in fact five date from the period *1693 to 1840*.[6] Further, certain unions, one of which was the International Telecommunication Union, were composed not only of States, but also of "private" members (miscellaneous non-State bodies), a fact which was liable to give rise to misunderstanding.

Becoming increasingly numerous—222 international unions were founded before 1919[7]—they more and more became "powerful instruments of rapprochement between peoples, ... the reforms achieved in the civil service of one country having been introduced into the international service and from there into the civil services of other countries."[a] The most characteristic factor which allowed these achievements to take place was the appearance of stabilized machinery and hence the enrichment of inter-State co-operation by the element of *organization*. To quote Georges Scelle:

> The public service conceived in this way remained fractional and truncated, at the mercy of the good will and special preoccupations of the State administrations, even when concerted co-ordination existed. [But] as a result of these different features, the system of the unions presents itself as a scaffolding, fragmentary no doubt, but sufficiently solid, on which international relations could be built...[b]

By virtue of the relevant treaties, each union was provided with a permanent organ responsible for administration. Generally called "bureau" in the texts, that organ played such an essential part that certain unions were themselves described as a "bureau" (e.g., the International Bureau of Weights and Measures, founded in 1875 at Sèvres) or "office" (e.g., the Central Office for International Transport by Rail, founded in 1893 at Berne). This "bureau" was supplied with a staff—numerically small—of officers representing the common will of the members of the union and not of any one member. The work of this organ was carried on by "borrowed" personnel. Either one of the States members, usually the host State, was entrusted with the conduct of affairs which came within the scope of its own civil service, or else the same State (or possibly several States members) seconded its own officials to the union to perform international functions for a specified period in the office of the union. In the first case the State concerned acted on behalf of the members of the union as a whole—i.e., in the name of the community; it has even been said that it was then acting as an "international organ." In the second case it was a matter of lending competent personnel who belonged or had belonged to the corresponding national administrations (e.g., retired civil servants). In both cases the officials were tied by uninterrupted links of national allegiance, or even of subordination to the national administration, and did not incur, as a result of their temporary attachment to the international union, any new psychological or moral obligations. There was therefore no question of autonomous or independent recruitment by the union itself, and still less of giving the head of the office the freedom to select his staff, whatever the nature and structure of the union. There being a complete absence of any international *cadre*, the officials of the unions worked as did the other administrative departments of the host State, and contacts with a view to the selection of staff between the latter and the organs of the union were never more than consultative.

(a) L. Renault, "Les Unions internationales. Leurs avantages et leurs inconvénients", in *Revue générale de Droit international public* (Vol. III, 1896, pp. 16-17).
(b) G. Scelle, *Manuel de Droit international public*, (Paris, 1948, pp. 557, 561/562).

In any case, as the need to reinforce the interdependence of countries increased, and ideas concerning international organization developed, there arose a growing tendency to bring about a relative autonomy *sui generis* of the unions vis-à-vis the States members. The unions had their own budget, and the contributing State was no longer in sole control of the funds paid to the union in this connection. Next, the unions' own powers, while relatively limited, remained separate from those of the member countries and extended beyond the traditionally conventional relationships. Thus, it became less and less a question of a simple juxtaposition of national services entrusted with certain international tasks. The more the international unions extended their sphere of action, and the stronger they grew, the greater became the trend towards a new type of international action marking an important step in the development of the techniques of close co-operation between States. Lastly, the personnel of the "bureaux" was also evolving in the direction of a "hybrid" situation, thanks to a sort of "functional duality" recognized in fact if not statutorily.

This strengthening of the internal hierarchy within the "offices" was accompanied by an increase in the moral and functional authority of the organs themselves, which were sometimes even provided with powers of arbitration (e.g., article 33 of the Universal Postal Convention). The "offices" in question came to be regarded as international civil services, created on a permanent footing, which were no longer content with internal work of a material nature, but increasingly exercised a consultative influence, preparing the discussions of the union's organs, guiding the action undertaken for immediate purposes and even anticipating somewhat in order to adapt the union's work to foreseeable needs. Accordingly, it became necessary to give the officials of these "offices" a special position more or less independent of the national administrations. A whole series of different factors here came into consideration—the question of pay, the problem of disciplinary responsibility within the office, the sending of officials to the places where they were needed. By placing these officials if not "above" at least "in the midst of" the battle, by giving them in practice the status of agents of the community of States, a situation was automatically created which required their *impartiality*. In order that they should be in a position to carry out the task entrusted to them, it was essential that—without arrogating to themselves any authority of their own—they should approach problems from an elevated viewpoint, taking into account the interests of all, not being content with any "particularist" point of view and not favouring anybody. It was the nature of the international task itself which compelled the officials of the unions to adopt a special mentality in keeping with the common interests of the States members. The fact that most of them were familiar with the administrative traditions of Western

Europe, since they came from the civil services of those countries, facilitated this psychological process to some extent. The said civil services having slowly evolved an impartial attitude towards individual interests, this attitude had simply to be transposed to the international plane and the necessary consequences drawn with regard to national interests. The high standard of most of the staff "lent" to the unions and the specialization of the tasks entrusted to them also constituted elements favouring this process.

Thus, we see an evolution both of the unions and of their officials as factors of international unification. The unions were to be *a form of organization* "proceeding from a functional and organic minimum to a maximum—namely, the constitution of an *entity* considered (for legal purposes) as distinct from its components, and the *personification* of that entity.... This form of organization became specialized in what may be termed 'international administration'."[a] To enable international co-operation to advance another step, it was sufficient, at a given moment of this process, that a *"union of unions"* should be established,[b] accompanied by an increase in powers (also on the political plane, but without losing sight of administrative action). As far as the officials were concerned, this evolution demanded a modification of the régime originally adopted. In the first place, the international organizations had to be given a mixed composition— first multi-national, then international; in the second place, the officials had to be provided with a genuine legal status with all the psychological consequences resulting therefrom. These changes imposed by the nature of things were to take place only later.

An example of an international union: the Universal Postal Union[8]

The Universal Postal Union may serve as an illustration of this evolution. Its creation was preceded by a series of bilateral conventions relating to postal communications between States. After the international conference held in Paris in 1863, continuous efforts were made to replace the existing multiple conventions by a single type of multilateral convention, and these efforts proved successful at the Berne Conference of 1874, when the Universal Postal Convention was drawn up. In addition to the congresses (which were convened every five years and which constituted "a real Universal Postal Parliament"[c], and the committees, the Union had an "international bureau" at Berne which served as a link between the postal adminis-

(a) A. Rapisardi-Mirabelli, op. cit., p. 390.
(b) Ibidem, p. 387.
(c) Mr. E. Garbani-Nerini (Director of the U.P.U.), "Les bases, l'organisation et le développement de l'Union postale universelle", in publ. No. 34 of the Société suisse de Droit international, (1935).

trations and as a centre of information, clearing operations, preparation of meetings and publications. Its attributions were therefore clearly delimited and in the sphere of indirect administration; in no case did the bureau of the Union substitute itself for the national postal administrations. The size of the bureau was deliberately modest (the staff comprised twelve persons at the time, and subsequently never exceeded forty-three). Under the Convention, the Swiss Federal Council was called upon to supervise the administration of the bureau; up to 1914 this supervision was exercised throught the Federal Department of Posts and Railways, and after 1915 through the Federal Political Department. While the Government of the Swiss Confederation was also entrusted by the Convention with certain diplomatic duties, which it was to perform in the name of the Union and on its behalf (e.g., the notification of accessions of members or communications between members), it exercised definitely administrative attributions in connection with the supervision of the bureau—recruitment of the entire staff, auditing of accounts and management control, disciplinary power over officials, etc. Hence, the personnel of the bureau of the Union enjoyed no special immunity or privilege for seventy-three years. Its status did not differ in practice from that of Swiss officials. The legal theory of the time regarded it, indeed, as consisting of "employees of the association", including, in addition to States, various bodies which were not autonomous but had separate postal administrations; it was this "*societas*" which had entrusted to one of its members (*socius*) the task of managing this sector of the common business. From the outset the staff displayed exemplary impartiality. Although the higher officials were Swiss, and sometimes former holders of high office in the Confederation,[10] they made remarkable efforts to recruit competent persons of other nationalities.

It is interesting to note that when in 1947 a formal international status was granted to its staff,[11] the bureau of the Universal Postal Union remained under Swiss supervision, unlike what was done in the case of the International Telecommunication Union, whose legal position vis-à-vis the Swiss Confederation had hitherto been identical to that of the Universal Postal Union.[12] But henceforward this supervision was limited, because new executive organs of the Union had powers of decision in administrative matters, and the director of the international bureau was responsible for the personnel.[13] In practice, the supervision of the Swiss authorities ("haute autorité de l'administration supérieure") never prevented the director of the bureau from enjoying a wide measure of autonomy.

This evolution of an international union of nearly a hundred years' standing—which, despite its present membership of the United Nations family, has kept its traditional name—seems instructive from the point of view of understanding the passage from the stage of unions to the next stage of development of international co-operation, the birth of the international civil services.

The birth of the international civil services

The régime granted in 1905 to the staff of the International Institute of Agriculture at Rome may be regarded as the true precursor of this transformation. "With the creation of the International Institute of Agriculture, the existence of persons who, while not representatives of any State, are agents of administrative activity of a purely international nature, was definitely established."[a] This is the more interesting became in its own sphere of action this Union[14] did not differ from other organizations of the same type and of the same period, since its primary role was one of co-ordination and consisted in the exchange of information and in the preparation of technical documents; it had no powers of decision.

Nevertheless, for the first time the Italian Government had conferred on the Institute itself and on its officials certain privileges and immunities. These officials became international civil servants; their staff regulations stipulated (article 2) that they could not seek or receive instructions from anyone but their own superiors, to whom they were responsible. Thus the organization itself having since its foundation been independent of the host State (although founded largely on the initiative of its king), its bureau was not to be subordinate to any State, even that of the host country. Whatever the nationality of its officials, they were not to be considered as representatives of their respective countries.

The international civil servant and the international civil service were born.

(a) J. Gascón y Marin, "Transformations du Droit administratif international", (*Recueil des cours A.D.I.*, 1930, IV, p. 53).

NOTES

(1) Quoted by Le Fur & Chklaver, *Recueil des textes de droit international public* (pp. 2-3). Cf. also, e.g. G. Ferrero, *L'unité du monde*, (Paris, 1927, p. 15 ff.).

(2) Particularly P. Kazansky, "Théorie de l'Administration internationale", in *Revue générale de droit international public*, (Vol. IX, 1902, p. 358 ff.).

(3) L. Renault, (op. cit., p. 21 ff.).

(4) E.g. P. Kazansky, (op. cit., p. 366) and his writings in Russian.

(5) P. Kazansky, (op. cit., p. 364): "It is in the creation of these organs (the unions) that the principal legal problem of international organization resides. But after their creation certain necessities appear. The need for definite rules governing their activity makes itself felt. International administrative law appears, and is destined to occupy an extremely important place in the system of the law of nations. It may be said that with it public international law is now complete...."; (pp.

365/366): "The international administration has not yet reached the development of which it is capable.... It is undeniable that international administration has a great future before it and that its development will involve that of the law of nations. ... Thereafter the extension of these organs and the creation of similar new institutions may be anticipated...." L. von Stein, *Handbuch der Verwaltungslehre*, Vol. I, Stuttgart, 1888, p. 249 ff.): "In a hundred years, it will be difficult to understand how States were able to exist without international administration. The international unions are truly the first elements of universal organization. And this organization will go on improving...." (cf. also L. von Stein, *Die Verwaltungslehre*, 2nd part, Stuttgart, 1866, p. 98, annex: "Die Idee des internationalen Verwaltungsrechts"; and "Einige Bemerkungen über das internationale Verwaltungsrecht", *Schmollers Jahrbuch*, 1882).
Cf. also: G. F. de Martens, *Précis de Droit des gens moderne*; K. Neumeyer, "Les Unions internationales", in *Revue de Droit international des sciences politiques et sociales*, (Geneva, 1923-1924, p. 139 ff.) and "Internationales Verwaltungsrecht" (3 Vols., Munich-Berlin, 1910-1922); P. S. Reinsch, "International Unions and their administration", in *American Journal of International Law*; (Vol. 1, 1907, p. 579 ff.) and *Public International Unions, their Work and Organization*, (Boston, 1911).

(6) *Les 1978 organisations internationales fondées depuis le Congrès de Vienne*, (Brussels, Union des Associations internationales, 1957).

(7) *The Handbook of the League of Nations for 1939* mentions ninety-one unions established before 1907, 121 established between 1901 and 1918, 246 similar organizations appearing after 1919.

(8) Cf., e.g. *L'Union postale universelle—Sa fondation et son développement*, (Memorandum published by the International Bureau on the occasion of the 50th anniversary of the Union 1874-1924) (Einsiedeln, 1929), "Bureau de l'Union Postale Universelle", in *Annuaire suisse de Droit international*, (1947, IV, p. 323 ff.), *Weltpostverein*, ibid., (1944, I, p. 310 ff.); J. Buser, "Zur Entwicklung des Weltpostvereins und des Weltpostrechts", in publ. No. 34 of the Société suisse de Droit international, (1935); H. Sasse, *Der Weltpostverein*, (Frankfort-Berlin, 1959).

(9) G. Jellinek, *Die Lehre von den Staatenverbindungen*, (Vienna, 1882, p. 167), Toll, *Die internationale Bureaux der allgemeinen völkerrechtlichen Verwaltungsvereine* (1910); K. Strupp, "Verwaltungsgemeinschaften", in *Wörtenbuch des deutschen Staats— und Verwaltungsrechts*, (1914); F. Fleiner, *Schweizerisches Bundesstaatsrecht*, (Tübingen, 1923, par. 74).

(10) C. Schröter, *Der Weltpostverein. Geschichte seiner Gründung und Entwicklung in 25 Jahren*, (Berne, 1900, p. 62 ff.).

(11) *The Universal Postal Union. Its Foundation and Development*, (Berne, 1955, *passim*); "Statut des bureaux internationaux placés sous la surveillance des autorités de la Confédération suisse", in *Annuaire suisse de droit international*, (V, 1948, p. 176 ff., particularly art. 9-12).

(12) G. A. Codding, *The International Telecommunication Union. An Experiment in International Co-operation*, (Thesis, Geneva, Leiden 1952, p. 296): "It is interesting to note that the Universal Postal Union, at its first postwar conference in 1947, did not attempt to change its International Bureau, but left it under the aegis of the Swiss government. The variation in subject matter treated by the Universal Postal Union and the International Telecommunication Union was the basis for the difference in treatment of their respective bureaux. The Secretariat of the International Telecommunication Union was 'modernized,' because radio, rather than the postal services, was in the process of a remarkable development, fraught with political implications. A truly international secretariat would be more above

suspicion of national influence than a secretariat recruited from, and under the aegis of, one member country. . . . "

(13) Cf., for example, H. Sasse (op. cit., p. 31 ff.).

(14) As regards the attempts to establish a doctrinal difference between "union" and "institute," cf. Ph. Cahier, *Etude des accords de siège conclus entre les organisations internationales et les Etats où elles résident,* (Milan, 1959, p. 55 ff.).

CHAPTER 2

THE HUMAN ASPECT

The function creates the organ

The function appeared first, and then, as in biology, the organ was created to perform that function. It began in the "unionist" era; but it was the creation in 1919 of the League of Nations and of the International Labour Office which completed this evolution. "There can be no doubt," says the Spanish scholar Gascón y Marin,[a] "that there [then] existed a sphere of activity which naturally belonged to international administration, that is the performance of public services in the direct interest of the international community or the indirect interest of the States composing it, and that individuals exercising purely international *functions* had been legally deprived of all representative national character, retaining only the capacity of true *international agents....*"

The gradual building up of permanent structures supporting the preparation, deliberation and execution of the resolutions of the international organizations was inevitably accompanied by the creation of organs ensuring their continuity and impartiality. It was a natural process, well known in the history of all public bodies and tending to ensure the stability and equilibrium essential to action.

Although unknown in the first two thousand years of the history of international agreements, the international civil servant nevertheless did not appear as a *deus ex machina*, springing full-blown into existence. Nor is his creation directly linked to any particular ideology. He may be said to have grown up naturally like a plant. Once the Universal Postal Union had begun to organize successfully postal services and other interchanges on a world-wide scale; once the International Telecommunication Union had harmonized national activities, maintaining and extending international co-operation in the use and improvement of telecommunications; once the Pan-American Union had promoted, by common action, the economic, social and cultural development of the States of the American continent; once the International Institute of Agriculture, thanks to the vision and creative spirit of David Lubin, had undertaken to carry out the motto "*fiat*

(a) Op. cit., p. 57.

panis"—it was absolutely essential that a permanent nucleus of international officials should appear; it was a practical necessity.

The formation of the State itself, and the creation within it of decentralized bodies and subordinate administrations, answered to a similar necessity. It is nowhere possible to *administer* without *administrators*. At every level this remains axiomatic. Theories and ideas are added *afterwards* to a practice already established. The requirements of life, the objective circumstances, have already entrusted these functions to organs created for the purpose; the subsequent ideology aims at justifying—morally or intellectually—what has already been done, in order to build an adequate theoretical framework and to enable the phenomenon already in existence to take root in the popular mind. If, as we have seen, the origin of the international civil servant dates back to the period of the "unions" based on various social interests and not on political interests (in so far as such a separation is practicable), the role of this official must become even more important as soon as the properly political element becomes a determining factor as in the modern international set-up. First of all, we have the *liaison officers* between the co-operating peoples. The closer the links between States, the greater the possibility of friction. Faced with the interplay of political forces, with the action of various pressure groups, with conflicting interests and controversies, any deliberate and continuous action would have been impossible without this element "emancipated" from direct dependence on the parties to the dispute. The international civil servant plays the essential role of connecting link, moderator, animator, collaborator and executor of the common will. It was only a matter of common sense to create a series of conditions making it possible for him to become the collective conscience of the international organization, to remain independent of particularist influences and thus to maintain the balance.

In order that the international organization should be able to act and survive, it was not enough that the founding States should set it up and determine the main outlines of its policy. They had also to be induced to accept *in the thick of the battle* the action of the international "secretariat"; that is to say of the executive organ constituted by the officials of the organization. The term "secretariat" goes back first to the early attempts to manage international meetings; secondly, to the technical services operating between two meetings and providing a link between them, and lastly to the "offices" of the era of the unions; it also reflects the terminology employed in private associations. Although inadequate to describe the task which now devolves on this international organ, the term has come to be generally accepted; it is preferable to that of "office", which suggests a purely material and technical function. This "secretariat" is an administrative mechanism, outside the national administrations and acting by definition in the interests of the whole community of States members of a given organization, under the control of the latter's deliberative organs. Despite appearances and illusions which were especially frequent at the time, its proper role is not essentially subordinate. When we describe it as a particular sector of public administration—namely, that of *international administration*—we are not simply employing a common term in order to counteract the "polycentrism" of the international organizations, we are also accentuating its true character, that of public *administration*. This is both desirable and necessary.[1] Even when an administration, as at present, does not possess a true *power of decision*, and when, unable to impose its will, it has to be content with proposing, suggesting, investigating and implementing, it nevertheless exercises a creative function—*creation* is inseparable from any public administration. The international secretariat is an irreplaceable instrument of liaison and transmission; it is also the permanent working cell of the organization; it plans, persuades and reminds member States of their obligations. While its duties are those of any public administration, it has a special role to play in the international arena for several reasons.

In the first place, the absence of traditions peculiar to such international action is accompanied by the absence of rules of reference. Whereas administrative action in the State is subject to legislative provisions containing precise rules, international action is determined by inter-State treaties and by the resolutions of the deliberative bodies of the organization. Both, being the result of compromise, must inevitably remain vague and leave wide scope for administrative interpretation. This specific character of international administrative action—apart from various peculiarities of environment—powerfully contributes to increase the real importance of the international secretariat. This is not always realized.

Secondly, in international organizations, in the absence of any "government" (to which by definition the public administration is amenable in any State), the secretariat enjoys a degree of autonomy greater than that which exists in state systems. If we compare the relations between the legislature and the executive in the State on the one hand and those between the deliberative organs and the secretariat in the international organizations on the other, we shall realize that despite deceptive analogies the set-up is entirely different, since on the international plane there is no "parliament" or "government". The international secretariat is not subject to the strict and continuous control of political organs of a ministerial character. The secretary-general is not a "Minister," and, where deliberative organs of limited composition exist (e.g., the Executive Board of UNESCO), they do not play the part of a "cabinet". We therefore find nothing (or almost nothing) of the constitutional system of checks and balances traditionally considered as essential in the apparatus of the State; a special situation arises which is liable to upset the balance of the mechanism and accentuate the role of the secretariat. "In the absence of normal ministerial guidance the Secretariat provides the main element of continuity and may occasionally have to take decisions which British officials would in the normal course of events refer to Ministers."[a]

Lastly, the international secretariat is characterized by its stability. In the international arena, it is in practice the only cog of the machinery which acts with visible continuity. While all the other cogs are multipersonal bodies or "councils", the secretariat is the *only* organ with a "bureaucratic" structure—i.e., comprising administrative services linked to one another by relations of hierarchic subordination and authority subject to the régime of single direction at all levels (principle of "unity of command"). Thus, all the services, however heterogeneous, are simply working instruments of the secretary-general who is at the apex of the hierarchical pyramid. For this reason, the secretariat can act with the necessary continuity and energy, with rapidity too if this is necessary, though suffering, of course, the effects of any tension or disagreement between the States members. If the balance of political forces is upset—those forces which have themselves created the international organization—the situation of the secretariat is delicate and frequently precarious. The less a given organization is technically specialized, the more it is exposed to political uncertainties: everything is in a state of flux as a result of the views (themselves continually changing) of the States members of the organization, views on international co-operation in general and on the action of the secretariat in particular. Hence, incessant improvisation is necessary—improvisation and re-improvisation in successive adjustments of the structure and operation of the secretariat to the unforeseeable demands of the States. Hence, too, the incessant empiric search for guiding principles, and the pragmatism which characterizes evolution. All these are elements which enhance still further the importance of the role of the international secretariat as a stabilizing and regulatory factor.

The "*stronghold of internationalism*"[b]

While the wheels of an international organization are set in motion by the spokesmen of the national governments represented in it, only the international civil service (apart from the International Court) is composed of persons who, by their permanence, their technical knowledge and their autonomy, can attempt to act as catalysts

(a) G. L. Goodwin, *Britain and the United Nations*, (New York, 1957, p. 399).
(b) G. Scelle, "Essai sur la crise de la Société des Nations et ses remèdes", in *Esprit international*, (April 1934, No. 3, p. 164 ff).

of the international spirit. That is the product of the process of growth and the essence of the international civil service.

"An international civil servant is a person to whom the representatives of several States, or an organ acting on their behalf, have entrusted, in virtue of an inter-State agreement and under their supervision, the continuous and exclusive exercise of functions in the common interests of the States in question subject to special legal rules".[a] Since serious disequilibrium would lead to the paralysis of the organization and threaten its survival, the international secretariat (and all its staff without exception) must undergo a radical change in their mental processes. It is essential to grasp the meaning of this change, and try to understand its manifestations. It grows out of the special circumstances of each people in the modern international world, and leads towards a wider outlook, a greater unity based no longer on a system of "invisible solidarities",[2] but on a conception of universality embracing the individual characteristics of the components.

It is his positive attitude to the world-wide interests of the international community which constitutes the *differentia specifica* of the international civil servant thus conceived. It is here that we find his principal *raison d'être*, the *sine qua non* of his usefulness. Whatever the purpose of the international organization, whatever the special function of each official, the general task of the international administration remains fundamentally the same: it serves institutionalized international co-operation—that is to say unity in plurality. What was unthinkable at a still recent stage of international relations—a nucleus of officials in the service of all the States of which the organization is composed—thus becomes, thanks to this vital "conversion", a fundamental condition of the latter's existence. Moreover, it will be seen on reflection that the international civil service, while preserving what has already been won, constitutes in itself a stimulus towards the achievement of a "universal civilization". Acts previously undertaken only under the stimulus of a catastrophe[3] are now performed every day by people whose scale of values is adjusted to the end pursued.

It is bearing in mind this special scale of values that we speak of the new "human category" which has come into being with the international civil servant. He has a new system of preferences with a unitary basis and centripetal tendencies, the practical consequence of working in an international organization embracing wider societies. If the international secretariat thus becomes logically a "stronghold of internationalism", it must not be forgotten that this "internationa-

(a) This definition, which has become a classic, was proposed by S. Basdevant (Bastid), *Les fonctionnaires internationaux*, (thesis, Paris, 1931, p. 53).

lism" is nothing else than the natural product of the relationships, the interactions and the interdependence of nations. It is a short-sighted attitude, taking no account of the practical necessities of today, to magnify temporary conflicts of interest into an opposition of principle. The phenomenon of the international civil servant must be viewed from the right angle if the picture is not to be distorted.

The importance of this fundamental criterion is the greater since, as in all relations between States, the international administration is continually obliged to compromise. As regards the fundamental international character of the secretariat and its staff in the service of the international community, however, no concession is admissible. Any attempt at compromise here would only enlarge the gap between principles and practice, a gap which is natural in a period of transition. As we shall see, the "internationalism" of the international civil servant by no means signifies a break with his nationality, with his own civilization, with his previous sentimental and legal ties. On the contrary, the contribution made by each of these elements to international co-operation serves to enrich the general climate and widen the horizons of all. As we shall see, this "almost complete dedication to international public affairs"[a] of every international civil servant is not in conflict with the maintenance of the civil servant's links with his own country; but it situates him in a hierarchy of values in which "the necessities peculiar to an international organization should completely exclude the idea of *representation*".[b]

Thus, the international civil servant, the embodiment of internationalism, will have to draw the conclusions which will determine his obligations and enable him to perform his task. Nevertheless, the official in no way "denationalizes" himself in accepting this special scale of values, corresponding as it does to the fundamental necessities of the international community of which his own national community forms part. This constitutes a reversal, or at least an adjustment, of the mental habits of centuries which cannot fail to create difficulties, and which calls for an effort of individual and creative comprehension with which we shall deal later. In the absence of such effort, there is a risk that the gap between statutory rules and common practice may become a deep chasm which, even though concealed and accepted with resignation, would deprive the common work of its effectiveness and deflect its purpose.

In the earliest days of the first comprehensive and multilateral international secretariat, the Secretariat of the League of Nations, this *international* criterion of international civil servants was defined in A. J. Balfour's famous report of 19 May 1920:

(a) Ibidem, p. 50.
(b) Ibidem, p. 324.

"...the members of the Secretariat once appointed are no longer the servants of the country of which they are citizens, but become for the time being the servants only of the League of Nations. Their duties are not national, but international....

Nothing should be done to weaken the sense of their international allegiance; ..."[a]

These "Balfour principles" have since become part of the constituent instruments and staff regulations of all the international organizations. Thus the ideal blueprint of the machinery of the international secretariats has been embodied in its original purity in the texts in force. The vicissitudes in the growth of the international civil service have demonstrated that these principles do not find ready acceptance, and that it is precisely in this sphere that there is a clash of contradictory conceptions, although neither side calls in question the "verbal façade" embodied in the legal texts.

The empirical growth of the international civil service

The function having created the organ, the latter's role had to be adjusted pragmatically to the growing needs of international life. This is a natural process, the spontaneous creation of the original process characterizing the establishment of the international administrations. History shows that the authors of the texts—including those of 1919—which were to govern this problem, did not fully realize the scope of the administrative phenomenon in international co-operation.[4] Thus once the successive secretariats had been established and set in motion, the force of circumstances continued to produce its effects.

Events were to show that, in spite of initial distrust and complex technical obstacles, these administrations could be set up and made to work. The rapidity of this process may even be found surprising, in view of the precedents in the individual States and the difficulties of all sorts on the international plane. An excellent judge has said in this connection: "The creation of a secretariat international alike in its structure, its spirit, and its personnel, was without doubt one of the most important events in the history of international politics—important not only in itself, but as the indisputable proof of possibilities which had hitherto been confidently denied...."[b] Several factors contributed to and hastened the growth of the role of the secretariats.

First of all, as we have already emphasized, they everywhere represent a stabilizing element and, working without interruption, they see to the implementation, directly or through the States members, of the resolutions voted by the deliberative organs of the inter-

(a) "Personnel of the Secretariat", (Report presented by the British representative, A. J. Balfour, to the Council of the League of Nations). (League of Nations, *Official Journal*, No. 4, June 1920, pp. 137 and 139.)
(b) F. P. Walters, *A History of the League of Nations*, (London, 1960 ed., p. 76).

national organization. These deliberative organs, in view of their multinational composition and the representative character of their members, are hampered by the diversity and sometimes the opposition of national interests; to this should be added the infinite variety of their crushing and sometimes incompatible tasks.[5] On the other hand, the international character (added to the multinational composition) of the secretariat, its capacity as an administrative organ and its internal hierarchical structure, make it easy to handle, its point of view is objective and it is technically capable of firm and effective action in the interest of the organization as a whole.

Next, it should be borne in mind that, in modern conditions, the role of the public administrations is everywhere increasing within the framework of the State, and that this increase of public intervention in contemporary life requires increased efficiency and speed and constant modernization. This continual transfer of the centre of gravity in the modern State—from the legislature to the executive— is a well known phenomenon and a parallel movement in international affairs must be expected.[6]

Lastly, an important point to be borne in mind is a change in the character of international action, from the traditional "political diplomacy" to a new sort of "diplomatic administration".[a] Thus, whatever the labels given to this tendency, it is easy to observe daily attempts to concentrate co-operative efforts on new issues, displacing the centre of gravity. We shall have occasion hereafter to revert to this point repeatedly. Hence, it is indispensable to think out afresh the classical analysis of the phenomena in question. Even if the political aspect of international co-operation remains the more spectacular and appears to be the most important, it is misleading to be content with it and not to take into account the other aspects of international action, of which there are a great variety, particularly of an economic, social and cultural nature. It is certainly here that we should now seek the principal instrument of any active (and not purely verbal) solidarity and of co-operation as defined in Article 1 of the Charter of the United Nations (particularly in paragraphs 3 and 4).[7] But what is more, even in the sphere of properly political action for the maintenance of international peace and security, the vigilant action of the secretariat becomes—in the respective organizations—increasingly one of the "peaceful means ... to bring about in conformity with the principles of justice and international law the adjustment or settlement of international disputes or situations which might lead to a breach of the peace."[b]

(a) Terminology used by Dag Hammarskjöld, "Introduction to the Report of the Secretary-General of the United Nations" of 1955/1956, (4 October 1956, doc. A/3137/Add. 1, p. 9.)
(b) Quoted from Article 1, paragraph 1, of the Charter of the United Nations.

Obviously, this process, substantially illustrated by many examples, leads to a displacement of responsibilities and reinforces the secretariat's position in the structure of the international organizations. Thus, as evolution goes on, it becomes increasingly clear that the secretariat is not an auxiliary and secondary creation responsible only for material tasks carried out mechanically and destined in fact to be entrusted more and more to machines. While carrying out the elementary operations of office work in the broadest sense, and constituting an essential material support of the international structure, the secretariat has begun to play a real part in the achievement of the purposes of the international organization. Faced with ideological differences and sometimes with radical opposition between the objectives proclaimed, the position of the element symbolizing the common interest—that is to say the identity of certain national interests despite differences of all kinds—grows *inevitably* in importance provided that it effectively enjoys the general confidence. This problem of confidence, with which is bound up a series of apparently technical questions (particularly that of *recruitment*), is the key to an understanding of the symbol which the international civil service has become; in seeking the meaning of that symbol, whatever branch of international administration we are studying, we inevitably come up against this problem.

As soon as the presence of international officials on the international scene was accepted, this unprecedented human category had to be placed in an appropriate psychological and legal framework. An adjustment of structures and methods to international needs became indispensable. Naturally, at first there was a wide choice of solutions based on analogies with existing structures. The idea of loaned personnel was abandoned, and it was realized that the juxtaposition of a series of national delegations in the secretariats[8] would be contrary to the "internationalization" (particularly from the psychological point of view) of the international civil service; how then were officials to be appointed? There were many suggestions: election by the States members (at least in the case of key and supervisory officials), or co-option (which was widely practised in private international associations), or drawing by lot, or the seconding of national officials in rotation, or, lastly, a combination of all these methods or some of them. Each of these solutions clearly had drawbacks, and none could be simply applied in such novel circumstances. Nevertheless, a choice had to be made in order that administrative action, recognized as necessary, could begin.

As it turned out, without sufficiently weighing the consequences or allowing an experimental period, it was decided to apply on the international plane the system of the national civil service which had grown, slowly and laboriously, in the countries of western Europe.

As we have said, the "growth" of the international civil service must be considered as a natural and spontaneous phenomenon imposed by circumstances, and its framework—legal and psychological—primarily modelled on a mixture of the British and French systems,[9] was deliberately transposed in 1919-20 to the international plane. It was the system established, not without hesitation, by the first Secretary-General of the League of Nations, Sir Eric Drummond,[10] and afterwards embodied in legal texts, which was to win the day. Corresponding to the "Balfour principles," and of the same date, this practice was accepted by the deliberative organs of the League and was afterwards imitated by all the other international organizations.

This audacious choice of an administrative model, the creation of a world-civilizing force which had been maturing for centuries, was clearly a risk. The civil service systems of western Europe not being those of other parts of the world and corresponding only partly or not at all to the ways of other civilizations, it was not easy to secure universal understanding for the principles on which they were based. For instance, it is well known that in many countries—for instance, the United States of America—the national civil service does not offer a stable career. Some countries lack a general guiding line of political continuity, nor do they understand the political impartiality and the continuity which are the essence of the British Civil Service and of the national public services of most of the countries of continental Europe such as France, Germany, the Netherlands, Belgium, Italy, Austria, the Scandinavian countries, etc. The degree of training needed to secure admittance to the national administrations of those countries is not required everywhere. Many countries, for lack of trained personnel, have to be content, at least during a period of transition, with an inadequate intellectual level for their civil servants. Hence, there is much hard feeling and misunderstanding of the system chosen. Though the consequences of the choice are evident, it is sometimes identified with the giving of preference to the countries possessing permanent civil services, and thus in a position to supply the international secretariat with properly trained officials capable of carrying out satisfactorily the international tasks assigned to them. This is regarded as deliberate discrimination against countries having different administrative systems, or not yet having reached a degree of development similar to those whose administrative system has been adopted as an international standard. Naturally, the intention of Sir Eric Drummond and the other founders of the international civil service was quite different. In choosing the type of service which seemed to them the best, and based on long experience, they wished to ensure a high level of efficiency in the international administration, the selection of the best candidates from all over the world, and the optimum conditions of work to be performed in common in the general interest. They certainly regarded it as out of the question that, taking into account the disparity of conditions existing throughout the world, an attempt should be made to strike an average between systems of unequal value, thus deliberately accepting a standard less than the highest. The political conditions of the crucial period 1919-20 were indeed in favour of such a decision. The League of Nations was in the nature of an enlarged "European Club". It was natural that it should adopt the administrative model which predominated in Europe and formed an integral part of its tradition.

But the more universal the international organizations have become, the more difficult it has been to adjust them to a system whose foundations frequently escape the comprehension of many countries. Even some highly developed countries fail to understand the various necessities of the system. An example of this is the widespread misunderstanding of the jurisdictional control function of the public administration and of the special symmetry of parallel set-ups, political, administrative and judicial. Thus international administrative action encounters a series of difficulties owing to differences of conception, different acceptances of similar terms, misunderstanding of texts voted which may be perfectly clear to some and mysterious to others. Hence *compromises* have been resorted to which complicate the general picture but are necessary to satisfy all the States members holding different viewpoints. So we have a *vicious circle;* since some compromises have been accepted, there is an urge to compromise further on fundamental principles which many of the participants in international action do not fully understand. But once compromises are tolerated on principles, and not merely on secondary or technical matters, the entire edifice is endangered. In seeking a *modus vivendi* in the circumstances of the moment, and in thus going on from one compromise to another, one often exceeds the limit of what is acceptable, and runs counter to the essential nature of international administration.

To this should be added another series of difficulties, connected with the need to reconcile principles usually applied on the national level with the special features of international work. Unlike the national civil servant, the international civil servant acts without any geographical limitations (at least in the world-wide organizations); he is governed by treaties and not by laws; he acts within a framework which is multinational as regards the composition, the training and the orientation of the staff; he belongs to organizations which are often fractional or functionally specialized; as we have said, he is not given precise instructions or established terms of reference or adequate precedents; he is not directed by a "government". Taking them all in all, these differences may be greater than the apparent resemblances. Far from home, working in an unusual environment, in constant contact with varied civilizations and traditions, obliged to retain his objectivity in spite of his own national predilections, the international civil servant must have the benefit of certain immunities and guarantees, must have a sense of his own worth and security. The compromises accepted as regards recruitment having led also to the acceptance of temporary appointments, of secondings by States of their national civil servants for a given period, and various similar arrangements, it is essential, in order to prevent the international civil servant's morale from being lowered by doubt as to the stability of his employment, to offer him technical advantages of various kinds (promotion by seniority and by merit, pensions, family allowances, international schools for his children, regular home leave, a system of privileges and immunities, encouragement of staff associations and participation of the elected representatives of the staff in the official direction of affairs, regular scales of increment, etc.). While several of these methods already existed on the national plane, the peculiar climate and special features of international administration must not be forgotten when they are applied to the international civil service.

In consequence of its empiric growth, the international civil service, from small beginnings, has acquired imposing proportions. Round the large nucleus of international officials have gathered several related categories of miscellaneous agents (experts, consultants, auxiliary employees of various associated organs, etc.). In spite of the persistent institutional *polycentrism* and of fundamental differences between the tasks of the various international organizations (particularly between those with multiple aims and those which are functionally specialized, and between political organizations and those which are predominantly technical), a single conception of the international civil servant has duly made its appearance. This conception is based on the regulations or inter-institutional agreements in force and on arrangements for staff representation; but it is above all worked out daily by force of circumstances. Independently of the dimensions and work of each organization, the identity of fundamental principles and the similarities of duties and status help to prepare the ground for a future unification. Despite obstacles and disillusions of all kinds, the evolution of ideas in this direction seems continuous and relatively rapid.

NOTES

(1) D. C. Stone, "Administrative Aspects of World Organization", in *Approaches to World Peace, Conference on Science, Philosophy and Religion*, (New York, 1944, p. 885): "Public administration is generic in character—applicable wherever organized activities are carried out in a continuing manner. There is no practical support

to the contention that International Administration is different in nature from any other kind of administration...."

(2) G. Ferrero, *L'unité du monde*, (op cit., p. 20): "There are no longer any nations with isolated destinies; the direct or indirect repercussions of events from one end of the globe to the other are unforeseeable but inevitable; the whole world, in spite of, and even because of, the strife between nations, is gradually being formed into a system of *invisible solidarities*."

(3) Ibidem: "The world unifies itself under the stimulus of catastrophes...."

(4) Thus, according to authoritative documents, no national delegate called upon to take part in the initial discussions of the League of Nations had any definite idea as to the dimensions and true role of the secretariat which was to be set up. There was only a vague idea of the tasks it would have to perform in international co-operation, in the light of the fragmentary examples of the "unions", (cf. in this connection: E. F. Ranshofen-Wertheimer, op. cit., p. 16). At most, some consideration was to be given to the question of a "permanent secretariat" and its staff, whose task was to "keep the minutes and records of the Council, conduct all correspondence of the Council, and make all necessary arrangements in the intervals between the meetings of the Council...."

Mention was also made of the Secretariat as a sort of "general staff which studies and watches closely all conditions anywhere developing which might call for action or counsel on the part of the League", (cf. Gen. Smuts' Plan, D. H. Miller, *The Drafting of the Covenant*, New York, 1928, Vol. 2, p. 43). Woodrow Wilson also spoke of a "secretariat to act as their ministerial agency....", (cf. Pres. Wilson's 1st draft, ibidem, p. 12). There therefore seems to have been no general plan, no trace of "perspective", essential though that was. Thus, in international political circles, the habit grew up of considering the international secretariat as an auxiliary creation of a secondary character, of underestimating the possibilities arising out of its permanence and the professional qualifications of its staff. This opinion dated from the time of the *unions* and had then taken firm root. While the achievements of the Secretariat of the League of Nations and of the I.L.O. contradicted this opinion, it was maintained by the force of inertia and for other reasons. A "minimalist school" had already grown up at the time of the League of Nations, tending to confine the Secretariat within the bounds of the organization as a centre of documentation, exchange and diffusion, called upon to perform multiple technical functions, but with no true *international* role of its own. This conception was based on the fact that the political factor, in contrast with the period of the unions, was playing a growing part in the international organization, and on the fear of a nucleus, however embryonic, of "world government". As we shall see later, the British influence on the establishment of the secretariats in 1919, modelled on the British civil service and its political passivity, encouraged the same conception. The consequences were to persist for a long time, even when belied by practical experience and in spite of the clear-sightedness of the Preparatory Commission of 1945, as regards the organization of the Secretariat of the United Nations. This but further proves the spontaneous character of the growth of the international civil service, stimulated or retarded by individual initiatives, and its principles, the constant subject of debate.

(5) The methods of action of the deliberative organs, when dealing with administrative affairs (even indirectly or in a supervisory capacity) were more reminiscent of those of an "embryonic parliament" than of an effective administrative body. (Cf. A. Loveday, *Reflections on International Administration*, Oxford, 1956, p. 236). These supervisory organs were somewhat sporadic in the specialized agencies. It is worth noting, however, the continuous action in this sphere of the Supervisory Commission of the League of Nations and of the Advisory Committee on Administrative and Budgetary Questions of the United Nations.

(6) To be compared with James Burnham's conception of the "localization of sovereignty in modern societies", (*The Managerial Revolution*, New York, 1941, chapter X).

(7) Article 1 of the Charter: "The Purposes of the United Nations are:...3. To achieve international co-operation in solving international problems of an economic, social, cultural, or humanitarian character, and in promoting and encouraging respect for human rights and for fundamental freedoms for all without distinction as to race, sex, language or religion; and 4. To be a centre for harmonizing the actions of nations in the attainment of these common ends."

L. M. Goodrich & E. Hambro, *Charter of the United Nations. Commentary and Documents*, (Boston, 1949, p. 96): "This paragraph [paragraph 3] affords clear evidence that the framers of the Charter recognized that the maintenance of peace and security is not solely a matter of settling disputes or dealing with threats to the peace or cases of actual aggression. There is also the need of creating conditions, other than purely political ones, favourable to the existence of peace."

(8) This was the basis of the plan of Sir Maurice (later Lord) Hankey, who was the first British candidate for the post of Secretary-General of the League of Nations. His plan provided for nine parallel national secretariats staffed by nationals of the respective countries (members of the Council of the League of Nations). The duties of Secretary-General were to be exercised in rotation and to consist in super-vising these national secretariats (cf., in this connection, D. Hammarskjöld, *The International Civil Servant in Law and in Fact*, address at Oxford University, 30 May 1961, (doc. PM/85, p. 2)).

As regards other similar plans of the time—cf. Philip Noël-Baker, *The Making of the Covenant from the British Point of View;* Rask-Ørstedfondet, *Les origines et l'oeuvre de la Société des Nations*, Copenhagen, 1924, Vol. 2, p. 41; and F. P. Walters, op. cit., pp. 75-76. The same idea of "national sections"—which would be "on duty" in rotation and which would be attached to the "Principal Secretaries" for each session of the League Council, is also to be found in the secret memorandum of Sir Eric Drummond (later Lord Perth), first Secretary-General of the League, dated 25 March 1919 (cf. Sir Eric Drummond's Memorandum (secret) on the "organization and functions of the League of Nations", Archives of the Palais des Nations, Geneva). The contrast between Sir Eric's initial idea and his final plan is interesting. His views seem to have evolved very rapidly in contact with reality. As early as 1919-20 he put into practice the *contrary* of what he had previously planned in theory.

We shall refer later to the Soviet proposals at the San Francisco Conference of 1945 regarding the division of the U.N. Secretariat into separate branches. Article 101, paragraph 2, of the Charter contains traces of these proposals, the purpose of which was to provide each principal organ of the United Nations with a separate secretariat.

This idea was actually carried out in the U.N. for reasons of security, but was confined to the secretariat of the Military Staff Committee (Article 47, paragraph 1, of the Charter) whose personnel (although forming part of the Secretariat) was, until 1957, recruited directly by the Military Staff Committee, each national delegation appointing its own nationals to the staff, subject to the approval of the Secretary-General.

By its resolution 1098 (XI) the General Assembly of the U.N. decided on 27 February 1957 to merge the secretariat of the Military Staff Committee with the Secretariat of the United Nations.

The juxtaposition of national delegations was also practised at times in the inter-national administrative organs set up temporarily during the First World War.

(9) The traditions of the British Civil Service were of course well known to Sir Eric Drummond, who had formerly belonged to it. The French participation,

first that of Jean Monnet as Deputy Secretary-General of the League of Nations and then of Joseph Avenol as Sir Eric's successor, and the role of Albert Thomas in the I.L.O., led to a combination of the British and French administrative models, permanence and political neutrality being characteristic of both systems.

(10) See above, chapter 2, note (8) and below, chapter 5, note (2).

CHAPTER 3

THE ADMINISTRATIVE UNDERTAKING

The two levels of administrative action

In any administrative undertaking, whether international or not,[1] action takes place on two levels simultaneously, whatever the subject matter and locality.

First, as in any composite mechanism, there is action on the level of management. This covers technical operations, and particularly those of planning, organization, command, co-ordination and supervision.[2] It is known in the United States as "servicing functions" or "housekeeping", and elsewhere as "self-administration".[3] Obviously, any collective action becomes impossible if internal affairs are not properly managed: planning, organization, direction, co-ordination, information, finance,[4] the handling of staff and the administration of property constitute internal management and call for continuous effort, on which the progress, success and survival of the undertaking depend. The more complex and varied the task of an organization, the more important this internal management becomes and the more vital resources it absorbs. It may be termed "auxiliary" to illustrate the relation between ends and means, but this in no way diminishes the importance of such work as accountancy, documentation, organization and methods (O. & M.) and general office work (minutes, verbatim records, interpretation, translation, sound recording, etc.). These are administrative tasks which should not be underestimated. Taking an illustration from the army, the public administration here acts like the supply services and to some extent like the general staff; subordinated to the combat activities (pursuit of the predetermined aim), the routine activities keep the combatant troops in a state of efficiency, enabling them to go into battle. The division of labour, the horizontal and vertical links of the internal framework, are therefore bound up with the general administrative phenomenon and constitute its static aspect. To this should be added the dynamism of the high-level staff: their drive and initiative frequently play a part which, although kept discreetly in the background, is of great importance. The experience of the last half-century clearly proves that the breadth of outlook and human qualities of international officials, even though working behind the scenes, are an important factor of international co-operation.[5] Such work may even be of greater importance than the determination of the budgetary ceiling and the preparation of programmes of action by the deliberative organs. Thus, on the basis of his professional knowledge and of the continuity of his administrative action, the international official can, as animator and executive agent, work consistently through the clash of events and individual interests, and indirectly exercise an influence on those who have the power of decision.

Secondly, we must consider administrative action directed "outwards", the "primary" (and no longer "derivative") action of the undertaking.[6] This is no longer a supporting function working by "internal" methods; it is, on the contrary, a matter of fulfilling the purpose of the organization, of spending money, of raising standards of living or of performing other tasks of a social, cultural, humanitarian, financial or educational nature—tasks innumerable and continually changing according to the requirements of the community. Atomic energy utilization and research have recently become important, and we now see an attempt to extend international action to the exploration of outer space.

We must briefly remark on three aspects of this "external" work of international administration.

In the first place, it was precisely the satisfaction of social interests of this kind that was the objective of the international unions of the nineteenth century and the early twentieth century. As we have already pointed out, it was from this kind of specialized action—although it was then only indirect—that the modern international organization was born.

Secondly, since the management of such public action serving the general interest is entrusted on the national plane to specialized departments, it is not surprising that when similar needs were felt on the international plane, similar special departments, though on a different scale, should have been set up. The extension of administrative activity from the traditional branches to new kinds of research, information and enterprise is one of the characteristic features of the work of public administrations in general today.

Thirdly, international work of this kind, at first sporadic and highly specialized, steadily increased in volume, spread in all directions and played an extremely important part in international co-operation. Apart from organizations with special functions, the new many-sided organizations with political aims were not content to practise "concerted diplomacy" in order to promote the peaceful coexistence of nations, but combined it in one way or another with social and non-political activities.[7] It is in this way that the idea of the "indivisibility" of peace[8] grew up.

At the time of the League of Nations, only Article 23 of the Covenant dealt indirectly with non-political international action. The absence of explicit legal provisions did not, however, prevent the League from doing very important social and humanitarian work—for example, the protection of refugees, the campaigns against narcotics and epidemics, etc. This was, indeed, the only work of the League of Nations with which the United States of America was associated.[9] The Special Committee of Experts on the Development of International Co-operation in the Economic and Social Spheres (Bruce Committee) set up by the Council of the League of Nations in August 1939, adduced the following arguments in support of its plan to set up a semi-independent central committee apart from the Council of the League of Nations to direct this international "non-political action".[10]

> "There has never been a time when international action for the promotion of economic and social welfare was more vitally necessary than it is at the present moment.... The world, for all its political severance, is growing daily closer knit.... These changes inevitably give rise to new problems that can only be solved by joint effort.... Neither the economic nor the physical contagion—nor, indeed, the moral—can be checked by national action alone, except by recourse to almost complete isolation. Indeed, to attempt such isolation is one of the first national reactions to the more frequent and intenser impact of these world forces. But it reflects rather a blind instinct to ward off these impacts than a desire of the constituent parts of a changing world to adapt themselves to what in the long run must prove the irresistible dynamism of these changes."[a]
> "The League is not and never has been an institution concerned solely with the prevention of war."[b]
> "It is to the great problems of international social and economic policy that the League is devoting its attention to a constantly increasing extent— to such problems as those raised by changes in the rate of growth and in the composition of populations, to public hygiene, nutrition, housing, the mitigation of economic depressions, taxation, the economic repercussions of armaments production—in a word, to all those forces and factors that affect directly the daily lives of all classes of the peoples of the world."[c]
> "...Few will disagree with the view that 'each sound step forward in these fields is a step towards the establishment of that national and international order which is essential to real peace'."[d]

The growing importance of economic and social action on the international plane, although in view of subsequent events it had no direct consequences,[11] was also recognized by writers who tried to separate the "political" side of international action from the "economic and social," in order to preserve the second from the repercussions of the failure of the first.[12]

In the United Nations, economic and social action was formally consecrated in the text of the Charter, particularly through the creation of the Economic and Social Council (Chapter X of the

(a) League of Nations publications, General, 1939, 3 (A. 23, 1939, pp. 7/8).
(b) ibidem, p. 7.
(c) ibidem, pp. 11/12.
(d) ibidem, p. 18.

Charter) and the detailed provisions concerning international economic and social co-operation (Chapter IX), particularly those relating to the specialized agencies attached to the U.N. (Article 57). As the international organizations develop, as the interdependence of all parts of the world is clearly seen, as new ideals and new methods of co-operation between nations arise, this kind of work acquires even greater importance and represents the major part of the continuous effort of the international organizations. The various programmes of development and co-operation in this connection (technical assistance to underdeveloped countries, postal communications and telecommunications, civil aviation, meteorology, customs, health, monetary and financial affairs, education and culture, food and agriculture, labour, statistics, housing, child welfare, social welfare, etc.), must be classed in this sector of international co-operation whatever its general title and even in the absence of such a title.[a] This leads to the following conclusion:

> "The idea of an international administration is recent. . . . But it has imposed itself . . . both on the League of Nations and on the International Labour Organisation. In relation to the past it represents a much more radical and revolutionary change than the constitution of inter-governmental organs, derived from the old system of international conferences. Moreover this idea, after proving its value in the period between the two wars, made possible the development after 1944 of the major specialized agencies . . . which are nothing less than international administrations in the technical field. Their daily activity escapes the notice of the public, which is concentrated on the great political debates in the General Assembly and the Security Council. It has, however, contributed much more than these to the progress of international solidarity and co-operation. . . . "[b]

The failure to grasp the complementary character of these two aspects of international administrative action—which are not always easy to separate from the structural point of view—leads to unfortunate misunderstandings. It is a mistake to try to confine the administrative factor in international organization to the function of "secretaryship", and to regard the whole staff of the secretariat as "secretaries" of the Secretary-General, as if this aspect were exclusive. The general picture is also distorted if the second aspect is regarded simply as auxiliary, as a sort of by-product of politics. Internal and technical management by no means exhausts the administrative element in international co-operation, and economic, social, humanitarian and other work does not constitute a roundabout form of diplomatic action even though its ultimate aim—beyond its immediate object— is the maintenance of international and "indivisible" peace and security. Here and there the administrative phenomenon is revealed by the acts and the ideas peculiar to the civil servant, by a certain

(a) See "Some terminological observations by the author", (p. 13).
(b) M. Virally, op. cit., (*L'O.N.U.* . . . , pp. 117/118).

style of thought which, as in architecture, is characterized not only
by the quality of the material and the methods used, but still more
by a general distinguishing outline. Hence to speak of an administrative undertaking, to use terms belonging to administrative science,
is not to play upon words. It helps to a better understanding of the
essence of administrative action,[13] and especially of the strategically
important role of the civil servant.[14] It excludes *a priori* the incorrect
idea of the public administration simply as an instrument, since it
is unjustified in theory and unrealistic in practice. Within the framework of a unitary conception, necessarily somewhat vague in the
present state of our knowledge, we can determine the criteria which
are essential to an understanding of the mechanism.

In short, to consider these types of international action as belonging
to the sphere of public administration—as the theorists of the international unions of the nineteenth century did intuitively—facilitates
the classification, systematization and comprehension of essential
data and makes it possible to choose among them. We are thus led
to conclusions which are an important contribution to international
relations, where confusion of thought has been traditional.

The public administration as stabilizer and organizer

Apart from the creative character of any public administration
and the dynamism of administrative action, we must briefly emphasize
certain consequences of our choice of criteria in order to explain
certain later developments and avoid repetition.

The principal product, both material and non-material, of any
administrative action is the element of *order*. The administration
regulates conditions in order to create and maintain some sort of
balance, to limit the alternatives, to smooth away all kinds of friction,
and to promote the carrying out of a predetermined policy.[15] Thus,
in its double task of execution and creation, it regulates and co-or-
dinates, unifies and stabilizes,[16] ensuring both continuity of action
and the direction of energy and initiative in the social sphere. It
represents the passage from the *association*—a voluntary group of
participants wishing to undertake certain concerted activities—to
the *institution*, an organized mechanism operating according to a
definite plan to ensure the performance of a given service. In simply
striving to avoid disorder, the administration continually promotes
order by establishing a system of "communications," and collecting,
processing and distributing all kinds of necessary information. Its
function in the social body is therefore not unlike that of the nervous
system in the human body.[17]

While this continuous action against disorder is the purpose of
all public administrative activity, in the international milieu it is of
course particularly important in that it has to contend with strong

centrifugal and disruptive forces. As we have already pointed out, any international organization is the result of conflicting forces: rivalry between Powers, nationalist and autarkic tendencies, the endeavours to achieve immediate results, misunderstanding of inevitable interaction and interdependence, differences in systems of government, age-old militarist traditions. In a world composed of national States, the international organization inevitably suffers from the failure of co-operation amongst them, and is constantly exposed to pressures of all kinds.[18] The search for world unity is hampered by prejudices, emotional pulls or repulsions, particularism, conflicts of interest. The introduction of administrative order therefore constitutes the first factor in the process of institutionalization.

Next, the administration as a public service, acting in the general interest and not in any particular interest, finds itself in a special situation politically. Obliged to carry out the decisions of political bodies, it is of course bound by the values established by others, which it has to translate into practice. This differentiation between the political will on the one hand, and administrative execution on the other, calls for a distinction between sources of authority and executive operations. The former must take decisions on the objectives to be pursued (programme of action), on the main line of action (methods to be employed) and on finance (budget). The latter put the decisions into effect with the means available. The "strategy" is obviously different in the two cases. But this distinction does not mean that it is necessary to proceed to a categorical "separation of powers" according to the classical doctrine. On the contrary, the conclusion has long ago been reached—although by a roundabout method—that these two processes are not mutually exclusive,[19] but co-ordinated, complementary, and linked by the interaction of many elements.[20] The administration, indeed, always plays some part in the formulation of policy, both as regards its elaboration (by means of its reports, investigations, draft programmes, and the personal influence and advice of the leading civil servants) and, in particular cases, as regards its formation (either through the liberal interpretation of decisions or by recourse to special tactics). Consequently, while ultimate responsibility rests with him who takes the political decision on the basis of values which are subjective, non-rational and founded on knowledge which is political rather than expert, the administrator plays an important part by carrying out that decision and by establishing his own "administrative policy". Thus, whatever degree of autonomy he may enjoy in law or in fact, he remains "always on tap and never on top"; subordinated as a matter of principle to the "political" will in every way—the fundamental values, the aims to be pursued, the "strategy" to be employed, and so on. The result is that "politics and administration are the opposite sides of the same coin, the currency being human relations".[21]

Lastly, these two symmetrical elements impose standards which guide administrative action,[22] standards which are universally accepted today,[23] but which none the less do not rule out specific solutions for specific problems.[24] Here, as always in public administration,[25] "account must be taken of diverse and changing circumstances, of men also diverse and changing, and of many other varying factors. Hence, the principles are elastic and capable of being adapted to requirements. The difficulty is to know how to use them. This requires intelligence, experience, decision and moderation".[a]

We shall confine ourselves to indicating here some of these standards:
—Hierarchical authority based on unity of command (supreme power of direction, co-ordination and internal control—leadership) at the highest level[26] and subordination at the lower level,
—Unity of personnel thanks to internal communications, teamwork and an understanding of the value of collective endeavour; the importance of the psychological aspect of this element in relation to the international administration is connected with the idea of "convivencia",[27]
—Spirit of initiative at all levels, despite the division of labour and of discipline; this is fundamental to the creative character of any administration,
—Planning and control, regarded as continuous and closely linked processes ensuring order and discouraging pure improvisation, which might deflect the administration from its purpose.

The importance of these standards in the international administration—for whose general application precepts have already been formulated[28]—is obvious. They prevent ceaseless experimentation; without predetermined criteria, every idea passing through the heads of the national representatives in the deliberative organs would be put into practice; experience shows that where precise texts and definite rules of conduct are lacking, abuses, most of them unintentional, are frequent.[29]

Here is further proof of the undoubted advantage to public administration of a mixture of scientific research and practical experience.

The civil servant

The prime mover of the modern administration is the civil servant as he has evolved in the West. Apart from national peculiarities and variations of approach by different legislations or administrations, we find him possessed of certain characteristics which we have al-

(a) H. Fayol, *Administration industrielle et générale* (Prévoyance—organisation—commandement—coordination—contrôle). (1956 edition, Paris, pp. 19-20.)

ready noticed in the previous chapter; characteristics which correspond to the above-mentioned standards, long-standing traditions having been gradually adapted to modern requirements. This model has been copied with more or less success in different parts of the world, the result depending primarily on the degree of civilization, on material and moral conditions, on the level of political conduct, on respect for the law and on the human element.

In a public administration, as in any other undertaking, it is the human factor which counts. Whatever the importance of the framework in which he must act, whatever the type of organization, the working technique or the machinery employed, it is always the human individual and he alone who, carefully chosen and trained, with sufficient instruction and guidance, working in harmony with his colleagues, aware of the purpose of his work and of its justification, satisfied with his legal and moral status, ensures success. The individual is never reduced to the role of a tool; his true contribution becomes evident when we contrast him with the subordinate instruments used by the group. Thus, human values, the psychic, intellectual and moral contribution of personality, remain decisive.

We have considered the standards to which the model civil servant conforms and may now sum up his characteristics:

Since his work is a public service, and since administrative action and established policy are closely linked, the civil servant's devotion to the public interest[30] and his possession of "political sense"[31] are taken for granted;

Such a necessarily political sense being far removed from a partisan attitude, political impartiality (but not political "virginity")[32] is also required of the civil servant;

The civil servant's identification, in the psychological and deontological sense, with his service is of fundamental importance to the cohesion of his group,[33] his loyalty to the public administration even constituting a legal obligation;

The same applies to the duty of discretion, of professional secrecy and of generally reserved behaviour on the part of the official, and to the anonymity of his public action;

Professional knowledge (the "expertise" and the "professionalization" of civil servants) becomes a characteristic feature of at least the nucleus of the civil service; this is due, first, to greater opportunities for a life career and, secondly, to stricter criteria of selection such as the requirement of previous professional experience, competence, period of probation and compulsory in-service training.[34]

This description of the type of civil servant who has been the model for international administrators serves as our introduction to the problem of the international civil servant.

NOTES

(1) The idea of an "administrative undertaking" has been used, for example, by S. Bastid in her preface to Mohammed Bedjaoui's book *International Civil Service,* (London, 1958, pp. VIII/IX).

(2) Cf. H. Fayol, op. cit., *passim,* (particularly p. 48 ff.).

(3) The expression "administering ourselves" is sometimes used, not without irony, on the international plane (cf., for example, E. F. Ranshofen-Wertheimer, op. cit., pp. 3 and 4).
As regards the differentiation between the two planes of administrative action, it should be compared with that between "auxiliary services" and "line services", in accordance with the terminology generally adopted by administrative science in the United States of America (cf. G. Langrod, *Science et enseignement de l'Adminis-tration publique aux Etats-Unis,* Paris, 1954, pp. 30 ff., 55, 130 ff.).

(4) To be compared with the well-known formula "POSDCORB" employed by L. Gulick in *Papers on the Science of Administration,* (New York, 1937, p. 13).

(5) W. H. C. Laves & D. C. Stone, "The United Nations Secretariat" in *Foreign Policy Reports,* (15 October 1946, p. 183): "under the League of Nations..., there seems to have been a strong preference for civil servants who were 'seen and not heard...'. "

(6) It is in this sense that, with reference to the international administration, the first Secretary-General of the U. N., Trygve Lie, speaks, on the one hand, of the "internal administration of the secretariat," and, on the other hand, of "its external projection", (*In the Cause of Peace,* New York, 1954, p. 47).

(7) The difference between two categories of international organizations, those with *multiple aims* (general competence) and those which are *functionally specialized* also deserves attention from the administrative angle. The first category includes the League of Nations, the United Nations, the Organization of American States, the Council of Europe: the second, the majority of the specialized agencies of the United Nations family (for example, the Food and Agriculture Organization, the International Civil Aviation Organization and the World Meteorological Organ ization, but since this second category contains organizations whose purposes are determined constitutionally, certain of these specialized agencies pursue shifting and mobile aims, resulting from periodically established programmes and initia-tives of States members in the given branch (UNESCO); the latter do not, therefore, differ very greatly from the first category (general competence and multiple aims), although their purposes are limited. The aims pursued have, of course, a visible influence on the character of the administrative work.
In the first place, the predominantly *political* (first category) or *technical* (second category) character operates in this direction although this line of demarcation is neither formal nor precise. Already, at the time of the unions, it had been proposed to limit international organizations solely to organizations with "social" purposes and of a mainly technical character. The transition from this period to the next, that of the League, is marked by the appearance of organizations of a political character; it should be borne in mind, however, that even among the first-mentioned, as at present in the specialized agencies or similar bodies (outside the United Nations family), preoccupations of a political nature are not entirely absent. This manifests itself, in particular, on the level of the relations of these organizations with the authorities of the States members. In view of their specialization, these contacts are maintained no longer exclusively through the Ministries of Foreign Affairs, but also through the technical Ministries (Post Office, Health, Labour, Economic Affairs etc.); even in these Ministries, political considerations continue to operate, and there is the further difficulty of ensuring interministerial co-ordination in the

government in question. Moreover, the already-mentioned phenomenon of the "indivisibility" of peace inevitably creates, in any problem of this kind, a mixture of political and technical preoccupations.

(8) L. Ledermann, *Fédération internationale. Idées d'hier—possibilités de demain*, (Neuchâtel, 1950, p. 165): "An international organization, the sole aim of which was the maintenance of peace, would no longer correspond to the requirements of our time and still less to the hopes placed in it by the peoples. Nowadays, peace has become truly 'indivisible'. The legal rules aimed at promoting peaceful coexistence of nations can no longer solve the international problem alone. Nowadays, the solution of economic and social problems rightly engages as much attention as the diminution of the risks of war. It is to these problems, to the construction of a true international community, that a reasonable organization of international society must dedicate itself if it wishes to fulfil the hopes which have been placed in it...."

(9) Cf. statement of the Secretary of State of 25 February 1939 (League of Nations, *Official Journal*, No. 3/4, 1939, p. 217): "The League has been responsible for the development of mutual exchange and discussion of ideas and methods to a greater extent and in more fields of humanitarian and scientific endeavour than any other organization in history...."

(10) According to the Bruce Committee's draft, the proposed new organ was to embrace all responsibilities apart from the political attributions proper, which would be retained by the Council of the League. This organ would be composed of representatives of States members chosen for their competence, and representatives of non-member States participating on a footing of equality with the former and without political preoccupations.

(11) The main lines of the Bruce Report were accepted unanimously on 14 December 1939, but the work could not be continued owing to the war (cf. E. F. Ranshofen- Wertheimer, op. cit., pp. 31 and 163 ff., "The United States and the League, the Labour Organisation and the World Court in 1939", in *Geneva Studies* (No. 1/XI, February 1940, pp. 24 ff.). It should be noted, in the same connection, that during the San Francisco Conference and the years which followed there was a tendency to regard Chapters IX and X of the Charter and the action of the Economic and Social Council as a kind of consequence of the principles of the Bruce Report; a similar connection was seen between the specialized agencies of the United Nations and the economic and social organizations of the League of Nations.

(12) For example W. H. Ayles, "An Economic League of Nations, the Report of the Bruce Committee", in *Peace* (No. 6, 1939, p. 49), M. Dendias, "Les principaux services internationaux administratifs", (*Recueil des cours A.D.I.*, 1938, I, pp. 354/355).

(13) In this connection, reference should be made to the characteristic remarks of Brooks Adams, *The Theory of Social Revolution*, (New York, 1913, p. 216): "Administration is the capacity of co-ordinating many, and often conflicting, social energies in a single organism, so smoothly that they shall operate as a unity. This presupposes the power of recognizing a series of relations between numerous special social interests, with all of which no single man can be intimately acquainted...."

(14) A. G. Coons, "Management's Professional Responsibilities", in *Advanced Management*, (December 1946, No. 11, p. 142): "The administrator's position (and that of his staff of assistants) is pivotal and strategic.... A confused and harassed world is groping for some economic and social philosophy possessing an explicable rationale for the modern world.... It asks that this rationale be capable of drawing all groups, classes and corporate entities into a more effective social coherence or sense of unity wherein the limits both of individual initiative or activity and of social control may be understood...."

(15) Alfred North Whitehead, "Science and the Modern World", in *Lowell Lectures*,

1925, (1929 ed., p. 207). Cf. also H. Hausmann, "Ordnung und Idee als Grundbegriffe einer allgemeinen Verwaltungswissenschaft", in *Schriftenreihe der Verwaltungsakademie Speyer*, (Tübingen 1949, p. 5): "*Order* being undoubtedly one of the most important foundations of human coexistence, the very conception of administration as a factor ensuring order makes it one of the most important elements of human action."

(16) Cf., for example, P. Pigors, *Leadership or Domination*, (New York, 1935, p. 267): "Administrators are the stabilizers of society and the guardians of tradition. They are stabilizers in both positive and negative sense, for not only they make possible the continuance of the ideas which they convert into institutions; they also frustrate many innovations to which they deny their support...."

(17) H. Fayol, (op. cit., p. 141) says: "Like the administrative service..., man's nervous system is not visible to the superficial observer; its action cannot be directly observed and yet the muscles, although they possess their own energy, cease to contract if the nervous system ceases to act. Without its action the human body becomes an insert mass and every organ rapidly deteriorates. The nervous system is present and active in every organ and in every part of each organ. By means of cells and fibres it receives sensations and transmits them first to subordinate nervous centres, reflex centres and, from there, if necessary, to the brain. These centres or the brain then send out an order which, in the reverse direction, reaches the muscle which must carry out the movement."

(18) R. M. Maciver & C. H. Page, *Society*, (London, 1961, p. 303): "... The vast majority of the earth's two billion inhabitants in their conception of community are limited to the nation, or, at most, hold a vague hope for an internationalized world. The hope is no doubt sharper among the members of certain of the smaller and weaker nations, for understandable reasons. The great powers, more "secure" in their strength and in their pride, to a large extent continue to rely upon international bargaining practices of the nineteenth century, following their own interpretations of national interests, rather than being guided by any clear recognition of world interests as such."

(19) M. E. Dimock, *Modern Politics and Administration*, (New York, 1937, p. 243): "The two processes of Administration and Politics or policy are co-ordinate rather than exclusive...."

(20) It is in this sense that S. K. Bailey (*Congress makes a Law*, (New York, 1950)) speaks of the four I's: ideas, institutions, interests and individuals.

(21) M. E. Dimock & G. O. Dimock, *Public Administration*, (New York, 1953, p. 50).

(22) The American literature of administrative science frequently refers to these standards as "principles of organization", (cf., for example, J. D. Mooney, *The Principles of Organization*, (New York, 1947), or L. Urwick, *The Elements of Administration*, New York, 1941), H. Fayol, (op. cit., p. 20 ff.. "Principes d'administration") sees the problem in the same way. But certain American authors regard them only as "pattern solutions" or even as "proverbs" (cf. H. A. Simon, "The Proverbs in Administration", in *Publ. Administration Review*, (No. 6, 1946, p. 58 ff.)). But even if they sometimes cast doubt on the rigid and definitive character of these standards (giving them rather the status of indicative theorems) they, too, agree that in the light of comparative experience they inevitably apply to *all* kinds of administrative action.

(23) It is characteristic that both Fayol in France and Mooney and Reilley in the United States have independently reached identical conclusions on these points (cf. L. Urwick, op. cit., p. 42).

(24) "There is seldom a '*One-Best-Way*' in Public Administration..." (quoted from "Standards and techniques of public administration") (considered more particularly from the point of view of technical assistance to the underdeveloped countries),

Report of the Special Committee on Public Administration Problems, United Nations (A.A.T.), 1951, (Doc. ST/TAA/M/I, para. 30, p. 12).

(25) The specific conditions of the international administrative environment must be taken particularly into consideration (cf. for example, T. Lie, op. cit., p. 43): "The disabilities of national bureaucracies are legendary and real. I was soon to find out that the difficulties in international Administration multiply these many, many times...."

(26) H. Fayol, op. cit., p. 27: L. Urwick, op. cit., pp. 43 and 49. The desire to avoid contradictory instructions (which are almost inevitable if unity of command is lacking) is closely bound up wich the standards of authority and hierarchy ("scaler chain").

(27) "A Latin American delegate to an Assembly of the U.N. once suggested that in international relations for the word 'coexistence' should be substituted the Spanish word '*convivencia*'. There is no English equivalent. A capacity for '*convivencia*', however, is one of the essential qualities of an international official. Those who lack it necessarily exercise a disintegrating influence in an international secretariat and, moreover, are unlikely to be effective in dealing with representatives of countries other than their own. Loyalty will be weak in a secretariat in which a large proportion of the staff lack this quality because group consciousness will be weak" (A. Loveday, op. cit., p. 35).

(28) We refer in particular to the following considerations chiefly concerning the international administration (D. C. Stone, *Perspectives*..., op. cit., pp. 428 ff.):

(*a*) The burden placed on administrative machinery (the permanent secretariats) should not be greater than the political structure is designed to sustain or heavier than the national governments will support;

(*b*) Objectives and purposes and *policies* should be clearly defined at the outset. The greater the ambiguity or uncertainty on these points, the greater will be the hesitations on the part of those who implement them, and this may lead to complete paralysis of all action; to avoid this they have to undertake the difficult and dangerous task of interpretation;

(*c*) A broad mandate is often an advantage, in order to keep open possibilities for growth, especially when future developments cannot be clearly foreseen. Deliberative bodies should not too rigidly prescribe administrative organization and procedures, since effective organization can never be static and must change continuously to fit evolving political, social and technical developments and harness most effectively the participants in it;

(*d*) The financial support should be assured so that the secretariat should not have to devote a great part of its energy to saving money where the expense would have been worth while, or obtaining payment from recalcitrant States or seeking means of covering the deficit by extra-budgetary methods.

(29) D. C. Stone (*Perspectives*..., op. cit., p. 429): "Individual delegates, as well as the Assemblies and their Committees, often consider the secretariats 'happy hunting grounds' for the imposition of their ideas on how affairs should be administered and for jobs for 'passed over' civil servants, army officers, diplomats and so forth...."

(30) In this connection it is worth recalling what Plato said (Republic, Book III, Ch. XIX): "Since those who command must be the best of guardians, should they not be those who are most competent to guard the State? And should they not have an intelligence directed towards this end, accompanied by authority and devotion to the public welfare?" As regards the French model: R. Catherine, *Le Fonctionnaire français. Droits – devoirs – comportement* (Paris, 1961, pp. 167 ff. and *passim*); as regards the British model: T. A. Critchley, *The Civil Service today*, (London, 1951).

(31) M. E. & G. O. Dimock (op. cit., p. 49): "Political sense, which is the ability to operate effectively in a political setting, is required if the administrator is to remain

alert to every opposing strategy of those with whom he deals...; consequently the administrator with a fine political sense is usually the most successful in furthering his programme and preserving the status of his agency...."

(32) Dag Hammarskjöld spoke in this sense in regard to the international civil service in his Oxford address in 1961 (op. cit., p. 3) of the difference between "politically celibate" and "politically virgin" (respect by the official for the scale of values established by (previous) political decisions and by tradition in spite of the personal opinions to which he is entitled).

(33) This mechanism has already been discussed by Freud in relation with the "mutual tie between members of a group, based upon important emotional common qualities" (S. Freud, *Group Psychology and the Analysis of the Ego*, New York, 1922, p. 62) and by Lasswell in relation to the different "symbols of identification" (nation, class, State, race ·= "*sentiment areas*"); H. D. Lasswell, *World Politics and Personal Insecurity*, (New York, 1935, p. 29 ff.). H. A. Simon, (*Administrative Behaviour. A Study of Decision-making Processes in Administrative Organization*, New York, 1948, p. 204 ff.) discusses particularly the application of this mechanism to the public administrations.

(34) P. M. Gaudemet, *Le Civil Service britannique. Essai sur le régime de la fonction publique en Grande-Bretagne*, (Paris 1952) and H. Finer, *Theory and Practice of Modern Government* (New York, 1949, pp. 614 ff. and 882 ff.).

CHAPTER 4

THE INTERNATIONAL CIVIL SERVANT

New human category

"The present extension...of international institutions is a major event in the evolution of the world, and there is no turning back from it, whether they are world-wide or regional institutions, or political or specialized organizations.... Short of a world-wide catastrophe, those [international] administrations are destined to become one of the permanent features of world organization....

The *international civil service* is, socially and professionally, a new departure which, in various forms, will be called upon to *break new ground in the development of the world of tomorrow.*"[a]

The international stage had hitherto been occupied only by States, and the individual had had no official place on it. The appearance on this stage of an *impartial third party* is a revolutionary event. This third party, the international civil servant, is not, like the international judge, called upon to settle occasional disputes (with the agreement of the States concerned), nor to give advisory opinions on legal questions when requested to do so; his task is to undertake *continuous* administrative action in the interest of the whole international community. Thus, his appearance symbolizes a new attempt—of capital importance because institutionalized—to introduce the element of *order* into international life.

Acting in international affairs side by side with the international judge, attached to an organ (the secretariat)[1] equal in importance to the Court of Justice which lays down the law in international disputes, the international civil servant has to be as impartial as the international judge.[2] This is the fundamental and unprecedented novelty of his contribution. There is no longer—as in the past—any trace of the "liaison officer" in the role of the international civil servant; he embodies the universal interest by representing only the organization which he serves. It is no exaggeration to say that he constitutes a new human category. The already large number of international officials, together with the special character of their job, makes it possible to speak of a human "category" no longer playing an intermittent part on the international scene, but already possessing rights of citizenship under international law.

(a) A. Molitor, "Public Administration towards the Future", *Revue internationale des Sciences administratives*, (Brussels, No. 4/1961, pp 381-383).

This position is of a special kind, as is the status of the international civil servant in relation to the classical legal framework. What is more, despite deceptive appearances, the novelty of this new category is above all psychological. It is important to grasp all the special features of the situation—hybrid in a sense—of the international official in a world in which, in principle, every human being "belongs" (legally and psychologically) to a State as its national. Many difficulties arise from the fact that, clinging to acquired mental habits, people often shrink from the intellectual effort required to understand the complex facets of reality. The same difficulty arises, indeed, in regard to the international judge, the difference being mainly one of degree. Both cases pose new problems which must be solved by an effort of the mind.

It is not surprising that this attempt to bring order into international relations should be accompanied by disorder in the realm of ideas. The international administration is a comparatively recent creation. As we have said, the international civil servant has come into being under the pressure of necessity, his theoretical justification following only slowly his "spontaneous generation". The very idea of the *impartial third person* among sovereign States, accepted—grudgingly and with many legal and mental reservations—in the case of the arbitrator and the international judge, runs counter to diehard conceptions of the State. Hence, the frequent misunderstanding of the work of the international civil servant. Hence, too, frequent attempts to play down his role in order to prevent him from becoming, thanks to his continuity and his competence, an impartial influence in international relations. Even where the constitutions of international organizations contain clear and decisive provisions on this subject,[3] attempts are still made to find interpretations (*praeter legem* and even *contra legem*) depriving them of real value.

This explains the persistence of the "minimalist" contention[a] that the international secretariat should perform only material and therefore subordinate tasks. Its proponents are, first, those who—in the absence of any accepted theory of international administration[4]—prefer a norm which suits their political ideas; secondly, those who cling to their own administrative traditions and wish to transplant them on to the international plane. Among the former are to be found some of the great Powers, who are in principle against any international factor liable to oppose their wishes.[5] Among the second we find, for example, Great Britain, who, owing to the tradition of political effacement in her civil service, favours a purely administrative conception of the secretariat's powers, and the "*seconding*" of international officials to deal with political affairs.[6] It was on the basis of

(a) See above, chapter 2, note (4).

the British traditions that the first Secretary-General of the League of Nations, Sir Eric Drummond, introduced a characteristic practice which will be discussed later. It seems useful in this connection to recall the fundamental declarations which at the time determined the principles of action of the League Secretariat:

> "We recommend with special urgency that, in the interests of the League, as well as in its own interests, the Secretariat should not extend the sphere of its activities, that in the preparation of the work and the decisions of the various organizations of the League, it should regard it as its first duty to collate the relevant documents, and to prepare the ground for these decisions without suggesting what these decisions should be; finally, that once these decisions had been taken by the bodies solely responsible for them, it should confine itself to executing them in the letter and in the spirit.
> "Once the decisions have been taken it is for the Secretariat to apply them. Here again a distinction must be made between application and interpretation, not of course that I ask the Secretariat never to interpret; that is its job! But I ask it, and you will certainly all ask it, to interpret as little as possible, as faithfully as possible and particularly never to substitute its interpretation for yours."[a]

It seems characteristic of the tenacity of the "minimalists" that, in spite of Sir Eric Drummond's being still in office and despite the extreme effacement of himself and his subordinates in political matters, they did not relax their efforts. The representatives of four Member States constituting the minority of the famous Committee of Thirteen[b]—Germany, Italy, Venezuela and Colombia[c]—defined their views in 1930 as follows:[d]

> "The field of activity of the various organs of the League, which have steadily increased in number, has been so enlarged that at the present time it covers almost every aspect of international life. The staff of the Secretariat, which at the beginning consisted of about 100 persons, now numbers nearly 700.... The political influence of the Secretariat and especially of its principal officers is in fact enormous and it would be a mistake to close our eyes to this fact.... [the question of] the organization of the higher direction of the Secretariat (is of capital importance); to a certain extent it determines the future of the League."

Although there was an element of exaggeration in this appreciation, for reasons due to the politics of the time, some writers concluded that the theory of the international civil service as an administrative, and thus in a sense as a creative phenomenon, was bound to win the day despite the restrictive tendencies which were then accepted and encouraged by the head of the Secretariat.

On the other hand, the "maximalist" theory regarded the inter-

(a) Quoted by Dag Hammarskjöld in his Oxford address of 1961, (op. cit., p. 3).
(b) Committee of Enquiry appointed to examine what steps could be taken to ensure, in the future as in the past, the best possible administrative results for the Secretariat, the I.L.O. and the Registry of the Permanent Court of International Justice (10th Assembly of the League, pp. 144, 166, 173).
(c) Bernstorff (Germany), Scialoja, later Giuseppe Gallavresi (Italy), I. C. Parra-Perez (Venezuela), Urrutia (Colombia).
(d) See chapter 5, notes (13), (14), (15), and (17).

national secretariat not as a mere "conference machine", fundamentally static, but on the contrary as:

"a dynamic instrument...through which...[to] seek...reconciliation and through which they should also try to develop forms of executive action, undertaken on behalf of all Members, and aiming at forestalling conflicts and resolving them, once they have arisen, by appropriate diplomatic or political means, in a spirit of objectivity and in implementation of the principles and purposes of the Charter."[a]

As we shall see, this conception sees in the Secretariat the elements of an "independent executive",[b] called upon if necessary to fill the gap left by the resolutions of the deliberative organs of the international organization in order to ensure the continuity of administrative action and to safeguard the interests of the international community.

Between these two extreme viewpoints we find a middle way: the Balfour principles mentioned above and embodied in the texts in force point the way to a sensible conclusion from the point of view of administrative science. If we begin by considering administration and "politics", as complementary rather than as conflicting processes,[c] we may come to understand the role of the administrator as appointed guardian of the public interest.

We have now sufficient length and variety of experience to enable us to draw valid conclusions from an objective analysis of the international civil service.

The independent status of the international civil servant

While indirectly under the authority of all the member States—which are represented in the deliberative organs—the international civil servant is not, as regards the performance of his task, subordinate to any of them, not even to the State of which he is a national. His situation is delicate and exceptional: whatever his rank and function in the secretariat he is subordinate in service matters exclusively to his own administrative superiors. The whole staff from top to bottom of the scale consists of officials whose status is the same.

The result is that while certain international officials, in view of their particular responsibilities, are directly or indirectly in touch with the governments of member States and may be subject to their (sometimes conflicting) influences—their task remains by definition outside and above any national or other preconception. This is the capital difference between the international official and any national official,

(a) Introduction to the Report of the Secretary-General of the United Nations of 1960/1961, p. 1 and *passim*) – an idea of Dag Hammarskjöld's.
(b) Introductions to the Reports of the Secretary-General of the United Nations of 1959/1960 and of 1960/1961 (Chapter 3); statement by the Secretary-General, Dag Hammarskjöld, to the Security Council in connection with the Congo question on 14 December 1960.
(c) See above, chapter 3, notes (19), (20), (21).

whatever analogies there may be between them in other respects.[7]

This distinction is clearly brought out by the provisions of the relevant international agreements and is characteristic of the international civil service.

Experience has shown that as impartiality is undoubtedly a necessary quality of the international civil servant, his independent status has become a *sine qua non* of his non-representative character. The international official, like the international judge, is chosen for his personal qualifications of efficiency, competence and integrity. While in both cases (subject to different methods of appointment in view of Article 9 of the Statute of the Court) national and cultural origins play a part[8] which has to be taken into account, they do not confer *representative* status on either. This must be continually stressed owing to the very unfortunate terminological misunderstandings which frequently occur. In speaking of international civil servants, the term "representative" is often used, referring to national allegiance;[9] hence a confusion—unintentional but serious—between national representatives (delegates) who actually represent their respective Governments, and international civil servants chosen *ad personam* who, without any national authority and representing nobody, nevertheless contribute to the international civil service a particular intellectual training, a certain culture derived from national or regional tradition. Even if they come from the civil service of a State, of which of course they still remain nationals; even if they will subsequently return to that civil service, they are *never* in a situation comparable to that of diplomats appointed by and responsible to their governments. Contrary to the examples we have seen during the unionist period, there is therefore no question here of a sort of "functional duality". The appointment of the international civil servant involves *a choice on his part:* we shall now consider the many consequences of this choice.

It is precisely this choice—voluntary acceptance of his psychological "identification" with and of his legal membership of the international organization—which is decisive in the case of the *international* civil servant. The idea of the international civil service, the realization of a centuries-old myth, is added *ex post facto* to its practical necessity, and contributes to the unity of the staff of the international secretariat in spite of differences of culture and training. The essential elements of this choice are connected, and that is why no concession is admissible without risk of destroying the whole edifice.

In view of his independent status, the international civil servant finds himself, as far as his international work is concerned, outside the authority of States, as follows:

first of all of the *host State* of the organization which he serves; since agreements concluded between the international organizations and the States in which they establish their headquarters[10] have allowed him certain limited privileges;

next of his *State of origin,* although he retains its nationality; since as soon as he is appointed, the rule *ne impediatur officio* comes into play, whereby the international civil servant enjoys, in the performance of the international task entrusted to him, certain immunities and exemptions (particularly as regards civil and penal liabilities).[11] He may therefore escape from the jurisdiction of the ordinary law, perhaps even that of his own country as far as his international functions are concerned, and this tends to preserve his impartiality. This immunity therefore goes even farther than that of diplomats who represent a national Government. But it must not be forgotten that the various privileges and immunities granted to international civil servants are granted in the interests of the organization, that these privileges and immunities are therefore "attached to the function and not to the person"[12] and that, according to the rules laid down in the relevant texts, the Secretary-General remains the sole judge of their application in any particular case;[13, 14]

lastly, of all the other States (whether or not they are members of the international organization in question) in virtue of treaties regarding the said privileges and immunities, in so far as they have been ratified by the State in question, or in virtue of generally accepted custom. Here the States accept certain uniform provisions even without treaty obligation "pending the conclusion or entry into force of a convention on this subject or even before".[15]

Independent status has various consequences. Once the basic principle is recognized, these consequences depend on compromises in its application. For the sake of clarity we shall divide these consequences under the three following heads:

psychological consequences (with deontological repercussions). The international civil servant must have a world-wide approach to his work (attitude of "togetherness") if he is to be really impartial;

legal consequences: special legal status;

Primarily *administrative* consequences—i.e., those connected with the operation of the machinery, although exercising an influence on the international civil servant's status in general. This category includes recruitment problems, the bond between the civil servant and his organization (degree of international allegiance while maintaining nationalities) and career problems.

Psychological consequences

Whatever the purpose and nature of the international organization (multiple-purpose or functionally specialized;[a] political or mainly

(a) See above, chapter 3, note (7).

technical; large, medium-sized or small), it is the international outlook of its officials which provides the psychological foundation of its independent status.

This international outlook is bound up with an idea or a philosophy—namely, the idea of co-operation between nations, the collective ideal as a matter of conscience, the vision of the international community rising above all obstacles. A conviction that this community, based on human solidarity, is inevitable, must be an integral part of the official's philosophy and independent of the vicissitudes of international life. There thus appears a system of ideal values, a philosophy which explains the labels of "international-mindedness, international outlook or international understanding";[a] it is both a centre of attraction for the creative imagination and a point of departure for the widening of traditional perspectives. The picture thus created by the intellect clearly portrays a community of interests as well as of sentiments. It is not a question of a negation of national outlooks, but of their co-ordination.[b] Thus, the international ideology is not in contradiction with national sentiment, although a traditional opposition tends to separate them. The two sentiments, both equally natural, can be reconciled as soon as the *mores* of the period which gave them birth allow it. The international ideology anticipates history and absorbs it. As Edouard Claparède says (*Morale et politique*), "The national must cease to be in opposition to the international; it must be absorbed into it as the individual is absorbed into society, being his own master only in order to be a better servant of the community. This revision of our scale of values is the great task to which we must apply ourselves without loss of time."

Further, the *international outlook* is more than an ideology or a state of mind, since it is not only "a matter of conviction and intention, but a matter of comprehension and training".[c] It is in fact a psychological attitude which can be acquired by proper training: "The international outlook is rather like a knowledge of foreign languages: it is acquired by practice provided that one has a certain degree of ability and willingness to learn...."[d] So it is a matter of education:

"The formation of an international outlook becomes an educational and cultural question, a question of scientific study of international relations, a problem of the development of understanding between peoples."[e]

(a) Cf., for example, International Civil Service Advisory Board, *Report on In-service Training in the U.N. and the Specialized Agencies* (Doc. Co-ord/Civil Service/4, p. 4).
(b) S. Basdevant (Bastid) (op. cit., p. 324).
(c) E. Giraud (op. cit., p. 70).
(d) Ibidem.
(e) O. Leimgruber, General Report of the VIIth International Congress of Administrative Sciences, Berne, 1947 (Minutes of the Congress, p. 109).

Setting out from an ideological conception, we construct by a process of reasoning a *principle of unity* which places the international element above national aspirations, without conflicting with them, but adding to and absorbing them. We thus arrive at the following conclusion: "The highest interests of one's own country are served best by the promotion of security and welfare *everywhere*, and the steadfast maintenance of that conviction without regard to changing circumstances."[a] By taking duly into account the interests of each country and the conditions of modern life, we are thus able to construct a political philosophy which determines the behaviour of the international civil servant:

> "The international outlook required of the international civil servant is an awareness made instinctive by habit of the needs, emotions and prejudices of the people of differently-circumstanced countries, as they are felt and expressed by the peoples concerned, accompanied by a capacity of weighing these...elements in a judicial manner before reaching any decision to which they are relevant...."[b]

This is clearly a totally different attitude from that ridiculed by Canning when he spoke of the "friend of every country but his own".[c] The experience of the international secretariats is that the daily work in common of people of different race, language, nationality and training, and the feeling of comradeship which goes with it, lead inevitably to a common denominator, to a mutual fertilization, to an increase in comprehension and to a sort of "control" of the impartiality of the team as a whole (except in a few isolated cases where the fundamental international outlook is lacking).

The sum of the psychological contributions of all the members of the staff of an international secretariat creates a common atmosphere—the spirit in which the staff works; it is on this spirit that the exclusively international character of the secretariat depends.[d] The element of *identification* derives from it[e] and plays an essential part in any civil service. Thus, from the *esprit de corps* which animates a team at work,[16] we come to the obligation of *loyalty*, the direct result of each official's feeling of "belonging" to his organization.[17] This feeling of loyalty is the complex outcome of both the fundamental philosophical conception and of the intellectual training of the official;[18] it applies in the first instance to the organization in which

---

(a) "The International Secretariat of the Future", in *Lessons from Experience by a Group of Former Officials of the League of Nations, Post-War Problems* (London, 1944, p. 18).
(b) C. W. Jenks, "Some Problems of an International Civil Service", in *Public Administration Review* (No. 2, 1943, p. 95).
(c) Ibidem.
(d) Introduction to the Report of the Secretary-General of the United Nations, 1960/1961, chapter IV, p. 16.
(e) See above, chapter 3, note (33).

the official is serving, but extends to international co-operation in general, embracing particularly the "associated organizations".

International ideological conception, international outlook, international loyalty—these three fundamental elements of the international civil service were clearly not intended by its founders to lead to a sort of "spiritual statelessness", to the creation of an "international man" (or "international globetrotter"),[a] "indifferent to the emotions and prejudices of those whose world is bounded by the frontiers of a single State".[b] The problem of administrative policy on the international plane (and *mutatis mutandis* in the central service of any federal State, particularly when it is multinational) is to create a series of conditions appropriate to the requirements of modern times and thus ease the transition from one period to another. If there are apparent contradictions between the national and the international elements, these are simply characteristic of the period of *transition* in which we live: "The degree of civilization," says Paul Valéry, "may be judged by the number of contradictions which it accumulates"; and he emphasizes the role of "a League of Nations which presupposes a league of minds...."

By definition, the psychology of the international official is neither that of a "rootless cosmopolitan" who has broken all ties with his country of origin (so that the classical adage *"nemo potest exuere patriam"* applies to him), nor that of a chauvinist mentally circumscribed by national frontiers. It is not a question of rejecting the system of thought, sentiments or emotions based on the national idea, nor of feeling superior to other human groups. There should be neither nationalism nor denationalization. This combination of sentiments is a common-sense solution. By retaining and in a sense accentuating[19] his attachment to his country of origin, the international official subordinates and reconciles it to the feeling (quite as *natural*) of belonging to the human community. Although a man brought up according to the ideas of the last century can only by an intense effort of self-determination adjust his mind to the new scale of values, it has been proved that this readjustment is only a matter of education. It has been advocated by great thinkers of the past. For example in Montesquieu's *Mélanges inédits* we find the following:

> "I was truly patriotically inclined; I loved my country not only because I was born there, but because it was part of that great fatherland which is the universe.
> ..."

The international official is therefore a pioneer who must harmonize these apparently contradictory but reconcilable extremes. With

(a) E. F. Ranshofen-Wertheimer, (op. cit., p. 240).
(b) C. W. Jenks, *Some Problems...*, (loc. cit.).

the international judge, he symbolizes this reconciliation in his own person and thus anticipates the future progress of human ideas. But the judge at the Hague Court has an objective legal statute creating favourable conditions for his impartiality as the basis of all justice. Such a guard, based on existing documents, is absent in the case of the international official. Therefore it is all the more essential that his "exclusively international" character should be respected. Thus the *dual loyalty* required of him—loyalty to his country and loyalty to the organization he serves (which, although international, is by no means *a*-national)—is essential to his integrity.[20]

Indeed, these new values tend to harmonize all ideologies, affinities and emotions and to find a compromise between national identification and universal identification: such a compromise is made possible by the accession of the country concerned to the international organization and by recognition of the "community of thought" binding peoples together, regardless of the often artificial frontiers of States, and calling for common action based on human solidarity. Thus national sentiment, alive, but without aggressiveness and intolerance, will help the international official to serve the needs of the international community, conceived as a synthesis of its components and based on generous comprehension of the diversity of peoples and the variety of civilizations.[21]

The international official's first duty, defined in the staff regulations and freely accepted at the time of his appointment, is to be faithful to his organization in the event of a conflict between his two loyalties, and even at the cost of painful sacrifice. In such a situation the extreme consequence of joining an international administration becomes plain. But even if no such extreme case should arise, international loyalty is not only a limitation imposed on the official, but also a source of positive obligations. It forbids prejudice, partisanship, narrow conception of the national interest, exclusiveness with regard to other groups, "ideological totalitarianism"—in a word, typical nationalist behaviour. But it also makes many positive demands—discipline, discretion, reserve in the expression of personal opinions,[22] and so on.

Indeed, "truly international officials are possible but very difficult to find. You have to transform into devoted servants of the international community men who are naturally attached to their native soil, and this is almost a miracle".[a] In the first place these officials have learnt to distinguish between "national loyalty" and "state loyalism";[23] the first means attachment to one's country, to its history, to its customs and to its civilization, which is perfectly compatible with international loyalty; and the second takes the form of

(a) Speech by W. Rappard, Swiss delegate in the 4th Committee of the 11th Assembly of the League of Nations, 1930, p. 74.

unconditional fidelity to one's national government, which is of course completely contrary to the essence of the international civil service. In the second place, they must defend consistently their character of international officials in the service of the international organization, even where the obligations of this service do not coincide with the views of the government of their own country. It is true that in most cases no important political questions are involved, but the attitude taken by certain officials "against their country" has been remarkable and created some stir at the time in their respective capitals. A famous example is that of Albert Thomas, Director of the I.L.O., who defended the interests of the International Labour Organisation before the Hague Court in direct opposition to his Government as regards the I.L.O.'s competence in agricultural matters;[24] and there have been other similar examples.[25]

> "Early in 1938 I was forced greatly against my will to resign the post of Director rather than make an appointment which one of the leading governments pressed relentlessly upon me, but which would have set a fatal precedent for all future international administration. In the critical position that then existed in Europe, it was not even possible to thresh the matter out in public without serious political consequences. Some day the story may perhaps be told. In itself it was of minor importance, but it turned round a vital question of principle, as subsequent events have amply shown."[a]

Even in cases of serious political conflict—for example, when the Governments of Fascist Italy and Nazi Germany ceased to be Members of the League of Nations and exerted pressure on their nationals to leave the international civil service, several of them, in spite of the "crisis of loyalty" thus created, resisted the pressure and remained at their posts in the Secretariat.

While officials acting in directorial, co-ordinating or supervisory capacities or exercising diplomatic functions[26] are more exposed to conflicts of loyalty than their colleagues whose work is of a material, purely advisory or executive nature, it must be emphasized that they may all be faced from time to time with serious questions of conscience. This is especially the case when they are nationals of a great Power or of a State with far-flung interests. Even an ordinary translator, interpreter or précis-writer may find himself in such a situation. That is why, on the basis of the texts in force, the international character of the service is identical for the whole staff regardless of rank or function.

Further, the problem of the independent status of the international civil servant has legal or administrative as well as psychological aspects.

Legal consequences

As soon as the appearance of this "new human category" outmoded

(a) H. Butler, *The Lost Peace*, (London, 1941, pp. 56/57).

the old conception of "functional duality", it became necessary to give it an adequate status outside the national sphere. First of all, it was important to avoid the legal vacuum in which the international official would find himself for lack of new rules applying to his special situation. Next, it was necessary both to guarantee the international organization the quality and continuity of service which it was entitled to expect from its staff, and to give the international official security of tenure and to draw up general rules for the whole conduct of his affairs. Such a statute was an inescapable necessity,[27] in spite of the lack of precedents and of the institutional *polycentrism* which complicated the picture and still does so today.

In spite of difficulties, this idea has won increasing acceptance. A domestic law of international organization ("infra-international law"), conceived as an autonomous legal branch, but really a part of public international law,[28] began to make its appearance in 1919. While the Covenant of the League of Nations remained silent on the subject, the statutory rules concerning the staff and reflecting the Balfour Principles tended to become a sort of ordinary law applicable to the staff of all the international administrations.[29] As a result of the League's experience, the San Francisco Conference took an interest in these problems and a few fundamental principles were inserted in the Charter of the United Nations. The aim was to provide the Secretariat in this way with better protection against pressure and interference from outside, while at the same time imposing a stricter rule of conduct on the staff. As the constitutions of other members of the United Nations family repeated the same rules, this process of systematization and unification increased. Both legally amongst the affiliated organizations and in practice outside the latter, and on the regional plane, statutory staff rules were henceforward more or less adjusted to the basic model—that is to say to the staff regulations of the United Nations. Ever since the days of the League of Nations, jurisprudential and doctrinal action has powerfully contributed to this tendency.

We thus see the progressive appearance of a *real* international administrative law, the legal status of the international civil servant being the precursor of the complete legal system.

"At its present stage of development, international administrative law is primarily a law governing the international public service and the administration of international public funds; as it develops further, it may well be increasingly concerned with the exercise of administrative powers directly affecting third-party interests.... As international administrative law develops further, it will be necessary to resolve the series of dilemmas already brought into focus in the preliminary stages of its development. They will not necessarily be resolved in a clear-cut and uniform manner....

If these varied dilemmas are to be successfully resolved, the future development of international administrative law must be nourished by a wide and deep understanding of administrative law generally, and disciplined by a full and instinctive awareness of the practical realities of international administration. . . . "a

These new statutes have a fundamentally dynamic character. There is here no static, purely individualist or conservative conception of international administrative law, but a reasonable reconciliation of the respect due to the rights of the staff with the overriding purpose of safeguarding the interests of the organization—two aspects of the legal consequences of the independent status of international officials, considered as a legal expression of institutionalized and continuous international co-operation.

"International administrative law, as all law, is directed to ensuring the preservation and fullest expression of an idea in action. When that idea is expressed in the complex and permanent system of action which we call an organization, law is concerned with preserving the integrity of the organization as an expression of its essential idea. It is concerned with preserving those ways of action which are necessary to enable the fullest expression of the idea which is at the heart of the organization. Its control of conduct flows from the necessity of maintaining the integrity of those patterns of action to which the system must adhere, if it is to maintain itself and be vigorous. International administrative law is, accordingly, more than an individual necessity in the functioning of the secretariat as a system of authority. It is an organizational necessity. . . . Ultimately, the rules of international administrative law represent a compromise between the values of the organization and the values of the individual participant in the day-to-day functioning of the secretariat. The organizational values of flexibility and discretion in the exercise of authority often clash with individual values of stability and security. International administrative law discharges its functions when it harmonizes these conflicting values upon a viable basis, assuring to administration a reasonable degree of authority and flexibility for the accomplishment of administrative goals and to individuals a reasonable degree of protection against abuse of authority . . . "b

The sources of the legal status in question are:
—first, the rules of the constitutions of the individual international organizations, which are almost always identical. When the United Nations came into being, these rules determined the "exclusively international" character of the staff, imposing both a service obligation on each official (positive obligation—subordination only to the authority of the secretariat; negative obligation—abstention from seeking or receiving instructions from any outside authority), and an obligation on Member States not to seek to influence that official. This legal consequence is of capital importance (though, as regards the obligation incurred by the member countries, it is not expressly stated in the texts in force);[30]
—next, the "internal" provisions of the staff rules and regulations, which are abundant and detailed, although subject to frequent changes. Thanks to the standards established and generally followed,

(a) C. W. Jenks, *The Proper Law of International Organization*, op. cit., pp. 128/129.
(b) K. S. Carlston, "International Administrative Law. A Venture in Legal Theory", in *Journal of Public Law*, (2 August 1959, Atlanta, pp. 334 and 337).

at least in principle,[31] we have uniformity in all similar international organizations.[32] In particular, the principle of the independent status of the international civil service in relation to the member States is universal, any offence being dealt with according to the organization's own disciplinary rules;

—lastly, jurisprudence. Since the immunity conferred on international officials prevents national judicial authorities from intervening in matters between the staff and the organization,[33] it is essential to have an administrative tribunal which will ensure stability in the international civil service by guaranteeing staff rights and at the same time protecting the organization against legally unjustified complaints on the part of the staff. This impartial judicial control represents an element of order in the relations between the staff and the organization and is considered by some writers as essential to the introduction of a "legal system" in this sphere.[34]

Before the creation of an Administrative Tribunal in the League of Nations in 1927 (initially as a temporary measure), various expedients had been resorted to in the settlement of disputes arising out of the non-observance by the organization of the clauses of contracts or of the regulations. It was soon found that neither an appeal by a dismissed official to the Assembly, nor the establishment of joint advisory committees, nor (obviously) reliance by the injured official on the diplomatic protection of his national delegation, nor even the *ad hoc* creation of a quasi-juridical body (Monod precedent of 1925)[35] "half-way between an administrative and political court of appeal and a jurisdictional court of appeal",[36] could suffice to ensure the smooth working of the Secretariat. In order to put an end to the "very natural feeling of insecurity which tends to diminish efficiency by destroying confidence in the future",[37] a permanent element of control based on "judicial" impartiality had to be introduced.

Since then, the jurisprudence of the Administrative Tribunal of the League of Nations (1927-1946), of the Administrative Tribunal of the International Labour Organisation since 1946[38] and of the Administrative Tribunal of the United Nations since 1950,[39] has contributed to the building up by interpretation of a body of precedents of general application. Thus the judgments of these tribunals have defined in detail the legal situation of the staff of the international secretariats by consistently emphasizing its *international* character and striking a balance between the old exclusive conception of the contractual character of the appointment of officials and that of its statutory and impersonal character. The contractual character is limited to the particular situation of each official (nature of the appointment, salary, rank), and the statutory character is decisive with regard to the organization and efficient operation of the international civil service.[40]

These jurisprudential principles are discussed, confirmed and interpreted in three important advisory opinions of the International
Court of Justice—namely:

(a) The case of *Reparations for Injuries suffered in the Service of the
United Nations* (*Bernadotte* Case of 11 April 1949). Considering the
problem of the U.N.'s right to claim compensation from the State
responsible for injuries suffered by an agent (who was not even in
this case an official of the United Nations), the Court emphasized the
international character of the relations between the international
organization and its agent:

> "To ensure the independence of the agent, and, consequently, the independent
> action of the organization itself, it is essential that in performing his duties he
> need not have to rely on any other protection than that of the organization
> (save of course for the more direct and immediate protection due from the State
> in whose territory he may be). In particular, he should not have to rely on
> the protection of his own State. If he had to rely on that State, his independence
> might well be compromised, contrary to the principle applied by Article 100 of
> the Charter. And lastly, it is essential that – whether the agent belongs to a
> powerful or to a weak State; to one more affected or less affected by the compli-
> cations of international life; to one in sympathy or not in sympathy with the
> mission of the agent – he should know that in the performance of his duties he
> is under the protection of the organization . . . ".[a] "The ordinary practice whereby
> a State does not exercise protection on behalf of one of its nationals against
> a State which regards him as its own national, does not constitute a precedent
> which is relevant here. The action of the organization is in fact based not upon
> the nationality of the victim, but upon his status as an agent of the organization.
> Therefore, it does not matter whether or not the State to which the claim is
> addressed regards him as its own national, because the question of nationality
> is not pertinent to the admissibility of the claim . . . "[b]

Thus, the Court,[41] taking into account the opinions of various States
represented during the proceedings,[42] drew important conclusions
from the relationship between the agent in the service of an international organization and that organization. It dealt pragmatically
with this new legal situation and applied in particular the "theory of
implied powers".

(b) The case of the *Effect of Awards of Compensation made by the
United Nations Administrative Tribunal*, 13 July 1954. In considering
the alleged right of the General Assembly of the U.N. to refuse to
execute a judgment of the said Administrative Tribunal granting
compensation to an international official whose appointment had
been terminated without his consent, the Court pointed out the fully
judicial character of the Administrative Tribunal, clearly distinguishing
between, first, the powers of the General Assembly, which was
responsible for laying down rules, and of the Tribunal, which, in
virtue of its Statute, took decisions in individual cases, and, secondly,

(a) Cf. *I.C.J. Reports*, (pp. 183-184).
(b) Ibidem, p. 186.

the powers of the Secretary-General, who was responsible for staff appointments and for the work of the organization which he represented.

"The Charter does not confer judicial functions on the General Assembly.... By establishing the Administrative Tribunal, the General Assembly was not delegating the performance of its own functions: it was exercising a power which it had under the Charter to regulate staff relations. In regard to the Secretariat, the General Assembly is given by the Charter a power to make regulations, but not a power to adjudicate upon, or otherwise deal with, particular instances."[a]

"...the Tribunal is established...as an independent and truly judicial body pronouncing final judgments without appeal within the limited field of its functions."[b]

"According to a well-established and generally recognized principle of law, a judgment rendered by such a judicial body is *res judicata* and has binding force between the parties to the dispute...."[c]

"...the function of approving the budget does not mean that the General Assembly has an absolute power to approve or disapprove the expenditure proposed to it..."[d] "Acting under powers conferred by the Charter, the General Assembly authorized the intervention of the Tribunal to the extent that such intervention might result from the exercise of jurisdictions conferred upon the Tribunal by its Statute. Accordingly, when the Tribunal decides that particular action by the Secretary-General involves a breach of the contract of service, it is in no sense intervening in a Charter power of the Secretary-General, because the Secretary-General's legal powers in staff matters have already been limited in this respect by the General Assembly."[e]

"Such a contract of service between the United Nations and its staff is concluded between the staff member concerned and the Secretary-General in his capacity as the chief administrative officer of the U.N. acting on behalf of that organization as its representative. When the Secretary-General concludes such a contract of service with a staff member, he engages the legal responsibility of the Organization, which is the juridical person in whose behalf he acts..."[f]

In this opinion,[43] which is important both in general and in the particular circumstances of the moment,[44] the Court, in admitting the existence of an organized legal system of the United Nations, seems to have implicitly established a line of demarcation between this "internal" law concerned with "internal disputes" on the one hand and the relations between States and disputes between them on the other.[45] Characteristic of this difference is the imperfect nature of the arrangements regarding inter-State disputes, which is contrasted with those concerning internal disputes, thanks to the existence in the internal legal system of a common authority or judicial organ.

(c) The case of the *Judgments of the Administrative Tribunal of the International Labour Organisation upon Complaints made against UNESCO*, 23 October 1956. The Court decided against a restrictive interpretation of the competence of the Administrative Tribunal, and empha-

(a) Cf. *I.C.J. Reports*, (pp. 47-87, at p. 61).
(b) Ibidem, p. 53.
(c) Ibidem, p. 53.
(d) Ibidem, p. 59.
(e) Ibidem, p. 60.
(f) Ibidem, p. 83

sized the importance of the administrative practice followed on the international plane as a basis for custom in administrative matters. In this way the legal status of international officials is partly based on an unwritten law which transcends the strict wording of the contract and is an important factor in its interpretation.

> "The arguments, deduced from the sovereignty of States, which might have been invoked in favour of a restrictive interpretation of provisions governing the jurisdiction of a tribunal adjudicating between States are not relevant to a situation in which a tribunal is called upon to adjudicate upon a complaint of an official against an international organization."[a]
> [With regard to staff appointments] "this has developed...a body of practice to the effect that holders of fixed-term contracts, although not assimilated to holders of permanent or indeterminate contracts, have often been treated as entitled to be considered for continued employment,...in a manner transcending the strict wording of the contract."[b]
> "The practice as here surveyed is a relevant factor in the interpretation of the contracts in question."[c]

Thus the Court drew interpretative conclusions from its above-mentioned previous opinion (1954) regarding the distinction between public international law proper, governing relations between States, and the "internal" law of the international organization, governing relations between the latter and its staff. In the latter case, the Court rejected the "exceptional" or *a priori* limited character of the judge's powers even if he should be an *ad hoc* judge; the Court made the judge's competence exclusively dependent on the contents of the relevant statutory text, without referring to interpretations, whether restrictive or extensive. Moreover, the Court, in the interests of equity[46] and drawing conclusions from the fact that an *administrative* action is concerned—in which precedent, custom and tradition play an important part as regards the interpretation of texts (and even as regards their possible lapse into desuetude)—has attributed to customary practice an interpretative importance deserving the greatest attention.[47]

It goes without saying that, side by side with this factor, we find, both in the practice of international secretariats and in the jurisprudence of the administrative tribunals, "general principles of law" taken either from the legislative texts of civilized nations or from their administrative practice, although this analogy is not clearly stated.[48] These general principles supplement the explicit statutory rules concerning the independent status of the international civil servant.

Administrative consequences

Here we have to consider a number of administrative provisions

(a) Cf. *I.C.J. Reports*, (pp. 77-168, at p. 97).
(b) Ibidem, p. 91.
(c) Ibidem, pp. 91/92.

regarding the situation of each official and affecting directly or indirectly his recruitment, his selection, his length of service, the character of his appointment, his hierarchical subordination, his dismissal, etc. Some of the provisions are dictated primarily by the interests of the international public service. Conditions have to be created which will ensure the normal operation of the international administration and above all its continuity in spite of fluctuating international relations. At the same time, these conditions must safeguard the legitimate rights and interests of the staff in order that they can do their work efficiently, despite its inherent difficulties.

These provisions are concerned in the first place with the independent status of the international civil servant, and it is only on this account that they interest us here. Administrative measures are provided to defend the international civil service against "pressure groups", whether the pressure is exercised by States or not; it is pressure from the State of origin of each official which must chiefly be considered. Owing to his national allegiance, his professional past, his habits of thought and his ideological conceptions, the official is exposed to constant, though perhaps unconscious, pressure from his State of origin, and it is here that the safeguard of his international loyalty as an essential psychological factor is indispensable. If we speak frequently of the "independence" of the international official, this label must not be misunderstood: it comprises firstly the principle of independence of the Secretariat vis-à-vis all third parties (as laid down in the constitutions of the international organizations), and secondly the principle of the political neutrality[49] of the international official (in the sense of the exclusion of all external influence on the performance of his task).

Thus the official is not "independent," since, like any civil servant, he is naturally subordinated to the hierarchy to which he belongs, owes obedience to his superiors and through the Secretary-General is amenable to the deliberative organs of the organization, composed of representatives of States; but he is legally and administratively protected against any attempt by States to exercise any pressure on him. Similarly, the official is not "neutral", since he is not debarred from having political opinions of his own, provided that he maintains the reserve which is indispensable in the interests of his service. Furthermore, the Secretariat may be called upon to take stands on politically controversial issues in response to requests from the General Assembly or the Security Council.[a] But here again, like any civil servant in the Western European tradition, he is above partisan controversies in his official capacity and must approach individual interests objectively, from a "superior" viewpoint "in order to

(a) Dag Hammarskjöld, Oxford address, (op. cit., pp. 9/10).

dominate the problems at issue." This same tradition lays down the principles of the official's anonymity, his disinterestedness, his continuity (this last being a further guarantee of impartiality, since the official's service goes on even if national and international policy changes).

On the national plane, this conception of public service, traditional in Europe, has established itself in the course of centuries, not without difficulty owing to the tenacity of the old "spoils system", traces of which persist, and of the system of "ownership of offices," which, on the contrary, has disappeared. Thus, the civil servant, assured of the stability of his employment, has been weaned from his partisan attitude and from the confusion between his free political opinions and his official duties; and the public service has been subordinated to the deliberative political bodies, although retaining the duties of drafting and implementing political resolutions. Subsequently, this administrative model has been imitated more or less successfully in central and eastern Europe and elsewhere.

By analogy, the same criteria and administrative framework have been introduced on the international plane. But the special features of international administration, together with the lack of traditions, have created and still create uncertainties, ambiguities, and hesitations. The essential criteria of the "independence" of the international public service are continually being called in question, and its full consequences are still insufficiently understood despite its apparently final acceptance. Hence the repeated crises marking the development of the international civil service. "The idea that the status of the international civil servant is analogous to that of national civil servants does not exist in the minds of government representatives, because governments do not yet recognize a collective international interest transcending their individual national interests...."[a] In view of these repeated crises, reference has even been made to "some evidence of a decline in the status of international civil servants since the Second World War",[b] that is to say precisely at the period of the greatest development of the international civil service. This contradiction is only apparent. The more the international administration develops, the greater the pressure exercised by governments on their nationals and the greater the danger of serious restriction of their "independence."

The administrative provisions concerning the careers of international civil servants are one of the first questions to be considered. We shall see later that the choice between temporary and permanent contracts creates apparently insurmountable difficulties. Two points have to

(a) *Conference on the Concept of a True International Civil Service* (Carnegie Endowment, Vevey, 1958, p. 5).
(b) Ibidem.

be considered: first, the *administrative* character of the service in the international secretariat, requiring stability, continuity, impartiality; secondly, the desire of States to attach temporarily to the international secretariats some of their own officials who will afterwards resume their duties in the national civil service. The States members of the international administrations constantly express the wish to have nationals of their own in the international secretariats as temporary or permanent international officials. This desire to "participate" in international administrative action through the medium of nationals, although the latter do not *represent* their States of origin, is paralleled by the wish of the international administrations themselves to recruit varied talents for the international service on condition that talent rather than variety remains the first consideration.

The problem of the method of appointment to posts in the international civil service, (with those of recruitment and selection and of the duration of the appointment), is administratively of fundamental importance to the international civil service.

In the first place, we have the exclusive competence of each Secretary-General to appoint all his staff. This is a general constitutional rule and an essential guarantee of the "independence" of the secretariats. Appointment in an international administration is obviously different from any previous national appointment, and this is a condition of the international organization's autonomy vis-à-vis the member States. The entire responsibility for this falls on the Secretary-General. Hence, nobody can impose a candidate on the latter nor exercise a decisive influence on his choice. This principle is expressed as follows in the Report of the International Civil Service Advisory Board "on recruitment methods and standards for the United Nations and the specialized agencies":[a]

> "The Board notes with satisfaction that the constitutional basis for the independent selection of staff by the Secretary-General and Executive Heads of the specialized agencies has been well established. It attaches the greatest importance to this principle and is convinced that an international secretariat of the desired high standards can be achieved only if this principle is maintained in practice as well as in theory.... The Board wishes to point out that governmental officials and delegations, in particular, have a high responsibility in supporting the Executive Head in his independent application of the basic criteria to the selection of his staff."

But there are some objective limitations of the freedom of selection which do not constitute infringements of the said independence. The Secretary-General remains always the sole judge of the abilities of each candidate for the Secretariat. Nevertheless, the tendency to consider the Secretariat as a sort of "mirror"—as faithful as possible —of the composition of the organization as a whole, was noticeable

(a) Doc. Co-ord/Civil Service/2/Rev. 1 – publ. U.N. 1950. X. 4, (p. 6).

in the early days of the League of Nations in spite of the silence of the Covenant on this point.[50] The aim is variety of recruitment in order that the Secretariat should have the benefit of different cultures, trainings and traditions. This guiding principle is to be found in any composite human community and particularly in the federal State.[51] The purpose is to widen the range of intellectual and cultural contributions and at the same time so to proportion these contributions as to avoid the undue preponderance of any one civilizing influence, of one mode of action or thought, or of a single national training and tradition. It is hoped "that the Secretariat [will be] enriched by the experience and culture which each Member nation can furnish and that each Member nation ₍will], in its turn, be satisfied that its own culture and philosophy make a full contribution to the Secretariat".[a]

The seriousness of the problem is evident and is constantly emphasized by writers on the subject who speak of "institutional efficiency versus geographical distribution" and of "the paradox of the international civil service."[b] An effort must be made to reconcile what at first sight seems irreconcilable: on the one hand the autonomy and relative freedom of choice given to the Secretary-General and to him alone in the interest of the organization and of efficiency; on the other hand the "fair distribution" of posts in such a manner as to ensure the international character of the Secretariat, its independence from any government influence and its role as a melting pot of different currents and national traditions. Since the "international man" does not exist in the present-day world, harmony must be sought through variety. The aim, which is incompatible with national privileges, is to establish a balance between the various essential contributions, but at the same time there is a risk of upsetting the criteria of selection. Such factors as the personality, ability, competence and integrity of the candidate are liable to be subordinated to his national origins, and this, in the absence of a proper comprehension of the problem, may lead to the revival in another form of the old "spoils system."

In order to escape from this dilemma, a compromise has been adopted in the international organizations which is expressed in most characteristic fashion in Article 101, paragraph 3, of the Charter of the United Nations:

> "The paramount consideration in the employment of the staff and in the determination of the conditions of service shall be the necessity of securing the highest standards of efficiency, competence, and integrity. Due regard shall be paid to the importance of recruiting the staff on as wide a geographical basis as possible."

(a) General Assembly of the United Nations, 3rd session, meeting of 2 September, 1948 (Doc. A/652, para. 7).
(b) T. C. Young, *International Civil Service: Principles and Problems* (op. cit., p. 89).

Thus, the geographical "quota system" has been evolved, which is intended to prevent the appearance of national "fiefs", not to create them.

> "...the paramount consideration...is to be the efficient performance of staff duties and not political expediency. In other words, those specific qualities of personnel which are usually demanded in the organization of an efficient national administrative service are to be given proper recognition. Positions are not to be regarded as 'spoils' to be divided among the more influential Members with a view to advancing the national interests of these States....
> "It is also stated that the staff should be recruited on as wide a geographical basis as possible. This principle might on occasion conflict with the principle enunciated in the first sentence of this paragraph. In a sense it is a concession to political considerations. However, it is stated here as a consideration of a secondary nature. The main thing is to get a good staff. If this staff can be made international, not only in outlook, in loyalty and in work, but also in composition, this should be done. It is easy to see that the Secretariat will command greater confidence if it is also international in this repect. The League of Nations took this principle of geography into consideration to a very great extent. There are those who feel that the effectiveness of the League Secretariat was restricted by this fact. A balance (in the U.N.) must be struck."[52a]

The compromise in question, therefore, rests on the following bases:

(*a*) In the first place, "The exclusively international character of the Secretariat is not tied to its composition, but to the spirit in which it works and to its insulation from outside influences...."[b] A varied composition, corresponding as far as possible to that of the organization as a whole, is desirable, but this is an additional administrative arrangement, designed not to weaken but to reinforce the independent status of the staff.

(*b*) The essence of the international civil service is the *independent status* of the official. If this criterion disappears or is undermined, the international official loses his *raison d'être*. It therefore goes without saying that psychological factors—namely, the international-mindedness, the international outlook and the international loyalty of the candidate—are decisive. The criterion of a "balanced distribution of posts on all levels among all regions... is clearly something entirely different from a balanced representation of trends or ideologies".[c] A balanced regional distribution of posts must not therefore be allowed to disturb the essential criteria or hierarchy of values, for it must be remembered that, apart from recruitment criteria as a whole, it is worthless. It is too weak to stand unsupported by the essential spirit of the international civil service.

(*c*) While, referring to geographical distribution, one considers

(a) L. M. Goodrich and E. Hambro, *Charter*...(op. cit., pp. 386/387). Cf. below, chapter 5, p. 130 and chapter 10, p. 296.
(b) Introduction to the Report of the Secretary-General of the United Nations for 1960/1961, (p. 16, chapter IV).
(c) Ibidem, p. 16.

the "nationality" of the candidate, it must not be forgotten that the rule may be applied not only on a national, but also on a regional or continental basis, thus enlarging the area of recruitment, mitigating the harmful aspects of a rigid national formula and putting the main emphasis on cultural affinities and intellectual training.

(*d*) For reasons of convenience, the regulations do not apply the principle of geographical distribution to several categories of staff, thus sanctioning a freedom of selection by the Secretary-General without limitations as to the candidate's origin. This applies in particlar to the general services, which, with a few exceptions (in the case of supervisors), are "locally recruited"—i.e., expressly excluded from the rule of geographical distribution.[53] The same applies to language staff (interpreters, translators, etc.) and to experts, although in this latter category there is a tendency to pay greater attention to geographical distribution. It should, however, be remembered that, whatever the rank and function of the international official, the same criteria of "independence" apply. The intimacy of the ties between *all* international officials and the work of international co-operation does not allow of the neglect or even the attenuation of any of the essential values. While, on occasion, certain adjustments may be made in law and in fact in the general rules, this is solely for utilitarian and practical reasons, and in no way affects the autonomous nature of the selection of all candidates by the Secretary-General, and the real importance of the qualifications required (integrity, international outlook, proper mental attitude, ability for teamwork, adjustment to colleagues with different trainings, ability to take decisions and to handle men, etc.). In view of the fact that an international outlook and "dual loyalty" are required of *all* officials, and that there are large categories to which geographical distribution does not apply (about seventy per cent of the staff), it is evident that the international idea takes precedence over the international composition and can alone ensure the impartiality of the staff, subject to prudent and careful selection.

(*e*) Geographical distribution (in the directorial and professional categories) applies only to initial recruitment, whether or not the higher posts are filled from within the service or from outside. It does not apply to the future career—that is to say to promotion. That principle is laid down in the regulations. Its advantage is to assure the international official that once the initial screening has taken place, formal considerations of a geographical (or cultural) nature will not prevent the normal development of his career. Its drawback is that, in order to achieve a balanced and varied composition of the higher posts, the international secretariats tend to recruit direct from abroad in filling these posts (particularly the top ones) thus limiting opportunities of promotion. In fact, experience shows that certain promotions are made on the basis of geographical criteria as a result of external pressure, which has a disastrous influence on the morale of officials and runs counter to the principles laid down.

This compromise has in practice led to greed, quarrels for prestige, incessant recriminations and even fickleness on the part of governments, so that "the appointing authority has to navigate between the Scylla of becoming a tool of the individual government in personnel matters and the Charybdis of antagonizing the Member States...."[a]

This practice has been called the "football" of international policy.[b] Be that as it may, it is regarded in fact as a necessary evil. Furthermore, it prevents the use of scientific methods of recruitment based on socio-psychology ("aggressive recruitment"), a constructive experiment in which modern civil services are engaged. To resist the constant pressure of States wishing to secure a large "representation" in the international secretariats and frequently misunderstanding the essence of the problem, it was found necessary to introduce quantitative standards—namely, the quota system. In spite of efforts to prevent too rigid an application of the quota, its very existence cannot but contribute to lowering the level of efficiency. Consequently, in order to maintain that level, it has been necessary to introduce empirically a number of correctives, even if they may have to be modified later as a result of governmental pressures. The continual changes in the composition of the international organizations owing to the entry of new member States further complicate the efforts to ensure some sort of geographical balance. At the same time, the technical difficulties of international recruitment resulting from distances, differences of education and other obstacles, may lead to the interference of national governments in the process of recruitment. This interference may be spontaneous or may even be requested by the organization in order to apply the principle of geographical distribution. Thus the national authorities can influence recruitment in a number of ways, which often lead to the reversal of the proper procedure, the national governments in reality deciding on the choice of candidates, appointment by the Secretary-General becoming a mere formality. It is doubtful whether the prestige of the government concerned is enhanced thereby, and the prestige of the international organization certainly suffers. The administrative arrangement introduced to safeguard independent status thus operates against that very independence. Here we have a vicious circle: national ambitions, competition and amour propre make appointments the prize of a struggle for prestige. The Secretary-General is obliged to take this into

(a) E. F. Ranshofen-Wertheimer, (op. cit., p. 326).
(b) T. C. Young, (op. cit., p. 110).

account in the interest of the organization, while doing his best to save face and to limit the damage. Once they have succeeded in enforcing their demands regarding recruitment, governments give free play to their political or other sympathies, which are frequently a cloak for pure nepotism. Of course, they seek to keep control of their nationals among the staff of the Secretariat: having "proposed" they "impose". This "remote control" of officials recalls the old idea of "liaison officers" of the time of the unions, but this time with a political tinge. A further factor is that States which have recently achieved independence want to give their officials periods of training by seconding them for a specific time to the international administrations. Hence elements foreign to the essence of the international service tend, often unconsciously, to destroy it and to impede administrative efficiency.

Thus, during the discussions on the Report of the Committee of Thirteen of the League of Nations (1930), the opinion was expressed that if the officials of the League of Nations were really international civil servants, their nationality would be irrelevant.

If, nevertheless, we adopt the compromise imposed by circumstances and take into account the national origins of candidates for the international civil service, they can be accepted only as a subsidiary factor and in accordance with the letter and the spirit of the constitutions of the international organizations.It must be remembered, too, that standards of modern administration, modelled on the European civil services, are now universal. "... it is the government above all that should respect the international character of the secretariat officials, and it is the duty of the governments to refrain from exercising political influence in the League of Nations through the members of the Secretariat.... It would be better to insist on governments solemnly pledging themselves to refrain from exercising any pressure whatever on their nationals who are employed in the Secretariat".[a] If that was desirable in 1930 in the days of the League of Nations, the United Nations, a generation later, has found it still more necessary. The international civil service will be what the States make of it. If they reduce an institution to a simple façade or to a myth out of contact with reality by upsetting, whether deliberately or not, the values on which it is based, that institution will cease to play the part which was assigned to it by its founders, which was confirmed by its constitution and which has become the main pillar of international co-operation in our time.

(a) Statement by the Swedish delegate Erik Boheman, at the 11th Assembly of the League of Nations, (4th Committee, 1930, p. 58; discussion of the Report of the Committee of Thirteen).

NOTES

(1) Neither the Covenant of the League nor the Charter of the United Nations contained any details on the organization of the secretariats. The Charter contents itself with a provision to the effect that the Secretariat constitutes a single unit in the service of all the organs of the United Nations, and not a number of parallel institutions as had been proposed (cf., however, Article 101, paragraph 2, of the Charter.

(2) Cf. Articles 100 and 101 of the Charter and Articles 2 and following of the Statute of the Court. Nevertheless, in the case of the judges of the Court, carefully chosen among the leading protagonists of international law, the Statute of the Court provides a series of institutional guarantees (Articles 3, 17, 24, 31 of the Statute and Article 13 of the Rules of the Court).

(3) Cf., for example, Article 101 of the Charter of the United Nations, Article 8, paragraph 2, of the Constitution of the Food and Agriculture Organization of the United Nations, Article XII, Section H (c) of the Constitution of the International Monetary Fund and Article V, section 5 (c), of that of the International Bank for Reconstruction and Development.

(4) Cf., for example, R. Kaplan, "Some Problems in the Administration of the International Secretariat", in *Columbia Journal of International Affairs* (No. 2/II, 1948, pp. 35 ff.).

(5) Cf., for example, S.M. Schwebel, *The Secretary-General of the United Nations. His Political Powers and Practice*, (Cambridge, Harvard Univ. Press, 1952, p. 170 and *passim*).

(6) Ibidem, pp. 169-170 and G. L. Goodwin, (op. cit., pp. 402-403).

(7) The elements which characterize the close link between the administrative staff and the public interest are *esprit de corps* (in the sense of solidarity between colleagues), anonymity, the sense of dedication to the public service, etc. It is these elements, which characterize any civil service based on the western European model, which make of any body of officials a sort of "lay clergy" – a "closed" organization directed from the top and based on hierarchy and subordination (cf., for example, F. Fleiner, *Beamtenstaat und Volkstaat*, 1916).

(8) Like the judges of the Court and the members of the two present international administrative tribunals, those of the United Nations and the I.L.O., international officials are appointed in a strictly personal capacity, although now and then the factor of nationality or of representation of the main forms of civilization plays a certain part.

(9) Cf., for example, L. Bourgeois, *L'oeuvre de la Société des Nations, 1920-1923* (Paris, 1923, p. 437): "Sir Eric Drummond *represents* England and Jean Monnet *represented* France in the Secretariat of the League."

(10) Cf. J. K. King, *The Privileges and Immunities of the Personnel of the International Organizations*, (thesis 66, University of Geneva, 1949): P. Cahier (op. cit.), M. Bedjaoui, (op. cit., pp. 192 ff.). Cf., for example: Headquarters Agreement between the United Nations and the United States of America of 26 June 1947 (U.N. *Treaty Series*, Volume 2, pp. 11-35), Agreement between the U.N. and the U.S.A. on the provisional headquarters of the United Nations, 18 December 1947 (ibidem, Vol 2., pp. 347-359), Provisional Agreement on the privileges and immunities of the United Nations, concluded by the U.N. with Switzerland of 11 March – 14 November 1946 (ibidem, Vol. 1, pp. 163-181), Agreement of the World Health Organization with Switzerland of 21 August 1948, Agreement of the International Labour Organisation with Switzerland of 11 March 1946, Agreement of the International Civil Aviation Organization with Canada of 14 April 1951 (ibidem, Vol. 96, 1951, p. 169), etc.

(11) This is broadly the opinion of the Institute of International Law based on the reports of Politis and of Lapradelle (1924).

Cf. also: F. R. Scott, "The World's Civil Service", in *International Conciliation* (No. 496, 1954, p. 305), A. Hammarskjöld, "Les immunités des personnes investies de fonctions internationales", (*Rec. A.D.I.*, 1936, II, pp. 128 ff.), C. W. Jenks, *International Immunities* (London, 1961, *passim*), M. Bedjaoui, (op. cit., pp. 207-209).

(12) L. Delbez, *Manual de droit international public. Droit général et droit particulier des Nations Unies* (2nd edition, Paris, 1951, p. 115), M. Bedjaoui, (op. cit., pp. 196 ff.), M. Hill, *Immunities and Privileges of International Officials. The Experience of the League of Nations* (Washington, 1947).

(13) According to the General Convention on the Privileges and Immunities of the United Nations of 13 February 1946 (U.N. *Treaty Series*, Vol. 1, pp. 15-33), and according to that concerning the specialized agencies of 21 November 1947, (resolution 179 (II) of the General Assembly of the United Nations) and in virtue of the staff regulations, it is only officials of directorial rank and of the professional category who enjoy these various "privileges and immunities" (with certain differences between these categories as regards the extent of the exemptions granted). A distinction between these various categories of staff had already been made at the time of the League of Nations, in spite of the general formula used in Article 7, paragraph 4, of the Covenant. The same applies to the United Nations *laissez-passer* which is not issued to locally recruited staff.

(14) Cf. C. McC. Croswell, *Protection of International Personnel Abroad: Law and Practice affecting the Privileges and Immunities of International Organizations* (New York, 1952, pp. 127 ff.); K. Zemanek, *Das Vertragsrecht der internationalen Organisationen* (Vienna, 1957); F. J. Lalive, "L'immunité de juridiction des États et des Organisations internationales" (*Recueil A.D.I.*, 1953, III, pp. 209 ff.).

(15) Cf. M. Bedjaoui, (op. cit., p. 174 and *passim*).

(16) L. Ledermann, (op. cit., pp. 164-165): "The legal structure of an organization is one thing and the spirit which animates it is another. No policy is worth more than the spirit which inspires it and the men who implement it; this is true of constitutions, treaties, the most solemn pacts and in general of all human institutions. The international organization does not escape this rule. Thus in the last resort it is moral and psychological considerations rather than diplomatic, legal or political subleties, which determine the good or bad progress of the international organization. For the same reason we believe that education to this end will be one of the most important undertakings of humanity...."
Taking into account the necessity of an adequate psychological development, it can be said that "international civil servants are not born, they are made...." K. J. Ewerts, *New Technique and Old in Building for Peace* (New York, 1951, p. 11).

(17) As regards the "sense of belonging", cf. R. N. Swift, "Personnel Problems and the United Nations Secretariat", in *International Organization*, (No. 2, 1957, pp. 246/247).

(18) A. Loveday, (op. cit., pp. 32/33): "Most writers put loyalty to the institution for which the official is working first in their general scale of values. This is probably right; but a blind loyalty is not enough. The loyalty must spring from an understanding of and a belief in the ultimate value of the work and purposes of the institution. It will prove stronger if buttressed by a sense of history.... This loyalty, composed as it should be of understanding and sympathy, as well as fidelity, constancy and honesty, may be subjected to great strains.... It can only stand that test if the official has a firm and enlightened belief in the value of the organization for which he works...."

(19) This is the reason for "home leave" every two years, to which the regulations entitle officials of the organizations in the United Nations family, recruited on an international basis and not serving in their countries of origin. "A system of home leave was embedded firmly in the administrative philosophy of the U.N. No such system could serve its purpose unless leave was given frequently enough to preserve

national characteristics and to neutralize that extraordinary influence which ... certain localities had on newcomers" (statement by the Deputy Secretary-General, Summary Record of the 265th meeting of the Fifth Committee, 17 November 1950, para. 24). The Staff Council expressed the belief that "an arrangement whereby staff members could return to their home countries every two years guaranteed that they would preserve their national characteristics and thus be able to make a richer contribution to a truly international secretariat."

(20) Dag Hammarskjöld said in this connection: "I am not neutral as regards the Charter; I am not neutral as regards facts; ... but what I do claim is that even a man who is in that sense not neutral can very well undertake and carry through neutral actions, because that is an act of *integrity* ... " (Press Conference of 12 June 1961, note No. 2347, p. 11).

(21) E. Giraud, (op. cit., pp. 69/70): "An international official must believe in the usefulness of his function and to do this he must possess a certain international philosophy. He must believe that humanity is a great family, all the members of which are entitled to respect and must work in common. He must believe in the value and possibility of a peaceful organization of the world. A person who is inspired by nationalist or xenophobic sentiments, who thinks that he has duties only towards his own country, should not be a candidate for an international appointment.... While the international official must have an international faith, it by no means follows that he must be as it were denationalized, that is to say that he should regard his country with indifference and that he should have lost the characteristics of the nation to which he belongs. To appoint people who claim to be world citizens would, as a rule, be a bad choice ... but they are comparatively rare and it is not from them that the secretariats of the international institutions have suffered, but rather from the presence in their midst of nationalist elements who have behaved in a conscious and premeditated fashion, or in a more or less instinctive and spontaneous fashion, as agents of their country's government or as defenders of that country's particular interests.... "

(22) Although only about five per cent of the staff of the United Nations (and still fewer in the specialized agencies) work in direct contact with "diplomacy" – and then not continuously – (W. R. Crocker, "Some Notes on the U.N. Secretariat", *International Organization* No. 4, 1950, p. 600) reserve in the expression of personal political opinions is essential in all cases. In this connection, we may recall the Bang Jensen case (in connection with the events of 1956 in Hungary) and its diplomatic consequences (cf. *Le Monde diplomatique* (Paris, No. 58/1959)). As regards the obligation of the international official to be "constantly on the alert" – an obligation going far beyond professional secrecy alone – cf. T. Aghnides, "Standards of Conduct of the International Civil Service", *Revue internationale des Sciences administratives* (No. 1/1953, p. 179).

(23) M. Bedjaoui, (op. cit., pp. 163/164): "*National loyalty* is not only tolerated but recommended, whereas *State loyalism* should be banished from the international official's duties. By national loyalty we mean the easy conciliation of international obligations with *sentimental* attachment to one's country ... and by State loyalism we mean the inescapable incompatibility between the same obligations and a *political* attachment to one's Government. It goes without saying that a person cannot be a perfect international official while having opinions which cause him to prefer a particular form of government or a particular Government, whether in power or not. This is not a problem of State loyalism, it is simply a conviction, an intimate political opinion, which as we have seen cannot be restricted. State loyalism may be regarded – and this emphasizes its incompitability with international loyalty – as unconditional *fidelity* to the Government in power and hence as an undertaking to *defend* it and serve it as long as it is in power, and to *combat* it if it falls from power and goes into opposition, and to serve its successor with equal zeal.... Clearly this

form of loyalism is absolutely incompatible with international loyalty because it misconceives the very essence of the international civil service...."

(24) When the French Government opposed the placing of agricultural questions on the agenda of the International Labour Conference, since it did not recognize the I.L.O.'s competence in regard to those questions.
Cf. also *The I.L.O.: Thirty Years of Combat for Social Justice* (I.L.O., Geneva, 1950, p. 36).

(25) Thus Henri Laugier, as Deputy Secretary-General of the United Nations, "in a number of important cases had had to take up positions conflicting with those adopted by the government of his country... [which had] been sufficiently international in its outlook to agree to his taking up those positions without accusing him of disloyalty towards it" (statement by H. Laugier in the Executive Board of UNESCO on 16 April 1953, doc. 33 Ex/SR. 4, p. 6).

(26) See above, chapter 4, note (22).

(27) K. S. Carlston (op. cit., p. 329): "A unique situation in law developed. The organization of the international Secretariat required that employment contracts be made, grades of service established, regulations promulgated and pension systems created. Effective administration required that authoritative commands be sanctioned. From the standpoint of the individual staff member, his reasonable expectations in the performance of his role under his contract and the regulations required protection. He must not be vulnerable to abuse of authority. Yet, as an organization, the international agency functioned beyond the control of the law of any individual State. Thus we see that a highly articulated corporate mechanism was brought into being, required to function efficiently at the very heart of the society of nations, but excluded from the sphere of control of any legal system of a State. To establish order a legal system was imperative...."

(28) As regards this expanded conception of public international law, cf. S. Basdevant (Bastid) (op. cit., pp. 68-69 and 283); Verdross, "On the Concept of International Law", *American Journal of International Law* (No. 3. 1949, p. 435); P. Reuter (oral statement to the International Court of Justice of 11 June 1954 in the case of the *Effect of Awards of Compensation Made by the United Nations Administrative Tribunal* (I. C. J., *U.N.Administrative Tribunal-Pleadings, Oral Arguments, and Documents*, p. 343; cf. below, chapter 4, note (45) and *Organisations internationales et évolution du droit* ("Etudes offertes à Mestre" (Paris, 1956, p. 457 ff.)). Cf. also: L. Focsaneanu, "Le droit interne de l'O.N.U.", *Annuaire français du Droit international*, (Paris, 1957, p. 315 ff.).

(29) Cf. S. Basdevant (Bastid), (op. cit., p. 90).

(30) Cf., for example, the following constitutional provisions: Article 100 of the Charter; Articles 9 and 40 of the Constitution of the I.L.O.; Article 8 of the Constitution of F.A.O., Articles 6 and 12 of the Constitution of UNESCO; Articles 35, 37 and 67 of the Constitution of the World Health Organization; Articles 9 and 12 of the Constitution of the International Monetary Fund; Article 5, section 5, and Article 7, International Bank for Reconstruction and Development; Article 4, section 5 and Article 6, International Financial Corporation; Article 6, section 5, and Article 8, International Development Agency; Articles 58 to 60, I.C.A.O.; Articles 37 and 50, Intergovernmental Maritime Consultative Organization, Article 11, International Telecommunication Union; Articles 20-22 and 27, World Meteorological Organization; Articles 7 and 15, International Atomic Energy Agency. Cf. also, outside the United Nations family, Articles 89 to 91, 104 and 105 of the Charter of the Organization of American States; Articles 36 and 40 of the Statutes of the Council of Europe; Articles 6 and 9 of the Convention of C.E.R.N.; Articles 9 and 86 of the E.C.S.C. Treaty; Article 157 of the Treaty on the European Economic Community; Article 126 of the Treaty on EURATOM; Articles 18 and 26 of the Constitution of the Intergovernmental Committee on European Migration.

(31) Such standard provisions, particularly in the financial field and that of staff

questions, are drawn up in the United Nations family under the auspices of the Administrative Committee on Co-ordination. In several organizations (and the same was the case for a time at the U.N.), an administrative manual kept continually up to date contains all the rules applicable to the staff.

(32) Thus banking or financial institutions constitute a separate group as far as administrative arrangements are concerned (cf. C.W. Jenks, *Proper Law...*, op. cit., p. 34).

(33) National jurisprudence also plays a certain part in the international field: cf., for example, the judgment of the British Court of Appeal in the case of *Godman v. Winterton* (Case No. 111, *Annual Digest and Records of Public International Law Cases*, 1919-1942, suppl. p. 205); the judgment of the French "Conseil d'État" in the case of *"Dame Adrien et autres"* (ibidem, Case No. 11, 1931-1932, p. 33); the judgment of the Italian Court of Appeal in the case of the *International Institute of Agriculture v. Profili* (ibidem, Case No. 254, 1929-1930, p. 413); the judgment of the City Court of New Rochelle, New York State, in the case of *Westchester County v. Ranollo*, 1946 (cited in Lawrence Preuss, "Immunities of Officials and Employees of the U.N. for official acts: The Ranollo Case", in *The American Journal of International Law* (No. 41, 1947, p. 555 ff.).

(34) K. S. Carlston (op. cit., p. 341): "Postulate V. The statement of a body of administrative law for the international organization is only the initial step in the establishment of a legal system within the organization; not until means of judicial recourse against contested administrative action are provided through the establishment of a judicial organ does the organization become fully organized as a legal system...".

(35) As regards the François Monod case, cf. S. Basdevant (Bastid), op. cit., p. 79 ff., and *Official Journal of the League of Nations* No. 10/6, 1925, p. 1443.

(36) Cf. S. Basdevant (Bastid), (op. cit., p. 272).

(37) Report of the Fourth Committee of the Assembly of the League of Nations on 17 December 1920, 600th plenary meeting (1921).
Cf. above, chapter 4, note (34).
Cf. also Report of the Supervisory Commission of the League concerning the creation of the Administrative Tribunal of the League in 1927: "The establishment of a tribunal such as is now proposed is expected not merely to remove a grievance which may be felt by the staff..., but also to be in the interest of successful administration. ...The international status of the League prevents officials from bringing actions in the ordinary courts to enforce the terms of their appointments. It is not, however, satisfactory that a class of employees amounting to several hundreds of persons and engaged on terms which are necessarily complicated and may give rise to disputes as to their exact legal effect, should have no possibility of bringing questions as to their rights to the decision of a judicial body.
It is equally unsatisfactory for the administrations to be both judge and party in any dispute as to the legal rights of their officials.... The special position of the League makes it difficult to refer claims by its officials to the jurisdiction of national courts. The remaining possibility, namely the reference of such disputes to a body constituted *ad hoc*, although it has been adopted in one case, is open to objections on many grounds and does not furnish a solution for the general problems...." (8th Assembly, 4th Committee, Annex 13, p. 251. Cf. *I.C.J.Rep.* 1954, p. 54).

(38) Cf. C. W. Jenks, *The Proper Law...*, (op. cit., p. 40 ff.), and *Annales de la Faculté de Droit d'Istanbul* (No. 7/1957, pp. DJ/3-DJ/159, No. 8/1958, pp. DJ/297-DJ/337).

(39) Ibidem: (No. 7/1957 pp. DJ/160-DJ/294 and No. 8/1958 pp. DJ/339-DJ/394).

(40) The passage from the *contract* (bilateral consensual ties) to the *status* ("legal situation") settled and, in theory, modifiable unilaterally, at least as regards the other than purely personnel clauses) took place gradually and not without difficulties

or restrictions. Initially, opinion was unanimous in giving a definite preference to contractual elements and full respect for "vested rights". There was no question then of transferring to the international plane elements of "public service", since the latter were regarded as part of the classical attributions of public authority which did not exist in the international organization. It was therefore considered that the international official's position rested on a contractual basis, and there was confusion between the latter and the state of private law (cf. S. Basdevant (Bastid), op. cit., p. 78 and *passim*)), both doctrine and jurisprudence having long hesitated on this subject (cf. M. Bedjaoui, op. cit., p. 115 ff.). This conception, at that time, was a result of the preponderance of Anglo-Saxon tradition and doctrine.

It is only since 1925, and the important opinion of the Committee of Jurists in the Monod case (cf. above, chapter 4, notes (35) and (37)), at the time of the League on Nations, that it has no longer been possible to avoid an analysis of the functional relation in the international administration, despite repeated hesitations and confusions of a terminological nature (obstinate application of the idea of "contract"). According to this opinion the idea of contract, as such, should be excluded in the case of an international organization; the functional relation should be considered mainly in the light of the principles of public law and administrative legislation, while taking into account the statutory character of the appointment. As far as doctrine was concerned, an attempt was made to approach the problem in a less general fashion, taking into account the "institutional" (or "non-institutional") position of each official, the contract applying only to the latter category and not to the former (cf. S. Basdevant (Bastid, op. cit., pp. 105 ff.).

In the same connection, but on the basis of the distinction between the different aspects of the official's position, the Administrative Tribunal of the United Nations, under the chairmanship of Mrs. Bastid, in its important Judgment No. 19 of 11 August 1953 (*Kaplan case*) established a distinction between the "contractual elements" (affecting the personal status of the person concerned) and the "statutory elements" (capable of being changed without the consent of the person concerned)– i.e., those which are not of a purely personal character, but affect the organization and operation of the international civil service (cf. below, page 191).

Cf. C. W. Jenks, *The Proper Law...*, (op cit., p. 68): "It is important to maintain an appropriate balance between the statutory and the contractual elements, but the determination of such a balance remains one of the major unsolved problems of international administrative law.... In seeking for the appropriate balance, conflicting considerations of public policy have to be reconciled. An international public service cannot be constituted on the basis of intangible contractual guarantees and legally protected vested interests. The objection to such a concept is not primarily that it is intellectually untenable; it might be preferable on balance to a concept which affords no effective legal protection of the *independence* of the service. The decisive objection to it is that it is not sufficiently widely acceptable to weather a serious crisis, as the discussions of the Assembly of the League of Nations in 1932 and 1946 and of the General Assembly of the U.N. in 1953 show. The stability necessary to the *independence* of the service, and to the high morale which is so essential to its effectiveness, presupposes, however, a degree of respect for the rights and expectations of its members which, in the present stage of development of international organization, is unlikely to be secured if the status of the international official is unaccompanied by any element of contract. The protection necessary to ensure the independence of the service cannot be ensured by giving the official an unqualified contractual right; but it can be, and in large measure has been, secured by giving him the right of appeal to an international administrative tribunal whenever he alleges failure to respect a legal right or to fulfil a legally protected expectation and by providing that the decision of the administrative tribunal can be challenged only by referring the matter to the International Court of Justice. As such judicial protection of the rights of the official becomes well established, the question whether his rights are statutory or contractual loses much of its importance...".

But cf., also, judgment No. 61 of 4 September 1962 of the Administrative Tribunal of the I.L.O. (case of *Lindsay v. I.L.O.*) tending to establish a difference "of kind" between national civil servants and international officials and to draw limitative conclusions as regards the administration's power to modify unilaterally certain statutory conditions of employment.

(41) Cf. dissenting opinions of the judges: Hackworth (*I.C.J. Rep.* 1949, pp. 201 ff.): "The bond between the Organization and its employees, which is an entirely proper and natural one, does not have and cannot have the effect of expatriating the employee or of substituting allegiance to the Organization for allegiance to his State..."; Badawi (ibidem, p. 210): "Would it be conceivable that the constitutions of all these specialized agencies can have created so many allegiances involving a right of protection for their staff similar to that accorded by States to their nationals?"; Krylov, (ibidem, p. 217): "The relations between a State and its nationals are matters which belong essentially to the national competence of the State. The functional protection proclaimed by the Court is in contradiction with that well-established rule...."

(42) In its written memorandum France expressed the opinion that, in supporting its staff member, the U.N. "did not defend him personally, but ensured respect for the international civil service which the signatory States of the Charter had instructed its organs to set up" (I.C.J. Pleadings, Oral Arguments, Documents: *Reparations for Injuries suffered in the Service of the United Nations*, (1949, p. 15); cf. also the oral statement of the French representative C. Chaumont (ibidem, pp. 104 ff.): "The legal situation of a United Nations official is... very special. He acts on behalf of the international organization, to which he is subordinate, and from which he receives orders. In virtue of Article 100 of the Charter he is responsible to it alone and cannot obey instructions from his own Government. His functions are exclusively international. He is therefore tied to the Organization by a special link, that of the function, that of participation in the public service".

In its written memorandum, the United Kingdom (ibidem, pp. 37 ff.) expressed the following opinion: "When a member of the regular staff of the U.N. is injured in the course of the performance of his duties, and in circumstances entailing the responsibility of a State or government,... it would be a reasonable inference to draw from *the special nature of the connection* and the normal allegiance owed by every individual to his own national State, that the Organization should have the right to claim compensation on behalf of the individual concerned...";

In his verbal statement, the U.K. representative (Fitzmaurice), (ibidem, pp. 123 ff.) expressed the following opinion: "The requisite basis may be found in Article 100 of the Charter which creates a *special relationship* of international allegiance between the Organization and its servants, a link going beyond the ordinary relationship of master and servant.... This special allegiance partially displaces the normal allegiance owed by individuals to their national State...";

Cf. also the statement of the Belgian representative (Kaeckenbeeck), (ibidem, pp. 100 ff.) and of the representative of the Secretary-General of the United Nations (Feller), (ibidem, pp. 86 ff.).

(43) Cf. also the dissenting opinions of the judges: Alvarez (I.C.J. Rep. 1954, pp. 67 ff.), who refuses to admit the judicial character of the Administrative Tribunal and refers to the "new international law" whose "social character," deriving from the "new regime of interdependence," tends to replace the "traditional individualistic régime" (p. 70); Hackworth, who points out the delegated authority of the Administrative Tribunal and the fact that disputes coming before the Tribunal are not between the United Nations and a staff member but between the Secretary-General and a staff member. "This would seem to be confusing two quite distinct procedural processes, i.e. that of review in the political or administrative sense and

that of review in the judicial sense"; Levi Carneiro, who denies the independence of the Administrative Tribunal, a "quasi-judicial organ of an administrative nature (p. 95) whose decision does not bind the United Nations...."

(44) The Administrative Tribunal was passing judgment in 1953 during a grave crisis of the international civil service (cf. below, chapter 9, p. 212, and chapter 9, notes (14) and (15)), and was, as it were, in the thick of the battle and acting as arbitrator on the battlefield. It might reasonably have been anticipated that this objective arbitration would help to smooth matters over. But this was not the case and the Tribunal's judgment provoked a violent reaction, particularly in the United States of America. It was in this atmosphere that the Hague Court was called upon to give its advisory opinion.

(45) Cf. statement by the French delegate (P. Reuter), *Effect of Awards of Compensation made by the United Nations Administrative Tribunal*, (I.C.J.—Pleadings, Oral Arguments, Documents, p. 343): "The rules defining the relations between employees of the United Nations and the United Nations arise from the Charter and constitute the internal law of an international organization; in this sense they derive to a certain extent from international law, but to a certain extent only, for it is in fact the internal law of an international organization. But whatever terminology may be adopted, all the rules which apply to relations between States are not applicable to relations between the United Nations and its employees, and this is the case in particular as regards the theory of the nullity of arbitral awards." Cf. also the written memoranda of the Governments of France, (ibidem, pp. 26 ff.), the Netherlands, (ibidem, pp. 97 ff.), Sweden, (ibidem, p. 92), the United Kingdom, (ibidem, p. 128), the United States of America, (ibidem, pp. 135 ff.), Mexico, (ibidem, pp. 258 ff.), Chile, (ibidem, pp. 264/265), Iraq, (ibidem, p. 267).

(46) The role of custom (administrative precedents) in the realization of the "equalitarian régime", in the preparation of written rules for the future, in the gradual establishment of a *"usus fori"* and in the orientation of doctrine (and vice versa) is emphasized by writers on comparative administrative law (cf., for example, G. Langrod, *Institutions of Administrative Law*, Warsaw 1948, in Polish, Volume II, pages 324ff, "Custom in Administrative Law").

(47) Cf. also the dissenting opinions of judges: Hackworth (I.C.J. Rep., *Judgment of the Administrative Tribunal of the I.L.O. upon Complaints made against UNESCO*, (1956, p. 121)), who objects to the identification of "legitimate expectancy" with "vested rights"; Badawi, who claims that "the jurisdictions of the Administrative Tribunals of international organizations are in no way comparable to that of the various national judicial systems which include a body of the *Conseil d'État* type" (ibidem, p. 134), and opposes the extension of international administrative jurisdiction in the sense of authoritative action embracing "judicial control of the discretionary exercise of the powers of the Administration" (ibidem, p. 136); Read (ibidem, p. 153), who contends that "the subjective appreciation of the Tribunal has been substituted for the rule of law in deciding disputes between officials and the Organization. By asserting its competence to deliver its judgment on abusive rights, the Tribunal has substituted its own notions of 'the good of the service' and 'the interest of the Organisation' for the control by the General Conference and Executive Board over the exercise by the Director-General of discretionary powers conferred on him by the General Conference". Cf. also for example R. de Lacharrière, in *Annuaire français de Droit international* (1956, pp. 383 ff.) and "advisory opinion" of P. Reuter and J. H. W. Verzijl, in publication of the Federation of International Civil Servants' Associations, (November 1955, Doc. FICSA/INF/15 of 15 February 1956).

(48) Cf., in particular, P. Guggenheim, "Rechtsfragen der inter nationalen Organisation", in *Festschrift für Hans Wehberg* (Frankfurt, 1956, p. 133 ff.).

(49) Cf. H. Finer, *Theory and Practice of Modern Government* (New York, 1949, pp. 614 ff., 882/883) and S. D. Bailey, "*The troika and the future of the UN*" (International Conciliation" No 538 1962 p. 30 ff.).

(50) As regards the Spanish proposal concerning the inclusion of the rule of geographical distribution in the draft Covenant of the League, cf. D. H. Miller, *My Diary at the Conference of Paris, with Documents* (New York, 1924, Vol. 4, p. 89) and Article 6, paragraph 3, of the Covenant. The League's practice in this sphere appears clearly in the reports of Balfour (*Official Journal*, No. 4, 1920, pp. 136 ff.); Allen (1st Assembly, pp. 654 ff.), Noblemaire (2nd Assembly, 4th Committee, Annex 2, pp. 174 ff.); Committee of Thirteen (11th Assembly, 4th Committee, Annex 8, pp. 290 ff.).

(51) Cf., for example, J. M. Howe, "The Geographic Composition of the International Secretariat", in *Columbia Journal of International Affairs* (No. 2/1948, pp. 55 ff.).
An equitable realization of geographical distribution in federal States is notoriously difficult. Thus, in the United States of America, since the introduction of this rule simultaneously with that of the "merit system" in 1883 at the federal level, it has never been possible to respect everywhere the population factor adopted as a criterion. Although only ten per cent of the federal posts were subject to this rule, any attempt at geographical distribution had to be dropped at times of emergency. Thus, during the whole of F. D. Roosevelt's presidency (1933-1945), this rule was never observed. During the period 1945-1955, thirty-four States out of forty-eight never reached the quota due to them. Similarly, in the U.S.S.R. it has been found that, for example, the Ukraine, in spite of the big part it plays in the Union and its relatively advanced degree of development, was "represented" in the federal staff only to the extent of three to four per cent, although its population amounted to eight to ten per cent of the population of the Soviet Union (cf. A.K. Srivastava, "Geographical Distribution of Personnel in the United Nations", *The Indian Journal of Public Administration*, (New Delhi, No. 4/1957, p. 364)).

(52) Cf. *Report on Recruitment Methods and Standards*... (op. cit., p. 7): "Without variation, the Charter or basic constitutional provision of each international organization prescribes two basic criteria in the selection of staff. The first is efficiency, competence and integrity, which is either expressly or by clear inference considered paramount; and the second is wide geographical distribution of the staff. It is of the utmost importance that appointments to the staff of the respective organizations be made solely according to these criteria, and without regard to personal or political pressures."

(53) As we have already pointed out, even an official doing purely office work in an international administration may frequently be placed in a delicate situation in which his loyalty to the organization comes into play. Hence, even if in the Secretariat national rivalries and antagonisms do not make themselves felt with the same force as regards such posts as in the case of the directorial and professional categories, it is obvious that *local* recruitment does not imply any lessening of the "exclusively international" character of the officials concerned. Any mistake on this subject as a result of loose terminology would be disastrous. Account should also be taken of the influence on geographical distribution of temporary appointments (fixed term or indefinite) and of "semi-local" recruitment (intermediate category of general service staff which, as a rule, is locally recruited, but in regard to which the Secretary-General is entitled to appoint nationals of neighbouring countries; cf. below, p. 250-251).

Part III: Its Evolution

CHAPTER 5

THE PIONEER PERIOD:
THE LEAGUE OF NATIONS

The origins: Sir Eric Drummond's role

The creation of the League of Nations was a quasi-revolutionary event because, unlike the *unions*, it extended its activities to the political domain; nevertheless no major complication accompanied the birth of its Secretariat. The operation took place in two stages, first in the Organizing Committee of the League at Paris (May 1919) and then at the fifth session of the Council of the new organization at Rome (May 1920). The Secretariat was housed at Sunderland House in London until its transfer to Geneva in August 1920. Its early days were characterized by the indifference of its founders—an indifference to which we have already referred.[a] When Sir Maurice (later Lord) Hankey, at that time British Secretary to the Paris Peace Conference, after having been Secretary to the British War Cabinet during the First World War, declined the post of Secretary-General of the League, this post was entrusted to Sir Eric Drummond (later Lord Perth) in virtue of Article 6 of the Covenant. He was a close collaborator of Arthur Balfour's and had previously occupied an important position in the British Foreign Office. He was chosen for his personal qualifications and his administrative competence; his discretion and his political effacement were considered as assets. This appointment had been included in the annex to the Covenant even before the Council of the League had been set up. The latter authorized Sir Eric Drummond to engage the staff of the Secretariat subject to the Council's subsequent approval, but gave him a free hand and relied—rightly, as it proved—on his sense of moderation and impartiality.

His appointment as "Secretary-General" and not as "Chancellor", as certain early plans had proposed,[b] showed a preference for the model of a British Under-Secretary of State—permanent and non-political—lest he should become a sort of "international dictator". He was thus debarred from playing a political part of his own. An international Secretariat was set up with limited powers, following

(a) Cf. above, chapter 2, p. 57, note (4).
(b) Lord Cecil plan of 14 January 1919, Cecil-Miller Draft of 27 January 1919 (cf. D. H. Miller, *The Drafting of the Covenant* (New York, Vol. 2, p. 61 and pp. 133-143)).

the example of similar organs during the "union" period, and of the temporary inter-allied organs of the First World War. This was the consequence of the conception of the League of Nations as an organ whose *task* was "to give reality to international life... by conferring moral and real authority on a central organization truly representative of the wishes of all the contracting States...";[a] but whose *structure* was to appear as a sort of limited liability company "transplanted onto the international plane",[1] devoid of any character as a "super-State" and with a secretariat which "could in no way be compared to any kind of government".[b]

Sir Eric Drummond had plenty of time to build up a secretariat *ab nihilo*. During the first eighteen months of the League's existence there were no important meetings. There was nobody to prevent him from putting his ideas on the international civil service into practice. In any case his administrative principles, in conformity with the traditions of the British Civil Service, were well known, and it was rightly expected that he would follow the administrative model of his country. It should be remembered that ideas regarding the technique of recruitment for the new Secretariat were vague at first, even in the Secretary-General's own mind. They were clarified by experience. At the same time the principle of the "international character" of the members of the Secretariat was proclaimed from the very outset on the basis of the Balfour principles of which Sir Eric Drummond was a part-author.[2] "In making these appointments he had primarily to secure the best available men and women for the particular duties which had to be performed... but in doing so, it was necessary to have regard to the great importance of selecting the officials from various nations".[c] The same principle—namely, the particular importance of the competence of candidates, but without losing sight of the international character of the Secretariat—was confirmed in Sir James Allen's report[3][d] and in the resolutions of the Council and the Assembly.[e] There was therefore no question at the time of geographical distribution's impeding the "international outlook" of the staff, which was already considered as an essential criterion of the international civil service. Thus the "international character" of the members of the Secretariat of the League became a firmly established principle and one which was frequently confirmed later.

(a) L. Bourgeois (op. cit., pp. 74/75).
(b) Ibidem, p. 39.
(c) Balfour Report to the Rome session of the Council of the League, May 1920, *Official Journal*, 1920, No. 4, p. 137.
(d) Report to the First Assembly of the League of Nations at Geneva in November 1920 (pp. 654 ff.).
(e) Resolution of the Council of the League (Fifth session, Rome, May 1920, Official Journal No. 4, 1921, p. 139); resolution of the First Assembly of 17 December 1920, pp. 663-664).

Such was the enthusiasm which greeted the new League of Nations and the pioneer spirit which characterized the first recruits of the Secretariat "who relied on their imagination to make good their lack of experience",[a] that candidates were taken on trust, without worrying too much about their previous relations with their respective governments, or even the part played by the latter in their selection. The experience of the first few years was soon to prove that this trust was justified.

"The Secretariat has accomplished a considerable task and has given proof of a devotion from which it has not departed for an hour or a moment.... The preparatory work for the discussions and decisions has always been carried out by the Secretariat with the greatest impartiality and with a profound feeling of the role which the League of Nations is called upon to play...."[b]

Further, the fact that the organization was small and geographically restricted made recruitment easy, and the general situation less complex. The *esprit de corps* thus formed contributed powerfully to the creation of the "Geneva spirit":

"The Secretariat of the League guarantees permanence and coherence in its work of rationally organizing the world. In its numerous offices has been formed, little by little... a school of international officials skilled in the study and resolution of conflicts, and immune from national prejudice. Yet they are in no way men denationalized. One does not expect them to betray the cause of their fatherland, or even to show indifference towards it: one expects them to realize that this cause is but part of a whole.... How often has the hesitation of a delegate been overcome by arguments and by a courage supplied to him by a member of the Secretariat whose name the public will never know! How often has a President of the Assembly been pleased to see, placed on his desk, ready drawn up and typed, the speech which he will deliver the next day amidst applause! And how many distinguished persons have been saved from making howlers by this or that diligent and well-informed official, ever attentive and smiling! In proportion as the Council is hesitant and long in coming to a decision, the carrying out of it by the Secretariat, once the decision has been reached, is rapid and fruitful.... The administrative services of the whole world might well take the Secretariat as a model...."[c]

"I would add that it is edifying to discover that many officers of the general staff have not only a considerable taste for hard thinking and a love of work well done, but also the conviction that they are collaborating in a noble enterprise. How many times... I felt myself discouraged by pacifist verbosity and the feeble inanity of arguments! There is a sententious way of being 'international,' a pontifical manner of speaking about peace, the 'rapprochement of peoples' and complete and immediate disarmament, which is horrible.... But there exists—and one finds it at the Secretariat—an intelligent and accurate way of conceiving the community of Nations, and of rendering service to humanity without boasting about it...."[d]

(a) E. Giraud (op. cit., p. 7).
(b) L. Bourgeois (op. cit., pp. 96/97).
(c) R. de Traz, *The Spirit of Geneva*, (London 1935, pp. 66-69).
(d) Ibidem, pp. 117-119.

It would, however, be wrong to think that the work of the Secretariat of the League, efficient though it was, did not arouse criticism. In the first place there was opposition from nationalists of all kinds, who, as soon as the League appeared, voiced their disapproval and described it as an ideological chimaera, dangerous to national sovereignty. A powerful section of the press conducted a furious campaign against the League throughout its existence. This campaign, being based among other things on financial considerations, inevitably affected the Secretariat. It was accused of waste of money, bad financial administration and unfair allocation of budgetary burdens, especially to the detriment of Great Britain. This led to exaggerated parsimony, and the League always suffered from an unfortunate shortage of funds. The Secretary-General therefore spent a large part of his time balancing the budget by reducing expenditure (thus putting the brake on initiative) and defending the Secretariat's action in the Committees.[4] These reasons, among others, led the First Assembly of the League to set up the Committee of Enquiry known as the "Noblemaire Committee". This was the first direct consequence of an incipient crisis, the first of a whole series of crises which were to follow one another owing to the hesitations of the Member States as to the basic principles of the organization, and to the difficulty they found in adjusting themselves to the idea of an international civil service. This state of affairs produced some unrest in the Secretariat, whose members supposed that their efficiency was doubted and feared that the Committee's activities would waste a lot of their time without tangible results.

> "But they soon perceived, as more experienced administrations would have perceived from the beginning, that if they were in truth established on solid lines and working with proper economy, they had everything to gain from a thorough and impartial inquiry...."[a]

This remained true as long as the fluctuations of international relations permitted some degree of stability. The situation remained stable in fact until the Tenth Assembly of the League, in 1929.

Secondly, in spite of this quiescence, certain criticisms against the Secretariat came from within the organization. They came first of all from two countries which from the outset had played a dominant role in the Secretariat, France and Great Britain. "In France the Secretariat was represented as being entirely in the hands of England, and in England as being entirely in the hands of France."[b] This view was expressed by various isolationist and nationalist elements, and reflected the importance attached at that time for political reasons to the nationality of the heads of the international secretariats. From

(a) F. P. Walters (op. cit., pp. 131-132).
(b) L. Bourgeois (op. cit., 437).

1919 to 1933 the head of the League Secretariat was an Englishman, Sir Eric Drummond, and he was succeeded after his resignation by a Frenchman, Joseph Avenol; the latter resigned in 1940 and was succeeded by the Irishman Sean Lester.[5] During the same period the heads of the I.L.O. secretariat were first the Frenchman Albert Thomas, after his death in 1932 the Englishman Harold Butler, and then the American John Winant. As Léon Bourgeois said:

> "In speaking of the part played by individuals...I cannot forget the services rendered by our Secretariat...giving to all an example of the most perfect correctness and impartiality....What better proof can I give of this correctitude and impartiality than by recalling the attacks simultaneously made on the Secretariat by France and Britain?...Truly I have never met in any organization such disinterested good will, hard work and dedication to the common task...."[a]

Next, during the early period grievances were expressed by certain non-European Members, particularly India,[6] as regards the absence of "representation," or the insufficient "representation" in the Secretariat of countries other than the great Powers. The operation of the rule of geographical distribution—vague and at that time not based on any definite criterion—had created difficulties from the outset in the League Secretariat. Neither the Middle East nor Latin America nor the Far East was "represented" on the Secretariat, or, if they were, had only a small number of "representatives" quite out of proportion to their budgetary contributions.[7] Even when this situation was later adjusted in favour of this category of Member States, they were dissatisfied by the slowness of the improvements. Though the problem of geographical distribution never became acute in the League of Nations, it was nevertheless constantly raised and remained a cause of friction at successive Assemblies.

The Noblemaire Report

The report of the Committee of Enquiry appointed by the First Assembly on 17 December 1920 under the chairmanship of the Frenchman Georges Noblemaire,[b] was submitted on 7 May 1921 to the Second Assembly by the Fourth Committee, after which it was adopted by the Assembly on 1 October 1921. It was to become a sort of Magna Carta containing the principles of the administrative and budgetary organization of the Secretariat. This report sets out from following consideration:

> "The Secretariat, which might well have given way to the temptation to be unduly expansive in scope and thus have run the grave danger of awakening justifiable apprehensions on the part of the Nations, seems to have grasped its

(a) Ibidem.
(b) Doc. C. 424, M. 305, 1921, X and A. 140 (a) 1921; 2nd Assembly, 4th Committee, annex 2, pp. 174 ff.).

duties correctly and to have kept its activities well within the bounds described in the Covenant. The secretariat as such has of course no executive power except in so far as the general direction of its various branches is concerned. Its functions are confined first to the preparation of the necessary material, whether for the meetings of the Council or of the Assembly or for those of the various technical committees, and secondly to the promulgation of the decisions and recommendations made by those bodies. From these wise limitations of its activities the Secretariat has in no way deviated...."[a]

The Committee thus came down decidedly on the side of the "minimalist" view, following the direction given to the Secretariat by its first Secretary-General.

The Committee considered the moral and intellectual quality of the Secretariat staff to be outstanding, but suggested several legal and administrative provisions which were later inserted in the staff regulations. The following points deserve attention:

—As the Balfour Report had already recommended that salaries should be calculated in such a way as to attract highly qualified candidates, the Noblemaire Committee proposed that the level of salaries offered to the Secretariat of the League should be higher than those of the best-paid national administrations. The British Civil Service was to be the standard in this connection, nor was the expatriation factor to be neglected. "Otherwise," said the Report, "it would be impossible to obtain the services of Britishers of the required standing or later on of Americans".[8]

—The introduction of recruitment by competition was recommended in principle, promotions from one step to the next being automatic and promotions from one category to another being by selection. But the principle of recruitment by competition (on qualifications or by examination) did not debar the Secretary-General from filling certain vacancies without resort to this method of selection.

—The international civil service being regarded in principle as a life career, a certain automatic rotation was provided for in regard to normal vacancies. Thus long-term appointments were generally recommended, stability of employment being increased in inverse proportion to the weight of responsibilities involved. This principle was expressed as follows:

> "The international character of the League of Nations and the legitimate desire of the States Members to take a full part in its working render it essential that such changes should take place in the higher posts of the Secretariat as will enable them to be filled by persons of whatever country, of recognized importance and widespread influence among their own people, whose views and sentiments are in agreement with their national public opinion. This principle of frequent changes in the higher staff is essential to make the League a living force among the nations. *Per contra* there can be no question of depriving

(a) 2nd Assembly, 4th Committee, annex 2 (p. 177).

the Secretariat of its leaders too rapidly and thereby losing the benefit of an experience which will be the more valuable the longer they are retained...."[a]

As regards the administrative staff of the conference and office services, the Committee proposed a high degree of stability. The members of the intermediate "professional staff" should also enjoy relative stability in view of the fact that "they carry out all the intellectual and administrative work of the Secretariat, which requires high educational qualifications, and in the upper ranges demands very considerable capactiy and qualifications of initiative and resource...".[b]

Hence the principle of frequent changes should be applied only in cases where high officials could be detached from their national administrations for a definite period of service, after which they would return to their national duties (so that they should not be troubled by doubts as to their future careers). This method of recruitment should not, however, be the general rule.

Thus a reasonable balance was sought between life careers and temporary appointments or the seconding of officials from national administrations, the latter method of recruitment being accepted only for certain posts. This was necessary in order to ensure stability of employment, which at that time seemed uncertain at the League.

"The Noblemaire Report...was...regarded as a kind of basic charter of the budgetary and administrative organizations of the League. In due course, an elaborate system of financial regulations and staff regulations was built up by later Assemblies. These expanded, defined, and, where necessary, amended the recommendations of the Noblemaire Report; they preserved its main substance, just as the Report itself preserved the main lines of the organization as Drummond had planned and built it...."[c]

The provisional staff regulations of 1 June 1921, based on a draft by the Norwegian Eric Colban, were replaced on 1 January 1922 by new regulations based on the principles of the Noblemaire Report.[9] To fulfil the requirement concerning stability of employment, the Fourth Assembly of 1923 decided to set up a compulsory pensions and retirement fund. This decision clearly illustrated the change which had taken place since the early days of the organization, when no provision had been made for a general pensions scheme. To provide the necessary guarantees to the staff, an obvious requirement of good administration,[d] the Eighth Assembly in 1927 established the Administrative Tribunal of the League, "a judicial body set up to determine the legal rights of officials on strictly legal grounds... to pronounce finally upon any allegation that the administration has

(a) Ibidem, p. 189.
(b) Ibidem, p. 190.
(c) F. P. Walters (op. cit., p. 132).
(d) Cf. above, chapter 4, notes (34), (35), (36) and (37).

refused to give an official treatment to which he is legally entitled or
has treated him in a manner which constitutes a violation of his legal
rights under his appointment...".[a]

The creation of this body corresponded to the wish expressed in
1921 by Albert Thomas, and to the views stated in the Noblemaire
Report; by giving the staff of the Secretariat access to a court of law
in the full sense of the term in its disputes with the organization, it
greatly contributed to the internal balance of the organization.[10]
In this connection it has been stated that:

> "the whole evolution which found its conclusion in the establishment of the
> Tribunal may perhaps best be characterized as a fair and workable compromise
> between the concepts of Anglo-Saxon law with respect to civil service tradition
> and Latin and Germanic concepts of civil service rights and safeguards...."[b]

The period of teething troubles having been left behind, the Secretariat of the League of Nations, whose legal skeleton had thus slowly
and empirically developed, rapidly began to attain maturity and
"had in fact established its reputation more rapidly than any other
organ of the League. The consequence was that the Governments
of the Member States began to take a more active interest in the
question of appointments".[c] A crisis of growth followed, the second
since the start of the League, the Secretariat being the target of
frequent attacks on the part of governments, some of them dissatisfied
with its composition and others with its relative importance.

The 1929-1931 crisis

Although at the time of the League's creation the launching of a
new type of international civil service was accomplished without
too many obstacles in an atmosphere of some indifference, as we have
noted above, and although the first crisis was allayed by the
Noblemaire Report, the general atmosphere gradually deteriorated
as complications arose in international relations, as the Secretariat's
role expanded and as its membership increased. "Each year the
League's sphere of activity was extended, not with a view to its
harmonious and methodical development, but in an impromptu
fashion".[d] At the same time "the administrative and secretariat
work falling on the Secretariat has increased in a proportion very
much greater than the staff itself."[e] Moreover, from 1929 onwards

(a) Report of the Sub-Committee (of the 4th Committee) of the 8th Assembly on
the establishment of an Administrative Tribunal (p. 251).
(b) E. F. Ranshofen-Wertheimer (op. cit., p, 262).
(c) F. P. Walters (op. cit., p. 419).
(d) Speech by the Venezuelan delegate, C. Zumeta, in 1931, (12th Assembly,
4th Committee, p. 9).
(e) Report by the Secretary-General, (8th Assembly, 4th Committee, annex 9,
p. 205).

international relations were suffering from a latent political crisis, and the growing tension could not fail to have direct repercussions on the Secretariat.

Thus the Ninth and Tenth Assemblies of the League in 1928 and 1929 were the occasion of bitter criticisms, which for the first time were directed against the Secretariat. These attacks came simultaneously from two sources: firstly from the small and medium Powers which opposed the privileges of the great Powers in the matter of recruitment; and secondly from Fascist Italy. While the delegates of both parties "for one reason or another objected to the actions or the membership of the Secretariat, and took the opportunity to express their dissatisfaction and their grievances,"[a] the aim of the group consisting of the smaller Powers was the readjustment of the geographical distribution of the Secretariat's staff in favour of small countries. Owing to Germany's admission this distribution was indeed liable to become still more unfavourable to them than in the past. Italy, on the other hand, aimed at weakening the Secretariat in general and at limiting the Secretary-General's power in particular.

The first group pointed to the Balfour principles and alleged that the Secretariat had departed from them in practice, which had led to the "loss of its international character".[b] Thus

> "The smaller Powers in the Assembly had always looked on the Secretariat as being, with themselves, the defender of the international spirit which, as they believed, the great Powers were inclined to despise; and they doubted whether this role could be maintained by professional diplomatists whose training and experience might naturally lead them to think primarily of the interests of their own governments. and who would look to these governments and not the Secretary-General for future promotion. They saw in the new development a further sign that the great Powers intented to guide and control the activities of the League...."[c]

They criticized vigorously the fact that the great Powers which had founded the League constituted a sort of "privileged caste". They proposed that there should be a "partial and gradual demobilization of the great Powers in the higher posts," in order to arrive at an equitable if not equal representation of the various nationalities among the staff, which was to consist of two parallel bodies—"a permanent and highly impartial body and a body of technicians; only the latter would remain in close touch with their respective governments and stay a short time at the League".[d] Speakers in favour

(a) F. P. Walters, (op. cit., p. 419).
(b) Speech by the Norwegian representative, C. J. Hambro, 9th Assembly, 4th Committee, pp. 32/33 and 61. Cf. also 10th Assembly, 4th Committee (pp. 38/39).
(c) F. P. Walters (op. cit., p. 419).
(d) Speech by the Swiss representative, W. Rappard, 10th Assembly, 4th Committee (pp. 45/46).

of this view considered that "the international character of the Secretariat depends not only upon the spirit of its members, but also upon the extent to which it really represents the different nations", this being "particularly true in respect of the higher posts".[a][11] Norway in particular "constituted itself a champion of the small Powers against the great, of the Assembly against the Council, and of the principle that the League should be a political rather than a diplomatic institution".[b] Thus in successive Assemblies the representatives of the small countries objected to the appointment of a growing number of diplomats either as high officials of the Secretariat or as national delegates (particularly in the case of Italy and Germany). They extolled the doubtful advantages of the system of rotation in the higher posts of the Secretariat, and, not without creating unfortunate misunderstandings at times,[12] raised categorically the problem of geographical distribution in the Secretariat.

Italy opposed the formation of an international civil service on the model of the national administrations on grounds of efficiency.[c] The Act of 16 June 1927 of the Fascist régime in Italy obliged Italian candidates to the international civil service to obtain the formal permission of the Italian Ministry of Foreign Affairs and to leave the international service when instructed to do so by their government.[d] This school of thought accordingly combated the international character of the Secretariat on the pretext of rationalization. As the Swiss delegate to the League, William E. Rappard, pointed out: "The responsible heads of the international organizations were asked to reconcile two incompatible principles—the *maximum* rationalization in their administration and the *maximum* internationalization. Neither of those conditions could be fulfilled without violating the other....".[e] As political tension increased,[13] "Governments put forward strong claims for a sort of proportional distribution of posts, particularly the more important ones, among their nationals. The result was that recruitment became a diplomatic affair, that promotion was blocked and that it became difficult for international officials to follow a normal career. This was an obvious danger to the quality of the international staff...".[f] A judicious observer commented:

"But while Britain, France and Japan wished to maintain the existing system, Germany and Italy tried to diminish the powers of the Secretary-General by

(a) Speech by the Indian representative, Homi Mehta, 10th Assembly, 4th Committee, (p. 44).
(b) F. P. Walters (op. cit., p. 421).
(c) Speech by the Italian representative, Stefano Cavazzoni, 10th Assembly, 4th Committee, (pp. 35/36).
(d) *Raccolta delle Leggi d'Italia*, 1927, Vol. VI, p. 5932.
(e) Speech in the 4th Committee of the 12th Assembly (p. 16).
(f) G. Scelle, *L'organisation internationale du Travail et le B.I.T.*, (Paris, 1930, p. 100).

transferring the political direction of the Secretariat to a committee of its principal members. The consequence was that the structure and membership of the Secretariat became henceforth, what it had never been hitherto, a matter of obstinate controversy...."[a]

The adoption by the Ninth Assembly, in 1928, of a resolution confirming the Balfour principles and asking for the drawing up of fresh staff regulations did not settle the crisis. The Tenth Assembly accordingly reverted in 1929 to the British suggestion for a fresh enquiry into the organization of the Secretariat. The British plan described in the Fourth Committee set out from the principles laid down in the Balfour and Noblemaire Reports—namely, the existence of an international civil service, the need for security of tenure for international officials, greater importance to be given to competence than to geographical distribution, and the idea of a genuine career in the Secretariat accompanied by proper personnel management, regular promotion and a pension system. It was proposed that the whole problem should be studied in order to ascertain "whether the spirit of the Balfour Report had always been observed".[b] This plan was adopted by the Assembly, which appointed the thirteen members of the new Committee of Enquiry afterwards known as the Committee of Thirteen. This Committee was instructed "to examine what steps should be taken to ensure in the future as in the past the best possible administrative results for the Secretariat, the I.L.O. and the Registry of the Permanent Court of International Justice".[c]

The clash of ideas: majority and minority in the Committee of Thirteen

The report of the Committee of Thirteen[d]—whose main suggestions were adopted by the Fourth Committee of the Eleventh Assembly, which approved on 3 October 1930 the provisions concerning the duties of the staff and the duration of appointments—was to play an important part in the history of the international civil service.

"With regard to general principles concerning staff problems, the Balfour, Noblemaire and Thirteen Reports should be regarded as classics by all responsible for world organization...."[e]

This report indeed marks an epoch. The Secretariat of the League, which had developed rapidly during the first ten years of the organization's existence, was acquiring maturity and had reached the crossroads. After a period of pragmatic experimentation in which definite principles were lacking and in which the Secretary-General laid down

(a) F. P. Walters (op. cit., p. 420).
(b) Speech by the British delegate, Hugh Dalton, 10th Assembly, 4th Committee, (p. 33).
(c) 10th Assembly, pp. 144, 166, 173.
(d) 11th Assembly, 4th Committee, Annex 8 (p. 290 ff.).
(e) C. W. Jenks, *Some Problems...* (op. cit., p. 97).

the lines to be followed, a decision had to be taken as to the future. States were showing growing interest in fundamental ideas and in the future development of the Secretariat (as though taken by surprise by the role which the latter had begun to play), and the staff of the Secretariat was dissatisfied with the conditions of employment, the possibilities of normal promotion and the atmosphere in which it had to work. Both were in favour of the establishment of a more stable basis: the "heroic era" had been left behind and a choice between different conceptions was necessary.

At the same time there were two conflicting ideas as to the task of the international Secretariat. This confusion had been present from the outset but serious clashes had hitherto been avoided, the problem not having been considered sufficiently important. It now began to be appreciated at its true value; in fact the tendency was to go to the opposite extreme. Thus, setting out from common premises, two opposing schools of thought, that of the majority and the minority, clashed, first in the Committee of Thirteen, and then in the Fourth Committee of the Eleventh Assembly of 1930 when the report of the Committee of Thirteen was debated. Both sides made ample statements during these debates which enable us to diagnose the crisis.

The majority of the Committee of Thirteen (nine against four) concurred in the main with the Noblemaire Report. The new administrative bodies (the Secretariats of the League of Nations and the I.L.O.) were to retain a strictly international character, to enjoy the powers essential to enable them to do satisfactory work and to be organized according to the rules of a public administration adjusted to the needs of an international organization.

> "... In the course of the last ten years proof has been given over and over again that it is possible to reckon on the existence of a body of good international officials, loyal to the League and ready to discharge faithfully the obligations which they accepted on entering its service. [The Committee] does not consider that the special interests of each country can best be secured by the existence, side by side in the Geneva organizations, of representatives of these interests who would naturally feel bound to defend them. That, in its judgment, is the business of the responsible delegates of Governments and the representatives of national administrations; and if it were undertaken by League officials, they would inevitably lose that impartiality which it is essential they should possess. In the Committee's view, therefore, the Secretariat should be organized, as was contemplated by the Noblemaire Committee, in departments under a central authority which would correspond to the purposes of the various League organizations. Each of them should consist of a properly qualified staff under the direction of a responsible head."[a]

Consequently, recalling the principle laid down in the Balfour Report and reproduced in article 1, paragraph 1, of the Staff Regulations in force at the time, the Committee proposed that this provision should

(a) Report of the Committee of Thirteen, (11th Assembly, 4th Committee, Annex 8, p. 295).

be further emphasized in order to leave no doubt as to the international character of the Secretariat:

> "The officials of the Secretariat of the League of Nations are exclusively international officials and their duties are not national but international. By accepting appointment they pledge themselves to discharge their functions and to regulate their conduct with the interests of the League alone in view. They are subject to the authority of the Secretary-General and are responsible to him in the exercise of their functions as provided in these regulations. They may not seek or receive instructions from any Government or other authority external to the Secretariat of the League of Nations.... An official of the Secretariat may not during his term of office accept any honour or distinction from a Government except for services rendered before appointment."[a]

Permanence being "the foundation of any satisfactory administration",[b] the Committee unanimously recommended it in the case of officials of medium and lower ranks,[14] but not in the case of higher officials. Only a majority of the Committee was in favour of maintaining the Noblemaire Report's view concerning appointments of unlimited duration for most of the higher posts of the Secretariat. These posts were the subject of the principal difference of opinion.

The *majority*, noting that there was "a certain feeling of discontent" on the subject, emphasized a number of fundamental principles regarding recruitment:

The Secretariat should not only be technically efficient, "but it must, by its impartiality, command the confidence of all States Members";[c]

While this does not preclude the maintenance of contact between the Secretariat and the national governments, this contact being, on the contrary, highly desirable, "the official who transmits information about his own country must be careful not to become an advocate of its policy. The line to be observed in this matter is a narrow one and requires, particularly in the Secretary-General, a high degree of fairness and objectivity";[d]

Equality of all States Members as regards recruitment is essential and no Power should be "unduly privileged": "Any arrangement of the higher posts which excludes the nationals of certain States Members of the League would seem very difficult to defend".[e] Thus the majority of the Committee emphasized the need of stability for the nucleus of medium and lower staff and advocated temporary appointments of political and technical experts, and the temporary recruitment of officials to perform urgent and exceptional tasks;

(a) Ibidem, p. 296.
(b) Ibidem, p. 297.
(c) Ibidem, p. 298.
(d) Ibidem, pp. 298/299.
(e) Ibidem p. 299.

All categories of staff must be given the opportunity of pursuing their career in the League ("it is of great importance that every official in the Secretariat should have the opportunity of reaching the highest posts, not excluding that of Secretary-General").[a] This idea was not accepted by the minority, which wished to maintain the privileges of the great Powers in this connection;

Administrative control should be left in the hands of a single person. This was contrary to the minority's proposal which was in favour of management by a committee:

> "The Secretariat...is a purely executive body and for executive purposes rapidity of decision is often essential. For that reason in most organizations, whether public or private, the administrative control is left in the hands of a single managing director and, when necessary, of his deputy. In the case of the League of Nations this principle seems to be of special importance. Certain duties in times of emergency are assigned to the Secretary-General, and a delay of a few hours caused by a difference of opinion in an advisory body might well be fatal to the success of his action."[b]
> "Essentially the minority propose to maintain unimpaired the privileged position of the permanent representatives of the Council. But they go further. They propose that there shall be formed a consultative committee consisting of Under-Secretaries-General which any Director would attend for the discussion of the affairs concerning his department. The Secretary-General would be bound to consult this consultative committee. They further suggest that the Directors should be grouped under the various Under-Secretaries-General instead of being directly responsible to the Secretary-General. The result of this arrangement would, by depressing the position of Directors, be still further to accentuate the difference between classes of States and so, far from removing the grievance felt by some of those States, it would aggravate it. Further, from the administrative point of view it would be a less efficient system than that which now exists."[c]

On the other hand the *minority*,[d] without openly attacking the fundamental conception of the international civil service laid down in the Balfour principles, nevertheless undermined the stability of the staff and the essential role of the machinery set up in 1919. In particular, its report drew attention to the drawbacks of security of tenure, which might lead to bureaucratization and the complication of administrative machinery as a result of a spirit of routine and loss of initiative. In the opinion of the minority this danger outweighed the advantages of the system of permanent appointments, even if the latter gave officials a feeling of security "which is, generally speaking, undoubtedly in the interests of efficient administration".[e]

(a) Ibidem.
(b) Ibidem.
(c) Ibidem.
(d) Cf. above.
(e) Report of the Minority of the Committee of Thirteen, annexed to the Committee's Report (op. cit., p. 312).

The minority thus opposed the views of the majority regarding the stabilization of the position of medium grade officials (first division).[a] These officials, who are:

"the mainspring of the Secretariat, must possess very special qualities. It is not enough that their work should be first class from the purely administrative point of view. They must, in addition, be acquainted with public opinion in their own countries so that they may, as far as possible, contribute to the common stock the conceptions prevalent in the various parts of the world. Until the 'international man' has been created, the international character of the Secretariat's work, which is of such importance to the League of Nations, can only be assured by the co-operation of the nationals of different countries, which would make the Secretariat a kind of clearing house for the various currents of thought and ideas prevailing throughout the world...."[b]

Consequently, both officials in the upper and medium grades and the principal officers should, according to this conception, be employed only on a temporary basis—i.e., for seven years, renewable if necessary. This formula would lead to a certain degree of rotation, would allow of the introduction of fresh blood and would give the nationals of all countries access to these posts. The most valuable staff members would be able, thanks to the system of renewals, to remain in the service of the Secretariat more or less permanently while "the less highly qualified officials might be dispensed with without any special procedure through the mere non-renewal of their contracts." Such a system, in the opinion of the minority, in no wise implied that officials would be in any way dependent upon the governments of the countries to which they belonged, and would better ensure the international character of the work of the organization by reflecting national realities in the different countries.

On this basis, the minority recommended the maintenance of the monopoly given to the great Powers in the higher posts of the Secretariat:

"States not permanently represented on the Council should realize that the holding of the post of Under-Secretary-General by a national of a country with a permanent seat on the Council is not a constitutional rule or privilege, but has proved useful in practice for the reason that the nationals of countries with general interests are by their capacity to serve as liaison agents specially qualified to discharge these duties...."[c]

The monopoly was therefore regarded as justified on practical grounds, and the "dissatisfied" States could be granted certain secondary advantages suggested in the Minority Report.[15]

As already indicated above,[d] the minority continually emphasized the increase in the Secretariat's importance since the time of the

(a) Cf. below, chapter 5, note (41).
(b) Report of the Minority... (op. cit., p. 313).
(c) Ibidem, p. 316.
(d) See above, p. 76.

Noblemaire Report. In its opinion, developments in no way confirmed the idea that the Secretariat should act as a clearing house rather than as a source of political initiative and action. The Secretariat was represented as a creative organ permanently exercising an unobtrusive but undeniable influence even on the political plane. This idea led the minority to propose that the Secretariat should be directed not by a single person, but by a committee, which would sufficiently guarantee the international character of the higher direction.[16a] This proposal was submitted in the Minority Report as follows:

First possibility: "A system of joint control would be exercised by a limited number of high officials. The Under-Secretaries-General might form a Governing Board, with the Secretary-General in the chair, and on a footing of equality as between one another. The Governing Board would, for instance, discuss in plenary session all general questions of any kind whatever and all the more important matters affecting each section, calling in the competent Directors in succession to its councils..."[b]

Second possibility: "Less far-reaching".[c] The Secretary-General would remain solely responsible for the direction of the Secretariat, but would be *assisted* in his duties by a committee consisting of the Under-Secretaries-General. This committee would remain in close and constant touch with the Secretary-General and would "have the right to give its opinion if it so desired before any measures involving, important political issues or principles were taken by the Secretary-General".[d] The Secretary-General would act alone only in cases of extreme urgency.

The clash of ideas in the Eleventh Assembly and the efforts to find a compromise

Lively debates followed the Report of the Committee of Thirteen in the Fourth Committee (Eleventh Assembly of the League of Nations).[e] The adherents of the two schools of thought put forward their views in detail.

Thus, speaking for the minority, the Italian delegate[f] recommended a "steady balance" in the direction of the Secretariat,

> "an international organization of an extremely conplicated and delicate nature, unprecedented in the history of nations...so as to guarantee the international character of its structure and to place that character above all suspicion. [The hypothesis of an Advisory Board] is in the opinion of the Italian Government the minimum guarantee for real co-operation between the various Powers in the direction of the Secretariat....When we come to consider

(a) Report of the Minority... (op. cit., p. 315).
(b) Ibidem.
(c) Ibidem.
(d) Ibidem
(e) 11th Assembly, 4th Committee (pp. 52 ff.).
(f) Giuseppe Gallavresi, ibidem, pp. 52-53.

the recruitment of staff it seems impossible to subordinate everything to the much advertised idea of destroying all the influences which an official's national environment may have had upon him. If we go into the motives which dictated the scheme put forward [by the majority] to give the staff of the Secretariat a permanence which contrasts with the requirements of contemporary international life, we always come up against this same fixed idea...."

Similarly the Hungarian delegate, recalling the Swiss Confederation and its system of committees, said:

"In the life of the League and in all organizations belonging to the League every idea, every aspiration, every ambition, should play its part. This principle would be realized if we gave the Secretary-General an organized advisory body and if a system of rotation were established for the Secretariat....The Secretary-General should be not the brain but the arm, a member which has no initiative of its own and is commanded by the nerves of the League, which are the Assembly and the Council...."[11 a]

On the other hand, those who wished to maintain the structure of the Secretariat as established in 1919, condemned the "out-of-date ideas of national rivalry,"[b] rejected the idea of a joint directorate of the Secretariat, and pleaded in favour of stability of employment for the staff. Thus, the French delegate said:

"An advisory committee is suggested, where, as you have always recognized... the chief's authority must prevail. There can be no good administration without a responsible chief, and this is so true that the Covenant itself has given the Secretary-General sole responsibility for his administration.... But if you want more than this [to help this chief] you must be careful. You are going to kill the spirit and destroy the responsibility of the administration...."[c]

The British delegate said:

"You cannot in that way [by setting up an Advisory Board] build up an effective machine whether you are considering normal times...or critical times.... It is essential that [in critical situations] the Secretary-General should be able to act swiftly without being impeded by the necessity of carrying with him five other persons subordinate to himself.... High direction must still be confided to one man....We regard such monopoly [reserving all the higher offices for the great Powers] as completely unjustifiable in the light of general principles...."[d]

The Norwegian delegate said:

"That is just the idea [the idea of an Advisory Board] we are here to combat. It is the Council and the Assembly that represent the various Powers, and the bare idea that it would be possible for the League of Nations to exist if a group of five Powers has a guiding influence on everything that was done by it, seems to me a proof that we have to move forward and reach conditions which will make it impossible for any delegate to put forward such suggestions when we discuss matters of this kind."[e]

(a) de Hevesy, ibidem (pp. 98-99).
(b) Speech by the Norwegian delegate Hambro, ibidem (p. 91).
(c) Cahen-Salvador, ibidem (pp. 66-67).
(d) Hugh Dalton, ibidem (p. 56).
(e) Hambro, ibidem (p. 91).

The Swiss delegate also strongly pleaded in favour of maintaining and strengthening the impartiality of the Secretariat staff:

> "We must be unanimous...in recognizing that the strictest international impartiality is essential to the duties of the Secretariat; otherwise its most valuable mission—that of assisting in the work of conciliating disputes—cannot be exercised by it in an atmosphere of international trust.... The minority report contains phrases like 'until the "international man" has been created.' This naturally suggests that the authors of the minority report doubt that human beings in general can be inspired by absolute impartiality in international matters. The idea seems to be that a man who is impartial from the international point of view, as the Balfour Report seems to demand, would be rather abnormal from the point of view of his psychological situation. ...I think, however, that it is possible...to do international work in a spirit of perfect impartiality. There are historic examples of this.... It must be understood that to serve the League of Nations is also to serve one's country ..."[a]

Sir Eric Drummond himself, in spite of his well-known reserve on all differences between representatives of national Governments, thought it necessary to state his position on the subject in the interests of the service:

> "I quite frankly believe that the constitution of the advisory committee would be contrary to the efficiency of the Secretariat.... I hold that the constitution of an advisory committee such as is suggested would lead to so much delay in the ordinary course of work that it would put an intolerable burden not only on the Secretary-General but on the other members of the staff. I calculate that with the programme set up for the advisory committee, the Secretary-General would spend from one to two hours a day in consulting that committee. I do not think that is a practical proposition...."[b]

The Committee of Thirteen could not agree and contented itself with a majority vote and the submission of two conflicting opinions, but the Eleventh Assembly tried to find a compromise.

The Fourth Committee, after hearing the opinions of both sides, rejected, by a majority of 30 votes to 5,[c] the idea of a joint direction of the Secretariat and particularly of the advisory committee proposed in the minority report. The Eleventh Assembly approved this decision of the Fourth Committee's without debate.[d] The minority proposal was thus defeated.

At the same time the problem of the higher direction, and particularly of the Under-Secretaries-General (their number, their possible elimination),[18] was referred in the absence of agreement to a *new* Committee of Thirteen, which would re-examine it after a further

(a) W. Rappard, ibidem (p. 73).
(b) Ibidem (p. 153).
(c) Report of the Fourth Committee to the Assembly, ibidem (p. 428).
(d) 11th Assembly (p. 219 ff.).
(e) Committee appointed to give further consideration to certain questions relating to the organization of the Secretariat (Report, 12th Assembly, 4th Committee, pp. 93-98).

investigation and present its report[e] to the Twelfth Assembly in 1931. The fact that this controversial problem was left in suspense proved the Assembly's desire to reach a compromise. Further proof was the proposed co-existence in the Secretariat of career officials and technicians engaged on a temporary basis.[19] But the compromise appears most plainly in the conception of the Secretary-General's duties.

On the one hand, in rejecting the minority proposals the Eleventh Assembly indirectly but materially reinforced the prestige of the Secretary-General.[20] A new importance was attached to the administrative point of view by invoking the "proper principles of administration" combined with "unity of command" in the Secretariat and rejecting multipersonal direction. But at the same time stress was laid on the importance of practical politics at the apex of the pyramid. In endorsing the view of the majority of the Committee of Thirteen, Assembly acknowledged the strength of political considerations and their influence on administrative action.[21] It is in this way that we must interpret the compromise implied by the Assembly. It was opposed to administrative arrangements which would further accentuate the differences between large and small Powers and between different groups of Powers, but it did not put an end to the paramount position of the great Powers in the higher posts of the Secretariat, and it emphasized the importance of the dual role of their holders as international officials and as qualified interpreters of the opinion and civilization of their respective countries. This has given rise to the following comment:

> "The outcome of these repeated debates, and vigorous, if often contradictory, attacks, was to prove in no uncertain manner that the Members of the League in general approved the record of the Secretariat and did not desire to make any radical changes. The malcontents were heard with courtesy: but when votes were taken, their proposals were rejected by overwhelming majorities. The long battle over what was known as the Higher Direction ended in a compromise which involved little change in the existing situation, and which was only to come into force after Drummond's resignation...."[a]

The result of the compromise: subsequent crises

The compromise reached at the Eleventh Assembly, and later compromises, prevented the question of basic ideas from being settled, and, while providing an immediate solution, carried the seeds of future crises. It consisted of makeshifts, refused to cross the t's and dot the i's and shelved rather than solved the difficulties. Unanimity was required in the League of Nations for all important decisions, so that the only way of reaching an immediate result was to be content with half measures. But, the choice being *fundamental*, a middle way could not

(a) F. P. Walters (op. cit., pp. 420-421).

provide a lasting solution. In fact temporary practical arrangements were sought to prevent the Secretariat from being torn by internal struggles and reduced to a sort of translation office and typing service. Thus the compromise nevertheless enabled the Secretariat of the League to keep enough authority and prestige to carry out with complete impartiality numerous tasks which were entrusted to it later. But the same difficulties inevitably remained.

The *new* Committee of Thirteen, set up by the Eleventh Assembly, submitted in 1931 its report on the question of Deputy and Under-Secretaries-General and similar problems.[a] Faced with three proposals aiming respectively at the abolition of all these posts, at increasing their number and at maintaining the *status quo*, the Committee contented itself with summarizing the arguments in favour of each, and proposed the third as an "essentially provisional solution" for three years, after which the problem was to be re-discussed. This compromise, which was adopted by the Twelfth Assembly,[b] merely prolonged the uncertainty. At the Thirteenth Assembly, in 1932, the same discussion was resumed, since Sir Eric Drummond's resignation made a categorical solution essential. On that occasion the "alleged acquired rights" of certain Great Powers to hold higher posts in the Secretariat was called in question:

> "When a French Under-Secretary-General left he was replaced by a Frenchman and when two Italian Under-Secretaries-General retired in succession they were replaced by Italians. The same thing occurred with regard to Japan. When Germany entered the League a post of Under-Secretary-General was created for her. It was not too much to suppose that the same methods would prevail in future if the Assembly did not immediately consider means whereby a certain amount of satisfaction might be given to the States who thought it unfair that in its composition the Secretariat should reflect the same national factors which were...represented permanently on the Council of the League. ..."[c]

The outgoing Secretary-General then stressed the importance of the Secretariat's having Under-Secretaries-General nationals of those Powers "provided they placed the interest of the League before the national interests of their own countries. If, on the other hand, they regarded themselves as representatives of their own countries, their value would be nil or worse than nil."[d] This view was in line with Sir Eric Drummond's consistent opposition to the establishment of permanent delegations of States Members at League Headquarters, and his preference for seeking contacts with these States through the principal officers of the Secretariat. It became increasingly evident,

(a) 12th Assembly, 4th Committee (pp. 93-98).
(b) 12th Assembly (p. 150).
(c) Speech by the Belgian delegate, Count Carton de Wiart, at the 4th Committee of the 12th Assembly (p. 23).
(d) 13th Assembly, 4th Committee (p. 56).

however, that the more impartial the Principal Officers were, the more the governments needed a permanent representative at headquarters. This was confirmed later, since governments, observing that they could no longer rely, as some of them had hoped, on their nationals in the Secretariat to represent their interest effectively, decided eventually to appoint permanent delegates. The latter, who were at first looked on in the Secretariat as a necessary evil, were soon recognized as performing a useful function.[22]

The Thirteenth Assembly decided on a compromise between diametrically opposed proposals which was to prove durable. In the first place, two Deputy Secretaries-General were appointed (instead of one as previously), in order to ensure that the "holders of the highest posts ... be chosen for their abilities, their personal qualifications and the contribution they can make to the performance of the tasks of the League of Nations ...".[a] As one of these higher posts was to be assigned to a national of a country not having a permanent seat on the Council, the right of these countries to participate in the higher direction was recognized. Secondly, the posts of Under-Secretaries-General were maintained and stabilized, their number being henceforward three.[23] "With this step, the right of smaller countries to a share in the higher posts was officially recognized";[b] "the 1932 Assembly ... put a stop to the discussion which had raged for four full years and had created unrest and uncertainty within the Secretariat ...".[c] Nevertheless, the claims of the medium and small Powers were not yet satisfied, and their dissatisfaction was accompanied by unrest in the Secretariat. The idea of inequality between States Members had again been confirmed in the Assembly. The Italian delegate[d] noted that the League had been successful where other great conceptions had failed, "because account had been taken of the inequality of States.... The Secretariat should mirror the political situation in the world and it would be very dangerous to distort its reflection of that situation". Similarly the German delegate,[e] while admitting the need for reform, expressed himself in favour of the maintenance of the *status quo* giving the permanent members of the Council a privileged position in the higher direction of the Secretariat. The Japanese delegate[f] held that "the Secretariat should be a sort of mirror of international life ... a body in which national interests should certainly be represented and whose officials should have a thorough appreciation of those interests ..."

(a) 13th Assembly, 4th Committee (annex 15, p. 252).
(b) E. F. Ranshofen-Wertheimer (op. cit., p. 64).
(c) Ibidem, (p. 59).
(d) Giuseppe Gallavresi (13th Assembly, 4th Committee, p. 59).
(e) Von Rheinbaben, ibidem (p. 61).
(f) Sato, ibidem (pp. 61/62).

Nor was there a perfect solution of the question of geographical distribution according to nationality for the staff in general. Even before the end of the Twelfth Assembly the problem was re-discussed in the light of the report of the new Committee of Thirteen—the latter having replied to the Irish draft asking for a strict application of the criterion of geographical distribution by saying that "this principle should not be made into a dogma".[a] During the debates of the Twelfth Assembly it was said that "there could be no true international spirit in an office in which all the members belonged to the same nationality as their superior",[b] and that "the best method of ensuring that the interests peculiar to each country were respected was not to collect at Geneva representatives of those interests who were bound to defend them; this was already the duty of the responsible government representatives".[c] During the same Assembly, it was again asserted that while the organs of the League were necessarily a combination of nationalities, the Secretariat was a body which should never acquire a character of that kind since: "if it did so the day of the League's collapse would be at hand. The Secretariat must be purged of all nationalist tendencies".[d]

In the end, the Thirteenth Assembly voted on 17 October 1932 a resolution which emphasized the primary importance of the *attitudes* of the staff of the Secretariat, including the holders of the highest posts, but pointed out the necessity of a "more equitable distribution of nationalities" and defined the practical consequences of this compromise between the two contentions.[24] This was henceforward to be the guiding line of administrative policy: it was to be considered as "the outcome of a protracted movement for reform".[e] Subsequent Assemblies frequently referred back to the "1932 rule." Thus, at the Sixteenth Assembly, in 1935, the Secretary-General, Joseph Avenol, stated in the Fourth Committee:

> "It is certain that the list of higher posts in the Secretariat now comprises a variety of nationals which represents an almost radical change as compared with the situation existing a few years previously.... [The 1932 rule] has therefore had good results...."[f]

At the Seventeenth Assembly, in 1936, the Norwegian delegate made the following remarks about the nationalist tendencies of the time:

(a) 12th Assembly, 4th Committee (p. 96).
(b) Speech by the Norwegian delegate, Hambro, ibidem (p. 30).
(c) Speech by the Belgian delegate, Count Carton de Wiart, ibidem (p. 22).
(d) Speech by the Spanish delegate, S. de Madariaga, in the 4th Committee of the 13th Assembly (p. 58).
(e) Speech by the Swiss delegate, W. Rappard, in the 4th Committee of the 16th Assembly, 1935 (p. 85).
(f) Speech in the 4th Committee of the 16th Assembly (p. 84).

"It is more essential than at any previous epoch in the history of the League to stress the international character of the Secretariat and the importance of keeping it free from the repercussions of nationalist conflicts.... No infringement of the principles laid down in 1932 can be tolerated. Everyone understands how often pressure from political quarters is brought to bear on the higher officials...."[a]

The Fourth Committee in its report to the same Assembly "was at pains to confirm emphatically that no infringement can be tolerated of the provisions adopted in 1932 to the effect that officials must discharge their functions and regulate their conduct with the interests of the League alone in view and not seek or receive instructions from any government or authority external to the League of Nations".[b]

As a result of this policy the number of nationals of permanent members of the Council holding principal posts in the Secretariat declined from 75% in 1922 to about 25% in 1938.[c]

But another crisis was looming on the horizon, owing to the existence of the Fascist régime in Italy, the Nazi régime in Germany and authoritarian movements in several other European countries. Governmental pressure soon made itself felt in the Secretariat, and Italy and Germany in particular openly tried to influence their nationals. Certain higher officials belonging to these countries appeared to consider themselves in control of all the officials of their nationality, to the detriment of the proper hierarchy and the needs of the service.[d] One writer spoke of the "gradual nationalization of the Secretariat", of a transformation which appeared to "mark the triumph of the national factor over the international idea", in consequence of "the importance which governments attached to the Secretariat".[e] The morale of the staff naturally suffered.

There were many practical proofs of the regrettable disregard by several Member States of the homogeneity and impartiality essential to the Secretariat. Perceptive writers of the period speak of this. Thus Professor William Rappard, on the basis of his intimate knowledge of an organization in which he played an active part as representative of his country, compared the initial conception of the international administration with the practice of the time, in which "the fiction of the purely international character of the Principal Officers of the Secretariat was becoming more and more difficult to

(a) Hambro (17th Assembly, 4th Committee, pp. 10/11).
(b) Ibidem, (p. 89).
(c) "Issues before the XVIth General Assembly," *International Conciliation* (No. 534, 1961, p. 216).
(d) Cf. E. F. Ranshofen- Wertheimer (op. cit., p. 251 ff.).
(e) W. Rappard, "Où en est la Société des Nations?" in *Esprit international* (No. 18, April 1931, p. 241).

maintain".[a] Similarly, Professor Georges Scelle[b] spoke of "decomposition... going so far as to make the Secretariat a multi-sectional branch of the different Foreign Offices... the prey of that diplomatico-parliamentary deliquescence which is the congenital disease of the League of Nations." He condemned the practices which made the recruitment of the staff of the Secretariat "the subject of inter-governmental bargaining," and the allocation of posts "a diplomatic negotiation" and attributed the causes for this state of affairs to the "common effort of the Wilhelmstrasse and the Consulta." It would be easy to quote other similar opinions from the literature of the same period.

Although as a result of nationalist pressure, particularly on the part of those two governments, "the only organ of the League which, owing to its permanence, its technical character, its independence, might have been able... to counterbalance the anarchical policies of the governments"[c]—that is to say, the Secretariat— suffered a great deal, it has to be recognized that it did not give way under the strain as might have been feared. Most of the staff stuck to their guns, including the Italians and Germans. It was learnt by experience that a show of character and determination was enough to resist pressures of this kind. As we shall see later, the final results of this serious test were positive. It was shown that, even in the most perilous situations, in the face of direct pressure and personal threats, international work could be carried on with perfect impartiality and objectivity.

Be that as it may, in view of the constant "preoccupation [of States] to maintain their acquired positions, and the absence of truly international spirit",[d] the Secretariat appeared more and more as an international island in an ocean of nationalism, which of course disrupted it internally by creating serious conflicts and putting a brake on progress. Several governments obstinately continued to demand that their nationals occupying positions in the Secretariat should be *personae gratae* recognized as such by themselves. At the same time they exercised pressure on the latter to leave the international civil service when their countries withdrew from the organization.[e] The illegality of these two attitudes, in view of the principles laid down, the resolutions adopted at the various Assemblies,[23] and the upsetting of fundamental values which was likely to be the result, necessitated a "constant struggle between the Secretary-General and the governments to make the institution truly international—a struggle against the

(a) Ibidem.
(b) G. Scelle, "Essai sur la crise de la Société des Nations et ses remèdes", (op. cit., pp. 179-180).
(c) Ibidem.
(d) J. Paul-Boncour, *Dictionnaire diplomatique*, vol. IV, p. 989.
(e) Cf. above, chapter 4, note (23).

encroachments of the governments on the Secretariat itself".[a]
This crisis was to last until 1939.

The decline and the inheritance

The progressive deterioration of the political situation in the world
during the thirties, culminating in the war of 1939, naturally had
serious repercussions on the work of the Secretariat. There were also
internal reasons [26] which contributed to increase external difficulties.
Nevertheless, the work of the Secretariat, although on a reduced
scale, continued in spite of the difficult financial situation of the
League, the number of members having declined by one-third (it
had fallen from sixty-three to thirty-nine in 1946), and the cutting
off of communications. It was desired to make this continuity an
act of faith in the re-establishment of the international organization
at the end of the war, after the failure of attempts to impose by force
an order founded on conquest.[b] At the same time, the Secretariat
undertook, on a small scale, economic and social work which had
been begun earlier by the League and which, during the war, branch-
ed out in several directions in order to help the suffering peoples.[c]
This continuity of administrative action was made possible by the
transfer of certain services to Great Britain, the United States of
America and Canada.[27] Thus the only existing nucleus of specialists
of international administration remained intact until after the war,
to carry on to some extent work previously begun and to prepare plans
for the international collaboration of the future.

When the formal liquidation of the League was voted by the
Twenty-first Assembly at Geneva in April 1946, the new world
organization had the benefit of the experience, the expertise and the
spiritual and material heritage of the old League of Nations, which
certainly helped it to make a good start. Although the U.N. theoretically began *ab nihilo* (being regarded as an entirely new organization),
the rich experience of the League proved extremely valuable. It was
in fact "a development which is quite natural and which history can
explain".[d] Lord Cecil of Chelwood said in this connection:

> "It is enough... to insist that, but for the great experiment of the League of
> Nations, the United Nations could never have come into existence. The
> fundamental principles of the Charter and of the Covenant are the same, and it
> is gratifying to some of us that, after the violent controversies that have raged
> for the last quarter of a century, it is now generally accepted that peace can

(a) G. Scelle, *Essai sur la crise*... (op. cit., p. 179).
(b) Cf. Report on the Work of the League, 1943/1944, quoted in *The League Hands over* (Geneva, 1946, p. 114).
(c) Cf. Report on the work of the League, 1942/1943, ibidem (pp. 116/117).
(d) Speech by the Greek delegate, T. Aghnides, at the 21st Assembly (April 1946, p. 52).

only be secured by international co-operation, broadly on the lines agreed to in 1920.[a]

It was particularly the administrative inheritance of the League that proved important. Administratively speaking, the Secretariat had successfully stood the test of time.

> "In retrospect, and by comparison, it seems amazing that work of such quality, and in such quantity, should have been performed year after year by an organization so limited in numbers and resources.... The Secretariat was an institution widely and deeply rooted: it did not depend for its spirit or its efficiency upon individual leadership. Under Avenol it maintained to the full the technical qualities which it had developed under Drummond. Nor did it ever lose its unity and *esprit de corps*, though at the end these were considerably impaired by that ideological conflict whose corroding power no institution and no nation could altogether resist...."[b]

In spite of repeated disruptive assaults, in spite of many unfortunate examples of "spiritual unpreparedness," a valid machinery constituting a judicious blend of Anglo-Saxon and French administrative methods had been set up. It has rightly been said that:

> "The experience of the League of Nations Secretariat has afforded conclusive proof that international administration is possible and that it can be highly effective; that an international civil service can be created which compares favourably with the best civil services of the world. The League has shown that it is possible to establish an integrated body of international officials, loyal to the international agency and ready to discharge faithfully the international obligation incumbent upon them. It was not for lack of executive efficiency that the League system failed."[c]
>
> "The League experience has proved beyond the shadow of a doubt that international administration can function competently and successfully even under signally unfavourable circumstances. It has shown that international administrative methods can be developed and that persons from all corners of the inhabited globe can be brought together for a common purpose, to work and act together as a team. In addition, League practice has conveyed the unique and somewhat unexpected lesson that nationality plays a less disintegrating role in a multinational administration than was expected. Common ideals, a common purpose, common conditions of work and life have proved potent factors in developing an *esprit de corps*, a common psychology capable of surviving the severest crisis imaginable...."[d]

In fact, a sort of automatic process of selection had led to the irreconcilable nationalist elements gradually leaving the service and to the staff's acquiring a psychological unity by remaining true to its international tasks. This had enabled the League to survive its successive crises.[28] Thus the "Geneva spirit" was preserved and transmitted to the organization which succeeded it. The binding

(a) 21st Assembly (p. 29).
(b) F. P. Walters (op. cit., pp. 559/560).
(c) E. F. Ranshofen-Wertheimer (op. cit., pp. 427/428).
(d) Ibidem, p. 439.

force of the Secretariat had become an element of psychological integration which was not to be destroyed by conflicts and disruptive influences.

The contradiction between the sometimes successful attempts to demoralize League officials by nationalist and governmental pressure and the positive achievements is more apparent than real, since the two opposing forces coexisted and clashed frequently during the whole of the League's life. While disruptive and centrifugal forces from outside caused damage to the Secretariat, the "Geneva spirit," of which the Secretariat was the principal depository, counterbalanced their effects by always pulling in the opposite direction. Events constantly oscillated between these two forces, which in the eyes of the superficial observer seemed to prevail alternately. History was to show that the international factor, personified by the permanent Secretariat, had stood its ground and had been strengthened by its trials. In spite of the League's political failure, the administrative sector had survived intact, and was able to provide a model for its successor.

This experience also showed that every international organization must include an administrative element conceived as a public service and designed to exercise a stabilizing, co-ordinating, unifying and creative influence.[29a] Never before the League had an international administrative enterprise of this scope been realized. It was therefore a veritable pioneer enterprise which, in general, had met with success. It is true that the experience was geographically limited (in spite of its aims, the League never became universal); that the administrative body was comparatively small (the total staff of the Secretariat amounted to 658 in 1930 and never exceeded 706); and that the administrative action undertaken was primarily regarded as "indirect." Its work was reminiscent of that of national Ministries in that it was in direct contact, not with the persons administered, but with other administrations. This work[30] consisted principally of "laboratory" work: preparation of resolutions and treaties, diplomatic activities (conciliation, consolidation, negotiation, etc.), research, documentation, information, implementation of decisions, etc. ("headquarters organization").[31] Nevertheless, the League had also conducted several "field operations"—first of all in application of the Treaty of Versailles, and then in relation to refugees, transfers of populations, financial reconstruction and what would afterwards have been called technical assistance in several countries (Austria, Hungary, China). At the time, these activities were strikingly novel. The work was usually entrusted to experts enlisted outside the Secretariat and assisted by members of the latter. Nevertheless, certain missions,

(a) Cf. above, chapter 3 (particularly notes (15), (16) and (17)).

such as the Lytton Commission in Manchuria (1932), had a secretariat of their own consisting almost entirely of League officials. It should also be remembered that certain Secretariat organs of a semi-autonomous character were called into being by urgent international necessities—the Economic and Financial Organization, the Communications and Transit Organization, the Refugees Organization (directed from 1921 to 1930 by Fridtjof Nansen), and the Health Section, or the bodies dealing with traffic in opium and other dangerous drugs and the traffic in women; and that these new forms of administrative activity appeared in spite of the shortage of funds and the inadequacy of the administrative machinery. Thus, despite marked opposition and although the Secretariat itself often apathetically regarded attempts thus to widen its powers, fearing that it had neither the equipment nor the financial resources necessary, some of its work was to be the model [32] for future international administrations, preparing the way for action undertaken after the Second World War (health, epidemics control, etc.).[33] The League's work in the Saar Basin is a well-known example of its direct administration.

Nevertheless, the structure of the Secretariat remained integrated during the whole of the League's existence. We find no true delegation of powers, even sporadic or temporary, by headquarters to the outposts, and no expansion of the tasks of outlying offices except as regards liaison and information. Although the Secretariat, with the help of committees of experts, made enquiries regarding forced labour, housing, child welfare, nutrition and refugees, "taken as a whole, these external activities of the League were never a major feature of the administration".[a] They were, however, a hesitant first experiment, handicapped by improvisation and by disruptive nationalist influences; and their importance was underestimated by people in general: in fact, "public relations" were bad. In these circumstances this large-scale international administrative undertaking was severely tested. Although in essential matters (geographical distribution, higher direction, recruitment, training) it had to be content with half measures in view of aggressive and threatening tendencies, the League nevertheless took a decisive step in the direction of giving reality to an intellectual conception.[b] It thus illustrated the role which can and must be played by public services in satisfying the common needs of modern societies and in seeking the means and methods of ensuring administrative order in the field of international co-operation.

This was pioneer work, and when the time came for the League of Nations to be dissolved, it was rightly said that:

(a) E. F. Ranshofen-Wertheimer (op. cit., p. 189).
(b) Cf. M. Dendias, "Les principaux services internationaux administratifs" (*Recueil A.D.I.*, 1938, I. p, 338 and *passim*).

"to these pioneers ... belongs the merit of having, for the first time in human history, recruited and trained a great international civil service, actuated by a spirit of co-operation and genuinely attached to its duties, whose assistance and example will surely facilitate the work of tomorrow...."[a]

(a) Speech by the Belgian delegate, Count Carton de Wiart, at the 21st Assembly of the League of Nations, (April 1946, p. 44).

NOTES

(1) Cf. L. Bourgeois (op. cit., p. 39 and *passim*). It is in *The Aims and Organization of the League of Nations* (published by the Secretariat of the League, 1929) that we find this comparison of the League to a *limited liability company* with the Covenant constituting the Statutes, the Council the Board of Directors, the Assembly the shareholders and the Secretariat the staff. This analogy takes no account of the conception and evolution of international organization. It illustrates the modesty of the initial conception and may also be explained by the limited resources placed at the League's disposal.

(2) In the Fourth Committee of the Ninth Assembly of the League, in 1928 (pp. 37 ff.), Sir Eric Drummond "revealed a secret and said that he had been at least a part author of the Balfour Report." He at the same time emphasized the guiding ideas of the Balfour principles, firstly, that "the members of the Secretariat were the servants of every individual nation which was a member of the League" and, next, that "it would be intolerable that there should be a monopoly" of the great Powers.

(3) The duration of appointments at the Secretariat of the League remained indefinite and was continually being discussed afresh. The Balfour Report set out from the idea of appointments for five years, which would be renewable, and of the "introduction of fresh blood," in order to avoid the danger of getting into a rut and to provide vacancies for the nationals of non-represented countries. The Allen Report reverted to the same suggestion, while pointing out the necessity of retaining a sufficient number of persons to ensure continuity (1st Assembly, 4th Committee, p. 91). The opposition of the British delegate, G. N. Barnes, prevented a decision from being taken in this connection. "Immediately a man starts his work he will have in his mind that he may be dispensed with after five years.... He will immediately start to look out for another job, and if he gets another job in a year or two he will leave.... You will not promote international spirit by five year appointments. ..." The First Assembly entrusted the examination of this problem and of the situation of the staff as a whole 17 December 1920 to a Committee of Enquiry on which produced the Noblemaire Report submitted to the Second Assembly in 1921.

(4) F. P. Walters has shown how unjustifiable were the criticisms of the Secretariat of the League which were based on alleged waste and were frequently the result of mere gossip. (op. cit. pp. 129 ff.)

(5) S. Lester was formally elected Secretary-General retrospectively as from 1 September 1940 (vote of the 21st Assembly of the League, of 18 April 1946).

(6) Even at the First Assembly, the Indian delegate had complained of the absence of any national of his country in the Secretariat. He repeated these grievances at the Seventeenth Assembly in 1936. At the Eighteenth Assembly in 1937, he pointed out that despite complaints repeated every year "there were only two Indians in the Secretariat, one of whom was in a subordinate post" (18th Assembly, 4th Committee, p. 15).

(7) Egypt, Iraq, Iran and Turkey contributed four per cent to the budget of the League, and yet in 1930 there was only one Iranian official (and later one Turkish

official) from that part of the world (cf. E. F. Ranshofen-Wertheimer, op. cit., p. 359). Whereas in 1930 the League had fifteen Member States from Latin America (12 in 1938), only six nationals of those countries were members of the Secretariat (1938); the total budgetary contribution of these countries was eight per cent. China, Japan and Thailand contributed twelve per cent and had, between them, only six of their nationals in the Secretariat (ibidem, pp. 359/360).

(8) The history of the problem of the salaries of the staff of the League Secretariat will be found in A. Lethbridge (secretary of the committee appointed in 1956 to examine United Nations salaries), "Note on the Establishment of Salary Scales in International Organizations since 1919, with particular reference to the criteria used or suggested as a basis for their determination" (mimeogr.).
Cf. also "Report by Sir Malcolm Ramsay", annex I to "Questions referred to the Supervisory Commission by the Council of the League of Nations at its meeting on 21 May 1932; Report of the Supervisory Commission" (doc. A. 5/a/1932.X, *Off. J.* special suppl. No. 107, p. 134 ff.).

(9) The final staff regulations of 1922 were amended in 1926, 1929, 1930, 1933 and 1937; they were on the way to becoming the "ordinary law of the international civil service". A. Cagne, *Le Secrétariat général de la S.d.N.* (thesis, Paris, 1936, p. 39). The last edition dates from 1933 and contains the amendments of the Supervisory Commission (reprinted in 1945).

(10) The Administrative Tribunal of the League had been set up by the resolution of 26 September 1927, at first provisionally for three years; but it was confirmed in 1931 as a "veritable court of law to deal with disputes" (J. Gascon y Marin, op. cit., p. 47), aimed at putting an end to the disequilibrium resulting from the fear that "a class of employees have no possibility of bringing questions as to their rights to the decision of a legal body" (Report of the Sub-Committee of the 4th Committee, 8th Assembly, on the institution of an Administrative Tribunal, p. 250 ff.). The Tribunal, which also had jurisdiction for the staff of the I.L.O., played a particularly important part, by its very existence creating an atmosphere ensuring a sounder operation of the Secretariat's services.
By a resolution of the Twenty-first Assembly of the League in April 1946, the Administrative Tribunal of the League was transformed into an Administrative Tribunal of the International Labour Organisation as from 31 October 1946 (cf. also the resolutions of the Governing Body of the I.L.O. of May 1946 and of the 29th session of the International Labour Conference at Montreal of 9 October 1946). At the time of the United Nations (after 1946), the Administrative Tribunal of the International Labour Organisation continued in existence at Geneva, its jurisdiction extending to the staff of the I.L.O., the World Health Organization, UNESCO, the International Telecommunication Union, the World Meteorological Organization, the Food and Agriculture Organization, GATT, the International Atomic Energy Agency (as well as to a regional organization: European Organization for Nuclear Research, or CERN, at Geneva). It is therefore a judicial organ on the same footing as the Administrative Tribunal of the United Nations (cf. below, p. 191).

(11) Views on the problem of geographical distribution were, in particular, expressed in the Fourth Committee of the Ninth Assembly of the League by the Norwegian delegate, C. J. Hambro, who was later to become Chairman of the Supervisory Commission of the League and, later still, President of the Norwegian Parliament (Minutes, pp. 32/33 and 71), and the Netherlands delegate W. J. M. van Eysinga (ibidem, pp. 34/35). These two speakers criticized the faulty geographical distribution and recalled the Balfour principles. In particular, the Netherlands delegate noted the "uneasiness" growing up among the staff and pointed out that out of sixty-six officials in the First Division, thirty-four were nationals of great Powers (out of eighteen persons drawing the highest salaries, the latter had fourteen).

(12) The Hungarian delegate, Paul de Hevesy, said in the Fourth Committee of the Tenth Assembly of the League (Minutes, pp. 66 ff.): "It was not merely sufficient, however, to have nationals within the Secretariat in order to exert a certain influence or to obtain information. The countries which had no high officials in the Secretariat were obliged to have permanent delegates at Geneva, and these delegates had the greatest difficulty in ascertaining what was passing within the Secretariat. The principle was excellent that the members of the Secretariat should not receive any instructions from their governments. No one, however, would believe that they did not inform the representatives of the countries of which they were nationals in regard to their work, or that they did not confide in their delegates and friends...." This is a typical example of a confusion of fundamental ideas regarding the international civil service.

(13) Cf., for example, Chapter IV of *The Geneva Spirit*, by R. de Traz (op. cit.): "The Crisis."

(14) Under article 8 of the Staff Regulations, "The staff of the Secretariat is organized in three divisions...according to the nature of the official's duties." According to the definition given by the Secretary-General (cf. Report of the Committee of Thirteen, annex I, p. 35): "*The First Division* comprises the staff which directly gives effect to the resolutions of the Assembly, the Council and the organizations of the League and carries out preparatory work on which their decisions may be based; it consists of the present Members of Section and officials occupying higher posts. *The Second Division* embraces the personnel performing strictly secretarial and routine administrative duties. *The Third Division* consists of personnel engaged in manual or chiefly manual work." In the present work the posts referred to as "lower" are certain posts in the Second Division and those in the Third Division; the posts referred to as "medium" and "higher" are those in the First Division.

(15) The concessions proposed by the minority of the Committee of Thirteen amounted only, in fact, to raising the Legal Adviser to the rank of Under-Secretary-General and making him a member of the Advisory Committee. He was to be the national of a country not having a permanent seat on the Council of the League. Moreover, out of five Under-Secretaries-General, one would "probably" be a national of a country of the same category. Lastly, "it might be provided that all posts of officials in charge of the different sections should, after a certain transitional period, be reserved for nationals of countries not permanently represented on the Council..." (ibidem, p. 316).
This conception was severely criticized by the majority of the Committee: "According to these proposals the only addition to the present Under-Secretaries-General should be the Legal Adviser. It is not clear whether they contemplate that this official should always be chosen from a particular group of States. If they do, such a suggestion seems contrary to the *good principles of administration*. There is no reason for supposing that any particular quarter of the globe has a monopoly of the best legal talent. In any case, their suggestion would be a quite insufficient admission of the principle of equality. To say that all the States Members of the League, other than those which have permanent seats on the Council, ought to be satisfied to be represented by a single technician, would not meet the difficulty felt by those States or remove their objections" (ibidem, p. 299).

(16) By "higher direction" was meant, in the Secretariat of the League, not a collective body, but all the individual officials holding higher posts and appointed for a specific period.

(17) It should be observed that the authors of the minority proposal of the Committee of Thirteen (cf. above, p. 124, notes (b) and (d)) themselves decided to support only a less far-reaching solution ("Advisory Committee"), "perhaps better suited to present requirements." (E. F. Ranshofen-Wertheimer, op. cit., p. 73).

The possibility of replacing the Secretary-General by a "collective direction" was neither maintained nor discussed.

(18) The Norwegian delegate Hambro proposed to the Fourth Committee (Eleventh Assembly) the pure and simple abolition of all Under-Secretaries-General ("their existence... has been the root of the feelings of national jealousy in the body of the Secretariat. The post should therefore be abolished"), (ibidem, p. 89). This view was supported in the same debate by the Swiss delegate, W. Rappard (ibidem, p. 74). The Committee of Thirteen had pronounced in favour of five Under-Secretaries-General.

(19) E. F. Ranshofen-Wertheimer (op. cit., pp. 28-29): "While retaining the principle of permanency for the majority of the members of the First Division laid down by the Noblemaire Report, the Report of the Committee of Thirteen put greater emphasis upon appointments of technical experts, persons with special political or other qualifications, and persons engaged temporarily for urgent and exceptional work...."

(20) Ibidem, pp. 30-31: "The Report of the Committee of Thirteen as agreed to by the majority of its members strengthened the hands of the Secretary-General in a difficult moment. The Committee backed his leadership in all internal questions and made it clear to recalcitrant governments that the chief League members were behind him in his resistance to any undue governmental pressure upon internal affairs, Furthermore, this report pointed out the importance of keeping intact the traditional international spirit of the Secretariat, of maintaining its organization in its essentials. and of preventing it from reacting nervously to all the ups and downs of international policies, while remaining permanently aware of political realities. In this the majority showed wisdom and statesmanship far beyond that displayed by the individual countries in their policy toward the League as a whole...."

(21) Ibidem, p. 31: "While backing the Secretary-General the Committee of Thirteen did not hesitate to show him what kind of concessions to political realities he was expected to make, and more especially to guide him in establishing a more satisfactory relationship with his principal collaborators. The passages referring to this should, however, be read with a view to what they imply rather than what they explicitly state, for on the surface they may seem nothing more than a reiteration of accepted policies and usages...."

(22) The problem of "liaison" between the Secretary-General and States Members was discussed in the Fourth Committee at the Twelfth and Thirteenth Assemblies in relation to the existence of the Under-Secretaries-General and the Deputy Secretary-General and of the permanent delegations of the States Members at League headquarters. (Cf., in particular, the speech of the Swiss delegate, W. Rappard, at the 4th Committee of the 13th Assembly in 1932, p. 57.)

(23) This number of three Under-Secretaries-General (four including the Legal Adviser) was maintained when Germany withdrew from the League (21 October 1935), a Soviet national then replacing the German Under-Secretary-General (who had resigned when his country left the League). When, in 1938, the Japanese and Italian Under-Secretaries-General resigned in their turn (Japan having left the League on 27 March 1935 and Italy on 13 December 1939) there remained only two Under-Secretaries-General in the Secretariat. After the exclusion of the U.S.S.R. from the League on 14 December 1939 and the departure of its Under-Secretary-General, there remained only one Under-Secretary-General in office.

(24) In virtue of the resolution of the Thirteenth Assembly dated 17 October 1932 (a) all officials, including the Secretary-General, were to make a "declaration of loyalty" (cf. E. F. Ranshofen-Wertheimer, op. cit., p. 245); (b) holders of the highest posts in the Secretariat were, like the other members of the staff, to be chosen "for their abilities, their personal qualifications and the contribution they

can make to the performance of the tasks of the League of Nations"; (c) to facilitate the application of this principle and in order to give the Members not permanently represented on the Council a larger share in the responsibilities devolving on the principal officers of the Secretariat, the number of Deputy Secretaries-General was increased from one to two (one of these posts being entrusted to the representative of a State not permanently represented on the Council, if the Secretary-General were the national of a country which was permanently represented on it); (d) the duration of appointments was to be ten years for the Secretary-General, eight years for the two Deputy Secretaries-General, seven years for the four Under-Secretaries-General (renewable for a limited period); (e) in order to ensure "a more equitable distribution of nationalities," not more than two nationals of any one Member of the League were to be included among the high officials of the Secretariat (13th Assembly, pp. 95-96).

(25) The Norwegian delegate, Hambro, said in 1938: "On the question of the retention of the services of officials belonging to States which had withdrawn from the League, it would be found on careful examination that very few such officials remained.... No League official was legally entitled to leave the service of the League because his government resigned its membership" (19th Assembly, 4th Committee, p. 25).

(26) The action of the Secretary-General, Joseph Avenol, in 1939/1940, and then his resignation on 31 August 1940, have been severely criticized (cf., for example, E. F. Ranshofen-Wertheimer (op. cit., pp. 378 ff.), F. P. Walters (op. cit., pp. 809/810)). At the time of writing, the relevant motives and facts are not yet sufficiently known. Avenol's successor carried on the Secretariat's work until the liquidation of the League.

(27) The technical services of the Secretariat (economic, financial and transit) under the direction of A. Loveday, took refuge in 1940 in the United States, chiefly at Princeton. The greater part of the Narcotics Section was transferred to Washington in 1941. The Health Section was able to set up a "research unit" in 1944 at Washington and was thus able to contribute to the formation of the corresponding services of U.N.R.R.A. and to the organization of the international conference on the standardization of penicillin in London in 1944. The Treasury of the League was set up in London. The I.L.O. settled at Montreal for the duration of the war. The Acting Secretary-General and the nucleus of the Secretariat remained at Geneva, the total staff of the Secretariat having been reduced to one-seventh of its previous strength.

(28) Cf. *Proceedings of the Conference on Experience in International Administration held in Washington on January 30, 1943* (Washington, 1943) and *Proceedings of the Exploratory Conference on the Experience of the League of Nations Secretariat, held in New York City on August 30, 1942* (Washington, 1942).

(29) E. F. Ranshofen-Wertheimer, (op. cit., p. 440): "In international as in national administration, the ideal must be to achieve a synthesis of initiative and discipline, of the executive and the administrative type, especially in the higher strata of the administration, rather than to establish a system of checks and balances in which the active type is paralysed by the sedentary and unimaginative element. ..."

(30) As regards the "operating field services" of the international administrations, and particularly of the League, cf., for example, E. F. Ranshofen-Wertheimer (op. cit., pp. 3, 6, 187 ff.) and Walter R. Sharp, *Field Administration in the United Nations System. The Conduct of International Economic and Social Programmes* (London, 1961, pp. 13 ff.).

Between a national administration of the "ministerial" type and an international administration, there is one difference which deserves to be noted. Unlike the former, the latter is not at the head of a vertical hierarchy or of a series of "non-central" (regional and local) organs. At that time it was only a question of geo-graphically detaching certain units of the Secretariat which nevertheless remained at the same horizontal level, their subordination being no greater than that normally applying to services at the same level.

(31) E. F. Ranshofen-Wertheimer (op. cit., p. 5) speaks, in this connection, of a "novel type of specialized foreign service."

(32) The Secretariat's resistance to "operational" activities was illustrated, for example, on the occasion of the resolution of the Conference concerning the traffic in women and children in Eastern countries (Java, 1937). The Secretary-General then definitely opposed the extension of the Secretariat's activities in relation with the proposal to create an "Eastern Office" aimed at co-ordinating police and other activities in this sphere (cf. E. F. Ranshofen-Wertheimer (op. cit., pp. 6/7)).
Furthermore, a policy of conciliation had to be practised towards certain States Members (particularly as regards refugees, cf. ibidem, p. 6). Nor should it be forgotten that the acceptance of principles of "economic liberalism" on a capitalist basis placed difficulties in the way of carrying out plans involving the use of inter-national instruments in economic action. In 1919 the "welfare State" was only vaguely appearing on the horizon (cf. W. R. Sharp, *Field Administration*... (op. cit., p. 15).

(33) Under Article 24 of the Covenant, the "international offices" of before 1919 could place themselves under the authority of the League if the signatories to the treaties agreed. There were only five "unions" in this situation and their relations with the Secretariat did not place them among the "technical organizations" of the League. (Cf., for example, L. Bourgeois, op. cit., pp. 363 ff.).

CHAPTER 6

THE PIONEER PERIOD: THE I.L.O.

The I.L.O. in the service of social justice

While the League of Nations could not function officially before the entry into force of the Treaty of Versailles on 10 January 1920, the International Labour Organisation went into operation immediately after the inaugural conference held at Washington in 1919. The success of this conference, in spite of many and apparently great difficulties, enabled the International Labour Office to begin its administrative work at once. The International Labour Office (I.L.O.) was the Secretariat of the International Labour Organisation and was established by the Treaties of Versailles, Trianon, Neuilly and St. Germain-en-Laye, as "part of the organization of the League of Nations".[1] Its work consisted in "the collection and distribution of information on all subjects relating to the international adjustment of conditions of industrial life and labour, and particularly the examination of subjects which it is proposed to bring before the [International Labour] Conference with a view to the conclusion of international conventions, and the conduct of such special investigations as may be ordered by the Conference".[a]

Part XIII of the Treaty gave the I.L.O. wide autonomy and a status of its own, despite links, particularly as regards its budget, with the League. It was the only specialized agency forming part of the international system created by the Treaty of Versailles. This agency had a "dual nature." It could be described on the basis of its purposes as constituting "on the one hand a recognition of the established order and on the other hand a revolt against this order and a determination to modify it".[b] At the same time, owing to its tripartite nature—unique in the international field—consisting in the simultaneous participation of representatives of governments, employers and workers, both in the International Labour Conference and in the Governing Body, the I.L.O. brought together all the social forces in the world of labour with a view to co-operation in the interests of social justice and hence of universal peace. This composi-

(a) Article 396 of the Treaty of Versailles.
(b) B. W. Schaper, *Albert Thomas—Trente ans de réformisme social* (Amsterdam, 1959 p. 358).

tion was to allow the I.L.O. to combine trade union socialism with employers' conservatism—"a paradox from both the capitalist and the socialist points of view"[a]—to embody "at the international level the orderly procedure of peaceful change[2] which capital and labour have introduced for the settlement of their disputes within their national boundaries...".[b] At the same time it must not be forgotten that "the I.L.O. was not set up to hold an equal balance between the interests of employers or firms and those of wage earners. It was created to promote an improvement in the situation of the workers and not to balance the two main factors of production, namely, management and labour".[c]

In this delicate situation the I.L.O. had to play an important part. It was responsible for all preparatory, documentary, advisory and executive action: its aim was universality (the participation of the United States of America in the I.L.O. though not in the League is important); it constituted a major international administration which was completely separate from the Secretariat of the League although subject to the same financial control (by the Assembly of the League); and it was characterized from the outset by its marked social orientation. While the whole organization of the League, including the Secretariat, had a predominantly conservative trend, aiming at the maintenance of the *status quo* established in 1919, the International Labour Organisation, and with it the Office, was essentially revisionist and reforming. The staff of the I.L.O. had to have an interest in social problems combined with a team spirit based on social ideals transcending national differences. In consequence, both the recruitment and the work of the I.L.O. staff was very complicated, and there was a fear of fundamental cleavages of opinion among the staff.

This fear, however, proved unjustified. Although of different nationalities and social origins, placed in a still more difficult situation than the staff of the League, the staff of the I.L.O., whether recruited from national Labour Ministries, trade unions or employers, always supported the policy of social progress set forth in the Constitution of the Organisation. "The I.L.O. scrupulously performs the duty placed on it by the Treaty of Peace by defending the interests [of labour]. It is not called upon to observe a cold impartiality, but to support the legitimate claims of the working class...."[d] There thus grew up in the I.L.O. a particular atmosphere rendering possible a community of fundamental ideas as regards the need to ensure social peace by combating poverty, since "poverty anywhere consti-

(a) B. W. Schaper (op. cit., p. 359).
(b) Ibidem.
(c) G. Scelle, *L'Organization internationale du Travail*...(Op. cit., p. 113).
(d) Ibidem.

tutes a danger to prosperity everywhere".[a] At the same time, this social orientation of the I.L.O., which remained steady despite fluctuations of current policy and which required previous "technical" knowledge, created an admirable *esprit de corps* which was a model of practical and effective co-operation. "It has taken the form of a sort of *international public service* which, owing to the nature of its representation, embodies a purer internationalism than the League of Nations, for example, where States have shown little cohesion...."[b]

The influence of Albert Thomas

The essential factor here was the personality of the first head of the I.L.O., Albert Thomas. This remarkable man had an ideological, psychological and administrative influence which was decisive for the future of the organisation. Although a politician with pronounced political and social opinions and a French statesman before, during and immediately after the First World War,[3] Albert Thomas rose above partisan conceptions, establishing cordial relations with the governments of the States Members and showing bold personal initiative. In exercising his "dynamic direction",[c] Albert Thomas played a very active role and did not hesitate to commit himself when defending his plans or his views; but in the stand he took, he always embodied the international spirit, thus becoming, as it were, the symbol of the defence of the general interest and never being suspected of bias of any kind. His impartiality, proved on several occasions in spectacular fashion and without hesitation,[d] gave him enormous prestige which enabled him to carry out his difficult task with a success universally acknowledged.

His conception of his duties was evident from the outset, when in July 1920 he transferred the headquarters of the I.L.O. from London to Geneva (an example followed later by the headquarters of the League).[4] There he was quickly able to set up, independently of the League Secretariat, a model organization with traditions of its own differing in many respects from those of the League. A strenuous defender of the Balfour principles, he fought for the "exclusively international" character of the I.L.O. staff, obstinately refusing any infringement of this principle. In particular he refused to follow the example of the Secretary-General of the League, who on several occasions, under pressure from governments, accepted compromises regarding the rule of geographical distribution.[e] It has been rightly said that

(a) *Declaration of the International Labour Conference at Philadelphia in 1944* (item I-c).
(b) B. W. Schaper, (op. cit., pp. 361/362).
(c) F. P. Walters (op. cit., p. 80).
(d) Cf. above, chapter 4, p. 74.
(e) Cf., for example, 4th Committee, 9th Assembly of the League, 1928 (p. 78).

"in the directing organs of the I.L.O.... he played a paramount role. He represented a policy, a point of view, those of the international institution itself, which none of its Members could have expressed in the same fashion. ... The greatest service he rendered to the International Labour Conference and especially to the Governing Body [of the I.L.O.] was to help them to rise to an international viewpoint, to become aware of their responsibilities, to form an opinion and to reach a decision."[a]

Within the I.L.O. his recruitment policy, largely based on competitive selection or examination, led to consistently high standards among the staff. But he succeeded in preventing over-bureaucratization by creating a strong "personalist" tradition through daily interviews with chiefs of service, monthly talks to the staff as a whole, and direct relations between the chief and his subordinates.[5][b]

Albert Thomas effectively created this *esprit de corps* despite many difficulties, and his leadership was to have a lasting effect on the I.L.O., even after his death in 1932. The chief's work and personality were the more effective as he had introduced into the I.L.O. the French system of the "Cabinet" of the administrative head. Thus, contrary to the system introduced by Sir Eric Drummond at the League, which was based on British administrative practices, there was from the outset in the I.L.O. a strong concentration of responsibility at the top which might have led to bureaucratization. This system was indeed criticized in the Noblemaire Report in 1920. In spite of a favourable estimate of the I.L.O.'s work as a whole, this report recommended for the future some degree of internal decentralization,[c] when "the work of the I.L.O. has attained greater stability than at present and when the need for centralization is less urgent." It should be recalled here that Albert Thomas was followed as head of the I.L.O. in 1932 by the Englishman Harold Butler, and that in 1933 Sir Eric Drummond resigned and was replaced by the Frenchman Joseph Avenol. As a result of these alternating French and English influences the procedures and methods of the two international administrations became similar in the end, despite the differences between them at first.

Having been entrusted by the Treaty with the appointment of all officials of the I.L.O. and jealously defending this prerogative, Albert Thomas collected a comparatively large staff (262 members in 1921, 399 in 1931, 425 in 1939). Everyone seemed to agree that an institution whose function was to see that equitable conditions of employment prevailed throughout the world was in duty bound to respect them in its own staff, thus giving an example to others: this

(a) E. Giraud (op. cit., pp. 56/57).
(b) B. W. Schaper (op. cit., pp. 229/230).
(c) Second Part of the Report, 2nd Assembly of the League, 4th Committee, Annex II, pp. 212-213.

made the work of organizing the I.L.O. easier. Moreover, in resisting any pressure from within or without—including pressure for financial economy—Albert Thomas usually had the support of the Governing Body of the Organisation, which shared his views. It has even been said that the International Labour Office "controlled" its Governing Body, rather than the other way round, thanks to Albert Thomas' dominant personality.[a]

Thus the impartiality of the I.L.O.'s staff was ensured despite the differences of opinion and interest represented in the Governing Body and the International Labour Conferences. Career diplomats were practically excluded from all organs of the I.L.O.; and, as there was a high degree of functional specialization, mutual comprehension, based on understanding of the social problem, was possible. Thus, as Albert Thomas put it, the I.L.O. was a kind of "social thermometer".[b] The stability of his staff was greater than that of the staff of the League Secretariat. Thus, around 1938, at the League only half the First Division (Members of Section) had permanent appointments, whereas the whole of the staff of equivalent rank at the I.L.O. were permanent. This ensured continuity of action and also gave the staff a stronger feeling of independence vis-à-vis government pressures.

The Noblemaire Report submitted to the Second Assembly of the League approved the work of the I.L.O. Apart from the suggestion regarding the internal decentralization of affairs mentioned above, no criticism was made against the Office's administrative action:

> "We are aware," says the Noblemaire Report, "that certain criticisms have been made...against the general policy which inspires the activities of that Office...we are, however, by no means convinced that this policy has materially deviated from the wise and elevating directions contained in the Treaties of Peace, nor do we consider that it is either just or correct to assert that the International Labour Office is a laboratory for the manufacture of a particular brand of 'social' or 'socialist' doctrines, and we are frankly of the opinion that the assertion that it is an actively propagandist body may be dismissed as without foundation."[c]

At the same time the Noblemaire Committee definitely came down on the side of the stabilization of the I.L.O.'s staff, so much desired by Albert Thomas, recommending that since its work "demands in a high degree intensive study, close research and the accumulated experience which can only be so acquired... it might often be disastrous to insist upon the premature replacement of individuals merely in order to give an opportunity to a subject of another nation."[d]

(a) B. W. Schaper (op. cit., pp. 234 ff.).
(b) Ibidem (p. 357).
(c) 2nd Assembly of the League of Nations, 4th Committee, annex 2 (p. 212).
(d) Ibidem (p. 209).

Commending the system of entrance by competition at the I.L.O., the Committee suggested the general application to that office of the standards which it recommended for the Secretariat of the League, particularly as regards staff salaries and internal organization.

Albert Thomas was particularly anxious that the I.L.O. should constantly appeal to public opinion throughout the world "The strength of the I.L.O. lay, he was never tired of insisting, in public support",[a] and it should endeavour to provide information and guidance even if it should thus engage in controversy and risk being accused of "propaganda". This desire for contact with the masses also influenced the atmosphere of the I.L.O., where the staff did not work in an "ivory tower", did not feel cut off from the outside world, but were committed to a common struggle for a "really humane labour system" in a better world.

Albert Thomas was able to measure the usefulness of his work by its results. As regards the numerous draft conventions voted by the International Labour Conferences, 1,044 ratifications had been notified to the I.L.O. by the end of 1949; fifty-seven conventions had actually entered into force; and eighty-seven recommendations had been addressed to States Members.[b] Thus, even if the ratifications did not always mean that the conventions were put into force, a gradual codification of social standards was taking place which, far from being "a mere registration of the legislation of the acceding countries, provided the foundations, the groundwork on which the labour and living conditions of the whole world could be constructed...."[c] The *social* character of the campaign undertaken by the I.L.O. to strengthen and accelerate this legislative process, guided by a consistent policy, meant that in spite of the slow rate of ratifications, most governments supported a policy favourable to the protection of labour. Though the resistance of the employers was sometimes stubborn and even aggressive, it was usually of a defensive and moderating character.

The draft conventions and recommendations of the International Labour Conferences differed from resolutions in that they had to be submitted to the competent national authorities, usually the parliaments, for action. While these conferences also voted resolutions which were suggestions rather than obligations, the recommendations concerning draft conventions were the essential factor. The I.L.O. was called upon to collect and circulate information regarding working conditions; to study the labour questions which were submitted to the International Labour Conferences, and to help govern-

(a) E. J. Phelan (op. cit., p. 87).
(b) *The I.L.O. Thirty Years of Combat for Social Justice 1919-1949* (Geneva, 1950, pp. 43-45).
(c) B. W. Schaper (op. cit., pp. 354-357).

ments to improve administrative practices. *Inter alia* the I.L.O. published works of international interest on industry and labour. These activities, together with a continuous observation of the steps taken by the different countries to implement the conventions adopted, constituted the main work of the I.L.O. staff. There were continuous contacts between its officials and the national administrations dealing with problems of labour, wages, social security, professional training, immigration, leisure and collective conventions. Good results were achieved by trustful co-operation with these special departments in the Member States. By-passing the Foreign Ministries, the I.L.O. achieved a certain interpenetration of specialized personnel and created links of comradeship and better understanding between the members of these administrations, both international and national. Thus there grew up among the specialists an "agreement for action"[a] in general terms, without political implications, which created conditions favourable for real co-operation.

The I.L.O. and the League Secretariat

In comparing the administrative experience of the League Secretariat and the I.L.O. at this period, three features stand out:

First, at the I.L.O. to a greater extent than at the League, the staff took an active part in the selection of new recruits. In virtue of the Staff Regulations drawn up in January 1923, taking into account the Noblemaire Report,[b] the Staff Union of the I.L.O., a professional body of a trade union character, appointed representatives to the joint administrative committee, an advisory body responsible for submitting to the Director of the I.L.O. proposals concerning all appointments. Similarly all examination boards were composed equally of members appointed by the Director and members appointed by the staff. The regulations also debarred from the examining board the officials of the service in which there was a vacancy, including its Director. Thus the staff played a large part in staff management, which paved the way for the future development of trade unionism in the international civil service. It was said of the "recruitment doctrine" of the I.L.O.:

> "The I.L.O. system reflects at once a mistrust by the staff in the good faith and judgment of the senior officials, a pride in the service itself, and a determination by the staff to prevent any lowering of standards through personal influence, prejudice and lack of acumen...."[c]

This system, with the philosophy on which it was based, was severely criticized. By ruling out any final decisions by the chief of the service

(a) As regards the meaning of this term, see, for example, P. H. Appleby, *Big Democracy* (New York, 1945, pp. 179 ff.).
(b) These regulations were amended in 1929.
(c) A. Loveday (op. cit., p. 54).

concerned as regards the selection of candidates, including the right to refuse candidates whom he considered unsuitable, it theoretically deprived him of any leadership. In order to remedy this, it was necessary in practice to circumvent the rule and to allow the chief of service some influence on the choice of his subordinates.[a]

Secondly, we have here a remarkable phenomenon of continuity. The I.L.O., since the creation of the Organisation in 1919, has gone on without interruption; the amendments of the Constitution in 1945 and 1946 prolonged its existence while bringing it into the United Nations family as a specialized agency. The I.L.O., set up by the same treaties as the League, was able, despite the provisions laid down in 1919 and despite certain permanent links and services in common with the League, to detach itself by degrees from that institution and to follow its own course of development. The I.L.O. did not share the fate of the League, which disappeared in 1946 and was replaced by the U.N., although it inherited its Administrative Tribunal.[b] But there is another aspect of the continuity of the I.L.O. which has to be considered—namely, that of the homogeneity of its staff despite all the upheavals which have taken place meanwhile, not least in the economic and social spheres. Moreover the changes which have taken place in the composition of the I.L.O. have not put an end to the tradition introduced by Albert Thomas nearly half a century ago, as regards the selection of staff in conformity with the principles of the international civil service.

Lastly, while the I.L.O. did not, at the time, undertake "operational" activities, even to the modest extent of the League Secretariat (it was to do so later under the programme of technical assistance), and while the two organs were of similar structure, nevertheless, thanks to Albert Thomas' initiative, the I.L.O.'s work outside headquarters became important. Here was one way in which the I.L.O. maintained contact with world opinion. It set up information services run by the "correspondence" offices in the principal industrial countries (including the United States of America as early as 1921, although it did not join the I.L.O. until 1924). Secondly, there were individual "correspondents" who were nationals of the countries concerned.[6] Another factor was the seconding of headquarters officials as advisers to States Members, which may be regarded as the first step towards future technical assistance. Lastly, the I.L.O. organized regional meetings dealing with various social problems. Nevertheless, in the absence of funds and long-term plans, it was unable to carry out continuous programmes of this kind over long periods.

(a) Ibidem.
(b) Cf. above, chapter 5, note (10).

Thanks to the indelible imprint of Albert Thomas, an example of the influence which a dynamic chief may have on international administrative action, the I.L.O. was, within its limits, a true model of international administration. "It is therefore not surprising that after the Second World War, this model and the experience it had acquired were taken into consideration in setting up the new functional organizations".[a] The I.L.O. was in fact a particularly instructive example of the successful solution of the practical problems involved.

(a) B. W. Schaper (op. cit., p. 362).

NOTES

(1) A union of mixed character (because it also contained "private members") had been in existence since 1901 at Basle, Switzerland, under the name of "International Labour Bureau" (cf. above, chapter 1, p. 36). As a result of public and private initiative, conferences of an international character concerning labour legislation had been held at Berlin in 1890, at Zurich and Brussels in 1897 and at Paris in 1900. After the creation of the Bureau, General Assemblies had been held at Basle in 1901, at Cologne in 1902 and at Berne in 1905; the latter was attended by fifty delegates from all the countries of Europe except Russia, Greece, Romania and Serbia. The action of the abovementioned bureau was supported by several national labour administrations, and its expenses were covered by the contributions of numerous national sections and particularly by the governments of the Member States, among which was Switzerland. This action has been commented on as follows:
"The extreme caution with which governments have proceeded in this matter is a characteristic mark of the jealousy which States feel in behalf of their legislative independence in such important matters as labour legislation.... Yet the governments have been very reluctant to commit themselves to any definite policy of uniformity in this matter" (P. S. Reinsch, "International Unions and their Administration" (op. cit., p. 601)). In this connection, the success of the I.L.O.'s action at Geneva since 1919, which was prepared for in a sense by that of its predecessor at Basle since 1901, is the more noteworthy.

(2) As regards the problem of *peaceful change* in general, cf., for example, L. P. Bloomfield, *Evolution or Revolution? The United Nations and the Problem of Peaceful Territorial Change* (Harvard University Press, 1957, chapter 1: "The Ideology of Peaceful Change").

(3) Albert Thomas was Armaments Minister in France during the First World War (1916/1917). He was a member of the French Parliament (elected in 1910 and re-elected in 1914 and 1919), but sat only until his definite appointment as Director of the I.L.O., in January 1920, after which he devoted himself entirely to international work. Thereafter, he made only brief appearances in the French Parliament and soon resigned, recognizing that membership of a national Parliament was incompatible with international duties.

(4) Despite the strong movement which existed at that time in favour of keeping the League in London or transferring it to Brussels, Albert Thomas played a decisive part in setting up the international organizations at Geneva. He regarded the establishment of the I.L.O. in London as inconvenient. The Treaties of Peace laid down that the headquarters of the League should be at Geneva and that the I.L.O. should be in the same city as the League. After fruitless discussions in London, Albert Thomas asked the Governing Body of the International Labour Organisation

to authorize the International Labour Office to settle at Geneva without awaiting the League's decisions, since the Covenant expressly mentioned Geneva and since, if the League transferred its headquarters elsewhere, it would always be possible to follow it.

At the end of 1920 the League followed Albert Thomas' example by transferring its headquarters from London to Geneva.

(5) In constantly seeking direct contacts with all his staff, among whom, particularly in the early days, he wished to create a "family atmosphere" (cf. B. W. Schaper, op. cit., pp. 229 ff.), Albert Thomas wished to avoid the appointment of a Deputy Director (in part XIII in the Treaty of Peace mention was made of the "Director *or* his Deputy"). Subsequently he realized that Harold Butler (who was to succeed him after his death) would have to be appointed Deputy Director to give satisfaction to the British Government, whose draft had been taken as a basis in 1919 for part XIII of the Treaty. As a matter of fact, relations between Albert Thomas and Harold Butler proved extremely cordial and fruitful.

Towards 1934 Harold Butler, as Director of the I.L.O., transformed the existing posts of chiefs of division into posts of assistant directors, each of whom became responsible for the supervision of a certain number of sections (since called "divisions"). The number of intermediaries between the Director and the staff was therefore increased, even though there was still only one Deputy Director.

(6) The "correspondents" of the I.L.O. were sometimes employed on a half-time basis and usually occupied a position in a government department of the country concerned. Some of them had a small staff for office work on the spot. They all had the nationality of the country in which they resided.

CHAPTER 7

THE PERIOD OF UNIVERSALITY:
THE BIRTH OF THE UNITED NATIONS

Origins

The United Nations—and with it the "United Nations family"—was established in successive stages, and the various problems of the Secretariat attracted increasing attention at each stage.

At first, general principles applying to the post-war period were laid down (Inter-Allied Declaration of London of 12 June 1941; Atlantic Charter of 14 August 1941, "United Nations" Declaration of Washington, 1 January 1942; and Declaration on General Security by the "Big Four" at Moscow on 30 October 1943). Only at the last of these early stages was there explicit recognition of the "necessity of establishing at the earliest practicable date a *general international organization*, based on the principle of sovereign equality of all peace-loving States, and open to membership by all such States, large and small, for the maintenance of international peace and security." This declaration was renewed at the Teheran Conference on 1 December 1943, where the chief executives of the United States, Great Britain and the U.S.S.R. spoke again of the "world family of democratic nations" based on "co-operation and active participation of all nations, large and small, whose peoples in heart and mind are dedicated... to the elimination of tyranny and slavery, oppression and intolerance."

The fundamental principles of the future international organization were laid down on the basis of the British proposals at the meeting of Prime Ministers held in London in May 1944; they were submitted at the international talks at Dumbarton Oaks, near Washington, which were attended between 21 August and 7 October 1944, while the war was still in progress, by the above-mentioned Powers and China. There for the first time a detailed discussion took place on the aims of this organization, its constitution and its general structure.[a]

Profiting by the experience of international co-operation between

(a) As regards the documents relating to this period, 1942/1944, cf. L. M. Goodrich & E. Hambro, *Charter of the United Nations. Commentary and Documents* (Boston, 1949, pp. 569 ff.). Cf. also *Postwar Foreign Policy Preparation, 1939-1945* (publ. 3850 of the U.S. Department of State, Washington, 1950).

the two wars and of U.N.R.R.A. (as regards "operational" activities away from headquarters),[1] a new international secretariat, this time truly universal, was set up at the end of the war. For psychological reasons it was decided that the new United Nations Organization should be an institution created *ab ovo* and not a formal continuation of the old League of Nations. It was nevertheless built on the experience of the League, particularly as regards the international civil service;[2] and it took over the supervisory and technical role assigned to the League by the treaties, together with the League's assets. It was realized that international conditions in 1945 were far removed from those of 1919 or 1939. The new organization would have both wider functions and a broader geographical base. New social, economic, humanitarian and cultural tasks were added to its first duty of safeguarding peace and international security. Consequently, from the outset, an adequate framework and appropriate instruments had to be created. It was easy to foresee that the work of the secretariat of the new organization would be very complex, and the experience of the League and of the I.L.O. showed that its scope should not be underestimated. Thus the problem of the secretariat had to be considered at all the preliminary stages, and its founders had to take urgent administrative decisions.

An important new feature was the Economic and Social Council, which was based both on the Bruce Plan of 1939[a] and on experience gained during the Second World War. This Council was to exist side by side with the Security Council, but its exact place in the structure of the organization had yet to be determined. According to the "Proposals" adopted at Dumbarton Oaks, the intention was to create "conditions of stability and wellbeing" by seeking "solutions of international, economic, social and other humanitarian problems" (Chapter IX), considerably enlarging the future scope of the organization and necessitating more extensive administrative services. Nevertheless, though dealing explicitly with the secretariat, these proposals did not go into detail. They simply assumed the existence or creation—particularly for economic and social questions—of specialized agencies on the model of the I.L.O. and parallel with the U.N., the various specialized tasks being divided among them. It was also assumed that there would be a link between these agencies and the U.N. in order to ensure cohesion.

The conference of the "Big Three" held at Yalta in the Crimea in February 1945 solved some important problems left in suspense at Dumbarton Oaks, such as the method of voting in the Security Council. The U.N.'s trusteeship of certain non-self-governing territories (this formula replacing the old mandates system of the League) was also

(a) Cf. above, chapter 3, p. 63, and note (10).

defined. It was at Yalta too that it was decided to summon a United Nations Conference on International Organization. This conference was attended by all the "United Nations" and was held at San Francisco from 25 April to 26 June 1945. The U.N. was formally set up and the Charter of the United Nations was adopted, defining in detail the constitutional framework of the future organization. Decisions were then taken regarding the new international civil service, which were decisively influenced by the example of the international organizations of the between-wars period. When the future role of the Secretariat and the Secretary-General's responsibilities came to be discussed, the "minimalist" and "maximalist" schools of thought once more came into conflict.

> "In San Francisco there were three principal issues in the discussion regarding the Secretariat. First, what is to be the role of the Secretariat in the framework of the United Nations and the specialized agencies? Secondly, what is to be the status of persons who work for the Secretariat? Thirdly, what is to be the role of Secretary-General? There were two opposing points of view already noticeable in San Francisco. The *one* group felt that the Secretary-General should be what the first part of his title indicated; he should be Secretary. He should not be much more than the Secretary of the Organization. He should follow the lead of the important Powers. He should do what the Council and the Assembly wanted him to do. The *opposing* view was that the Secretary-General, whatever he was called, had to approach, so far as it was possible, the position of chief executive of the United Nations. In an organization that did not establish an executive branch it was difficult to hammer out a position for the Secretary-General which would give him a position of stature, a position in which he could really be of influence; but if you will examine the Charter you will notice that the Charter does grant him in fact very considerable power and give him functions which are partly administrative and partly political...."[a]

Thus the San Francisco Conference did not accept Roosevelt's idea that the Secretary-General should be an "international statesman" with the title of "World Moderator," nor the idea discussed at Dumbarton Oaks of a division of functions between a "President" modelled on that of the United States of America and a "Secretary-General."[b] It nevertheless gave the Secretary-General a right of initiative going beyond his "internal" functions and thus deliberately departing from the "intelligent secretaryship" idea. The Conference's conception was a compromise which left the exact scope of the function to be defined in practice on the basis of the personality of the candidate appointed and the circumstances prevailing at the time.

Taking as a basis for its discussions the Dumbarton Oaks proposals,

(a) W. H. C. Laves, "The U.N. Assembly Meeting in London" in *Proceedings of the 8th Conference of Teachers of International Law and Related Subjects* (Washington, Carnegie, 1946, p. 92).
(b) S. M. Schwebel (op. cit., chapter 1); cf. also Dag Hammarskjöld, Oxford address (op. cit., p. 7).

supplemented by the comments and amendments of the sponsoring Powers and the comments of the participating countries, the San Francisco Conference[3] drew up the fundamental principles of the independence of international officials. Drawing the logical conclusions from the experience of the League of Nations, it not only defined constitutionally the duty of the staff to safeguard its own independence by refraining from seeking or accepting instructions from outside, but also laid down a corresponding obligation for States Members.[4] Contrary to the Dumbarton Oaks proposals, which conceived several parallel secretariats, the Secretariat was to be a coherent administrative unit despite the multiplicity of its functions, entirely subordinate to the Secretary-General as single chief of the whole staff. The principle of geographical distribution was introduced into the Charter as subsidiary, being explicitly subordinated to the efficiency, competence and integrity of the staff.

The result was that the San Francisco Conference had to accept several inevitable compromises, in spite of the agreement reached on fundamental principles. Chapter XV of the Charter came much closer to the "ideal" international secretariat than did the Dumbarton Oaks proposals. Nevertheless, only the main outlines were traced, and the details were left to be filled in later. The Conference was unable to agree on certain important questions which remained unanswered. Thus the serious problem of the political and administrative role of Deputy Secretaries-General—already a burning question at the time of the League and even more so in the U.N.—was not settled in the text of the Charter. There were differences of opinion both as to the method of appointment of these officials (election or appointment by the Secretary-General) and as to their number and "representative" character.

> "The Sponsoring Governments had proposed that the Charter should provide for a certain number of Deputy Secretaries-General who would be elected by the General Assembly on the recommendation of the Security Council. For a number of reasons this proposal was strongly opposed by a large number of delegations. Certain delegates of Great Powers admitted that the Secretary-General would hold a position of great political authority and maintained that the higher posts in the Secretariat would also be of considerable political importance and should be treated as political positions. They were anxious to secure political control of these high functionaries. Other delegates, while recognizing the need for Deputies, were against fixing either their number or their terms of office in the Charter. They also thought that the Deputy should be appointed by the Secretary-General like the other members of the staff. It would, they claimed, undermine the authority of the Secretary-General if his immediate subordinates were elected or appointed in the same manner as he. This would destroy the homogeneous character of the Secretariat. Finally, they did not want the nomination of staff members to be politically controlled."[a]

(a) L. M. Goodrich & E. Hambro (op. cit., p. 498).

As no agreement was reached at San Francisco, the Charter remained silent on this point. Thus no distinction was made between Deputy Secretaries-General and the rest of the staff of the Secretariat and the result was that Article 101, paragraph 1, applied also to these principal officers. This was a success for the supporters of the Balfour principles.

By putting on one side a series of disputed questions, the participants in the San Francisco Conference were able to adopt the Charter of the United Nations, which was signed in that city on 26 June 1945 by 51 States who became founding members of the Organization.[a] As a result of ratifications the Charter entered into force on 24 October of the same year. A further stage in the creation of the Organization began on 16 August 1945 in London. On the very day of the signature of the Charter, in accordance with the "provisional arrangements" voted by the Conference, a preparatory commission was created "for the purpose of making provisional arrangements for the first sessions of the General Assembly and the three Councils, for the establishment of the Secretariat and for the convening of the International Court of Justice...".[b] This stage was particularly important:

> "It was a far cry from putting the provisions into the Charter to realizing the establishment of a Secretariat and the appointment of a Secretary-General who could in fact do the things that were contemplated by those of us who wanted a strong central executive of the U.N. Throughout the Preparatory Commission there was a strong battle (it was much more evident than it had been out at San Francisco) between those who still thought of the Secretary-General as a relatively unimportant person who called meetings and saw to the distribution of the agenda, and those who felt that this person should really be a driving force, a person who was in a way the only person continually at the headquarters with the conscience of the whole organisation in mind...."[c]

The Preparatory Commission had to think out afresh all the problems raised by the setting up of the Secretariat. It was inevitable that there should be repeated conflicts of opinion. Not only had the questions left in abeyance at San Francisco to be answered, but it was found that in spite of the decisions made when the Charter was adopted, those who had opposed these decisions had by no means given up the struggle. This clash of ideas with regard to the very foundations of the international civil service subsequently influenced the whole history of the United Nations, provoking periodical crises. On many occasions the provisions of the Charter were variously interpreted according to different political, national and international influences, thus reopening the discussion of basic principles.

Be that as it may, the Charter, the provisions of which were to be

---

(a) *Documents of the U.N. Conference on International Organization*, (vol. I, p. 654). There were fifty signatures of national delegates present, the fifty-first being that of Poland, which was given on 15 October 1945.
(b) Ibidem (vol. 15, pp. 516 ff., art. 1).
(c) W. H. C. Laves (op. cit., p. 92).

repeated in the constitutions of the specialized agencies in the United Nations family, remains a decisive and fundamental instrument. Being a treaty concluded between contracting parties, it is *legally* the constitution of the international organization, with all the rights and duties which that implies for its signatories; it is *morally* the expression of certain common values adopted as such; *psychologically* it represents a dynamic evolution of political and social forces; lastly, from the *administrative* point of view, its principles are the basis of the structural and functional framework of the organization. It may be regarded, despite its imperfections and omissions, as the Magna Carta of the international civil service, defining it and determining its future.[a]

The framework—the Charter of the United Nations

Article 7, paragraph 1, of the Charter, describes the *Secretariat* as one of the six *principal* organs of the United Nations; it is thus placed on the same footing as the General Assembly, the three Councils (Security, Trusteeship and Economic and Social) and the International Court of Justice. These "principal organs" are contrasted with "subsidiary organs" (Article 7, paragraph 2) (to be created should the need arise, and which would remain optional and subordinate). In classing these six organs as "principal," it was obviously not intended to indicate the effective degree of independent authority assigned to each. Thus the Economic and Social Council and the Trusteeship Council are in any case legally subordinate to the General Assembly. The Secretariat is "in the service" of the whole organization and particularly of the first four "principal organs" whose decisions it prepares, inspires and implements. Moreover, neither the Secretariat nor the Hague Court, unlike the four other principal organs, is composed of representatives of Member States, but of persons chosen in an individual capacity. Nevertheless, the founders of the organization rightly emphasized at San Francisco the importance of the Secretariat in view both of the experience of 1919-1940 and of the purposes of the new organization as defined in the Preamble and Article 1 of the Charter.[5]

We must now define the position of the Secretariat in relation to the deliberative organs of the United Nations, on the basis of the four categories outlined by C. W. Jenks[b] in 1945:

(1) *Secretarial* relationship—that is to say that existing between the

---

(a) "The principles of the Charter are by far greater than the organization in which they are embodied" (statement by the Secretary-General, Dag Hammarskjöld, in the Security Council on 31 October 1956 (*United Nations Review*, No. 11, 1956, p. 13)). Cf. also below, chapter 10, p. 260 note (b) and 262 note (b).

(b) C. W. Jenks, "Some Constitutional Problems of International Organizations", in *British Yearbook of International Law* (No. 22, 1945, pp. 42 ff.).

Secretariat proper and a "group directorate"; it is this type of relationship which, according to the author, existed at the League of Nations.

(2) Relationship based on actual *management* by the Secretariat, whose principal officers are responsible for the conduct of affairs. It is this type of relationship which is to be found, for example, in the international banks and in the International Monetary Fund, which is a member of the United Nations family. It is particularly suitable for organizations whose tasks are mainly "operational." At the Fund the main executive action is in the hands of the executive directors by delegation of power from the Governors.

(3) *Quasi-parliamentary* relationship on the model of the British parliamentary system, where the representative organs have complete authority over their senior officer, who is merely their adviser and servant (even though he may acquire great personal influence); it was this type of relationship which was to be found at the I.L.O. under Albert Thomas, whose dynamic personality did not prevent him from respecting parliamentary traditions and from observing the limitations imposed by parliamentary customs.

(4) Relationship based on the strict *division of powers* as understood in the United States. The powers of the administration derive from the office of the Chief Executive as defined by the Constitution, and are not delegated by Parliament. This type of relationship was characteristic of U.N.R.R.A. during the Second World War.

Although at the time when he was writing the author placed the machinery created by the Charter on the model of the League in the first of these categories, it would appear that it should rather belong to the fourth category, thanks to Article 7 of the Charter. Thus Dag Hammarskjöld states in his analysis of the Charter:

> "It is not without some significance that this new conception of a Secretary-General originated principally with the United States rather than the United Kingdom. It has been reported ... that the United States gave serious consideration to the idea that the Organization should have a President as well as a Secretary-General. Subsequently, it was decided to propose only a single officer, but one in whom there would be combined both the political and executive functions of a President with the internal administrative functions that were previously accorded to a Secretary-General. Obviously, this is a reflection, in some measure, of the American political system, which places authority in a chief executive officer who is not simply subordinated to the legislative organs, but who is constitutionally responsible alone for the execution of legislation and in some respects for carrying out the authority derived from the constitutional instrument directly...."[a]

While therefore the vagueness of the constitutional text leaves the door open for different theories—theories which imperfectly fit the facts—it seems easy to understand the intention of the founders; when we

(a) Dag Hammarskjöld, Oxford address (op. cit., p. 7).

consider the fourfold activities of the U.N. as defined in Article 1 of the Charter[6] (maintenance of security and peaceful settlement of disputes; development of friendly relations among nations; international co-operation in solving economic, social, cultural and humanitarian problems; harmonization of common efforts) it is hardly conceivable that the role of the Secretariat should have been intended to be only the giving of *assistance* to the representative organs.

Under Chapter XV of the Charter this "principal organ" is the only one which is not "collective." Article 97 states that "the Secretariat shall comprise a Secretary-General and such staff as the Organization may require." It is thus the Secretary-General, "the chief administrative officer of the Organization," who personifies the latter in the same way as the President of the United States of America, who, *mutatis mutandis*, alone personifies the "executive power" under Article II (section 1) of the Federal Constitution. The staff of the Secretariat *assists* the Secretary-General in the performance of his tasks; it is therefore a working instrument of the Secretary-General's, acting under his responsibility.

> "The drafters of the Charter laid emphasis on the personal responsibility of the Secretary-General; it is he who is solely responsible for performing the functions entrusted to him for the appointment of all members of the Secretariat and for assuring the organization that the Secretariat will carry out their tasks under his exclusive authority. The idea of a "cabinet system" in which responsibility for the administration and political functions would be distributed among several individuals was squarely rejected...."[a]

But in the way in which Article 97 describes the post of Secretary-General we find evident traces of the San Francisco compromise. The Secretary-General is in fact an "official" like all the staff of the Secretariat, although he is *primus inter pares*. But "the idea of a civil servant would appear to exclude and be contrary to that of a master,"[b] although "in the diplomatic sphere the contrast between masters and servants loses much of its significance. Nowhere else is the frontier between decision and execution so uncertain and so shifting".[c] Be that as it may, it was intended to illustrate symbolically in this way the "submission" of the Secretary-General to the representative bodies with a view to providing a sort of graduation between the different "principal organs"; it is in fact the "Secretariat" as such, with the Secretary-General in its midst (and at its head), and not the latter alone, which constitutes the "principal organ" of the organization.

For the same reasons, in virtue of Articles 97 and 101, paragraph 1, of the Charter, all the members of the Secretariat are *appointed* and

(a) Ibidem (p. 8).
(b) M. Virally, "Le rôle politique du Secrétaire général des Nations Unies", in *Annuaire français du Droit international* (Paris, 1958, p. 362).
(c) Ibidem.

not elected: the Secretary-General by the General Assembly on the recommendation of the Security Council—the latter's part in his selection emphasizing the fact that the Secretary-General has also a political role [7]—and all the other officials by the Secretary-General under regulations established by the General Assembly (the Staff Regulations). Thus, the fact that the whole of the staff is *appointed* by the Secretary-General—without subsequent approval being required as at the League of Nations—may be regarded as a generalization of selection by appointment (unilateral) and not by consensual contract as had been the case previously. But when the word "appointment" is used in connection with the Secretary-General, it must not be taken literally. In fact the Secretary-General is *elected*, although this election is constitutionally represented as an "appointment":

> "The use of the word 'appointment' instead of the word 'elected' is intended to emphasize the administrative character of his duties.... The General Assembly may reject a candidate recommended to it by the Security Council; but if the Assembly does so, it cannot appoint a Secretary-General of its own choice. It must wait for the Council to make a new recommendation."[a]

A verbal compromise has therefore been resorted to in order to satisfy the opponents of the "promotion" of the Secretariat in comparison with the League model, without compromising in any way the effective role of the Secretary-General. If we compare this form of selection with that of the judges of the International Court of Justice[8] we cannot draw any substantial conclusions from the terminology employed.

In setting out from this conception of the Secretariat, the Charter defines as follows the respective roles of the Secretary-General and of the other members of the Secretariat.

A

The Secretary-General is called upon to take the following kinds of action:

(1) He "acts in that capacity in all meetings of the General Assembly and of the [three] Councils (Article 98). This *ex officio* action is widely conceived, and under the Charter includes all current administrative functions, *active* as well as *passive*.

(2) More specifically, as regards his relations with the other principal organs of the United Nations, he makes an annual report to the General Assembly on the work of the Organization (Article 98 and Article 15, paragraph 2); with the consent of the Security Council, he notifies the General Assembly at each session of any matters relative

---

(a) L. M. Goodrich and E. Hambro (op. cit., p. 491). Cf. also Hans Kelsen, *The Law of the U.N.; a Critical Analysis of its Fundamental Problems* (1951, p. 296).

to the maintenance of international peace and security which are being dealt with by that Council (Article 12, paragraph 2); he convokes special sessions of the General Assembly (Article 20, paragraph 2); he takes a number of steps in relation to the action of the International Court of Justice (Articles 5, paragraph 1; 7, paragraphs 1 and 2; 13, paragraph 4; 36, paragraph 4; 40, paragraph 3; Articles 67 and 70 of the Statute of the Court).

(3) "The Secretary-General performs such other functions as are entrusted to him" by the General Assembly or by any of the [three] Councils (Article 98). This procedure of 'delegation'—henceforward formally accepted outside the 'normal' scope of the Secretary-General's actions—constitutes a novelty, the importance of which was at once perceived by commentators. It means an enlarged sphere of action for the Secretary-General of the U.N. compared with that of the League. Since *each* principal organ (except of course the Court of Justice) may in virtue of the Charter entrust to the Secretary-General '*other* functions' without any constitutional limitation, he is liable to exercise politico-diplomatic powers in matters which are the subject of international controversy. There is not the least doubt that such delegations of authority are legal under the Charter, even if the Secretary-General should thus find himself in the thick of political disputes and even if he runs the risk of overstepping the generally accepted limits of his role of 'chief administrative officer.' In view of the possibility of disputes between Members of the United Nations— easy to anticipate, even in the optimistic days of victory in 1945—it is obvious that the founders of the U.N., in framing Article 98, intended to assign to the Secretary-General in case of need an important and difficult part which was to be played no longer behind the scenes but openly and with explicit powers.

(4) "The Secretary-General may bring to the attention of the Security Council any matter which in his opinion may threaten the maintenance of international peace and security" (Article 99). This constitutional provision, voted at San Francisco almost without discussion, gives the Secretary-General an important power of initiative to be exercised spontaneously in an essentially political sphere. This right of initiative was to prove important" less owing to the specific powers which it conferred... than owing to the political complexion which it gave to the function of Secretary-General and the general responsibilities thereby incurred by him in the sphere of international peace and security".[a] If we analyse this, we see that the Charter confers on the Secretary-General not only the right to act if he wishes and thinks it necessary to do so, but also, logically

(a) M. Virally, "Vers une réforme du Secrétariat des N.U.", in *International Organization* (No. 2/XV, 1961, pp. 236/237).

enough, the right to make enquiries or to take any kind of action, official or unofficial, in order to demonstrate the existence of danger. At San Francisco it was even proposed to replace the *right* by the *obligation* to take such steps, but in the end it was preferred to leave the matter to the Secretary-General's discretion.[a] A proposal to confer a similar power of initiative on the Secretary-General, not only in his relations with the Security Council but also in regard to the General Assembly, was rejected. Lastly, the proposal to extend the Secretary-General's power of initiative to any infringement of the principles of the Charter was turned down, chiefly in order to avoid placing too heavy a burden on the Secretary-General. Be that as it may, it is apparent from the documents of the period that "most delegates appear to share Smuts' opinion that the position of the Secretary-General should be of the highest importance and for this reason a large measure of initiative was expressly conferred".[b]

For this reason he could avail himself of the powers provided for in the Charter or transfer them to his representatives (the delegation of such powers being permissible in the absence of any statements to the contrary in the Charter) according to his personality, his courage and the circumstances of the moment—which gave him undoubted authority.

B

While the Dumbarton Oaks Proposals did not mention the staff of the Secretariat, at San Francisco it was decided to lay down certain principles in the Charter:

(1) The "exclusively international character of the responsibilities of the Secretary-General and the staff" (Article 100, paragraph 2). As already stated, two additional constitutional obligations arise from this:

> "In the performance of their duties the Secretary-General and the staff shall not seek or receive instructions from any government or from any other authority external to the organization" (Article 100, paragraph 1).
>
> "Each Member of the United Nations undertakes to respect the exclusively international character of the responsibilities of the Secretary-General and the staff, and not to seek to influence them in the discharge of their responsibilities" (Article 100, paragraph 2).

(2) The logical outcome of this was that all international officials were responsible to the organization alone (independent status: Article 100, paragraph 1). This service obligation was to be enforced by disciplinary and deontological sanctions and precluded any subordination of the staff to outside authorities. It entailed consequences

(a) "Documents of the U.N. Conference on International Organization" (op. cit., Vol. 7, p. 397 and p. 164; Doc. 1115, I/2/74 (2), p. 7).
(b) Dag Hammarskjöld, Oxford address (op. cit., p. 6).

regarding even the passive behaviour of the staff (receipt of instructions from outside).

(3) The obligation of international officials to refrain from any action which might reflect on their position as international officials (Article 100, paragraph 1). This clause widened the scope of the "passive" obligations of the staff beyond that indicated above in paragraph 2), it being understood that they would be defined in detailed rules of conduct.

(4) Although "appropriate staff shall be permanently assigned to the Economic and Social Council, the Trusteeship Council and, as required, to other organs of the United Nations, these staffs shall form a part of the Secretariat" (Article 101, paragraph 2). This clause confirmed the decision made in the Dumbarton Oaks Proposals as regards the principle of the unity of the Secretariat, the division of tasks between certain sections of the staff remaining an *internal* problem.

(5) In defining and classifying the standards of recruitment and the conditions of employment (Article 101, paragraph 3),[a] the Charter clearly distinguished between two sets of criteria. The first, consisting of the first three qualities (efficiency, competence and integrity) were compulsory, the Charter requiring the *highest* standards in these, which were broad enough to include some secondary qualities. The second consisted of a single criterion, that of geographical distribution, which was subordinated to the first criteria in several respects: (*a*) its application was confined to recruitment without extending to "conditions of employment" as was the case for the first set of criteria under the Charter; (*b*) its application was not a *sine qua non* condition as in the case of the first criteria, but represented a sort of constitutional requirement, which had to be "given due regard." A rigid formula was deliberately avoided; (*c*) the "geographical basis" was to be "as wide as possible," which meant that each individual case was to be considered on its merits and on the basis of existing circumstances. This provision precluded a rigid application as of a mathematical formula in every case. Such was the policy as regards recruitment, personal criteria being given "paramount consideration," whereas only "due regard" was to be paid to geographical distribution. At the same time the two sets of criteria were subordinated to the fundamental principles laid down in Article 100 of the Charter, which constituted an absolute rule in relation to which all the rest was subordinate.

The period of gestation: the preparatory work in London

Theory had now to be turned into reality and a paper constitution into a living institution. This was the work of the Preparatory Com-

(a) Cf. above, chapter 4, p. 94.

mission, which was held in two stages: firstly, from 16 August to 12 November 1945, the Executive Committee, consisting of representatives of fourteen States Members, appointed ten Committees, of which the Sixth, under the Chairmanship of the Netherlands representative, Adrian Pelt, prepared the "provisions concerning the officials of the Secretariat and other international officials"; secondly, from 24 November to 23 December 1945, the Preparatory Commission, consisting of representatives of all the States Members, set up eight "technical committees" of which the Sixth, responsible for administrative questions, was under the chairmanship of the Greek representative Thanassis Aghnides. The latter, like Adrian Pelt, was a former high official of the League Secretariat, a fact which inevitably had an influence on the work of both the Executive Committee and the Preparatory Commission.

It was thanks to the exhaustive reports of these two bodies, the first serving as basis for the second, and to the documentary annexes containing various draft regulations, that it proved possible to bring the organization into being in a very short time. The first session of the General Assembly (first part) was accordingly held in London from 10 January to 14 February 1946. It was entirely devoted to questions of organization, the final report of the Preparatory Commission serving as its agenda. This session elected as first Secretary-General the Norwegian Foreign Minister Trygve Lie, on 1 February 1946.

Meanwhile, since 28 November 1945 an advisory group of experts on administrative, staff and budgetary questions had been at work, on the invitation of the Executive Secretary of the Preparatory Commission, Sir Gladwyn Jebb (who, until the election of Trygve Lie, acted as Secretary-General of the first part of the Assembly). This group was composed of the representatives of nine countries and was assisted by twelve advisers and eighteen experts. Its first report, dealing with the internal operation of the Secretariat and personnel questions, dates from 8 March 1946.

The administrative machinery of the U.N. was put into operation without delay by the new Secretary-General, Trygve Lie, first at Hunter College, New York, then at Lake Success (Long Island, New York) in half of the Sperry Gyroscope plant; in 1950 the organization moved into the new "glass house" specially constructed at Turtle Bay, on the East River, Manhattan, New York.

Thus, in the early months of 1946, "the greatest undertaking of our time"[a] set to work.

The work of the Preparatory Commission deserves our particular

(a) Expression used by the Prime Minister of New Zealand, Peter Fraser, quoted by Trygve Lie (op. cit., p. 14).

attention. First the Executive Committee and then the Preparatory Commission dealt in their respective reports[9][a] with the problems concerning the six principal organs of the United Nations, and with five supplementary questions: treaties and international agreements; privileges and immunities and facilities of the United Nations; budgetary arrangements; the permanent headquarters of the United Nations; winding-up of the League of Nations and transfer of its assets. The recommendations and the report proposed by the Executive Committee were then adopted, with amendments, by the Preparatory Commission in plenary meeting. The latter unanimously adopted its final report for submission to the first session of the General Assembly (convened by the Preparatory Commission). The amendments made in the initial proposals did not concern basic principles, although attempts had been made in the Commission to call such principles in question. It was again the problem of the Secretariat which aroused controversy, although the attacks made against the San Francisco decisions finally proved unsuccessful.

The work of the Preparatory Commission as presented in its final report may be summarized as follows:

A

The *recommendations* of the Commission are based on certain fundamental principles formulated in preambles—namely:

(i) "The degree in which the objects of the Charter can be realized will be largely determined by the manner in which the Secretariat performs its task. The Secretariat cannot successfully perform its task unless it enjoys the confidence of all the Members of the United Nations."

(ii) "Heavy responsibilities rest upon the Secretary-General in fulfilling his obligations under the Charter."

(iii) "The administrative organization of the Secretariat should be so designed as to enable the work of the Secretariat to be conducted with the greatest possible efficiency."

(iv) "The United Nations cannot achieve its purposes unless the peoples of the world are fully informed of its aims and activities."

(v) "The system of classification, recruitment and promotion within the Secretariat will go far to determine the degree in which, in accordance with paragraph 3 of Article 101 of the Charter, the standards of efficiency, competence and integrity may be ensured, due regard being paid to the importance of recruiting the staff on as wide a geographical basis as possible."

(vi) "The conditions of employment in the Secretariat should be

(a) "Report of the Executive Committee to the Preparatory Commission of the United Nations," 1945 (PC/EX/113 Rev. 1, 12 November 1945); "Report of the Preparatory Commission of the United Nations," 1945 (PC/20, 23 December 1945).

such as will attract qualified candidates from any part of the world".[a]

These recommendations, based on the experience of the League, particularly as regards the roles of the Secretary-General and the Secretariat (the provision of public information, the priority of efficiency as a criterion for staff selection and the provision of adequate conditions of employment), are of a *general* character. The majority of the Commission opposed the attempts made during the discussions to impose *a priori* on the future Secretary-General certain detailed provisions which would restrict his freedom of action. It was here that the greatest differences of opinion arose.

> "There was a tendency on the part of the delegates of a good many of the countries to try to sit down during the Preparatory Commission stage and write out a bill of particulars as to how this Secretariat should be organized, what its departments should be, what each Assistant Secretary-General should do, how its staff should be recruited, what the staff regulations should be, the terms of appointment, salary scales, and all that sort of thing, and to tie the hands of the Secretary-General so that when he came in all he would have to do was to move into the little niche that had been made for him. The contrary view, which finally prevailed, I am glad to say, was that the Preparatory Commission and the Assembly should do only that much preparatory work in this area as was absolutely necessary to get the Organization started during the period of the Assembly and the first few weeks or months afterwards, but that the bulk of the job of deciding how his Secretariat should be organized, what his departments should be, what their functions should be, how he should hire his staff, who his personnel director should be, and all that sort of thing, had to be left to the Secretary-General himself to work out and submit to the Assembly for approval. It is true it put a tremendous responsibility upon him, but the alternative to that was to make a very weak figure of him. This was one of the big issues carried over from the Preparatory Commission into the Assembly, and efforts were made in Committee 5 to reopen the issue to try to clip the wings of the Secretary-General, but fortunately the forces of light prevailed...."[b]

Nevertheless twenty-five detailed recommendations were put forward regarding the organization of the Secretariat;[c] after the approval of the Preparatory Commission's report by the General Assembly, the first Secretary-General said, "the instructions .... were so detailed that they limited my freedom of action".[d] The Preparatory Commission's work was therefore another compromise between conflicting opinions which were to clash again later, although on the whole those who preferred to respect the prestige of the future Secretary-General and not to tie his hands too much prevailed.

In particular the Commission recommended, as regards the Secretary-General, that "the terms of his appointment should be such as

(a) Report of the Preparatory Commission (op. cit., chapter VIII, pp. 81-84).
(b) W. H. C. Laves (op. cit., pp. 92/93).
(c) Report of the Executive Committee (op. cit., chapter VI, pp. 71/72); Report of the Preparatory Commission (op. cit., chapter VIII, pp. 81-84).
(d) Trygve Lie (op. cit., p. 43).

to enable a man of eminence and high attainment to accept and maintain the position" (recommendation 5), and fixed the duration of his appointment (five years subject to renewal) and the conditions of appointment to the directorial posts (recommendations 6 and 22). The Secretary-General was called upon to take "immediate steps" upon his appointment to establish an administrative organization which would permit of the effective discharge of his administrative and general responsiblities under the Charter, and the efficient performance of those functions and services required by the several organs of the United Nations (recommendation 9). Recommendations 15 and 25 referred to the internal structure of the Secretariat, the consultative machinery to be set up, the selection of staff and duration of employment, promotions and dismissals, classification of posts and salaries. The Commission nevertheless stipulated that the Secretary-General could "make such changes in the initial structure as may be required to the end that the most effective distribution of responsibilities and functions among the units of the Secretariat may be achieved" (recommendation 12). It was for him to take whatever steps might be required to ensure co-ordination between departments (recommendation 11), and he had "full latitude" as regards the provisional allocation of posts, the fixing of salaries and temporary appointments (recommendations 15 and 20).

As to the *Secretariat*, the Preparatory Commission emphasized its international character by insisting that all officials should take an "oath or declaration" that they would discharge their functions and regulate their conduct with the interests of the United Nations only in view (recommendation 2).[11] The Commission recommended the "career principle" for the staff (recommendations 18 and 20). It emphasized the unity of the U.N. Secretariat (in contrast to the U.S.S.R. draft)[12] and even that of the whole international administration within the United Nations family. Thus recommendation 19 dealt, *inter alia*, with the "means by which common standards of recruitment in the Secretariat and the specialized agencies may be ensured." It was also recommended that an advisory committee should be appointed, possibly including representatives of the staff, to draft a statute for an Administrative Tribunal (recommendation 4).

The Preparatory Commission thus drew a number of fundamental conclusions from the principles laid down in the Charter. The same considerations are to be found in the draft staff regulations annexed to the Preparatory Commission's report[a] and in the sixteen additional recommendations of the Technical Advisory Committee on Information, concerning the policies, functions and organization of the De-

(a) Report of the Preparatory Commission (op. cit., chapter VIII, section 3, pp. 95 ff.).

partment of Public Information.[a] Lastly, in expressing its "general approval" of the report on the organization of the Secretariat, "as an explanation of the recommendations" to be presented by the General Assembly to the Secretary-General for his guidance, the Preparatory Commission made a point of stating its fundamental ideas in comparative detail.

B

This report on the organization of the Secretariat, which interprets and explains the recommendations adopted, is a document of the greatest importance both to the future of the U.N. Secretariat, whose general outlines it traces, and to the evolution of the international civil service in general. It is in fact impossible to analyse the latter without considering this text, and particularly its first part.

The report consists of four parts:

(1) The first, dealing with the general character of the Secretariat, lays down guiding principles on four subjects:

(a) The position of the Secretariat in the Organization:

> "The key position of the Secretariat in the United Nations is recognized in the Charter, Article 7 of which provides that it shall be one of the principal organs of the United Nations. While the responsibility for the framing and adoption of agreed international policies rests with the organs representative of the Members ... the essential tasks of preparing the ground for these decisions and of executing them in co-operation with the Members will devolve largely upon the Secretariat. The manner in which the Secretariat performs these tasks will largely determine the degree in which the objectives of the Charter will be realized" (*paragraph 1*).

(b) The truly international character which the Secretariat must possess, "if it is to enjoy the confidence of all the Members of the United Nations," is specified in Article 101 of the Charter (*paragraph 2*).

Drawing the logical inferences from this principle, the report expands the main points made in the recommendations as follows:

The staff is in no way representative, but is appointed and works in a strictly personal capacity:

> "Such a Secretariat cannot be composed even in part of national representatives responsible to Governments. For the duration of their appointments, the Secretary-General and the staff will not be the servants of the State of which they are nationals but the servants only of the United Nations (*paragraph 3, first two sentences*);

Hence there are both *negative obligations*:

> "Those (officials) appointed for two years or more must resign from any position they may hold in public or private employment, and none may accept any honour, decoration, favour, gift or fee in respect to services rendered during the period of his appointment or service in the Organization. Officials

(a) Ibidem (annex, pp. 102-103).

who become candidates for any public office of a political character must resign from the Secretariat" (*paragraph 3*, last two sentences);

and *positive obligations:*

"But the obligations of officials are not purely negative. It is essential that officials should be inspired by a sense of loyalty to the United Nations and devotion to the ideal for which it stands, and that they should develop an *esprit de corps* and a habit of daily co-operation with persons of other countries and cultures. Loyalty to the Organization is in no way incompatible with an official's attachment to his own country, whose higher interest he is serving in serving the United Nations. It clearly involves, however, a broad international outlook and a detachment from national prejudices and narrow national interests" (*paragraph 4*).

"All officials of the United Nations must recognize the exclusive authority of the Secretary-General and submit themselves to rules of discipline such as are normally enforced in national civil services. More especially, they are required to observe the utmost discretion in regard to matters of official business. Except by authorization of the Secretary-General, no official may publish anything relating to the activities of the Organization or to any political question, or make any public pronouncements on such matters" (*paragraph 5*).

(*c*) The *immunities and privileges of officials:*[a]

"An adequate system of immunities and privileges, as provided in Article 105 of the Charter, is essential if officials are to be free from pressure by individual governments and to discharge their duties efficiently. These immunities and privileges, however, furnish the officials who enjoy them no excuse for evading their private obligations, or for failing to observe laws and police regulations. Whenever these immunities and privileges are invoked, it lies within the discretion of the Secretary-General to decide whether they should be waived" (*paragraph 6*).

(*d*) Standards for the *recruitment* and *conditions of service* of the staff:

"The paramount consideration in the employment of the staff and in the determination of the conditions of service, as laid down in Article 101 of the Charter, is the necessity of securing the highest standards of efficiency, competence and integrity. Due regard is also to be paid to the importance of recruiting the staff on as wide a geographical basis as possible. How best to ensure the fulfilment of these two principles—which, as experience has shown, can in large measure be reconciled—has been one of the major preoccupations of the Preparatory Commission" (*paragraph 7*).

(2) The second part of the report deals with the *Secretary-General*. The principal functions assigned to the Secretary-General "explicitly or by inference" by the Charter, are grouped by the Preparatory Commission under six headings:

(*a*) General administrative and executive;

(*b*) Technical;

(*c*) Financial;

(*d*) Organization and administration of the Secretariat;

(a) Chapter VII of the General Report of the Preparatory Commission (op. cit., pp. 60 ff. and annexes).

(e) Political;

(f) Representational.[a]

Naturally, this division of functions is theoretical, since they are bound frequently to overlap. But their enumeration proves that the Preparatory Commission fully realized the extent of the future Secretary-General's role in virtue of the letter and the spirit of the Charter. Leaving till a future date the closer definition of this role by internal regulations, the Commission emphasized the varied responsibilities of the Secretary-General and made clear the true nature of his post, very different from that of the Secretary-General of the League. In describing the position of the head of the Secretariat of the U.N., the Commission did not hesitate to refer *a contrario* to past history, as will be seen from several clauses, for example *paragraph 19:*

> "Because a Secretary-General is a confidant of many Governments, it is desirable that no Member should offer him, at any rate immediately on retirement, any governmental position in which his confidential information is a source of embarrassment to other Members, and on his part a Secretary-General should refrain from accepting any such position."[b]

Anticipating future needs and with remarkable vision and foresight, the Commission regards the Secretary-General as the personification of international co-operation, as is shown by *paragraph 17:*

> "The United Nations cannot prosper nor can its aims be realized without the active and steadfast support of the peoples of the world. The aims and activities of the General Assembly, the Security Council, the Economic and Social Council and the Trusteeship Council will no doubt be represented before the public primarily by the Chairmen of these organs. But the Secretary-General, more than anyone else, will stand for the United Nations as a whole. In the eyes of the world no less than in the eyes of his own staff, he must embody the principles and ideals of the Charter to which the Organization seeks to give effect."

The report emphasizes that although the Secretary-General will naturally delegate many of his duties to members of "his" staff, the ultimate responsibility remains his alone (*paragraph 9*). In view of his "administrative and executive duties of a wider character, he is the channel of all communication with the United Nations or any of its organs" (*paragraph 12*).[13] More specifically, "as regards the work of the Economic and Social Council and Trusteeship Council, the expert technical assistance which the Secretary-General is able to provide and which he himself must control will clearly affect the degree in which these organs achieve their purposes" (*paragraph 13*). Apart from "wide responsiblities in connection with the financial administra-

(a) Ibidem, chapter VIII of the Report on the Organization of the Secretariat, (section 2 B, p. 86).

(b) Sir Eric Drummond, after resigning from his position as Secretary-General of the League, became British Ambassador to Italy (at that time under the Fascist régime).

tion of the United Nations,"[14] the Secretary-General is "the head of the Secretariat" and as such he:

> "... appoints all staff under regulations established by the General Assembly (Article 101, paragraphs 1 and 3) and assigns appropriate staff to the various organs of the United Nations (Article 101, paragraph 2). He alone is responsible to the other principal organs for the Secretariat's work; his choice of staff—more particularly of higher staff—and his leadership will largely determine the character and the efficiency of the Secretariat as a whole. It is on him that will mainly fall the duty of creating and maintaining a team spirit in a body of officials recruited from many countries. His moral authority within the Secretariat will depend at once upon the example he gives of the qualities prescribed in Article 100 and upon the confidence shown in him by the Members of the United Nations" (*paragraph 15*).

Lastly, as regards his role

> "as a mediator and as an informal adviser of many Governments... he will undoubtedly be called upon from time to time, in the exercise of his administrative duties, to take decisions which may justly be called political. Under Article 99 of the Charter, moreover, he has been given a quite special right which goes beyond any power previously accorded to the head of an international administration.... It is impossible to foresee how this Article will be applied; but the responsibility it confers upon the Secretary-General will require the exercise of the highest qualities of political judgment, tact and integrity" (*paragraph 16*).

(3) The third part of the report deals with the "*administrative organization of the Secretariat*" and emphasizes the need for interchangeability of staff, the existence of common as well as distinctive functions (*paragraphs 24 and 25*), the responsibilities of each section of the Secretariat and above all the indispensable unity of the Secretariat as a whole:

> "The principal reason for setting up the Secretariat as a single working body— though it will, of course, be internally organized so as to deal most effectively with the various aspects of the operations of the United Nations—is that all the organs it serves have their responsibilities in the primary common task of maintaining peace and security. This task is the unifying principle of the whole Organization, its organs, and the Secretariat" (*paragraph 28*).
>
> "Another reason is that by organizing the Secretariat according to the work performed by each part and not in Departments tied exclusively to one or the other organ, duplication of work, overlapping and waste of time, and confusion will be avoided. Again, the creation of Departments attached exclusively to a single organ would give rise to divided loyalties and undesirable rivalry between Departments" (*paragraph 29*).

(4) Lastly the fourth part of the report deals with *grading, promotion, recruitment* and *terms of employment*. Here again the report shows the paramount role of the Secretary-General in setting up the administration, and the importance of a wide and adaptable system of recruitment. The report then deals with the following questions: entrance examinations (to be used as far as possible) (*paragraph 50*);

appraisal of the temperament, character and general capacity of candidates (*paragraphs 51 ff.*); other methods of selection for candidates to whom the examination system is inapplicable (*paragraph 54*); staff participation on questions concerning them (*paragraph 56*), etc.

A few points dealt with by the Commission under this heading deserve particular attention—namely:

The provision of in-service training for members of the staff, particularly those whose earlier education has been inadequate and for those on probation (which "would have the great advantage of combining study of the theory and practice of their work") and courses in the working and official languages, administration, and the more technical aspects of the work:

> "This system would have the long-term effect of reconciling the two criteria for appointments laid down in paragraph 3 of Article 101 of the Charter, namely personal capacity and geographical distribution" (*paragraph 55*, last sentence);

The need to offer a permanent career to the majority of the staff—this was considered to be essential:

> "Unless members of the staff can be offered some assurance of being able to make their careers in the Secretariat, many of the best candidates from all countries will inevitably be kept away. Nor can members of the staff be expected fully to subordinate the special interests of their countries to the international interest if they are merely detached primarily from national administrations and remain dependent upon them for their future. Finally, it is important that the advantages of experience should be secured and sound administrative traditions established within the Secretariat (*paragraph 59*).
>
> "For these reasons, it is essential that the bulk of the staff should consist of persons who will make their career in the Secretariat. They should be given contracts for an indeterminate period subject to review every five years on the basis of reports by their superior officers. An appointment should not be terminated to make way for the appointment of a person of some other nationality or for other reasons not connected with the staff member's own work" (*paragraph 60*);

Provision in some cases for temporary appointments: for the Secretary-General and principal officers (five years, renewable); for "specialists in technical fields as well as persons with special political qualifications" (fixed-term contracts); for persons "from geographical regions inadequately represented in the Secretariat if suitable candidates from that region are not readily available for permanent appointment" (temporary appointments with or without fixed term); and for officials from national services seconded for the purpose (or who have been granted leave without pay);

The institution of periods of probation which would be "a genuine testing of the staff member's suitability for his particular post";

The provision of disciplinary measures;

Rules for the termination of appointments.

In its resolution 13 (I) of 13 February 1946 the General Assembly adopted the Preparatory Commission's proposals without essential changes.[a]

To sum up: in 1946, when the United Nations was set up, in contrast to the early days of the League in 1919 and 1920, and thanks to the preparatory work which had been done, a perceptive observer could understand the responsibilities and characteristics of the international civil service. The general principles of the Charter were supplemented by the comments, the postulates and the recommendations of the Preparatory Commission, particularly as regards the Secretary-General's functions and the "exclusively international character" of the staff of the Secretariat. All misunderstanding therefore seemed to be ruled out, and everything now depended on the willingness of States to co-operate effectively within the framework of the international organization.

Owing to the vicissitudes of international affairs, the U.N. has, in the course of years, departed in several respects from the Preparatory Commission's proposals. Problems which seemed to have been solved in principle at the outset reappeared, causing fresh disagreement and a number of crises. Nevertheless, we must acknowledge the constant tendency of the Organization to observe as far as possible the ideological and administrative principles laid down by the Preparatory Commission, and the repeated efforts it has made to revert to its original structure.

The start: Trygve Lie at grips with reality

The first Secretary-General of the League of Nations, Sir Eric Drummond (later Lord Perth), in analysing the initial period of the U.N., observed:

> "When I was appointed Secretary-General of the League I had the time and the opportunity to choose my colleagues at leisure. The various organs of the League were developing slowly so I only had to choose a small nucleus of men and women in the early days. But Mr. Trygve Lie was in a very different position. The exact performance of the Charter called for a Secretariat of considerable size immediately; and few States had eminent men available, since they needed them to reconstruct their own countries. And yet an international task possesses a special attraction, especially when those who undertake it realize that through it they are serving their country's highest interests...."[b]

The new Secretary-General was faced upon his election with the gigantic task of setting up *ab nihilo* an enormous international secretariat. He himself has said in this connection:

(a) Cf. A. Pelt, "Peculiar Characteristics of an International Administration", *Public Administration Review* (No. 2/VI, 1946).
(b) "L'ancienne Société et la nouvelle O.N.U." (*Dictionnaire diplomatique*, op. cit., p. 106).

"The central problem was that the United Nations was already a going concern which had to be serviced continuously, and with no delay whatever. It had been different in Geneva. Not a meeting of importance was held during the first eighteen months of the League's existence, when the world was far too busy implementing the peace treaties which—fortunately for the League—had already been concluded. Sir Eric could take the necessary time. I could not."[a]

Starting in 1946 with a temporary staff of about 300 persons belonging to the secretariat of the Preparatory Commission and of the first General Assembly, and relying as far as possible on such former officials of the League as were still available and whose international outlook was well known,[15] the first Secretary-General had to undertake the improvised recruitment of about 2,900 staff members in a few months. The demobilization of American troops and the difficulties of communication with Europe at that time meant that at first it was easiest to accept candidates from the United States of America: some 10,000 applications had been received. Speed was essential owing to the amount of work to be done at once, but at the same time the principle of worldwide geographical distribution could not be disregarded. He was thus faced with a difficulty which is usual when a new international organization is set up, but which in this case was multiplied at least tenfold. He had to improvise a complex piece of machinery capable of going into action with some degree of efficiency at once.

It is not surprising, therefore, that at the outset the Secretariat had all the characteristics of a house built in a hurry, and that later the early recruitment was criticized with some justice. This was a complication for the Secretariat, since it took years to redress the situation which had been compromised at the start. Further difficulties arose as regards the higher posts owing to the "cold war". The recruitment of candidates for these posts was to prove particularly difficult owing to dissension among the founding Powers.

The Charter was the outcome of a conception of a united and peaceful world determined to co-operate—that is to say of a fictitious world, the existence of which had seemed possible in the first flush of victory, but which in no way corresponded to reality. Born of a world war conducted in common against the common enemy, the "united nations" were united against that enemy, but in hardly anything else. Although the Charter had been accepted by all, positive action encountered major and even insurmountable difficulties at every step. It was to this "world of the Charter" that the idea of the international civil service belonged—an idea defined by the Charter and expanded by the Preparatory Commission. Its object was to realize, at the international level, unity in diversity and permanence in discontinuity. This ideal, up against hard facts, was often (even in the Secretariat) impossible to put into practice.

(a) Trygve Lie (op. cit., p. 44).

The first problem which the Secretary-General had to face in recruiting his staff was that of his deputies. The Charter said nothing on the subject, and the Preparatory Commission had confined itself to recommending that "Assistant Secretaries-General... appointed by the Secretary-General... should have responsibility for and supervision of Departments or Services" (recommendation 11) and that among them "there should always be one... designated by the Secretary-General to deputize for him when he is absent or unable to perform his functions" (recommendation 8). The object was to prevent these posts from developing on "ambassadorial" lines as at the League of Nations. But when the Secretary-General took office, he found himself faced with a "private" agreement between the five Great Powers dividing up these posts among themselves. According to this initial "gentlemen's agreement" imposed on the Secretary-General as a *fait accompli* and as "one of the basic political premises upon which the Secretariat had been built[a]", the U.S.S.R. had "reserved" the post of Assistant Secretary-General for Security Council Affairs ("first Assistant Secretaryship"), the United States that of Administrative and Financial Services, the United Kingdom that of Economic Affairs, France that of Social Affairs and China that of Trusteeship Council Affairs.

> "Strictly speaking," said Trygve Lie, "the Big Five had no right to arrive at any understanding regarding the distribution of the offices of Assistant Secretary-General which was binding upon the Secretary-General...."[b]

In practice he could do nothing but accept the situation. Although the agreement had no legal force whatever, the holders of the posts became *a priori* representatives of the States Members placed at the highest level of administrative responsibilities, and in addition to controlling the departments assigned to them, were attached to the Secretary-General "in a representative capacity with individual countries and groups of countries".[c] This unfortunate precedent of the "occupation" of key posts by the great Powers, which was severely criticized later in many quarters,[16] provided the basis for a custom— which became firmly established in spite of Trygve Lie's early hopes[d]— that when a post of Assistant Secretary-General "reserved" in this way for one of the great Powers fell vacant, a national of the same Power was entitled to fill it. What is more, the logical result of the agreement was that the Power concerned could, if it wished,

(a) "Issues before the IXth General Assembly", *International Conciliation* (No. 499, 1954, p. 126).
(b) Trygve Lie (op. cit., p. 45).
(c) "Issues before the IXth General Assembly", (op. cit., p. 124, and doc. A/2214 of 7 October 1952).
(d) Trygve Lie (op. cit., p. 45).

exercise a decisive influence on the choice of the candidate for the vacant post, even if it did not always exercise this right, and even though the appointment was officially made by the Secretary-General, who was the only authority entitled to do so.

Of course, regrettable though this arrangement was from the point of view of the letter and spirit of the Charter, it had certain practical advantages. Thus the Secretary-General had an additional source of information and contact independently of the permanent delegations accredited to the United Nations by the great Powers. Moreover, some of these Assistant Secretaries-General who were nationals of great Powers showed themselves capable of independence while ensuring good relations between the Secretary-General and their governments. The danger therefore varied according to the personalities concerned and according to the attitude of each government. Thus the clear violation of the Charter constituted by this "gentlemen's agreement," which placed the Secretary-General in a very difficult position and was of bad augury for the future, was counterbalanced to some extent by certain advantages. The actual influence of each of the Assistant Secretaries-General, whose post thus constituted the "property" of his home country, depended in the last resort on factors which had to be judged individually—for example, the respective influences of the Assistant Secretary-General concerned and the permanent delegate of his country. The appointment of permanent national delegations to the Secretariat—which had been opposed at the time of the League so as to preserve direct contacts between the Secretary-General and Governments—meant the presence at U.N. headquarters of liaison officers who were not members of the Secretariat.[17]

Administratively speaking, and independently of this complicated political situation, the Secretary-General was not relieved of any of his duties by the existence of Assistant Secretaries-General. Largely for reasons of prestige, it soon became the established practice for the government delegates to submit directly to him most of the cases which concerned them.[a] Even the problem of the Secretary-General's replacement in case of absence or inability to perform his duty was not adequately solved, despite the Preparatory Commission's explicit recommendations. In the absence of any definite statutory regulations, authority was delegated from time to time on an *ad hoc* basis, and the successive plans later put forward to create a permanent post proved unsuccessful.[c] Lastly, the continual insistence on economy

(a) Trygve Lie (op. cit., pp. 51/52).
(b) Cf. Note on the Press Conference No. 902 of 19 August 1954, p. 5. Cf. also Rules of Procedure of the General Assembly, articles 38 and 63; of the Security Council, articles 21 and 22; of ECOSOC, articles 23 and 26; of the Trusteeship Council, articles 23 and 26.
(d) Cf., for example, A/2554 (chapter 26) and A/2731 (chapter 28).

worked in favour of a reduction in the number of Assistant Secretaries-General, though such a reduction did not actually take place while Trygve Lie was in office.

As regards the consultation of governments in connection with each appointment of an Assistant Secretary-General and the apparent respect then shown for the letter of the Charter, the first Secretary-General himself remarked:

> "It would not have been politic of me to resist the Great Power accord. Moreover, I welcomed the understanding as a sign of good will and confidence between East and West....As became my custom in connection with filling of the highest posts in the Secretariat, I felt it was both necessary and desirable to secure nominations from the Governments, in particular for positions of the rank of Assistant Secretary-General. The decisions were always mine, but I had try to get the best talent and that sometimes took persuasion, as good people can seldom be spared...."[a]

As to the other posts in the Secretariat (even sometimes the lower ones) which had to be filled urgently, pressure on the Secretary-General came from all quarters, in spite of the fact that the texts in force and their interpretation by the Preparatory Commission were perfectly clear and ruled out any sort of government interference in recruitment. The geographical distribution rule, the practical application of which was undefined, was invoked from the start by several States for purposes which had little to do with the intentions of the authors of the Charter, and from motives of national ambition and considerations of prestige and emulation. At the same time, in setting up the Secretariat, the Secretary-General had had to employ whatever qualified persons were at hand, such as the London nucleus and former League officials, mainly belonging to the countries of western Europe. This fact gave that continent a numerical advantage and provided ammunition for the detractors of Trygve Lie's recruiting. Furthermore, for reasons of expediency, he sought the help of governments in finding recruits for the Secretariat. This resort to governmental facilities was later to become an established tradition for practical reasons, and it was not regarded as contrary to the Charter, since the final decision always rested with the Secretary-General and his formal rights were thus safeguarded. Nevertheless, this practice led to regrettable nepotism[b] and to the centre of gravity of recruitment being frequently displaced to the capitals of the Member States.

As a result of this confusion regarding the "right" of governments to propose or even to impose certain candidates; to give their views on the candidatures under consideration and to enter into official

(a) Trygve Lie (op. cit., p. 45).
(b) Cf. J. M. Howe, "The Geographic Composition of International Secretariats", in *Columbia Journal of International Affairs* (No. 2/II, 1948. pp. 46 ff.)

or informal negotiations on the subject; to receive lists of candidates in advance and screen them, the principle of the Secretary-General's exclusive responsibility for recruitment became more and more illusory. In the search for "varied talents" recommended by the Preparatory Commission, there was plenty of "variety," but often not much "talent". Recruitment thus became a matter of negotiation and even of bargaining, contrary to the principles of the Charter. Trygve Lie confesses in this connection:

> "It was my practice to ask Member Governments to propose candidates for the Secretariat and to check with them often on proposed appointments. Of course I always reserved the final decision in accordance with the constitutional authority of the Secretary-General under Article 100, and the international recruitment procedures were conducted on an independent basis. Nevertheless, help from Governments in getting the best people was obviously necessary, and advisable, so long as my independence of judgment and decision was respected …"[a]

This last reservation may be compared with Trygve Lie's statement of 10 March 1953:

> "I have resisted strong requests—in some cases what might fairly be termed strong pressures—coming from many quarters to appoint or replace Secretariat officials when to yield would have been against my own judgment and therefore would have weakened the constitutional status of the Secretariat as provided in the Charter."[b]

Thus it will readily be understood that during all this period the problem of geographical distribution and the various transactions which took place in its name was one of the major anxieties of the new organization. Naturally an attempt had to be made to find criteria for this distribution, in spite of the danger of tying the hands of recruiters by rigid formulas, in the hope—vain, as it turned out—of moderating the claims made from different quarters. The fear that the quality of the staff might be dangerously lowered was justified. One commentator has stated:

> "Among staff members who joined the field since World War II, there are those who arrived recommended or sponsored by certain governments, who can be regarded as little more than unofficial representatives of those governments seconded to do a period of service in the international organization in the interests of the home country."[c]

Despite all these obstacles the administrative machinery was set up and worked fairly smoothly under the direction of Byron Price, Assistant Secretary-General for Administrative and Financial Serv-

---

(a) Trygve Lie (op. cit., p. 387).
(b) Speech by the Secretary-General at the seventh session of the General Assembly (doc. SG/281 of 10 March 1953, p. 4).
(c) B. Akzin, *New States and International Organizations* (Paris, 1955, p. 97).

ices, acting on behalf of the Secretary-General and thus occupying a key position in the international administration at critical moments. Practices were improvised and methods worked out to ensure that the new machinery, which had continually to cope with new tasks, should be able to function within the prescribed constitutional framework and without too much friction. Whatever the disillusions and criticisms, chiefly caused by faulty recruitment and the initial instability of the staff, an experienced observer was able to say:

> "If there is any part of the structure of intergovernmental organizations that deserves to be called 'international' more than any other, it is the international secretariats that may lay claim to this distinction."[a]

(a) Ibidem, p. 98.

NOTES

(1) Cf. G. Woodridge and others: *U.N.R.R.A.: The History of the United Nations Relief and Rehabilitation Administration* (New York, 1950, 3 volumes). Cf. also W. R. Sharp, "Field Administration..." (op. cit., pp. 20 ff).

(2) L. M. Goodrich, "The United Nations," (op. cit., p. 133): "To a large degree, such successes as the League enjoyed, particularly in the areas of economic and social cooperation and the development of non-self-governing territories, were due to the existence and effective functioning of an international civil service". Cf. also A. Nussbaum, *A Concise History of the League of Nations* (New York, 1954, *passim*).

(3) Of the four Commissions appointed by the San Francisco Conference to prepare recommandations on the general principles for the guidance of its technical committees, Commission I (which drew up the "general provisions") prepared the draft clauses regarding the Secretariat to be inserted in the future Charter (Committee 1/2: chapters III, IV, X and XI of the Dumbarton Oaks Proposals). After six weeks of uninterrupted work and twenty-nine meetings, this task was successfully accomplished.

(4) Cf. C. W. Jenks, "Some Comments on the Dumbarton Oaks Proposals", paragraph 19 (published in *The Proper Law*..., op. cit., pp. 28/29): "A recognition of the importance of the matter born of a decade of experience led the Assembly of the League of Nations to require all League officials to make a solemn declaration that they would discharge their functions and regulate their conduct with the interests of the League alone in view, and would not seek or receive instructions from any government or other authority external to the League. League experience showed these arrangements to be seriously defective in that under them the obligation of officials to exercise the functions entrusted to them with the interests of the League alone in view was not paralleled by any corresponding explicit obligation of the governments concerned not to seek to influence their nationals in the discharge of international duties. In the case of some of the organizations now being created the matter has been dealt with in a more satisfactory manner by including in their constituent instruments provisions on the subject which will be binding on officials and governments alike. Important as this principle is in the case of the specialized U.N. organizations for which it has already been adopted, it is still more vital in the case of the proposed general organization...."

(5) Cf. Report to the President on the Results of the San Francisco Conference by the Chairman of the United States Delegation, the Secretary of State, (Depart-

ment of State, publication No. 2349, Conference Series No. 71, pp. 150-152):
"The proposed Secretariat of the United Nations will be, in effect, an international
civil service. It will be recruited on the basis of competence, promoted on the basis
of merit, and selected with due reference to linguistic and geographical considerations. Unlike a national civil service, however, it will not have the policy-making
authorities...constantly available for reference and guidance. The staff must
therefore be able to give effect to the decisions of policy-making bodies by exercising
a high degree of good judgment and responsibility. In this concept the Secretariat
becomes rightly one of the principal organs of the United Nations...."

(6) Article 1 of the Charter: "The Purposes of the United Nations are:
1. To maintain international peace and security, and to that end: to take effective
collective measures for the prevention and removal of threats to the peace, and for
the suppression of acts of aggression or other breaches of the peace, and to bring about
by peaceful means, and in conformity with the principles of justice and international
law, adjustment or settlement of international disputes or situations which might
lead to a breach of the peace;
2. To develop friendly relations among nations based on respect for the principle
of equal rights and self-determination of peoples, and to take other appropriate
measures to strengthen universal peace;"
(items 3 and 4, cf. above, chapter 2, note (7)).

(7) Cf. Dag Hammarskjöld, Oxford address (op. cit., p. 8): "The fact that the
Secretary-General is an official with political power as well as administrative
functions had direct implications for the method of his selection. Proposals at San
Francisco to eliminate the participation of the Security Council in the election
process were rejected precisely because it was recognized that the role of the Secretary-General in the field of political and security matters properly involved the
Security Council and made it logical that the unanimity rule of permanent Members
should apply. At the same time it was recognized that the necessity of such unanimous agreement would have to be limited only to the selection of the Secretary-
General and that it was equally essential that he be protected against the pressure
of a Member during his term of office. Thus a proposal for a three-year term was
rejected on the ground that so short a term might impair his independent role...."

(8) Article 4 of the Statute of the International Court of Justice is as follows:
"1. The members of the Court shall be elected by the General Assembly and by the
Security Council from a list of persons nominated by the national groups in the
Permanent Court of Arbitration, in accordance with the following provisions.
"2. In the case of Members of the United Nations not represented in the Permanent
Court of Arbitration, candidates shall be nominated by national groups appointed
for this purpose by their governments under the same conditions as those prescribed
for members of the Permanent Court of Arbitration by Article 44 of the Convention
of The Hague of 1907 for the pacific settlement of international disputes.
"3. The conditions under which a state which is a party to the present Statute but
is not a Member of the United Nations may participate in electing the members
of the Court shall, in the absence of a special agreement, be laid down by the
General Assembly upon recommendation of the Security Council".

(9) The Report of the Executive Committee (op. cit.) is divided into four parts:
I. Introduction; II. Statement of Recommendations; III. Committee Reports
and Supplementary Papers (Summary of the discussions of the Committee on the
General Assembly; Observations by the Acting Chairman on the Work of the
Committee on the Security Council; Memoranda by the Delegations of the United
Kingdom and the United States of America and Extract from the Summary
Report of the Seventh Meeting of the Committee on the Trusteeship Council;
Study on Privileges and Immunities; Minority Proposal submitted by the U.S.S.R.
delegation for the Administrative Organization of the Secretariat; Communication

by the Committee on the Economic and Social Council concerning the Economic and Social Departments of the Secretariat; Observations by the United States Delegation on the Organization of the Statistical Work of the Secretariat; Discussions of the Proposals of the United States Delegation for an Executive Office of the Secretary-General; Draft Provisional Staff Regulations; Statement of Assets and Liabilities of the League of Nations as on 31 December 1944; Extract from the Verbatim Record of the Twenty-First Meeting of the Executive Committee on the Permanent Headquarters of the U.N.), IV. Terms of Reference of the Committees of the Executive Committee.

The report of the Preparatory Commission (op. cit.) is divided into eleven chapters (The General Assembly; The Security Council; The Economic and Social Council; The Trusteeship System; The International Court of Justice; Treaties and International Agreements; Privileges, Immunities and Facilities of the United Nations; The Secretariat; Budgetary and Financial Arrangements; The Permanent Headquarters of the United Nations; The League of Nations). The appendices include a study on privileges and immunities; a draft convention on the same subject; a draft treaty on the headquarters to be concluded with the United States; recommendations of the Technical Advisory Committee on Information; draft provisional financial regulations; rules and discussions on the use of languages; observations on the organization of the statistical work of the Secretariat; report of the Advisory Group of Experts to the Administrative and Budgetary Committee; the Charter of the United Nations and the Statute of the International Court of Justice.

(10) Cf. D. C. Stone (op. cit., pp. 428-429): "The chief violation of principles in practice has been the habit of General Assemblies not only to tell Secretaries-General what to do but how to do it. Detailed instructions and minute prescriptions regarding organization, methods, personnel, financial administration and other administrative matters flow steadily from these bodies, with a deleterious effect upon responsible, efficient management. To the extent the Secretary-General and other top officials fall short of demonstrating executive skill, they contribute to this tendency of deliberative bodies...."

(11) Text of the oath or declaration (article 1.9 of the Staff Regulations, 1958 edition, ST.SGB/Staff Rules/1, p. 6): "I solemnly swear to exercise in all loyalty, discretion and conscience the functions entrusted to me as an international civil servant of the United Nations, to discharge these functions and regulate my conduct with the interests of the United Nations only in view and not to seek or accept instructions in regard to the performance of my duties from any government or other authority external to the Organization."

(12) Cf. the graph submitted by the U.S.S.R. delegation on behalf of the minority in support of the proposal (rejected by the Commission) for four parallel secretariats and three common departments (Report of the Executive Committee, op. cit., p. 84). This should be compared with the graph illustrating the plan of the initial organization adopted by the majority and reproduced in the final report (ibidem, pp. 102/103).

(13) Paragraph 12 of the Report: "[The Secretary-General] must endeavour within the scope of his functions to integrate the activity of the whole complex of the United Nations and see that the machine runs smoothly and efficiently. He is responsible moreover for the preparation of the work of the various organs and for the execution of their decisions in co-operation with the Members."

(14) Paragraph 14 of the Report: "It may be assumed that under the financial regulations which will be established by the General Assembly he will be made primarily reponsible for preparing the budget, for allocating functions, for controlling expenditure, for administering such financial and budgetary arrangements as the General Assembly may enter into with specialized agencies for collecting contributions from Members and for the custodianship of all funds."

(15) Cf. B. Akzin (op. cit., p. 97): "The not inconsiderable core of staff members taken over from the League of Nations days are, on the whole, extremely international-minded and have devoloped a perfect loyalty to the *ensemble* of international organizations as well as an admirable *esprit de corps.* . . . "

(16) Cf., for example, the speech of the Syrian representative at the Fifth Committee (428th meeting) of the Eighth General Assembly of the United Nations in December 1953 ("the so-called gentleman's agreement which had been reached informally in London in 1946").

(17) Cf. E. Jackson, "Developing the Peaceful Settlement Functions of the U.N." in *Annals* (Vol. 296, 1954, p. 31): "The heads of the sixty permanent delegations to the U.N. are continuously available. Some of them have had extensive diplomatic experience and many of them can be focal points of conciliation as issues are weighed and negotiated both before and during consideration by the Security Council or the General Assembly. The representatives of certain countries are often able, for reasons both of geography and interest, to be of special assistance to the Secretary-General on an informal basis. In making the United Nations a trusted instrument of political negotiation, there can be no substitute for the closest diplomatic relationship between the Secretary-General and the heads of delegations representing the Member States."

(18) There was no lack of criticisms. Thus, for example, W. R. Crocker, "Some Notes on the U.N. Secretariat", in *International Organization* (No. 1/IX, 1950, pp. 598 ff.), in critisizing the manner of conceiving and realizing geographical distribution, speaks of "inflation of personnel" and says that, in his experience, in certain branches of the secretariats, one official out of four was "dead wood" (p. 602). "Judged by its organization, by the manner in which it recruited its personnel, by the kind of personnel it found, by the environment in which it works and by the work it turns out, the U.N. Secretariat begins badly. In the two absolute essentials, the average quality of its chiefs and the average quality of the personnel, it has been unlucky. Instead of a small, carefully selected staff, the Secretariat got a mass of half-qualified or quite unqualified persons, collected by hazard under ill-advised pressure from [national] delegates, posted or graded by favouritism or whim and working according to standards—standards adopted and implemented because of the dominance of Americans—that are more suited to a mass production factory than to a secretariat . . . " (pp. 612-613).

CHAPTER 8

THE PERIOD OF UNIVERSALITY: THE GROWTH OF THE UNITED NATIONS

Trial and error

The United Nations seems to have been moulded much more by circumstances than by the principles laid down in the Charter and their interpretation by the Preparatory Commission. Events belied the anticipations of those who drew up the fundamental texts, and many compromises were needed to ensure the smooth running of the machinery and the survival of the institution. Thus practice departed from, and even sometimes contradicted, the texts. But the principles remained immutable and even if they were disregarded in the first place, they were frequently invoked by one side or the other in self-justification. Hence certain contradictions were inevitable.

The Charter presumed that the concert of great Powers would survive, a presumption which was proved only superficially correct; thus in the political sphere the Organization was unable to adhere strictly to the Charter. This led certain authors to speak of a "new United Nations"[a]—"new" because operating under a new "charter," written by the practical conduct of affairs, corresponding to the needs of the hour and justified by the desire to achieve the purposes of the Charter even when some of the methods laid down therein could no longer be applied.

In the administrative sphere, but closely related to political considerations, many compromises which affected the status of the international civil service were adopted in practice. Here the ground seemed to be solid; but, as in the past, it proved shifting and uncertain. Certain concessions made to the detriment of established principles, particularly as regards the recruitment of the Secretariat, are at the basis of the suggestion that the "*true*" international civil service[b] is not that which actually exists, but that which would exist if the rules were observed. Thus actual achievements, which are imperfect and

(a) Cf., for example, H. J. Morgentau, "The New United Nations and the Revision of the Charter", in *Review of Politics* (No. 1/16, 1954, p. 3) and S. Hoffmann, "The Role of International Organization: Limits and Possibilities", in *International Organization* (No. 3/X, 1956, p. 361 ff.).
(b) Cf., for example, *Conference on the Concept of a True International Civil Service* (Carnegie Endowment, Vevey, 1958).

unstable, are contrasted with abstract principles. This contrast is instructive.

In giving a brief outline of the practices followed, their empirical character must be stressed. In the first place certain governments have not fully understood the commitments into which they have solemnly entered, or have failed to take them seriously. Hence interference and pressure of a kind which had been condemned in the Charter with the approval of all the States Members. But, in addition to this, as the U.N. grew, an increasing proportion of Members— eventually more than half the total—were new States which had not taken part in the creation of the organization and were unfamiliar with the discussions and work which had preceded it. Inevitably this led to many misunderstandings and to complex, if not impossible, situations. The very existence in an *intergovernmental* environment— all the organs except the Secretariat were by definition intergovernmental—of an *"international"* organ which, in spite of its composition, was not intergovernmental, seemed to many nonsensical and merely a matter of splitting hairs. The public education undertaken by the U.N. in accordance with the Preparatory Commission's proposals did not seem able to put across this idea to the national Ministries, and, particularly in the case of administrative problems, had little popular appeal.

Moreover, there seems little doubt that the first Secretary-General was disinclined to insist too much on administrative principles and sometimes thought it expedient to sacrifice them to the political principles of the Charter or to give way if a government or group of States made difficulties. It is interesting to speculate as to how the administration of the Secretariat would have developed if, instead of Trygve Lie, the first Secretary-General had been Dag Hammarskjöld, who attached greater importance to principles. In any case, even the reluctant acceptance of compromises explicitly ruled out by the founders of the organization could not but be detrimental to the Secretariat by placing it out of line with the model laid down in the Charter. At the same time, even apart from political considerations proper, we observe in the evolution of the Secretariat hesitations, experiments, tentative attempts to apply different national models, and arbitrary fluctuations between different solutions. Thus the compromises which had been adopted underwent modifications, some of them only minor, but all playing a definite part in the evolution of the organization.

"Merit versus geography" :[a] *geographical distribution*

At the second session of the General Assembly, in 1947, Colombia

(a) Cf. H. G. Nicholas, *The United Nations as a Political Institution* (London, Oxford University Press, 1959, chapter 7, pp. 146 ff.).

proposed as a criterion for the geographical distribution provided for in Article 101, paragraph 3, of the Charter, the financial contributions made by each Member State to the budget of the organization, the minimum basic quota being from one to three officials per State. In spite of the support of the Latin American, African and Asian countries—that is to say those who complained most often that the Secretariat did not include a sufficient number of their nationals— this proposal was rejected by a majority, the countries of western Europe, the British Commonwealth, the United States of America and eastern Europe all voting against (20 votes to 19 with 7 abstentions).[a] Despite this result, the first Secretary-General, in seeking a basis of allotment, soon arrived at the conclusion that although any rigid mathematical formula would have grave drawbacks, there was no alternative to basing geographical distribution on the budgetary contributions of the States Members. Nevertheless, to allow greater elasticity, resolution 153 (II) of the General Assembly permitted a margin of twenty-five per cent above or below the national quotas on the understanding that this margin should not apply to States whose budgetary contribution exceeded ten per cent of the total (in practice the U.S.S.R. and the U.S.A.). Countries whose nationals in the Secretariat were within the limits of this margin ("desirable range") would not be regarded as "over-represented." Those having four nationals among the staff would also not be so regarded, whatever their budgetary contribution. It was also stated in staff rule 104.5 that the rule of geographical distribution contained in Article 101, paragraph 3, of the Charter and reproduced in staff regulation 4.2, did not apply to the greater part of the posts in the General Service category[b] or at similar salary levels.[1] This provision also applied to language staff regardless of grade.

This formula had many drawbacks. It was too rigid in spite of the exceptions indicated. Budgetary contributions were partly calculated on the basis of income per head of the population, and this gave underdeveloped countries a relatively small representation. The fact that budgetary contributions were based on the national income was also criticized by a number of States.

In view of the difficulties in the initial recruitment of the Secretariat, it was inevitable, as we have said, that nationals of the United States, Canada and the western European countries should represent about eighty per cent of the international staff (i.e., staff other than General Service). United States citizens alone constituted over fifty per cent of the staff. According to the statistics for 1947, 390

(a) General Assembly, second session, Fifth Committee, 82nd meeting, of 30 October 1947 (pp. 291/292) and 91st meeting, of 7 November 1947 (p. 372).
(b) Officials in the highest grade of this category (G. 5) at the U.N. were regarded under rule 104.5 as subject to geographical distribution.

officials of this category were nationals of two North American countries (the United States and Canada); 295 were nationals of western European countries, 72 came from eastern Europe, 41 from Asia (including 32 Chinese), 7 from the Middle East, etc. In 1951, out of 1,054 secretariat officials recruited internationally, 343 were United States citizens. If we add 1,233 United States citizens among the staff not subject to geographical distribution (totalling 2,288), it will be seen that the total number of U.S. citizens in the Secretariat was 1,576 out of 3,324. At the same time, among the officials of the Secretariat recruited internationally, there were 123 British, 74 French, 54 Chinese, 50 Canadians, 33 Indians, 23 Australians, Dutchmen and Poles, 14 Soviet nationals, etc.[a] Thus the disequilibrium continued in spite of the Secretary-General's persistent efforts to improve the situation and to give each country a fair share of the posts.

The process of improving the geographical distribution was retarded by several factors. In the first place, in virtue of well-established and respected principles, it was not possible simply to terminate an appointment in order to create a vacancy and thus reduce the disequilibrium. Secondly, the increase in the number of Member States was continually creating a fresh disequilibrium as fast as efforts were made to remedy the situation. Lastly the Secretary-General's instructions forbidding in principle the appointment of nationals of countries "over-represented" in the Secretariat[b] could not always be obeyed, owing to the difficulty of finding suitable candidates for vacant posts among the nationals of the under-represented countries. In addition, it was impossible in certain countries to look for candidates without going through governmental channels; the influence of such a government was therefore in practice decisive; it alone could announce vacancies (to be filled by its own nationals or by others); could choose the moment to claim such posts; could indicate which candidates were *personae gratae* in its own eyes and which were not. The recruiters were practically helpless, however much they wished to respect the principles of the Charter.

For all these reasons, *geography*—that is to say the various factors depending on the culture or nationality of a candidate—was likely to be diametrically opposed to *merit*—that is to say to the highest standards of efficiency, competence and integrity. Thus there was a constant conflict between the efforts to give the Secretary-General latitude in the application of the geographical principle and the incessant pressure, collective if not individual, of governments continually demanding observance of their "right" to a fair share of posts in the Secretariat. This pressure, dangerous in itself, was even more

(a) Cf. "Nationality Report" (doc. UN/AFS/60/010, of 1 March 1951).
(b) Secretary-General's instructions SGB/77, April 1948, Report of the Secretary-General dated 2 September 1948, doc. A/562.

so when it consisted, not in *counting* the number of posts "due", but in *weighing* their importance, and when it was applied not to the total number of posts in the Secretariat, but to certain particular departments, with a claim to a given quota of posts in those departments. When, at each session of the General Assembly, the debate on geographical distribution was reopened, critics went so far as to speak of the "sequels of the colonialist régime" and of the "remnants of the spoils system" which they saw in the recruiting methods of the Secretariat.

In order to escape from this vicious circle, recourse was had to the International Civil Service Advisory Board set up by General Assembly resolution 13(I) of 13 February 1946. This was a board appointed to advise the Secretary-General "on the methods of recruitment for the Secretariat and on the means by which common standards of recruitment in the Secretariat and the specialized agencies may be ensured".[2] This board, after discussions in 1949 and 1950, submitted in March 1950 an exhaustive report "on recruitment methods and standards for the United Nations and the specialized agencies".[a] This report confirmed the main contentions of the Preparatory Commission and added remarks on the methods to be followed:

> "Without variation, the charter or basic constitutional provisions of each international organization prescribes two basic criteria in the selection of staff. The first is efficiency, competence and integrity, which is either expressly or by clear inference considered paramount, and the second is wide geographical distribution of the staff. It is of the utmost importance that appointments to the staffs of the respective organizations be made solely according to these criteria and without regard to personal or political pressures.[b]
>
> "The Board notes with satisfaction that the constitutional basis for the independent selection of staff by the Secretary-General and Executive Heads of the specialized agencies has been well established. It attaches the greatest importance to this principle and is convinced that an international secretariat of the desired high standards can be achieved only if this principle is maintained in practice as well as in theory. Political or personal pressure for the appointment of individuals must be avoided. The extension of competitive examinations and the establishment of formalized appointments machinery... can go a long way towards strengthening the hand of the Executive Head in this field. The Board wishes to point out that governmental officials and delegations, in particular, have a high responsibility in supporting the Executive Head in his independent application of the basic criteria to the selection of his staff."[c]

While emphasizing the great difficulties to be overcome in achieving a reasonable balance between the criteria of competence and geographical distribution, particularly at the U.N. owing to the "general political character" of the Organization, the Board considered that such a balance was attainable, subject to certain conditions.[3] These

(a) Report Co-ord(CIVIL SERVICE/2/Rev. 1 (op. cit.).
(b) *Ibidem*, par. 8 (p. 7).
(c) *Ibidem*, par. 9 (pp. 7/8).

conditions included the limitation of geographical distribution to professional and administrative posts and to the top level of posts in the General Service category; the application of the regional rather than the national criterion in some cases; the calculation of the number of posts subject to geographical distribution in relation to the Secretariat as a whole, and not to its individual deparments; the inadvisability of attempting either a balanced geographical distribution in every grade and at every salary level or a purely numerical approach. At the same time the Board accepted as a subsidiary measure the seconding or loan of national officials on a temporary basis, provided that the percentage of persons recruited in this way was not large enough to detract from the international character of the service and the career principle.[4] In furtherance of this principle, the Board recommended recruitment at the junior level and the introduction of a programme of in-service training—two points contributing to a better balance from the point of view of geographical distribution. Mathematical rigidity was condemned outright:

"No strict quota should be adopted or recognized. The Board is aware that various bases for a quota system have been advenced, but it has the firm conviction that the fixing of any rigid quota for geographical distribution would be extremely harmful to an international secretariat,"[a]

and it was recommended that undue haste should be avoided:

"Every effort should be made immediately following the creation of an international organization to maintain a proper balance between competence and geography as the staff is recruited. If, from whatever reason, the balance of geographical distribution is poor, it must be recognized that the process of correcting this state of affairs must be gradual if the efficiency of the organization is not to be seriously damaged. Otherwise competence will be sacrificed for the sake of geography...."[b]

At the same time, as from 1 January 1951 at the U.N., and later in the specialized agencies, the system of nineteen grades (which had been in existence since 1946 and which was similar to the system used by the Bureau of the Budget at Washington, was replaced by a system comprising four categories "... a signal triumph for the protagonists of the League tradition in the classification of positions...".[5][c] In this way it was hoped to give international officials a salary scale capable of attracting the best candidates from all over the world. Resolution 470 (V) of the General Assembly, dated 15 December 1950, which set up the general system of salaries and allowances, was based on the work of a committee of experts appointed by the Administrative Committee on Co-ordination;[6] this committee of

(a) *Ibidem*, par. 10 (i), (p. 11).
(b) *Ibidem*, par. 10 (a), (p. 8).
(c) "The U.N. Secretariat" (*U.N. Studies 4*, New York, Carnegie Endowment, 1950, p. 75).

experts noted in its report[a] that definite security of employment, adequate remuneration and retirement pensions were essential conditons for the recruitment and retention of a high-quality staff.

In fact, despite repeated reaffirmations of basic principles, despite a variety of efforts to achieve a satisfactory balance and despite a slow and partial improvement, the effects of which were not felt until later, the situation remained confused and the dissatisfaction of the countries under-represented on the Secretariat was expressed with growing force. The complicated problem of geographical distribution, no longer a purely *administrative* one, was becoming more and more *political* and remained a major preoccupation.

Permanent versus temporary: the career problem

It will readily be understood that initially, the staff was only appointed on a temporary basis. Nevertheless, as the Preparatory Commission had suggested, the problem of a real career in the Secretariat was soon raised. In 1948 twenty-four per cent of appointments were already permanent (of indeterminate duration), and this percentage rose to twenty-five per cent in 1949 and 34.15 per cent in 1951.[7] This was in keeping with the stand taken on this point by the Civil Service Advisory Board in 1950[b] and by the Committee of Experts on staff salaries, allowances and leave.[c] Both committees agreed that, as the Organization became stabilized, the members of the staff who had undergone a successful probationary period should not (with few exceptions) remain on a temporary basis for more than four or five years. Furthermore the Joint Selection Committee (Walters Committee) set up in 1951 by the Secretary-General to clear up the position of the Secretariat from the point of view of careers,[8] recommended an increase in the number of permanent appointments to 70-75% of the total. The proportion of seventy per cent was reached in 1952.[d] At that date there were 884 permanent appointments in the professional category and 897 in the General Service category.

This reform, which partly offset the effects of the early large-scale recruitment, was aimed at stability of employment, in order both to give a feeling of security to the staff and to safeguard the independence of the international civil service. It was well understood that provisional appointments detracted from the independence of the staff. Obviously, a temporary official—whether he is seconded for a time from his national civil service or simply expects to return shortly to his own

(a) Doc. A/C. 5/331 and Add. 1-3, dated 31 October 1949.
(b) Report, Co-ord/CIVIL SERVICE/2/Rev.1, (op. cit., par. 55, p. 34).
(c) Doc. A/C.5/331 (op. cit.).
(d) Cf. doc. A/C.5/SR. 332 (statement by the Secretary-General on 23 January 1953 to the Fifth Committee concerning the data at the end of 1952). Cf. also doc. A/2364 (para. 36) and A/2141 (p. 178).

country—has a feeling of dependence which is contrary to the intentions of the founders of the Organization. The gradual "professionalization" of the staff, which was to find its legal expression in the staff rules and regulations, thus became the foundation of administrative policy. Nevertheless, for practical reasons, the system of temporary appointments was kept for some of the posts: posts of higher direction (in which a system of rotation was desirable), posts of specialists who would not have been ready to stay all their lives at the Secretariat and posts which were temporary owing to the nature of the work. These two methods of appointment, as well as the rule[9] that permanent appointments should be reviewed every five years, nevertheless allowed for the continual introduction of fresh blood into the Secretariat, preventing the staff from getting into a rut and combating bureaucratic tendencies, which were encouraged by a certain psychological isolation of the headquarters staff. While temporary appointments were retained only for a few posts, and the career element was emphasized, an attempt was made to find a compromise. As at the time of the League, "the Gordian knot cannot be cut: any simple solution is just a plain evasion of the real problem."[a] Be that as it may, the hybrid, or even irregular, situation[b] which characterized the Secretariat at the outset had been left far behind. In the clear interests of the service, an end had been put to the former method of "juggling" with appointments, making them temporary or permanent according to fluctuating criteria or even according to no criterion at all.

At the same time, the jurisprudence of the new Administrative Tribunal of the United Nations continually worked to strengthen the security of employment and to prevent arbitrary measures being taken to abolish posts or to reduce staff on the pretext of reorganization, in order that the experience acquired by an official might not be wasted as a result of his premature departure. The contractual element in the legal situation of international civil servants was reduced, and the statutory element increased.[c] The Tribunal always asked the Secretariat to make a serious effort to find a new post for any official legitimately dismissed, if his services had been satisfactory.[d] Even when the statutory provisions in force[e] gave the Secretary-General discretionary power to judge the interests of the Organization, the Tribunal objected to this power's being abused.[f] As to temporary

(a) Sir Arthur (later Lord) Salter, "The International Character of the League Secretariat" (*The United States of Europe*, London, 1930, p. 135).
(b) G. Palthey, "La fonction publique internationale", in *La Revue administrative* (Paris, No. 6, 1948, p. 17).
(c) Cf. above, chapter 4, p. 103, note (40).
(d) Judgment No. 4 of 25 August 1951 (cases 17 to 21: *Howrani* and four others).
(e) Staff regulation 9.1 (*c*) and resolution 590 (VI) of the General Assembly dated 2 February 1952.
(f) Judgment No. 18, of 21 August 1953 (case No. 26, *Miss Crawford*).

fixed-term appointments, the Tribunal took the line that the automatic termination of such appointments should not be taken for granted. In the first place, according to its jurisprudence, no prejudice, rational or otherwise, could in itself legally justify a dismissal of this kind, even after the expiration of a fixed-term appointment. In the second place, the question must be considered in each case whether the appointment really was for a fixed term, and not in fact a permanent appointment in the guise of a temporary appointment. Thus the Administrative Tribunal's jurisprudence and, subsequently, the Secretariat's administrative policy were opposed to the previous practice of making appointments which were temporary in form, but which, as a result of constant renewals, became "quasi-permanent". The tendency at the time was in fact to emphasize security of tenure at all levels. But as a result of the admission of many new States to the U.N., the geographical distribution rule soon brought the question of temporary appointments into prominence again and made it necessary to increase their number and range.

International recruitment and local recruitment

The problem of the limitation of "international recruitment" to the higher directorial and professional grades (except in the language services) had already risen at the League; it is closely related to that of geographical distribution, and illustrates the difference between international and local recruitment. For financial reasons—i.e., savings on travelling expenses, allowances, home leave, etc—local recruitment had been adopted for the great majority of the General Service staff[a] and for all manual workers. Consequently, office workers in the broadest sense (typists, stenographers, secretaries, accountants, etc.) were as a rule recruited locally regardless of nationality.

This dual recruitment, however, has several disadvantages. In the first place it may lead to misunderstandings, since, drawing superficial conclusions from the two types of recruitment, it may be thought that the "exclusively international character" of the staff referred to in Article 100, paragraph 2, of the Charter does not apply, or applies less, to locally recruited staff. But, as we have seen, this would be entirely erroneous. Whatever the method of recruitment, *all* staff without exception must have the benefit of the constitutional provisions; certain officials, owing to their particular work, need it more than others, but all, even the most humble, are by definition covered by these provisions.[10]

Furthermore it is liable to create an undesirable psychological rift between two groups of staff members. Locally recruited officials arc not entitled to some of the allowances and advantages enjoyed

(a) Cf. above, chapter 8, p. 186, note (b).

by the other group.[a] They do not receive the same immunities and privileges.[b] In several respects they are subject to the laws of the country in which they work.[c] Their salaries are based on local practice and on the best local rate. Thus there are difficulties of comparison and calculation,[d] and a risk of infringing the principle of equal pay for equal work.[e] A large proportion of the staff remains under the influence of the host State and carries on its work in a particular "climate" which may in some circumstances be prejudicial to the international atmosphere.

Lastly, it is often impossible to find competent candidates on the local labour market, particularly when several international organizations are located in the same city and when there is no common recruitment policy, or when the pay offered to this category of staff is not sufficiently attractive. "Semi-local" recruitment is then used,[f] candidates being sought outside and given a living allowance or other material advantages.[g] This type of recruitment may constitute a reasonable compromise and narrow the gap between the two categories of staff, but it certainly complicates the system of local salaries.

The double recruitment system has other advantages. It would be unnecessary, difficult and expensive to set in motion the ponderous machinery of international recruitment to select manual workers and office staff. The League's experience showed in fact that the international recruitment of young candidates for posts at the junior level created many special problems and complicated staff management.[h] Nor should it be forgotten that local recruitment does not determine the nationality of candidates, since in the large cosmopolitan cities locally recruited staff is multinational.[i] Moreover, the regulations do not preclude staff in this category from becoming members of the international staff in due course. The fact that most of the locally recruited staff are better acquainted with the geography, customs and language of the host country is also an undoubted advantage. Further, experience has shown that, while locally recruited staff enjoy fewer administrative and financial advantages than international staff, they are not considered and treated *in principle* as having a less "international" status: for instance, they enjoy tax exemption. Indeed, many kinds of manual work are done more efficiently and

(a) Staff rules 104.6 and 104.7.
(b) Cf. above, chapter 4, p. 79, and chapters 7, 8.
(c) Cf. C. W. Jenks, *The Proper Law* ... (op. cit., pp. 25 ff.)
(d) Cf. for example T. C. Young (op. cit., pp. 136 ff.).
(e) Cf. for example doc. A/C.5/331/Add. 1, appendix II (par. 25: statement by the Staff Association of the United Nations).
(f) Cf. Doc. A/C.5/331.
(g) *Ibidem.*
(h) Doc. Co-ord/CIVIL SERVICE/2/Rev. 1, (par. 13).
(i) Cf. B. Akzin (op. cit., p. 95).

cheaply by local staff. Persons recruited in these two different ways usually work together without friction, provided that the organizations scrupulously observe the rule that locally recruited staff is to be paid at the *best* local rates and that the pay is periodically reviewed. Nevertheless, at the higher levels of the General Service category the distinction becomes difficult to maintain, especially when special qualifications (linguistic for example) are required. International recruitment is then resorted to, and the system seems sufficiently elastic to obviate excessive injustice.

Experience has proved here again the importance of finding a middle way between administrative necessities and the principles of the Charter, so as to avoid establishing two watertight categories of staff, and so that the absorption of local elements should not detract from the "exclusively international character" of the Secretariat.

Structure and activity: stability and development

The practical difficulties of the early days, which increased as the "cold war" developed did not prevent the gradual establishment, stabilization and development of the administrative machinery of the United Nations family. A network of organs covering the whole world was created during the first few years; the U.N. Secretariat, without losing its unity, became a veritable *centre of operations*, an unprecedented development which surpassed all expectations:

> "It is not generally realized that the Secretariat of the U.N. is the greatest institute of social research in the world. A glance at the six catalogues of economic and social projects containing lists of 1663 projects of the U.N. Secretariat (together with 1910 additional projects of the specialized agencies) reveals a scope and extent of research work unparalleled in this field."[a] [b]

Moreover, the Secretariat's work evolved beyond the "laboratory" stage (whether diplomatic or technical) and ceased to be of a "departmental" type, as had been the work of the League. It increasingly took the form of operational missions, of "field" activities, implying contacts on the spot, links of a new type with national administrations[11] and methods of action proper to "direct administration." Examples are the enormous work of technical assistance to under-developed countries (Expanded Programme, inaugurated in 1950), aid to refugees (at first provided by the I.R.O. and then by the Office of the High Commissioner for Refugees at Geneva), the realization of a series of programmes—more or less concerted—in the economic and social spheres, health protection, education, child welfare, etc. The in-

(a) J. Robinson, "Strengthening the Secretariat", *Annals* (vol. 296, 1954, p. 137).
(b) These figures relate only to the period 1946-1954 (cf. doc. E/2398 of 13 May 1954, para. 27).

fluence of this type of international action on structure and methods was soon felt:

> "The most significant thing about the U.N.'s short history has been the growth of its executive operations. It is now a family of eleven agencies with 55,000 people at work as of this year. These agencies last year spent about $551 million. That is big business. The U.N. is not just the conference machinery with which we were familiar in the League of Nations, but something different, something new on the face of the earth.... The economic and social programmes of the U.N. and its specialized agencies now engage nearly 90% of all the people working on U.N. programmes...."[a]

As to structural changes, we note first of all the separation between the U.N. proper and the other members of the "family"—namely, eleven specialized agencies and one agency placed "under the auspices of the United Nations" (the I.A.E.A.). This separation was in conformity with the provisions of the Charter (Article 17, paragraph 3; Article 57; Article 63, paragraph 2; Article 64). Some of these specialized agencies dated from the days of the "unions" (Universal Postal Union, International Telecommunication Union); others from the time of the League, such as the I.L.O. and those which grew from embryonic organizations existing at that time. Thus UNESCO is the much expanded successor of the former International Institute of Intellectual Co-operation in Paris and of the International Committee on Intellectual Co-operation of the League; the World Meteorological Organization had previously been in existence in a more modest form at Lausanne; the World Health Organization has grown out of the Health Organization of the League created in 1923—Health Committee, Advisory Council appointed by the Permanent Committee of the Office international d'Hygiène publique in Paris, Health Section of the League Secretariat. The Food and Agriculture Organization carries on the work of the former International Institute of Agriculture at Rome, while the International Civil Aviation Organization is the successor of the former International Air Navigation Commission which had been in existence in Paris since 1919 under the auspices of the League, in both cases on a much larger scale. Certain institutions were new creations (International Bank for Reconstruction and Development, International Monetary Fund, Intergovernmental Maritime Consultative Organization). There is already the nucleus of an International Trade Organization—namely, the General Agreement on Tariffs and Trade (GATT), which dates from 1948. Lastly, the International Atomic Energy Agency, created in 1956, has a special position in the "family," its autonomy being even greater than that of the specialized agencies. The autonomy of each of these organizations is sometimes very jealously guarded by its

(a) H. Cleveland, "The Future Role of the United States in the United Nations", in *Annals* (vol. 342, 1962, pp. 70 and 71).

secretariat, not only vis-à-vis the U.N., but also vis-à-vis the other specialized agencies. This autonomy is indeed strongly encouraged by the national Ministries (public health, labour, etc.) responsible for relations with the organization concerned, each of which has its own "foreign policy". This policy has advantages from the point of view of practical achievement despite administrative drawbacks.

This horizontal separation was needed in order to spare the already overworked central organization from being overwhelmed by diverse demands, at the same time observing the principles of the Bruce Report of 1939. The multiplicity of tasks arising out of the political aims of the States Members tended to impose an unbroken succession of varied activities on the Secretariat. But its inevitably limited administrative resources seriously restricted its freedom of manoeuvre and created grave and growing difficulties. Resolution 310 (IV) of the General Assembly invited States Members "to refrain from initiating new projects other than those which are urgently required and which can be effectively carried out"; and it recalled the Economic and Social Council's recommendation concerning the need to concentrate manpower and resources. The Secretary-General therefore had to make an effort to review priorities, to adjust the resolutions of the representative organs to practical possibilities and to take into account repeated requests for economy in spite of the continual increase of day-to-day work.

Nevertheless a serious problem of co-ordination was raised by the parallel existence of several organizations, differing in their composition and attached to the U.N. by bilateral agreements concluded with the Economic and Social Council. Programmes and aims had to be brought into line and duplication eliminated within the United Nations family; co-operation must be as close as possible in spite of rivalry and of varying traditions.

> "This time we are not beginning with the world organization as a whole, but we are following a more practical method, setting up special organs for special purposes in a whole series of operations...."
> "But the present method of creating special organs for international action as they are needed, wise and necessary as it is, will eventually call for a coordinating centre in the field of politics...[a] central body, in which the various international activities would be represented and weighed against each other.."[a]

Thus, the need for co-ordination led to agreements in keeping with Article 63, paragraph 1 of the Charter.[12] The objects of the agreements were representation, action as regards placing certain subjects on the agenda of representative bodies, recommendations by the U.N., exchange of information and documents, organization of common services, assistance, relations with the International Court of Justice and other measures necessary for effective co-ordination. As regards,

(a) J. T. Shotwell, *The Great Decision* (New York, 1944, pp. 200 and 201).

for example, "arrangements concerning staff," we should note the provisions which recognize "that the eventual development of a single unified international civil serve is desirable from the standpoint of effective administrative coordination..."[a] and those providing for the "widest possible co-operation" in order

"to the fullest extent possible
"(a) To consult together concerning the establishment of an International Civil Service Commission to advise on the means by which common standards of recruitment in the secretariats of the U.N. and the specialized agencies may be ensured;
"(b) To consult together concerning other matters relating to the employment of their officers and staff, including conditions of service, duration of appointments, classification, salary scales and allowances, retirement and pension rights and staff regulations and rules, with a view to securing as much uniformity in these matters as shall be found practicable;..."[b]

In the same connection, apart from the co-ordinating work of the Economic and Social Council and its own permanent Co-ordination Committee (Article 63, paragraph 2, of the Charter), an Administrative Committee on Co-ordination was set up by the Economic and Social Council consisting of the heads of all the secretariats of the United Nations family, under the chairmanship of the Secretary-General of the United Nations, "the nearest approach to an international cabinet that exists."[c] It is a consultative body which reports to the Economic and Social Council, but whose decisions, if unanimous, are in practice binding on the administrations. The new tasks to be accomplished, and their many repercussions—which are usually dealt with on an *ad hoc* basis—make co-ordination continually more complex and difficult, although progress has undeniably been made. Nevertheless a real central organ of permanent co-ordination and standardization, as recommended in the agreements concluded between the various agencies, has not yet been set up.

We should also notice a compromise between the "organic" theory adopted in principle and the "functional" theory, sometimes going as far as the creation of subsidiary organs (Article 7, paragraph 2, of the Charter) within the U.N. itself. Under the pressure of international relations, such organs have had to be added, often for temporary reasons, to the initial structure, and some have been subordinated to the Secretariat. Thus the United Nations Children's Fund was made a part of the Secretariat when it became permanent.[13] The Office of the United Nations High Commissioner for Refugees, the United Nations Korean Reconstruction Agency and the United Nations Relief and Works Agency for Palestine Refugees in the

(a) Cf., for example, Agreement between the United Nations and I.C.A.O. of 13 May 1947 (U.N. publ., New York, 1947) (article XII, paragraph 1: p. 12).
(b) *Ibidem* (article XII, paragraph 2, p. 13).
(c) A. Loveday (op. cit., p. 274).

Near East are examples of these subsidiary organs. The Secretariat of the Military Staff Committee was the outcome of Articles 47 and 101, paragraph 2, of the Charter.[14]

The operational activities of all the members of the United Nations family became so multifarious that offices were set up "in the field," geographically detached from headquarters, but vertically subordinated to it ("advanced echelons"). This "outposting" is often described as decentralization by writers on the subject. This process must be distinguished from the establishment of "external departments" away from headquarters (thus the Narcotics Division of the Secretariat has been at Geneva since 1955);[a] from the grouping of several services away from headquarters into a single administrative unit (European Office of the United Nations); from the detachment of certain headquarters officials on prolonged missions in the field, etc. This "regionalization" of services is in fact an important phenomenon, manifested in many ways: for example, the four regional Economic Commissions, which have their respective secretariats at Geneva (for Europe), Bangkok (for Asia and the Far East), Santiago (for Latin America), and Addis Ababa (for Africa). In this case, organization by clearly defined geographical regions has been the main object. It is a tendency whose importance must not be underestimated. Its object is to simplify such work as liaison and direct public information work (cf. the regional information centres of the United Nations), public relations with adjacent States, and economic and social integration in a particular region in order to plan and promote work in that region.[b] The decentralized implementation of programmes for different countries is also considered to be more efficient and more economical.

The same reasons have led to the regionalization of the services of other members of the United Nations family. The most important cases are those of the *World Health Organization* (with its regional offices at Brazzaville for Africa, at Washington for the American continent,[c] at Alexandria for the eastern Mediterranean, at Copenhagen for Europe, at New Delhi for South-east Asia, and at Manila for the western Pacific); the *Food and Agriculture Organization* (regional offices at Bangkok for Asia and the Far East, at Santiago for Latin America, at Cairo for the Near East and at Washingon for North America); *UNESCO* (regional office for the western hemisphere at Havana, scientific co-operation stations at Montevideo for Latin America, Cairo for the Near East, New Delhi for southern Asia, Djakarta for

(a) Cf. doc. A/3137 (p. 65).
(b) Cf. W. A. Sharp, *Field Administration*... (op. cit., pp. 45-46).
(c) Pan American Sanitary Organization (P.A.S.O.) and particularly its Secretariat (Pan American Sanitary Bureau) which, in virtue of the agreement with W.H.O. of 24 May 1949, acts as the latter's regional office.

South-east Asia, etc.). Some of these regional offices are further divided into "subregional offices". The services detached from I.L.O. headquarters between the two wars (transformed in 1950 into general offices for the planning, negotiation and implementation of technical assistance projects) no doubt served as models to some extent.

Further, "regional arrangements" for the maintenance of international peace and security on a regional basis, as provided for in Chapter VIII of the Charter, form an integral part of the United Nations system[15] and have an influence on administration.

To sum up, both centripetal and centrifugal tendencies are at work, and this makes continuous co-ordination all the more necessary. The large number and wide dispersion of parallel activities means a constant danger of separatism, at least psychologically: "Elaborate regional organizations may tend to develop into semi-independent kingdoms and strengthen, if not create, pressure groups at Assembly meetings."[a] This danger in turn leads to attempts to reinforce the central organs.

Two further compromises have helped to build up stability.

First, concessions were made to the idea of group direction, although the principle of unity of command and hierarchical subordination was strictly applied in the Secretariat in accordance with the Charter and the Preparatory Commission's recommendations. Thus Trygve Lie carried on the League tradition of organizing periodical meetings of the principal officers of the Secretariat and treating them as a sort of advisory body which should be asked for its opinions on various questions, not only on the problems affecting the countries to which each of its members belonged. There thus arose a sort of "cabinet" consisting of Assistant Secretaries-General and later of their immediate subordinates. The Secretary-General tried in this way to reconcile two ideas: first, that collective direction should be excluded from an administrative and non-governmental structure, and secondly, that exchanges of views were necessary and teamwork an advantage. The result was not collective direction, but a strictly advisory body. But, for various reasons, this system did not work well either at the League or at the U.N. On the other hand, the Advisory Committee on Administrative and Budgetary Questions, an auxiliary body of the General Assembly presided over without interruption since 1946 by Thanassis Aghnides, former Under-Secretary-General of the League, played an important role and exercised a notable influence on the international civil service. This Committee is the direct successor of the Supervisory Commission of the League which was presided over before and during the Second World War by Carl Joachim Hambro, President of the Norwegian Parliament at that time. Further

(a) A. Loveday (op. cit., p. 246).

examples are the International Civil Service Advisory Board referred to above and the system of joint accountancy control of the United Nations.

The second compromise was between the stabilization of the international civil service accompanied by the reinforcement of hierarchical authority in the Secretariat and the giving of an opportunity to the Staff Association to co-operate closely in the management of staff affairs. In the light of experience, the problem of adapting the organization of the Secretariat to practical requirements was the subject of constant discussions in the Fifth Committee of the General Assembly and in the Advisory Committee on Administrative and Budgetary Questions. The Staff Regulations which replaced the original provisional texts were adopted by resolution 590 (VI), of 2 February 1952, by the General Assembly and came into force on 1 March 1952. They expand the provisions of the Charter which concern the independence, discretion, privileges and immunities, recruitment and role of the staff. For instance:

> "Members of the Secretariat are international civil servants. Their responsibilities are not national but exclusively international. By accepting appointment, they pledge themselves to discharge their functions and to regulate their conduct with the interests of the United Nations only in view" (regulation 1.1.). "Staff members are subject to the authority of the Secretary-General and to assignment by him to any of the activities or offices of the United Nations. They are responsible to him in the exercise of their functions. The whole time of staff members shall be at the disposal of the Secretary-General. The Secretary-General shall establish a normal working week" (regulation 1.2). "In the performance of their duties members of the Secretariat shall neither seek nor accept instructions from any government or from any other authority external to the Organization" (regulation 1.3).
>
> "Members of the Secretariat shall conduct themselves at all times in a manner befitting their status as international civil servants. They shall not engage in any activity that is incompatible with the proper discharge of their duties with the United Nations. They shall avoid any action and in particular any kind of public pronouncement which may adversely reflect on their status, or on the integrity, independence and impartiality which are required by that status. While they are not expected to give up their national sentiments or their political and religious convictions, they shall at all times bear in mind the reserve and tact incumbent upon them by reason of their international status" (regulation 1.4). [16] [17]

In order to ensure the better observance of these obligations, and despite the hierarchical subordination prescribed in regulation 1.2, not only are the rights of association of the staff recognized and protected in the international civil service, but at the U.N. all officials of the Secretariat are also automatically members of the Staff Association at headquarters.[18] [a] The Staff Council, elected every year, deals with numerous questions concerning the welfare and administration

(a) Cf. Article 4, paragraph 1, of the statutes of the Staff Association, adopted on 26 April 1950 and amended in 1952 and 1953.

of the staff, which are defined in staff regulations 8.1 and 8.2 and staff rules 108.1 and 108.2. Thus, as a consultative and representative organ, the Staff Council may submit to the Secretary-General any proposal for improving the position of the officials and is consulted on principles governing appointments, promotion, salaries and dismissals, etc. Moreover, a joint administrative body established by the Secretary-General advises him on personnel matters and general questions of staff welfare and submits to him proposals for the amendment of the Staff Regulations and Rules. *Ad hoc* advisory committees are set up whenever necessary, to give advice on individual questions. In practice, the elected representatives of the staff have played a very important part in safeguarding the careers of officials, and especially their promotion. A similar situation exists in the specialized agencies, and since 1952 there has been a Federation of International Civil Servants' Associations for the whole United Nations family. Steps have thus been taken to remove a handicap of the international staff as compared with national officials, who can appeal in defence of their interests to public opinion, parliament or the government. "This power of each citizen in his own country is a small matter in itself but it is multiplied by the right of association and by the existence of electoral groups, of numerous identical professional interests whose political influence may be considerable... the interests of officials being represented even in parliament, to say nothing of the numerous methods by which they can influence opinion."[a] The international official is less well armed from the legal point of view and has practically no means of political action. Thus the application to his case of articles 20, paragraph 1, and 23, paragraph 4, of the Universal Declaration of Human Rights of 10 December 1948, guaranteeing the rights of association and the right to join trade unions for the defence of common interests, is of particular importance.

The Secretary-General's dual role

The search for compromise can also be seen as concerns the Secretary-General's own activities. As we have seen, the Charter and the interpretation given to it by the Preparatory Commission calls upon him to exercise two kinds of function; firstly, the administrative direction of the Secretariat—a heavy burden—which may even involve military operations, as was the case in the Gaza Strip, Korea, Lebanon, Egypt, the Congo and more recently New Guinea; and secondly, political action as a result of the strategic position at the centre of world affairs assigned to him by the Charter. Already shouldering a

(a) P. Strohl, "Représentation et défense des intérêts professionnels des fonctionnaires internationaux" in *Journal du Droit international*, Clunet (No. 2-84, 1957, p. 352).

crushing administrative load, he is at the same time often expected to play the difficult part of negotiator, mediator and political trouble shooter. His duties vary from that of a "secretary" to that of a "general";[a] but "where are his troops?" asks Trygve Lie.[b]

In order to give meaning to this section of the Charter, a practical compromise had to be worked out between the "international leadership" of the Secretary-General—promoter, inspirer, living expression of international co-operation, continuous symbol of the international outlook—and his conduct of administrative affairs. To what extent should the Secretary-General appear *pro foro externo* as the informer and creator of world opinion as advocated by Trygve Lie?

> "The Secretary-General, who more than anyone else symbolizes the organization as a whole..., should not merely service U.N. meetings, but should seek to influence the course of the debates..., emerge as a bold leader of international thought and action, as a genuinely international figure stimulating the Member States to rise above their international dispositions...."[c]

But at the same time it was not possible to ignore those States Members which, despite the Charter, opposed for various reasons any political activity on the part of the Secretary-General, and tried not only to confine him to administrative work, but also to prescribe in detail the administrative methods which he was to use.

The first Secretary-General, however, often acted in a political capacity, placing himself in the centre of several important diplomatic negotiations—for example, during the tension between Iran and the Soviet Union with regard to Azerbaïjan, the Berlin blockade in 1948-1949, the partition of Palestine, the Greek question, the problems of Kashmir, Trieste and Korea. He did not hesitate to take a stand on international controversies; to intervene spontaneously and actively in plenary meetings of the General Assembly and of the Committees; or even to take the initiative in spectacular fashion. An example is his twenty-year peace programme, launched in 1950, which was to give the United Nations an essential role as "a bridge across the chasm."[d] He expressed general views on the problems of the Organization both in his annual reports and in a number of public statements. He visited the capitals of the great Powers specifically to plead for his proposals. He was therefore obliged to take a stand as regards the interpretation of the Charter. In his view, his position and that of the staff of the Secretariat was that of an "advanced post" with exclusively

(a) S. M. Schwebel (op. cit., title of chapter 9).
(b) Trygve Lie (op. cit., p. 48).
(c) *Ibidem* (pp. 40-41).
(d) *Ibidem* (p. 275). Cf. Trygve Lie's Memorandum "On Points for Consideration in the Development of a 20-Year Program for Achieving Peace Through the U.N." (*Ibidem*, p. 277 ff.).

international responsibilities which inevitably exposed him to criticism.[a] This role has been described as follows:

> "In taking the various political initiatives that he did, Trygve Lie did not violate the Charter in letter or in spirit, nor did he do anything for which he could not have found justification in the discussions which preceded the signing of the Charter or in the expectations that prevailed at that time. It is clear, nevertheless, that his experience demonstrated that the Secretary-General of an organization like the U.N. is subject to certain practical limitations, which prevent him from successfully undertaking the kind of political leadership which we are accustomed to expect from the chief executive of a parliamentary or presidential democracy. For one thing, in dealing with Member governments, the true repositories of governmental authority, he has only powers of persuasion, except as he may be given additional powers by explicit agreement. Second, he represents no independent constituency. Those who elect him are themselves jealous of their powers and apart form their wishes he has no independent source of authority.
> "Finally, unlike Albert Thomas, who was able as the first Director of the I.L.O. to achieve a role of leadership, the Secretary-General cannot depend upon the backing of powerful pressure groups either in U.N. organs or in the Member States who in the last analysis determine the decisions of these organs. It would appear that Trygve Lie, in attempting to provide political leadership, did not always take sufficient care to have the support of those whose approval was necessary to the success of his initiatives. Or perhaps it might be better said that he sought to provide leadership too openly and independently, thus putting governments in the position where they could not follow him without serious loss of face."[b]

And yet the first Secretary-General well realized that, although he deliberately rejected the "minimalist" views advocating the Secretary-General's effacement in accordance with the Drummond tradition, he could not go to the opposite extreme. He was in favour of a middle way, of compromises, of approaching problems in a pragmatical manner with his mind always open to the requirements of international politics. He recognized this himself and adds:

> "I would listen to all my advisers and be directed by none. I had no calculated plan for developing the political powers of the office of Secretary-General, but I was determined that the Secretary-General should be a force for peace. How that force would be applied I would find out—in the light of developments..."[c]

The question has been asked whether "Lie had gone as far as he could or as far as he should."[d] The question remains. Be that as it may, a comparison of his ideas as to the role of the Secretary-General and his activity, not behind the scenes, but in the forefront of the stage, is instructive for all who wish to understand this high office: an office so complex and so perilously balanced that it attracts criticism *a priori*, whatever its holder may do.

(a) *Ibidem* (p. 386 ff.).
(b) L. M. Goodrich, "The United Nations", (op. cit., pp. 139/140).
(c) Trygve Lie, (op. cit., p. 53).
(d) S. M. Schwebel, (op. cit., p. 202).

NOTES

(1) In order to avoid all abuses, the official interpretation of the Staff Regulations is that the candidate's nationality should not work to his advantage if he has only spent a short time in the country of which he is a national. Under rule 104.8 the U.N. does not recognize more than one nationality for each staff member in the applicaton of the Regulations and Rules. For the purposes of these rules an official having several nationalities is regarded as a national of the country with which, in the Secretary-General's opinion, he is most closely associated. Under regulation 4.3 officials are chosen without distinction as to race, sex or religion. As far as possible each post is to be filled by competitive examination.
Stateless persons (in law or in fact) may be appointed only in exceptional cases. (Administrative Manual pp. 183-185.)

(2) At its fourth session, the Administrative Committee on Co-ordination agreed to the establishment of the International Civil Service Advisory Board and defined its terms of reference as regards the provision of advice and information on recruiting methods. The Advisory Board was requested to advise the U.N., the I.L.O., the F.A.O., UNESCO, I.C.A.O., the International Bank and the International Monetary Fund, W.H.O. and the I.R.O. Its chairman at the time was T. Aghnides. Cf. the reports of the I.C.S.A.B.: Co-ord/CIVIL SERVICE/2 (1950), Co-ord/CIVIL SERVICE/4 (1952), Co-ord/CIVIL SERVICE/5 (1954), Co-ord/CIVIL SERVICE/7 (1961), etc.
Cf. also, as regards the widening of the Board's functions: doc. A/C.5/SR. 626 (p. 10), A/3209 (para. 295-303), A/3535 (para. 14), A/3558 (para. 137), A/3681 (para. 19), A/3656 (paras. 32 and 33), A/3681 (paras. 17-19), A/3797 (para. 27).

(3) As regards the role of the Flemming Committee, cf. A. Lethbridge (op. cit., *passim*). Cf. also doc. A/C. 5/331 (1950).

(4) Report of the I.C.S.A.B. on recruitment methods and standards for the United Nations and specialized agencies, March 1950 (op. cit., p. 27): "There is no doubt that for a small percentage of posts in the international organizations, the formal secondment or loan of governmental officials who will not make a career in the international service has many advantages; among others, it will provide good training for members of a national civil service and increase the numbers of such officials who have an intimate knowledge of international organizations, their problems, and the best methods of working with them. The number of such secondments to any international organization should, however, be proportionately small in order to preserve the international character of the service. It is, of course, inevitable that even though it was not foreseen at the outset, a few seconded officials might be employed on a permanent basis after the initial period, and become valuable international civil servants. In the Board's opinion all member governments should make provision for easy arrangements which would preserve re-employment rights, seniority rights, pension and security rights, etc., for its own civil service officials who are seconded to one of the international organizations...." (para. 45)

(5) Before the general reclassification of posts, at the beginning of 1951 in accordance with the proposal of the Committee of Experts (doc. A/C/331) the staff of the Secretariat was divided into some forty classes and nineteen grades, to each of which was assigned a salary varying between fixed limits at a number of steps varying between three and seven (cf. W. R. Crocker, op. cit., pp. 604-605). This system, based on that of the Federal Bureau of the Budget at Washington, took into account the nature of each function and achieved not so much an organization of the staff as an organization of the posts on the basis of a detailed "job description." Over 150 precise job descriptions (cf. Manual of Standard Post Descriptions, U.N. Secretariat, 1947) had been prepared in order to permit of the assignment of competent persons to specific jobs. This "grade system" having appeared compli-

cated and having the drawback, particularly in an international administration, of leading to certain "overclassifications" and of hindering regular promotion, it was replaced by a slightly modified version of the system employed at the League of Nations. Since 1951, the staff has been divided into four categories: directorial staff, professional staff, general services (manual and office staff) and specialists (technical services). This classification is in accordance with the European administrative tradition, and, without setting up impassable barriers between the different categories, allows of greater elasticity of assignments and transfers, while providing a solid foundation for a unified international civil service of high quality and based on the career principle (cf. Doc. A/1313 and A/1378, p. 3).

(6) As regards the history of the classification of international officials since the League, and particularly from Sir Malcolm Ramsay's report (1932) to the U.N.'s discussions (1948, 1950, 1956), cf. above, chapter 8, note (3).

(7) On 1 July 1951, out of a total strength of 3390 officials at the Secretariat of the U.N., 1156 had permanent appointments (34.15%) and 2234 had temporary appointments (65.85%); of the latter, 1902 were of indeterminate duration (56.15%) and 322 fixed term (9.70%).

(8) The Joint Selection Committee presided over by F. P. Walters, former Under-Secretary-General of the League, was replaced in 1953 by two committees, one for professional staff, under the chairmanship of Sir Ramaswami Mudaliar, and the other for general service staff, under the chairmanship of I. Kerno, former official of the League of Nations and former Assistant Secretary-General of the U.N. The work of these three bodies contributed to the conversion of temporary appointments into permanent appointments (cf. the three reports of the Walters Committee and doc. A/2364, annex II; cf. *International Conciliation*, No. 484 (p. 485) and No. 493 (p. 119 ff.).

(9) Since the amendment of staff rule 104.13, which entered into force on 11 November 1957 (doc. ST/SGB/94/Rev. 4/Amend. 10, and ST/ADM/SER. A/437 of 17 October 1957), both permanent and regular appointments (cf. below chapter 10, note (2), have been subject to a single review five years after the date of appointment.

(10) Report of the I.C.S.A.B. on recruitment methods and standards (op. cit., p. 12): "Quite apart from the question of promotional opportunities there is no doubt that a reasonable spread of nationality within the secretarial and higher clerical posts has many advantages. Staff members in these posts can to a considerable degree affect the tone and atmosphere of the Secretariat's work and reliance upon a single nationality for all such staff is extremely questionable...."

The institution of local recruitment, which does not take into account the rule laid down in Article 101, paragraph 3, sentence 2, of the Charter, is based on the provison of Article 101, paragraph 1, to the effect that the staff is appointed by the Secretary-General "under regulations established by the General Assembly." Certain doubts of a purely legal nature may, however, remain: The "regulations established by the General Assembly" should not be contrary to the specific provisions of the Charter, particularly those contained in Article 101, paragraph 3. Moreover, local recruitment is not prescribed by the Staff Regulations voted by the General Assembly, but by the Staff Rules (104.5 and 104.6) established by the Secretary-General in virtue of the Regulations. It therefore constitutes an extraconstitutional arrangement dictated by practical considerations and thus corresponding, on the model of the League, to the intentions of the founders.

(11) Cf. doc. E/3630 of 7 May 1962 (General review of the development, co-ordination and concentration of the economic, social and human rights programmes and activities of the U.N. and the specialized agencies as a whole, paragraph 6, p. 3): "there are many other links between the international community and the

internal administration of a country. Such links are to be found not only in agreements concerning international financial transactions and loans, but in the international conventions and regulations adopted in such fields as labour, social security, education, human rights, protection of health and safety affecting international movement of ships, aircraft, dangerous drugs, radioactive substances, communicable diseases, etc. This trend is also visible in the case of modern means of communication. Many of these not only establish policies and norms, but go more or less deeply into questions of how they are to be applied, and especially by what administrative procedures they can be implemented. Even when international regulations do not deal directly with public administration, the States have to adapt their services, law and practice to uphold the standards laid down in those instruments."

(12) Cf. agreements with the I.L.O. of 14 December 1946; with F.A.O. of 14 December 1946; with UNESCO of 14 December 1946; with I.C.A.O. of 13 May 1947; with the International Bank for Reconstruction and Development of 15 November 1947; with the International Monetary Fund of 15 November 1947; with W.H.O. of 10 July 1948; with the Universal Postal Union of 1 July 1948; with the International Telecommunication Union of 1 January 1949; with the World Meteorological Organization of 20 December 1951; with the International Financial Corporation of 20 February 1957. The agreement with the Intergovernmental Maritime Consultative Organization was approved by the General Assembly on 18 November 1948, that with I.A.E.A. on 14 November 1957, etc.

(13) The United Nations Children's Fund was set up on 11 December 1946 by resolution 57 (I) of the General Assembly in connection with the termination in August 1946 of the activities of U.N.R.R.A., which had decided to transfer its remaining funds to a children's fund. By resolution 4175, of 1 December 1950, the General Assembly decided to reconsider the fate of the Fund at the end of three years. By resolution 802 (VIII), of 6 October 1953, which was adopted unanimously, the Fund was renewed indefinitely.

(14) According to a well-established tradition, only nationals of the five great Powers were recruited as members of the Military Staff Committee (cf. Article 47, paragraph 2, of the Charter). From the outset "upon the insistence of the Chiefs of Staff" this Secretariat had had its own regulations which had never been submitted to the General Assembly for approval; "it may be presumed that each delegation designated the staff members of its own nationality [although] this secretariat formed a part of the staff of the U.N. Secretariat, but its personnel was nominated by the Committee subject to the formal approval of the Secretary-General.... These arrangements are not easily reconciled with Articles 100 and 101 of the Charter...." ("Issues before the Twelfth General Assembly," *International Conciliation* (September 1957, p. 183). The problem of the effective integration of this staff with that of the U.N. Secretariat had been discussed for a number of years (cf. doc. A/2731; A/C.5/ SR.626; A/C.5/709; A/3691; A/C.5/709 paras. 36 and 38). A resolution in this sense was adopted at the twelfth session of the General Assembly in 1957 (cf. *U.N.Review*, No. 7, March 1957, pp. 36 ff.).

(15) There had been some question at the San Francisco Conference, on the proposal of the Egyptian delegation, of extending the scope of the regional arrangements concerning problems of international peace and security to cover the development of economic and cultural relations, but this proposal was not adopted by the Conference.

(16) The Staff Regulations of the U.N. were adopted on 2 February 1952 by the sixth session of the General Assembly (resolution 590) and subsequently amended as follows: 9 December 1953 (res. 781 (VIII) and 782 (VIII)), 14 December 1954 res. 882 (IX)), 17 December 1954 (res. 887 (IX)), 15 December 1955 (res. 974 (X)), 27 February 1957 (res. 1095 (XI)), 14 December 1957 (res. 1225 (XII) and

1234 (XII)), 5 December 1958 (res. 1295 (XIII)), 28 November 1961 (res. 1658 (XVI)) and 20 December 1961 (res. 1730 (XVI)).

As regards the Staff Rules, "the Secretary-General as the Chief Administrative Officer shall provide and enforce such staff rules consistent with these principles as he considers necessary." (Cf. doc. ST/SGB/Staff Rules/1/Amend. 1-18).

(17) As regards equality of the sexes (Article 8 of the Charter) advocated by the Commission on the Status of Women of the Economic and Social Council (cf. docs. E/CN.6/132, 176, 180, 246), the problem was settled from the outset, the practice of the Secretariat being in conformity with the principles laid down. This is particularly important because the different international institutions bear a great responsibility in this connection. In different parts of the world women have at present only limited access to higher studies and still more limited access to the civil service and professional life in general. This is therefore an important element of social emancipation and democratization. The total number of women employed in the Secretariat of the U.N. and in the specialized agencies including all categories of staff (even the directorial posts, especially in social affairs) is comparatively large and amounts to almost half the total strength.

(18) Similar associations have been in existence at the European Office of the United Nations at Geneva since 1955 (doc. CPG/AP/4.55 and 7/AP/4/Rev.1) and in the specialized agencies.

The Federation of International Civil Servants' Associations, in its "declaration of principles" of 24 December 1952, emphasized that international officials should be protected by their respective organizations against any infringements of their international status.

CHAPTER 9

THE PERIOD OF UNIVERSALITY: GROWING PAINS

Two major crises

The United Nations, apart from going through a number of relatively minor trials, was deeply influenced by two simultaneous major crises in 1950-1953. Both these crises, though apparently widely different, originated in the Korean war, in which "in continental Asia the U.N. passed the test and set a first precedent for armed international police action in the field...".[a] By dramatically bringing the first Secretary-General face to face with his political responsiblities, the Korean war directly provoked the first crisis, subsequently exposing the Secretary-General to violent personal attacks. It was also the direct and indirect political repercussions of the Korean question which gave rise to the second crisis, changing a latent political disquiet into a veritable storm which for several years profoundly affected the internal life of the Secretariat. While the first crisis broke out suddenly, the second remained dormant for some time. The U.S.S.R. Government was the prime mover of the first, while the United States of America, its public opinion and its authorities, precipitated the second. The first was confined to the U.N. in the person of its Secretary-General; the second affected the whole staff of the Secretariat and spread to other members of the United Nations family. Nevertheless, both were *political* in origin and were not due to the functioning of the international civil service as such; in neither case, therefore, were administrative factors involved. The officials who were victims of these crises were not criticized from the point of view of their *administrative* and *professional* qualities.

Each of these two crises had lasting effects by provoking changes in the structures and operation of the United Nations: the first as regards the division of powers between the representative bodies, and the second as regards the status of the Secretariat staff, the legality of internal action affecting that status being put to the test. Both were a severe trial for the international civil service. The first was marked by the prolonged boycotting of the head of the Secretariat by one of the great Powers, which started a sort of breach (much the

(a) Trygve Lie (op. cit., p. 323).

same happened again in 1960-1961) between one group of States
Members and the Secretary-General, who was supported by the great
majority of the other Members. The work of international administration was disturbed and the morale of the staff seriously affected.
The second crisis caused profound and prolonged disturbance among
the whole staff because a second great Power, which was at the same
time the host of the United Nations, had disregarded the fundamental
principles of the international civil service for domestic political reasons. To quote Trygve Lie:

> "It was a cruel turn of fate that the Secretariat, the delegations and I should
> have been battered by all the turmoil of highly charged emotions, mutual
> misunderstandings, and even recriminations in those months...."[a]

These two conflicts arising from particular circumstances were in the
nature of growing pains and were to leave lasting traces. No description of the evolution of the international organization would be complete without some account of these crises. Moreover, they contributed,
owing to the violence of the clash between the international outlook
and national influences, to a better understanding of the position of
the international civil service, of the duties of the States Members
under the Charter, of the peculiar status of international officials
and of the need to ensure an impartial protection of their morale and
of their rights.

The first crises

The Korean crisis broke out in June 1950 when, faced with the
armed aggression in Korea, the Security Council took the decisions
of 27 June 1950, after its appeal of 25 June for a cessation of hostilities
had been disregarded. The U.S.S.R. had at that time stayed away
from the Council for over four months owing to the dispute over the
refusal to admit Communist China. Thus the Security Council's
resolution was not nullified by a Soviet veto. Nevertheless, owing to
the U.S.S.R.'s absence, the machinery of collective security provided
for in Articles 42, 43 and 47 of the Charter did not come into play.
Instead the Council appealed to States Members to assist the United
Nations in its efforts to restore the *status quo* in Korea. A "Unified
Command" was set up, the United States of America having been
asked to form an expeditionary force under American command.
Troops of sixteen countries took part in the military operations on
behalf and under the flag of the United Nations. For the first time
an international armed force was fighting for collective security.

The Secretary-General's duty was to carry out the Security Council's
resolutions in spite of the attacks of the U.S.S.R., a Power which
until then had constantly supported him. The Security Council's

(a) Ibidem (p. 386).

action was regarded as illegal by the U.S.S.R. (on the ground that it constituted an interference in Korea's "domestic affairs"), and the Secretary-General was blamed: by playing an "unseemly role" he had "obsequiously helped a gross violation of the Charter on the part of the United States Government and other members of the Security Council."[a] Thus the Secretary-General was reproached with not having set himself up as a judge of legality, with not having placed himself above the Security Council and with not having taken action against the majority and in favour of the legality which was said to have been infringed. The U.S.S.R. and the other Eastern Powers therefore accused him of being unneutral, of political involvement in the cold war and of improper action at a critical time.[1] These criticisms led Trygve Lie to define his position as follows:

> "The Secretary-General is not to be 'neutral' above all else, 'for neutrality implies political abstinence, not political action,' and in certain circumstances might well keep him from conscientious fulfillment of his Charter obligations. There is for example an 'unneutral' predisposition about the Secretary-General's calling the Security Council's attention, under Article 99, to a matter threatening the peace, since it is unlikely that it can ever be in the equal interests of the parties to a dispute, in an exact, precisely neutral degree, that a situation in which they are involved be brought before the Council. Rather, the duty of the Secretary-General is to uphold the principles of the Charter and the decisions of the Organization as objectively as he can. This is what I did in Korea...."[b]

The Korean war was in progress when, on 27 July 1950, the U.S.S.R. resumed its seat in the Security Council, although the reason for its previous absence still remained. By its resolution No. 377 (V), of 7 October 1950, the General Assembly then adopted the Acheson Plan, called "Uniting for Peace". In order to avoid the effect of a veto on the Security Council's action, a special session of the General Assembly could henceforward be convened either at the request of the majority of the States Members or as a result of a vote, not subject to veto, of seven members of the Security Council. In such a case the Assembly was to meet within twenty-four hours. Bodies were also appointed to observe the situation and take collective measures to reinforce international peace and security. These bodies were, in a sense, designed to learn the lessons of the Korean experience and to apply them.[c] This proposal, supported by the Secretary-General, led to fresh protests on the part of the U.S.S.R., to accusations of illegality and to reproaches of partiality made against the Secretary-General. In consequence, when the Secretary-General's term of office expired in October 1950, the U.S.S.R. vetoed Trygve Lie's re-election, proposed by Yugoslavia (9 votes in favour, 1 against,

(a) *Ibidem* (p. 335).
(b) *Ibidem* (p. 342).
(c) *Ibidem* (p. 346).

Nationalist China abstaining). Thus the Security Council was unable to recommend a candidate to the Assembly under Article 97 of the Charter (10 votes in favour of this conclusion, the U.S.S.R. voting against). The General Assembly, pointing out that the same candidate had been recommended by the Security Council in 1946, and that it was evident from its recent vote that no fresh recommendation would be forthcoming, extended Trygve Lie's term of office as Secretary-General for three years by 46 votes to 5 (Eastern bloc), with 8 abstentions.

Claiming that this election was illegal, the U.S.S.R. and the other Eastern countries refused to have anything more to do with the Secretary-General, an attitude which was far removed from that contemplated by the Charter, and which created innumerable difficulties in the day-to-day work of the Secretariat. The Eastern countries acted as if the Secretariat had no head; they maintained direct contacts with his subordinates and completely ignored Trygve Lie's existence. At the same time it was clear that the aim of the boycott was not to bring about Trygve Lie's resignation. It was directed against the function of Secretary-General rather than against the man holding the post. Through that function the whole Organization was attacked because it had thwarted a particular policy. It should be added that in a way these attacks helped to emphasize the importance of the Secretary-General's position in the U.N. system. But they greatly disturbed the normal conduct of affairs in the Secretariat, which continued to operate at the lower level, although sometimes complications in international relations created impossible situations. In refusing either to submit to the majority or to withdraw from the Organization, the Eastern countries deliberately transferred a political conflict between States to the level of the Secretariat by making the Secretary-General the target of their attacks and thus trying to block administrative action.

Nevertheless, that action continued in spite of increased obstacles until Trygve Lie's resignation on 10 November 1952. This resignation was specifically provoked by the untenable situation created by the boycott. Without the confidence of all the States Members— and even ignored by some of them—he could more or less despatch current business, organize the transfer of the Secretariat to its new quarters in New York and carry on in the name of the United Nations the war in Korea. But such an impasse could not last. On 10 April 1953 the new Secretary-General, the Swede Dag Hammarskjöld, who enjoyed the confidence of all the States Members, took the place of Trygve Lie.

These events have been represented as proving the vulnerability of the Secretariat because of the sabotage practised by certain States against its head. It is true that this experience has shown that a dissatisfied minority can more or less effectively block the action of the Secretariat's higher direction, provided that it is led or supported by one of the great Powers having a veto in the Security Council. In fact, despite the democratic vote of the majority of the States Members, a boycott against the first Secretary-General actually took place, and a group of countries prevented the re-election of the Secretary-General and obliged him to leave. Such an attitude on the part of States Members, showing a hiatus between constitutional theory and reality, can undermine the very foundations of the international civil service by endangering its international character.

It remained to be seen what lessons the United Nations could draw from this experience in order to prevent or reduce such risks and dangers in future. Subsequent events in Egypt and the Congo showed that the increase in the Assembly's prerogatives made it more difficult for the Great Powers to paralyse the action of the Organization. While the danger was not removed, it was reduced. The future was to show that the lesson of the Korean crisis had been learnt.

The second crisis

This crisis took place in two stages, each of them consisting of three acts. The first stage, 1946-53, covers the whole of the seven years during which Trygve Lie was at the head of the Secretariat. The second stage covers the years 1953 and 1954, the beginning of Dag Hammarskjöld's term of office. The crisis flared up or subsided according to the temperature of the cold war and the ground where it was being fought; it developed simultaneously or successively sometimes in the Secretariat, sometimes in the representative organs of the U.N. or the specialized agencies, and sometimes at the national level in the United States of America or elsewhere. In the United States the legislative, executive and judicial machinery were all brought into play. In the United Nations the Administrative Tribunal and later the International Court of Justice were obliged to take a stand. The very essence of the international civil service was again called in question, the exact significance of its "exclusive international character" was discussed repeatedly, and a battle for and against the international status of the staff and its rights took place on several fronts. Needless to say, staff morale suffered.

It should be added that both stages began with a judicial case. In the first stage, this consisted of proceedings brought in the United States courts against an international official who was a Soviet national; he was accused of spying and was convicted. In the second stage proceedings were initiated in the Administrative Tribunal by international officials who had been dismissed from the Secretariat for their alleged political conduct outside their duties and before their appointment.

Background

At first the policy of the United States towards the U.N. Secretariat had followed that laid down by Secretary of State James F. Byrnes in 1946, which consisted in categorically refusing to recommend candidates for posts in the Secretariat "owing to the fact that according to the Charter and the rules laid down by the General Assembly, the Secretary-General alone has full and exclusive authority to appoint and dismiss officials of the United Nations."[a]

The espionage affair—the only case of its kind which occurred at the United Nations throughout the crisis—broke out in 1949.[2] This affair, which did not affect the work of the Secretariat, apart from the fact that the offender was a U.N. staff member, greatly alarmed public opinion in the United States. At a time when relations between the Allies were deteriorating, the United States press began to make attacks against the Secretariat of the United Nations, alleging that it was "riddled with Communist elements," and with "pro-Soviet fellow travellers" left over from the days of F. D. Roosevelt, and that it was a centre of anti-American subversion. Accusations such as these were made by the Security Service of the Department of State in July 1948 before a Senate sub-committee in Washington, but a commission of investigation appointed by Secretary of State Marshall decided that they were without foundation. This did not prevent the press from continuing its attacks, taking as a fresh starting-point the evidence of a mysterious, unidentified witness called "Witness No. 8," who was alleged to have spoken in the same sub-committee of the existence of "communist terrorism at the U.N. with the complicity of Trygve Lie".[b]

In September 1948 the Secretary-General concluded with the Department of State a secret agreement intended to settle for the future the problem of political information concerning staff members of the Secretariat who were United States citizens. The Secretary-General gave a sort of undertaking in return for confidential information. In virtue of this agreement, "the U.S. Government was to '*identify*' for the Secretary-General the American officials in the United Nations and the American candidates who appeared either to be members of the Communist party or to be under Communist influence... It was agreed... that the 'operations' carried out under this agreement should be regarded as highly confidential."[c] At first only United States citizens who were *candidates* for the international civil service

(a) Doc. A/2364 (Statement by the Assistant Secretary-General for Administrative and Financial Services, 23 December, 1952, pp. 1/2 and annex I).
(b) Cf. U.N. Press release SG/11-12 of July 1949.
(c) Doc. A/2364 (op. cit., pp. 1/2).

were "screened", but gradually this procedure came to be applied to United States citizens already serving in the Secretariat.[a]

Although the Secretary-General had reserved the last word on each case subjected to such a check, this agreement, as soon as it was made known—somewhat belatedly[b]—was very severely criticized. Having concluded such an agreement with the government of the host country and then later consulted that government in each case, the Secretary-General found it difficult to refuse to accept the government's opinion; in practice he was bound to submit. Each case was considered on the basis of the loyalty of the person concerned to his own government and its policy, and the complaints made on such a basis might be ill founded. Further, the United States Government sent the Secretary-General unfavourable and laconic replies unsupported by proof; sometimes the replies were merely verbal and often there were none at all.[c] The inevitable result was an atmosphere of suspicion and uncertainty in the staff, and the process of clearing came to be regarded as a condition of admission to the Secretariat.

Stage I

The crisis was brought to a head by the outbreak of hostilities in Korea in June 1950, owing to the part played by the United Nations (and particularly the United States and its army) on the one hand and the U.S.S.R. and Communist China on the other. The subsequent breach between the countries of eastern Europe and the Secretary-General aggravated the situation. The ground, as we have seen, was already prepared, and public opinion in the United States was suspicious. It was Senator McCarthy's vitriolic anti-Communist campaign and the excitement which his "witch hunts" aroused in the United States in 1950 that were decisive. This agitation, claiming the need to defend the country against the Communist peril from within and without, and provoking a sort of mass psychosis, led to a series of resounding trials, parliamentary investigations and aggressive propaganda campaigns. Naturally, in the fight between McCarthyism and the old "New Deal," the U.N. Secretariat, which included several New Dealers, became a target of attack.

Act 1. The Federal Act of 23 September 1950 (McCarran-Kilgore Act, Internal Security Act) obliged all Communist organizations in the United States, and all their members and former members, to report themselves to the federal authorities, penalties being prescribed in case of non-registration.

In virtue of this law a series of judicial investigations were undertaken from 1951 onwards, without involving the U.N., by the Special

(a) M. Bedjaoui (op. cit., p. 585).
(b) Circular No. 52-297113 to the staff of the Secretariat (11 December 1952).
(c) Cf. Trygve Lie (op. cit., p. 389).

Federal Grand Jury of New York (responsible for investigations and indictments). Certain Secretariat officials were summoned before the Grand Jury as witnesses, without opposition on the part of the Secretary-General. After eighteen months' work the Grand Jury made public a presentment which contained no indictments and mentioned no names. Among the conclusions was a statement that there was "infiltration into the United Nations of an overwhelmingly large group of disloyal United States citizens," several of whom were still closely associated with the international Communist movement. This group included many individuals who, although for a long time in the United States Federal service, had at the same time been in contact with persons and organizations guilty of subversive activities against their country.[a] This conclusion was followed by recommendations by the Grand Jury which may be summarized as follows: (1) All United States citizens must obtain previous consent from the Government before being recruited at the U.N.; (2) all U.N. officials who were United States citizens must answer a questionnaire; (3) a further jury was to continue the enquiry. At the same time appropriate federal legislation was recommended to put an end to "subversion" in the United Nations.

This gives some idea of the background when the crisis entered its acute stage. The Grand Jury's recommendations were to be put into force one after the other.

Act 2. Several other investigations by judicial or parliamentary bodies followed that of the New York Grand Jury. In particular, that undertaken by the Internal Security sub-committee of the Senate, presided over by Senator Pat McCarran, enjoyed wide publicity in the country and powerfully contributed to aggravating unrest. Certain U.N. officials, having been summoned as witnesses, refused to give evidence, invoking their immunity as international servants, the prohibition to give evidence involving their official Secretariat activities, or the Fifth Amendment of 1791 against self-incrimination;[3] this was held by the sub-committee to be "contemptuous of the Senate." There were two consequences:

Firstly, the members of the Senate sub-committee publicly protested against any attempt to oppose it: "A Senate committee cannot be stopped in its endeavour to secure facts relating to subversive activities on our shores by Americans, regardless of their affiliation with an international organization."[b]

This protest rapidly degenerated into a new wave of violent attacks by Congressmen against the U.N., "an instrument conceived by the diabolical brain of the international agents of the U.S.S.R."[c]

(a) Cf. doc. A/2364 (op. cit., para. 49).
(b) Statement by Senator H. R. O'Connor, chairman of the sub-committee, dated 15 October 1952 /doc. A/2364, op. cit., pp. III 13).
(c) Statement by H. Wood, quoted in *The Nation* of 20 September 1952. Cf. also

Secondly, the Secretary-General decided to dismiss—usually in two stages ("compulsory leave," followed by dismissal pure and simple)— several U.S. officials of the Secretariat because they had refused, on the basis of the Fifth Amendment, to answer questions during the investigation, or because, after their evidence, they had been charged with actual subversive activities against their country of origin. The reason given for the dismissals was that the officials concerned had been guilty of a fundamental breach of their service obligations and were consequently unfit to remain in the employment of the Secretariat. Altogether there were eighteen dismissals, twelve of them for refusal to give evidence under the Fifth Amendment.

These dismissals, of course, caused more trouble among the staff, and this was further aggravated when, on 1 January 1953, the Senate sub-committee published in the press a list of thirty-eight Secretariat officials regarding whom the State Department had previously communicated to the Secretary-General "unfavourable comments"; after several resounding resignations of persons mentioned in the communiqué, seven were still in the service of the Organization. This publication put an end to the original anonymity of the charges— always extra-judicial ones—while proving that the number of international officials considered by their Government as "suspect" was after all small.

This brought the crisis among the staff of the Secretariat to a paroxysm and ended Act 2 of the drama.

Act 3. The indirect repercussions of these events were many.

First, the United States Government published two Executive Orders in succession. The first (Order No. 10422 of 9 January 1953) laid down the procedure to be used by the Federal Government in communicating to the Secretary-General of the U.N. information concerning candidates to the Secretariat. The second (Order No. 10450, of 27 April 1954) defined certain new principles and set up organs of investigation and execution. The first Order reproduced the provisions of Executive Order No. 9835, of 21 March 1947, concerning investigations regarding the loyalty of federal officials, making them applicable to relations between the Federal Government and the U.N.[4]

Secondly, in the Secretariat "tragedy and anxiety"[a] followed rapidly: *tragedy*—in the shape of the dramatic suicide of A. H. Feller, Legal Counsel of the Secretariat and a close colleague of Trygve Lie's from the beginning; *anxiety*—in the shape of a general feeling of insecurity among the staff. Moreover, in the confusion nothing was done to allay this anxiety; it was even intensified.

The Secretary-General chose an extra-statutory method of *external*

the statement of Senator A. Wiley, quoted in the *New York Times* of 12 December 1952.
(a) Title of an article in *Démocratie combattante*, No. 2, 1953 (p. 15).

expertise in order to introduce some objectivity into the controversy and at the same time to clear up the legal aspect of the situation. On 29 November 1952 three international lawyers of different nationalities, appointed *ad hoc*,[a] proceeded, in an advisory capacity, to lay down certain general principles and arrived at two conclusions: first, that any modification of the Staff Regulations was superfluous, since "the existing legal framework is adequate to contain harmonious relationships" between the U.N. and the host country; and second, that the invocation by an international official in a national enquiry of the guarantee against self-incrimination constituted a fundamental breach of his obligations—such behaviour furnishing presumptive evidence of an activity incompatible with the proper discharge of his duties.[b]

Moreover, the purists expressed the opinion that when the Secretary-General had reliable information that an official was engaging in activities considered as subversive by the host country, or that there was a *risk* of engaging in such activities, he should conclude— after investigation and after hearing the official concerned— that the latter should not, or should no longer, be employed in that country.

Preoccupied by the grave problems raised by the accusations made and the enquiries carried out, the Secretary-General accepted this advice as a basis of his future policy.[c] This statement was full of alarming possibilities for the staff. The consultation itself was criticized very severely. The Federation of International Civil Servants' Associations at Geneva asked Professor Henri Rolin for a second opinion.[5][d] In that opinion, Professor Rolin emphasized the principle of the Secretary-General's independence in assessing any information supplied by governments on candidates for the Secretariat and denied that a person's employment as an international civil servant was incompatible with his membership of a legal political party in his own country; moreover he held that the invocation of a constitutional privilege against self-incrimination by a staff member interrogated by a state authority was merely the exercise of a right which was unimpaired by his status of international civil servant and therefore could not render him liable to disciplinary measures.[6] Subsequently, the Administrative Tribunal of the United Nations found[e] that the opinion of the three jurists—namely, that the Secretary-General could,

(a) Sir Edwin Herbert (British), William de Witt Mitchell (American), Paul Veldekens (Belgian).
(b) Cf. doc. A/2364 op. cit., III-1 ff.) and *American Journal of International Law*, No. 3/47, 1953, (p. 87 ff.).
(c) Memorandum by the Secretary-General of 4 December 1952, No. 52-29591, and doc. A/Inf/51 of 5 December 1952.
(d) Cf. doc. MFICSA/4/53 and annexes I and II (10 October 1953).
(e) Judgments of the U.N. Administrative Tribunal dated 21 August 1953, Nos. 28-38 (cases Nos. 36-45). Cf. also judgment of 21 August 1953, No. 18 (case No. 26).

without reference to any particular clause of the Staff Regulations, dismiss an official on the basis of contractual relations existing between himself and that official—disregarded the nature of permanent contracts and the character of the regulations governing termination of appointments laid down by the General Assembly under Article 101 of the Charter.

The principle implied in the Secretary-General's attitude aroused criticism on the part of the Staff Council [7] and of public opinion,[8] but this did not prevent the Secretary-General from applying the opinion of his three advisers. He appointed an "Advisory Board" of five members to assist him in judging problems of this kind and so informed the staff.[a] Moreover, when the permanent delegation of the United States asked him to take steps for the immediate application of the Executive Decree of 9 January 1953, he agreed that questioning undertaken by the Federal Bureau of Investigation (F.B.I.) should take place on the Secretariat's premises with the help of U.N. staff and during office hours. The United States Government, in announcing these investigations, invoked the danger to internal security represented by the presence of 1,680 of its citizens in the U.N. Secretariat.[9] It also asked the Secretary-General to suspend any appointment of its citizens to the Secretariat until the candidatures had been studied by the United States authorities.

Thus, although he had announced his resignation on 10 November 1952, the Secretary-General asked the staff to submit to these investigations;[b] and out of 2,000 persons concerned, about 1,700 were actually subjected thereto.

The whole problem was discussed at the second part of the VIIth session of the General Assembly, in March 1953, in the light of the report on the administration of the Secretariat submitted by the Secretary-General on 30 January 1953 and the stand taken in this connection by the Staff Council.[10] In his speech of 10 March 1953 the Secretary-General mentioned the pressures to which he had been subjected,[c] and said that: "To place the problem in its proper setting, it should also be kept in mind that the Secretariat of the United Nations works in a glass house not only physically, but in every respect. Almost all meetings and documentation of the United Nations are open for all to see and hear. No military secrets are ever handled by the Secretariat. The policies and programmes of the United Nations in all fields ... are determined by the governments of Member States, not by the Secretariat. The work of the Secretariat in carrying out these policies and programmes is subject to the constant scrutiny of

(a) Cf. doc. A/2364 (op. cit., pp. 27 and 31) and ST/AFS/SER.A/192, of 16 January 1953.
(b) Press release SG/281, (p. 16).
(c) Cf. above, p. 179 note (b).

governments. It is not a profitable place for spies and saboteurs."[a]

The seriousness of the crisis and the anxiety caused by its harmful effects on staff morale were described and commented on during this session of the General Assembly's by the representatives of several countries who expressed criticisms and asked for steps to restore the balance.[b]

After rejecting the draft resolutions submitted by twelve Arab-Asian countries and proposing the appointment of a special committee to study all the aspects of the question, the General Assembly adopted, by 41 votes to 13, resolution 708 (VII), which recalled that the Charter had conferred on the Secretariat of the United Nations an exclusively international character and requested the new Secretary-General, Dag Hammarskjöld, to submit to the VIIIth session in autumn 1953 a full report on personnel policy.[11]

Stage II

When Trygve Lie handed over to his successor, on 10 April 1953, the crisis was far from over. The legacy of the previous period was a heavy one. The witch hunt set on foot by McCarthy was still in full swing in the United States. The hardening of politico-military blocs in the world and the cold war between these blocs was still going on. Apart from endless political complications, a battle of principles was being fought in the Secretariat between the "Administration," which had extensive and partly discretionary powers as regards staff matters, and the officials as a whole, whose professional solidarity was being increasingly displayed. The defence of the interests of these officials was henceforward undertaken by the Staff Association and its funds, and the individual cases became the symbol of a collective struggle.

Trygve Lie's successor was helped by a general predisposition in his favour. He did not consider himself bound by his predecessor's personnel policy and therefore had an entirely free hand. He displayed great prudence at first and avoided, as far as possible, all partial settlements based on particular circumstances. His intention was to establish gradually "a sound body of rules by decisions in individual cases, creating a kind of common law."[c] The staff had confidence in him. There was therefore reason to hope for a speedy settlement of the Secretariat's "domestic" crisis, particularly as, for the first time, the matter was in the hands of an impartial judge. These hopes were short-lived.

Act 1. An appeal had been made to the Administrative Tribunal of

(a) Doc. A/2364 (op. cit., p. 7), and *International Organization*, No. 2, 1953 (p. 243 ff.).
(b) *Ibidem*, (p. 246)
(c) Press release SG/318 of 10 July 1953, (p. 5).

the United Nations by the United States officials of the Secretariat who had been dismissed by the Secretary-General in the circumstances we have described.[a] The Tribunal settled the dispute by its judgments of 21 August 1953.[b] According to these judgments the fact of having invoked the Fifth Amendment in order to avoid self-incrimination, and of having refused to answer certain questions asked by the United States authorities, did not constitute "serious misconduct," which alone could have justified the dismissal of the international official without notice and without observing the guarantees offered by the ordinary disciplinary procedure.[32] An official could be dismissed only for "unsatisfactory services," under the Staff Regulations,[13] if the services in question were connected with the official's professional activities at the United Nations and not with his general obligations. Any dismissal should, in any case, be based on an express clause of the Staff Regulations.

Under these judgments, ten complainants—that is to say all the holders of permanent appointments who had refused to testify before the United States authorities by invoking the Fifth Amendment [14]— won their cases. As to the complainants who had temporary appointments,[15] their dismissal was considered as admissible in the interests of the Organization and to come within the scope of the Secretary-General's discretionary powers, but only if it were established that the decision to dismiss them had not been taken for improper reasons.

There were varied reactions to the stand taken by the Administrative Tribunal, whose judgments at that time were not subject to appeal. In the United States it was severely criticized.

Act 2. The Senate Internal Security sub-committee resumed its public hearings in the United States in September 1953 under the chairmanship of Senator W. E. Jenner and later of Senator O. D. Johnston. These hearings concerned the U.N. officials to whom the above-mentioned judgments of the Administrative Tribunal related and who, in view of the Secretary-General's refusal to reinstate them, received substantial compensation from the U.N.[c] Several of them again invoked the Fifth Amendment.

During these hearings, followed by attacks in the press, it was openly proposed to "correct" the Tribunal's judgments and to prevent the payment of the compensation which had been granted. In particular, the U.S. permanent representative at the United Nations, Henry Cabot Lodge Jr., insisted that "the finding of this Tribunal is not final" and that "the General Assembly has the power to over-rule it."[d] This contention, which called in question the binding force

(a) Cf. above, p. 216.
(b) Cf. above, p. 191, note (f), and 217 note (e).
(c) Cf. above, p. 219 (a), below p. 222.
(d) *U.S. News and World Report*, No. 16 of 16 October 1953 (pp. 29 ff.).

of the decision—the basis of all law—by invoking the alleged "insub-
ordination" of the Administrative Tribunal (a subsidiary organ)
to the General Assembly (the principal organ which had set up the
Tribunal) led to the launching of a veritable offensive at the VIIIth
session of the General Assembly.

The new Secretary-General, Dag Hammarskjöld, in his report of
2 November 1953,[a] submitted under resolution 708 (VII) of the General Assembly and concerning staff policy, proposed two kinds of amendments to the legal texts in force—an amendment of the Staff Regulations defining the "integrity" of officials,[16] forbidding them to engage
in political activities[17] and materially widening the Secretary-
General's discretionary powers to dismiss permanent officials. These
powers were to cover three possible cases: firstly, when the staff
member's conduct indicated that he did not meet the "high standards
of integrity required by Article 101, paragraph 3, of the Charter";
secondly, when the Secretary-General learnt of facts anterior to the
staff member's appointment and relevant to his administrative
suitability which, if they had been known when the staff member was
appointed, would, under the standards established in the Charter,
have precluded his appointment; and lastly, if his termination would
be in the interests of the good administration of the Organization and
in accordance with the standards of the Charter. In the latter case,
compensation not exceeding fifty per cent of what would normally
be due under the Staff Regulations might be granted, if the Secretary-
General thought fit and if the circumstances justified it;[b] an amendment to the Statute of the Administrative Tribunal to the effect that
in future, in the event of the annulment of a decision of dismissal, the
Tribunal should automatically fix the amount of compensation payable to the successful complainant if he was not reinstated (a decision
on this point having to be taken by the Secretary-General within
sixty days), and that the compensation granted should not exceed
the equivalent of two years' net base salary.[c]

These two proposals were the object of sometimes heated discussions in the Fifth Committee and afterwards in the General Assembly
at the end of 1953.

As regards the amendment of the Staff Regulations, the Secretary-
General "reaffirmed his opinion that in effecting dismissals under the
proposed amendments to the Regulations, it was his moral obligation to explain his reasons in each case."[d] Moreover, he accepted an
attenuation of his proposal by agreeing that a dismissal "in the
interests of the good administration of the Organization and in ac-

(a) Cf. doc. A/2533.
(b) *Ibidem* (pp. 10-23).
(c) *Ibidem* (pp. 27-29).
(d) Doc. A/C.5/SR. 414 (p. 22). Cf. also doc. A/2615 (p. 5).

cordance with the standards of the Charter" could take place only
if such a step was "not contested by the official concerned." The
other measures of dismissal provided for in his proposal should not be
applied "until the matter has been considered and reported on by
a special advisory board appointed for that purpose by the Secretary-General."[18] This was the line eventually taken by resolution
782 A (VIII), of 9 December 1953, which amended the Staff Regulations (regulations 1.4, 1.7, 9.1a, 9.3).[19] It also specified that at its
tenth session in 1955 the General Assembly would re-examine the
principles and standards which might have been drawn up and applied
by the Secretary-General.

As regards the amendment of the Statute of the Administrative
Tribunal, two diametrically opposed opinions clashed in the Fifth
Committee of the General Assembly. The *minority* supported the
United States view that the Assembly was entitled to overrule the
Administrative Tribunal's judgments. The *majority* opposed this view.
The debate provided an opportunity for a fresh review of the standards
of international administrative law and brought out the necessity for
an impartial judge in the legal relations between the Organization
and its staff. For example:

Minority Opinions:

"The General Assembly could not be bound by the decisions of any organ.... If
it were admitted that the recent judgment of the Administrative Tribunal
could prejudice the interests of the Organization, the General Assembly should
take the necessary steps to remedy the situation...."[b]

"Relations between the General Assembly and the Tribunal were by no
means the same as those between the legislature and the judiciary in a State.
For international organizations in general the International Court of Justice
was the judiciary. The Tribunal's decision was of course final for the parties
concerned—one of them being the Secretary-General—but it was not binding
on the General Assembly. That was the sole body to which appeal could be
taken against mistaken decisions...."[11c]

Majority Opinions:

"The General Assembly had not established the Tribunal to assist it in the
performance of a function which it could in principle perform itself. On the
contrary it had established the Administrative Tribunal because the General
Assembly could not perform judicial functions. The General Assembly could
admittedly abolish the Tribunal or amend its Statute but it could not review
the final judgments of the Tribunal. In a comparable case no parliament of
any Member State, however powerful, could do such a thing, even when the

(a) Doc. A/C.5/SR. 413 (p. 8); A/2615 (p. 19); A/C.5/414 (p. 22); A/C.5/415 (pp.
5/6); A/C.5/SR. 420 (p. 4); A/2533.
(b) Speech by the Cuban representative, Blanco (doc. A/C.5/SR. 409, pp. 2 ff.).
(c) Speech by the Chinese representative (Formosa) Kiang (doc. A/C.5/SR.421,
p. 3). Cf. also, for example, the opinions of the following representatives: Australian,
Brennan (doc. A/C.5/SR. 421, pp. 8 ff.); Argentine, Cafiero (doc. A/C.5/SR. 408,
pp. 13/14); Turkish, Vaner (Doc. A/C. 5/SR. 414, p. 6).

State's Constitution was silent on that point. A judicial organ, even though considered a subsidiary organ, was not an advisory body. Its decisions were binding on the parties, even on the party which had set it up.... It was the typical function of a tribunal to form its own independent interpretation of the relevant provisions.... The General Assembly would be exceeding its powers if it substituted its own interpretation for that of the Tribunal...."[a]

"Firstly the Administrative Tribunal was a judicial organ established by the General Assembly; secondly the General Assembly was empowered to amend the Statute of the Administrative Tribunal and even to abolish it; thirdly since the Administrative Tribunal was a judicial organ its judgments and decisons based on its statutes were not subject to revision by the political and legislative body that had established it; and lastly the Administrative Tribunal's decisions could not therefore be revised by the General Assembly...[b] The delegation of Uruguay could never have imagined that so clear an issue in law and justice could have given rise to any doubt in the General Assembly. [He] would therefore vote to support the principles of law involved; indeed they were so self-evident that they should not have needed any support beyond their intrinsic merit."[c]

"The Secretary-General's proposal would radically alter the existing situation. It would in any case deprive the Administrative Tribunal of its power to recommend the restoration of the applicant's rights by ordering either the revocation of the decision taken in violation of his contract or the specific performance of the obligation levied by the Administration. It would leave the Tribunal merely with the power to award damages and would limit even that power."[d]

The Secretary-General considered that "the competence of the Tribunal should remain unimpaired."[e] He agreed that the Tribunal should be able, in exceptional cases, to grant compensation greater than indicated as a *maximum* in his proposal.[f] The time-limit for the decision on the possible reinstatement of an official following a judgment by the Administrative Tribunal was reduced to thirty days. As a compromise the General Assembly adopted the other amendments to the Statute of the Administrative Tribunal proposed by the Secretary-General. But in the end the attacks of the governments of certain Member States, and particularly of the United States of America, upon the independence of the Administrative Tribunal and consequently upon that of the international civil service—whose principal guarantee was at stake—achieved very little. While there were reservations as to the Secretary-General's proposals for the

(a) Speech by the Dutch representative, von Balluseck (doc. A/C.5/SR. 508, p. 14 ff. and doc. A/C.5/SR.421, pp. 6 and 8).
(b) Speech by the Uruguayan representative, Vignale (doc. A/C.5/SR. 408, p. 208).
(c) *Ibidem* (doc. A/C.5/SR.422, p. 11).
(d) Speech by the Belgian representative, Robert Fenaux (doc. A/C.5/SR.408, pp. 6/7). Cf. also, for example, the opinions of the following representatives: Canadian, Cote (doc. A/C.5(SR. 409, p. 19); Lebanese, Rizk (doc. A/C.5/SR.412, pp. 4 ff.); Yugoslav, Popovic (*ibidem*, pp. 13 ff.); etc.
(e) Doc. A/C.5/SR.414 (pp. 13 and 22) and A/C.5/SR.415 (p. 5).
(f) Doc. A/2615 (pp. 5 and 19) and A/C.5/SR.413 (p. 8).

amendment of the regulations, the need for a proper judicial control of the conduct of personnel affairs in the Secretariat was confirmed by the debates.

Nevertheless, the Assembly made a gesture of concession to the minority. The political battle was still being carried on by the United States Government, this time using the purse strings. An item had to be entered in the U.N. budget to cover the substantial compensation granted by the Administrative Tribunal to the officials, all Americans, who had been dismissed by the Secretary-General. Attempts were made to rouse public indignation in America by alleging that that country's budgetary contribution was being used to finance "subversive activities." So the problem became a matter of public controversy. The Advisory Committee on Administrative and Budgetary Questions assented to this item of expenditure. World opinion was divided, some favouring the execution of the Administrative Tribunal's judgment.[21] Eventually, in its resolution 785(VIII), of 9 December 1953, the General Assembly asked the International Court of Justice for an advisory opinion on this subject, and postponed the vote on the items in question until it had received that opinion.

The advisory opinion of 13 July 1954, to which we have already referred,[a] and which was adopted by 3 votes to 1,[b] endorsed the views of the majority. In answering the questions put by the General Assembly,[22] the Court stated, inter alia:[c] "As this final judgment has binding force on the U.N. as the juridical person responsible for the proper observance of the contract of service, that organization becomes legally bound to carry out the judgment and to pay the compensation awarded to the staff member. It follows that the General Assembly as an organ of the United Nations must likewise be bound by the judgment."[d] In order that such judgments could be subjected to review by any body other than the Tribunal itself, "it would be necessary in the opinion of the Court that the Statute of that Tribunal or some other legal instrument giving it should contain an express provision to that effect."[e] In any case, any intervention by the General Assembly in individual cases was ruled out, and the Court rejected the idea of a dispute between the official and the "Secretary-General" without the Organization's being one of the parties.

The legal question having thus been settled, the General Assembly at its IXth session, unanimously adopted on 17 December 1954,

(a) Cf. above, chapter 4, p. 89.
(b) Cf. above, chapter 4, note (43).
(c) Cf. above, chapter 4, p. 89.
(d) I.C.J. Reports, *Effect of Awards of Compensation made by the United Nations Administrative Tribunal*, (1954, p. 53).
(e) *Ibidem* (p. 56).

resolution 888(IX), in which the Court's advisory opinion was noted, and it was decided that the compensation in question should be paid, although the United States House of Representatives had already formally opposed such a course. This solution of the dispute was favourably received. One author wrote:

> "It at least has led Member States to define for themselves the constitutional position of the organization, the Secretariat and the General Assembly in dealing with staff members as well as host and Member State relations...."[a]

Act 3. Nevertheless, the crisis continued.

In the first place the investigations undertaken by the United States Government in the U.N. Secretariat went on. The enquiry was concerned not only with the professional activities of the officials invited to testify, but also with purely personal questions past or present, even with the political activity of third persons and of non-American international officials. Special questionnaires continued to be distributed to the American staff members, and fingerprinting took place at the headquarters building itself. What is more, these investigations were extended to the "outside" services and the specialized agencies, the United States authorities having sent three American officials to a number of countries to investigate personally their citizens in the service of the international organizations there. The Swiss Government refused to allow them to carry out such investigations in Switzerland, regarding them as incompatible with its national sovereignty. Elsewhere, however, the enquiries actually took place, for example at UNESCO in Paris, at I.C.A.O. in Montreal and at F.A.O. in Rome. In the case of W.H.O. in Geneva, the Director-General, Dr. Brock Chisholm, and his successor Dr. M. G. Candau, refused to allow officials of W.H.O. to appear before the American Loyalty Board which was travelling in Europe at that time. While the general tendency was one of hesitation and the requests of the diplomatic representatives of the United States of America became more and more pressing, both directors of W.H.O. took a very firm attitude against any pressure considered as violating Article 37 of the Constitution of W.H.O. While agreeing to transmit to members of their staff any communication from their national authorities, both directors firmly maintained that the observance of the provisions of national legislation was a question between each individual and his government, and that the disciplinary powers possessed by international organizations in relation to their staff could be exercised only in connection with a staff member's conduct as an international official. This courageous and resolute defence of the international character of the secretariats of international organizations made a profound

(a) M. Cohen, "The U.N. Secretariat—Some Constitutional and Administrative Developments," in *American Journal of International Law* (No. 49, 1955, pp. 318/319).

impression at the time in international circles; other organizations subsequently adopted the same attitude, which certainly helped to influence the views of the United States Government in the long run.

There were further difficulties: in some cases the U.S. Government refused to grant residence or even transit visas to officials of the specialized agencies sent to U.N. headquarters in New York, to representatives of non-governmental organizations with consultative status at the U.N., or to journalists, contrary to the principle of freedom of information.[a] The Government justified this action on grounds of domestic security, recognized as valid by the Secretary-General "when there is clear and convincing evidence."[b] But such an attitude taken by the host State of the United Nations inevitably produced many immediate complications.

Lastly the United States refused to issue passports to certain of its citizens in the service of the United Nations "family" who were regarded by the American services as "security risks." Moreover, when, in the course of the investigations, the United States Government called upon officials to appear in person before the investigators inside or outside the country in which they worked, some of these, at the risk of having their passports withdrawn, referred to appear, which led to chain reactions. The Federal Immigration and Nationality Act of 24 December 1952 caused more difficulties for those international officials who had the status of immigrants in the United States; their privileges and immunities, their tax status and their classification from the point of view of geographical distribution were affected. The Secretary-General succeeded in negotiating individually rather than *en bloc* the question of United States entrance visas for nationals of other countries in the service of the U.N., but the problem of the United States Government's refusal to issue passports to its own citizens in the service of the United Nations remained unsolved. Moreover, such an arrangement, although it might be generally satisfactory,[c] called in question the whole conception of the independence of the international civil service, and aroused criticism in the press. On 1 August 1953 the Economic and Social Council unanimously expressed the hope that disputes concerning access to headquarters would be settled rapidly and satisfactorily;[d] and such proved to be the case.

But the pressure of the United States authorities continued to be strongly felt at UNESCO, which was repeatedly attacked by certain American state legislatures and certain American newspapers.[e]

(a) Cf. *International Conciliation*, No. 493, 1953 (pp. 121/122).
(b) Press release PM/2558 of 27 July 1953 (p.1.), and ECOSOC, 15th session, 679th meeting, of 9 April 1953 (p. 37).
(c) Doc. A/2364 (op. cit., annex II, pp. 18 ff.).
(d) *International Conciliation*, No. 493 (op. cit., pp. 122/123).
(e) Cf. below, chapter 12, note (4).

In 1952 the U.S. Government categorically demanded co-operation by the Secretariat in the investigation of its citizens in the service of UNESCO;[23] this pressure continued in 1953 and culminated in 1954-1955. The test case here was the "Leff case." Mr. Leff was an American, a temporary official of UNESCO, whose passport and those of his family had been withdrawn by his government in 1951. In 1953 he was summoned to appear before the Grand Jury in New York. He refused to go, in spite of an express order from the Director-General of UNESCO. He was then suspended, and later reinstated with the suggestion that he should agree to a transfer to New York, against which he and the Staff Association protested.[24] Mr. Leff asked in vain to be allowed to testify before the United States Governmental Commission in Paris, where he worked, and eventually the Director-General of UNESCO again ordered him "to satisfy the requirements of the judicial authorities of the United States," who had charged him with contempt of court owing to his non-appearance before the Grand Jury. He appealed twice to the Administrative Tribunal of the I.L.O.[25] Three other UNESCO officials, whose temporary and fixed-term appointments had not been renewed owing to their non-appearance before the Loyalty Board, which the Director-General of UNESCO regarded as "a breach of integrity," also applied to the Tribunal for the rescinding of these decisions.

These cases aroused considerable agitation in the world press.

All the UNESCO officials who had appealed to the Administrative Tribunal of the I.L.O. won their cases.

In the first case, by a judgment of 6 September 1954,[a] the Tribunal, relying on the provisions of article VI, paragraph 5, of the UNESCO Constitution and of articles 1.2 and 1.4 of the UNESCO Staff Regulations, stated the following:

> "Considering that it does not follow from the above-mentioned texts that the conduct of an official with regard to the Government of his country, although outside the actual service of the international Organization, is entirely outside the control of the disciplinary authority of the Organization, that on the contrary this is the case when that conduct is judged to be seriously likely to affect the dignity of the official and the prestige of the organization to which he belongs—a point of fact of which the appreciation will vary according to the circumstances of each case; that the validity of the order in dispute therefore depends entirely on whether... this fact was established to the point that the intervention of the authority of the Director-General was justified;
>
> Considering that the Appeals Board formally expressed the view that at that date disciplinary action was not justified, the circumstances required for such action not being met since there was only a question, in the case of the complainant, of abstention from appearing in New York as a witness in the investigation of the Grand Jury;

(a) Judgment of the Administrative Tribunal of the I.L.O., No. 15, (*D.N. Leff v. UNESCO*). Cf. *Annales de la Faculté de Droit d'Istanbul*, No. 7, 1957, op. cit.: *Décisions juridictionnelles internationales* (D.J., p. 65 ff.).

Considering that the opinion thus expressed by the Appeals Board should be subscribed to and that in consequence the order...should be rescinded...."[a]

In the other cases, by its judgments of 26 April 1955,[b] the Tribunal, on the same grounds, ordered that the decisions should be rescinded, and expressed the view that they constituted in law an abuse of rights causing prejudice to the complainant. In its statement the Tribunal laid down certain essential principles of the international civil service as follows:

"Considering that...the ground for complaint of the Director-General is based solely on the refusal of the official to participate in measures of verbal or written enquiry to which his national Government considered it necessary to subject him;
that the Director-General of an international organization cannot associate himself with the execution of the policy of the Government authorities of any State Member without disregarding the obligations imposed on all international officials without distinction, and in consequence without misusing the authority which had been conferred on him solely for the purpose of directing that organization towards the achievement of its own, exclusively international, objectives....
Considering that the fact that in this case the matter involved is an accusation of disloyalty brought by a Government which enjoys in all respects the highest prestige, must be without any influence upon the consideration of the facts in the case and the determination of the principles whose respect the Tribunal must ensure;
that it will suffice to realize that if any one of the seventy-two States and Governments involved in the defendant Organization brought against an official, one of its citizens, an accusation of disloyalty and claimed to subject him to an enquiry in similar or analogous conditions, the attitude adopted by the Director-General would constitute a precedent obliging him to lend his assistance to such an enquiry and moreover to invoke the same disciplinary or statutory consequences, the same withdrawal of confidence, on the basis of any opposal by the person concerned to the action of his national Government;
that if this were to be the case there would result for all international officials, in matters touching on conscience, a state of uncertainty and insecurity prejudicial to the performance of their duties and liable to provoke disturbances in the international administration such as cannot be imagined to have been in the intention of those who drew up the Constitution of the defendant Organization;
Considering therefore that the only ground for complaint adduced by the Director-General to justify the application to the complainant of an exception to the general rule of renewal of appointments, that is to say his opposal to the to the investigations of his own Government, is entirely unjustified.... Considering that it is irrelevant to seek whether or not the complainant was engaged in militant activities before being appointed to the international service and at a time when he was not bound by the obligations involved in joining this

(a) *Ibidem*, (D.J. pp. 76/77).
(b) Judgments of the Administrative Tribunal of the I.L.O., No. 17 (*P. Duberg v. UNESCO*); No. 18 (*D.N. Leff v. UNESCO*); No. 19 (*Mrs. A. Wilcox v. UNESCO*), *ibidem*, (D.J. pp. 86 ff., pp. 99 ff., pp. 103 ff.). Cf. identical grounds of the judgment of the Administrative Tribunal of the I.L.O., No. 21 (*Mrs. C. Bernstein v. UNESCO*), *ibidem* (D.J. pp. 116 ff.). Cf. also Judgment of the same Tribunal, No. 13 of 3 September 1954 (*G. McIntire v. F.A.O.*), *ibidem* (D.J. p. 44 ff.).

service, unless it has been proved that he had been guilty of dishonourable
or criminal acts;

that any accusation of this nature could only be admitted if drawn up both
in due form and with all the precision required to ensure respect for the right
of the accused person to defend himself; that it is not so in this case;...

considering that it has been shown that the attitude of the complainant towards
the Loyalty Board in no way justifies the existence of serious doubts as to his
integrity, judgment and loyalty towards the defending Organization; that it
does not therefore appear that the complainant placed his own interests the
true interests of the Organization which consist above all in safeguarding *erga
omnes* its independence and impartiality...on the grounds as aforesaid
the Tribunal...orders the decision taken to be rescinded ...."[a]

In spite of these judgments the dispute continued. An appeal to the
International Court of Justice [26] against the judgments was lodged
by the Executive Board of UNESCO under article XII of the Statute
of the Administrative Tribunal of the I.L.O. which "allows the Executive Board of the Organization concerned to submit the question
of the validity of the decisions given by the Tribunal to the International Court of Justice for an advisory opinion, this opinion being
binding." The Court is thus called upon to pronounce upon the validity
of the judgments of the Administrative Tribunal of the I.L.O. if the
above-mentioned Executive Board either challenges its jurisdiction or
considers that a decision has been vitiated by a fundamental fault in
the procedure followed. This was the first time that the Court's opinion
had been asked on the basis of article XII, which proves the importance of the problem. The examination of the case by the International Court aroused great interest. In its Advisory Opinion of
23 October 1956,[b] the Court accepted the decisions of the I.L.O.
Administrative Tribunal and rejected UNESCO's allegation that the
Tribunal had committed an excess of jurisdiction in pronouncing
on the constitutional obligations of the head of the Secretariat and on
his relations with a State Member of the Organization.

Consequently all the complainants received compensation from
UNESCO.

Later, the McCarthy agitation died away in the United States, and
towards 1955 the liberal atmosphere in western Europe, assisted by the
resolute and courageous attitude of certain national governments and
certain heads of international secretariats, gradually brought the
crisis to an end.

Epilogue and conclusions

The anxiety of the international staff was allayed by the decisive
and skilful diplomatic action of Dag Hammarskjöld and of certain
other heads of secretariats. The staff's confidence was restored when

(a) Cf. Judgment No. 17 (*Ibidem*, D.J. pp. 93-96 and 98).
(b) Cf. above, chapter 4, p. 90.

the fundamental principles of the international civil service were steadfastly upheld by the two international Administrative Tribunals and by the International Court.

Events had shown that the repercussions of the shifting attitudes of States Members towards international officials largely depended on the way in which the successive heads of the Secretariat reacted to governmental pressure. Thus, a decided reaction in favour of principles which, although solemnly established, had been continually challenged, revived hopes of a lasting improvement in international co-operation. Although traces of this troubled period remained, the two crises had psychologically fortified the staff to withstand the new trials which were rightly apprehended. They showed that the apparently established positions—ideological, legal and moral—remained insecure and must always depend on unforeseeable factors. But light had been thrown not only on the difficulties, but also on the greatness of the task. The need for an international spirit in every official was emphasized once more. The rules laid down in the Charter, their real validity regarded with scepticism by the public and challenged afresh by every temporary and empirical arrangement, depended for their survival on the permanent servants of the international organizations.

The crisis proved that although "the international organization is a tender plant which must be nursed carefully if it is not to wither before it has had a chance to grow,"[a] it can resist the most serious shocks if its chiefs are up to their jobs and if the staff, whatever their anxieties or their feelings of frustration and insecurity, can trust them. Furthermore, the States themselves, despite disputes between the blocs and innumerable political differences, had to take this element more and more into account. A direct attack having become increasingly difficult, all that they could do was to try indirectly to juggle with principles and with established institutional practice. Dangers still threatened on all sides: any stagnation, any psychological weakness on the part of the international staff, left a serious breach. The fight for international co-operation in the interests of humanity had to be carried on unremittingly, and it was symbolized by the international civil service.

The lesson to be drawn from the crises was not forgotten.

Retrospectively, Dag Hammarskjöld, faced in 1961 with a fresh crisis of the international organization, described the atmosphere and crises of 1950 to 1955 as follows:

"The conception of an independent international civil service, although reasonably clear in the Charter provisions, was almost continuously subjected to stress in the history of the organization. International tensions, changes in

(a) F. Honig, "International Civil Service. Basic Problems and Contemporary Difficulties," *International Affairs* (London, No. 30, 1954, pp. 175 ff.).

governments, concern with national security, all had their inevitable repercussions on the still fragile institution dedicated to the international community. Governments not only strove for the acceptance of their views in the organs of the organization, but they concerned themselves in varying degrees with the attitude of their nationals in the Secretariat. Some governments sought in one way or another to revive the substance of the proposal defeated at London for the clearance of their nationals prior to employment in the Secretariat; other governments on occasion demanded the dismissal of staff members who were said to be inappropriately representative of the country of their nationality for political, racial or even cultural reasons. In consequence, the Charter Articles underwent a continual process of interpretation and clarification in the face of pressures brought to bear on the Secretary-General.... It may be recalled that this problem assumed critical proportions in 1952 and 1953 when various authorities of the United States Government, host of the U.N. headquarters, conducted a series of highly publicized investigations of the loyalty of its nationals in the Secretariat. Charges were made which, although relating to a small number of individuals and largely founded upon inference rather than on direct evidence or admissions, led to proposals which implicitly challenged the international character of the Secretary-General and his staff. In certain other countries similar proposals were made and in some cases adopted in legislation or by administrative action. In response, the Secretary-General and the organization as a whole affirmed the necessity of independent action by the U.N. in regard to selection and recruitment of staff.... It should be said that, as a result of the stand taken by the Organization this principle was recognized by the United States Government in the procedures it established for hearings and submission of information to the Secretary-General regarding U.S. citizens."[a]

Lastly, as to internal rules, mention should be made, apart from the amendment of certain staff regulations,[b] of a further amendment[c] to the Statute of the Administrative Tribunal of the United Nations; both changes were the direct outcome of the crisis. In its resolution 957(X), of 8 November 1955, the General Assembly, after considering the report of a Special Committee,[27] approved by 33 votes to 17 (with 9 abstentions), despite the reservations expressed by the Secretary-General,[28] the establishment of special machinery for the possible review of United Nations Administrative Tribunal judgments. This resolution was a compromise[29] between opposite opinions. Taking as a pattern the Administrative Tribunal of the I.L.O., it set up a procedure for asking the International Court of Justice for advisory opinions. If a Member State, the Secretary-General or the person in respect of whom a judgment had been given by the Tribunal objected on the ground that the Tribunal had exceeded its jurisdiction or competence, or had failed to exercise the jurisdiction invested in it, or had erred on a question of law, or had committed a fundamental

(a) Dag Hammarskjöld, Oxford address (op. cit., pp. 9-11).
(b) Cf. below, chapter 9, notes (16) (17) and (19). As regards the staff regulations of UNESCO, cf. doc. ADM A/25, of 9 December 1954: amendment to regulation 9.1 of the Statute by the VIIIth session of the General Conference (Montevideo).
(c) Cf. above, p. 223.

error in procedure, steps could be taken to dispute the judgment; but a Committee composed of the Member States represented on the General Committee of the most recent regular session of the General Assembly must screen the request and decide whether or not it rested "on a substantial basis." This compromise safeguarded the Administrative Tribunal's prestige by making the review of its judgments difficult and by calling upon the International Court to undertake this review if necessary. The judge was therefore not subordinated to the politician. But the politician could screen the appeals, and the Administrative Tribunal's judgments were no longer final. This statutory amendment logically followed the Advisory Opinion of the International Court of Justice of 13 July 1954,[a] by confirming the possibility of a judicial review of administrative jurisprudence with an intermediate check by an extra-judicial body.

This reform was the legacy of the crisis and marked its end.

(a) Cf. above, p. 224.

NOTES

(1) It was during the Korean crisis that Article 99 of the Charter was formally invoked for the first time (in practice, it was frequently resorted to: cf. S. M. Schwebel, op. cit., p. 85). But before the Secretary-General had invoked it, the question had already been referred to him by one of the States Members. Thus, in practice, the machinery of Article 99 did not come into play on this occasion.

(2) He was a Soviet national who had been a Secretariat official from July 1946 to the day of his arrest. He was accused of espionage for the benefit of his country, but in a manner unconnected with his official duties (which were mainly technical). After conviction he was deported.

A point worthy of attention in this connection is that the U.S.S.R. Embassy assured the U.S. Government that the person in question was an official of the Soviet Embassy "seconded by order of the Government" to the international Secretariat and, as such, was entitled to diplomatic immunity. In point of fact, before entering the service of the U.N., he had been employed for a few weeks at the Permanent Delegation of the U.S.S.R. at the U.N. "This would seem on the face of it to be a significant admission of a choice imposed on the Secretary-General and of a recruitment decided upon by the U.S.S.R." (M. Bedjaoui, op. cit., p. 69, note (28)).

(3) Text of the Fifth Amendment:

"No person shall be held to answer for a capital or otherwise infamous crime, unless on a presentment or indictment of a grand jury, except in cases arising in the land or naval forces, or in the militia, when in actual service in time of war or public danger; nor shall any person be subject for the same offence to be twice put in jeopardy of life or limb; nor shall be compelled in any criminal case to be a witness against himself, nor be deprived of life, liberty or property, without due process of law; nor shall private property be taken for public use, without just compensation."

(4) Senator P. McCarran's Bill of 7 January 1953 aimed "to prevent citizens of the United States of questionable loyalty to the U.S. Government from accepting"—subject to penalties—"any office or employment in or under the United Nations."

Reminiscent of the Italian Fascist Act of 1927 quoted above, this Bill was a striking proof of the "witch hunt" going on at the time in the United States.

(5) The conclusions of Professor H. Rolin's counter-opinion were endorsed by Professors Tomasi Perassi and Charles Rousseau.

(6) The authors of the counter-opinion also express the view that none of the staff rules or regulations of any of the international organizations authorizes dismissal as a disciplinary measure, of a staff member who is merely suspected of present or future disloyalty to the organization and has not been found guilty of any violation of his obligations. Moreover, none of the staff rules or regulations directly provides that international civil servants must comply with the summonses of judicial or other bodies. In certain cases, however, the obligation to do so may follow from their duty to conduct themselves in a manner befitting their status as international civil servants and to keep the interests of their organization in view. Thus, apart from exceptional cases, in which the Secretary-General feels obliged to invoke privileges and immunities *in opposition to* compliance with a summons, an international civil servant will be committing serious misconduct if, by failing to comply with a summons, he renders himself liable to arrest, which would be injurious to the prestige of the organization.

(7) The fact that the Secretary-General accepted most of the recommendations of the three jurists was interpreted by the Staff Council both as an abandonment of the fundamental conception of an international civil service which was to be entirely free from national pressures, and as indicating the absence of any "natural reaction" on the Secretary-General's part against the idea of the undesirability of having any officials at the U.N. Secretariat in New York from countries other than the host country—an idea which was held by public opinion in the United States (cf. Doc. SCC/154, report of the Staff Council of 16 February 1953).

(8) For example, the Eighth Plenary Assembly of the World Federation of United Nations Associations adopted in Paris the following resolution: the 8th Plenary Assembly "Realizing the supreme importance to the development of effective international institutions of a body of civil servants well recruited, highly skilled, trustworthy and above all animated by a truly international spirit; expresses its high appreciation of the devoted services of the Secretariat of the United Nations and its specialized agencies, often performed in difficult or even dangerous circumstances; notes with concern the adverse effects which 'loyalty' investigations of United States citizens employed in the Secretariats have had upon the position and morale of the whole of the international secretariat; recalls that the Member States, by the terms of the Charter, are bound to respect the exclusively international character of the Secretariat; urges the Governments of the Member States and the General Assembly of the United Nations to reaffirm that the officials of the Secretariat and of the specialized agencies, in the execution of their duties, are responsible only to the United Nations and must be judged only upon their performance of their United Nations orders, and hopes that the studies now being undertaken will lead to an improvement of the situation and will give effect to these purposes."

(9) Although the Executive Decree of 9 January 1953 related only to internationally recruited American officials, the locally recruited staff were also investigated as to their loyalty to their government.

(10) "Every effort must continue to be made to preserve the independent authority of the Secretary-General, especially in such difficult circumstances as those now prevailing.... It is of fundamental importance that the Organization should comply with elementary requirements of justice and fairness in dealing with individual cases.... The rights of staff members can be fully protected only within the framework of a sound administration providing both for the clear definition of the rights of staff members and for the establishment and maintenance of representative

and judicial organs to safeguard those rights." (Statement by the Staff Council on 25 February 1953, doc. A/2367 and AT/R/12.)

(11) The invitation to the Secretary-General to review the staff problem as a whole and make a fresh report to the eighth session was contained in a draft submitted by thirteen countries, which included the United States of America, France and the United Kingdom; the Secretary-General was to give an account of "the progress made in the conduct and development of personnel policy, together with the comments of the Advisory Committee on Administrative and Budgetary Questions." (*International Organization*, No. 2/VII, 1953, p. 246).

(12) Cf. staff regulations 10.1 and 10.2 and staff rule 110 (1-5) concerning disciplinary measures, the Joint Disciplinary Committee and procedure.

(13) Cf. staff regulations 9.1 (a-c) concerning the dismissal of staff (below, note (18)).

(14) Cases Nos. 36-45 (Judgments Nos. 28-38 of 21 August 1953 and No. 51 of 11 December 1953.) Seven of the complainants had substituted a request for compensation for a request for reinstatement, and they were granted compensation. Three complainants whose reinstatement had been decided upon by the Administrative Tribunal (Judgments Nos. 28-30 and 32) were not reinstated, the Secretary-General having decided to maintain their dismissal. Compensation was granted to them afterwards.

(15) Cases Nos. 26-35. All these applications were rejected, except application No. 26 of Miss R. E. Crawford, Judgment No. 18 of 21 August 1953.

(16) The purpose of this amendment to the Staff Regulations was to obviate any further conflict between the Administrative Tribunal and the administration regarding the interpretation of the idea of "unsatisfactory services" and "integrity" (staff regulation 1.4, amended text).

(17) Staff members were forbidden to "engage in any political activity which is inconsistent with or might reflect upon the independence and impartiality required by their status as international civil servants," but their right to vote was admitted (staff regulation 1.7, amended text).

(18) Staff regulation 9.1 (a): "The Secretary-General may terminate the appointment of a staff member who holds a permanent appointment and whose probationary period has been completed if the necessities of the service require abolition of the post or reduction of the staff, if the services of the individual concerned prove unsatisfactory, or if he is for reasons of health incapacitated for further service." Amended text (resolution 782 A (VIII)): "The Secretary-General may also, giving his reasons therefore, terminate the appointment of a staff member who holds a permanent post:
(i) If the conduct of the staff member indicates that the staff member does not meet the high standards of integrity required by Article 101, paragraph 3 of the Charter;
(ii) If facts anterior to the appointment of the staff member and relevant to his stability come to light which, if they had been known at the time of his appointment should, under the standards established in the Charter, have precluded his appointment.
No termination under sub-paragraphs (i) and (ii) shall take place until the matter has been considered and reported on by a special advisory board appointed for that purpose by the Secretary-General.
Finally, the Secretary-General may terminate the appointment of a staff member who holds a permanent appointment if such action would be in the interest of the good administration of the organization and in accordance with the standards of the Charter, provided that the action is not contested by the staff member concerned."

As regards the special advisory board mentioned above (Kaeckenbeeck, later Gundersen, Board)—cf. staff rule 109.1 : (a) "The Special Advisory Board under staff regulation 9.1 (a) shall be composed of a chairman appointed by the Secretary-General on the nomination of the President of the International Court of Justice and of four members appointed by the Secretary-General in agreement with the Staff Council" (cf. docs A/C.5/574, A/2615, pp. 15-17, A/2777, and A/C.5/726). See below, note (29).

(19) Cf. above, chapter 9, notes (12), (16), (17) and (18).
Staff regulation 9.3: "(a) If the Secretary-General terminates an appointment, the staff member shall be given such notice and such indemnity payment as may be applicable under the Staff Regulations and Staff Rules. Payments of termination indemnity shall be made by the Secretary-General in accordance with the rates and conditions specified in Annex III to the present regulations." (b) *Amended text*: "The Secretary-General may, where the circumstances warrant and he considers it justified, pay to a staff member terminated under the final paragraph of staff regulation 9.1 (a) a termination indemnity payment not more than 50% higher than that which would be otherwise payable under the Staff Regulations.
As regards the rate and conditions of payment, cf. staff rules 109.3 and 109.4.

(20) The minority of the Fifth Committee referred particularly (cf. doc. A/C.5/SR. 420, pp. 9 ff.) to the precedent of 1946 when the last (21st) Assembly of the League refused to carry out the last thirteen judgments of the Administrative Tribunal of the League, invoking the following arguments in support of this refusal: "No outside body exists which can enforce the decision of the Tribunal against the Assembly, and this is a not irrelevant consideration in deciding whether the Assembly is sovereign in this matter and whether the dismissed officials have any right against it. By statutory provision and diplomatic usage, no remedy is available against the League; where then is the official's right against it? *Ubi ius, ibi remedium*, and the absence of any remedy in the circumstances of this case here leads to the conclusion that there is no legal right. If only an ethical right is claimed, the protection against its abuse is not a legal but a political one lying in the hands of the States Members of the League. Sovereignty is a question of fact from which a conclusion of law is drawn: it arises from the presence or absence of overriding and controlling powers." (I.L.O., *Official Bulletin* of 31 August 1946, Vol. XXIX, No. 1, p. 40). Professor Georges Scelle observes in this connection (*Cours de Droit international public*, Paris, 1948, p. 568): "Such a distortion of the idea of sovereignty in the contractual relations of an international organization, which is thus placed beyond the reach of any judicial decision, is hardly believable. Nevertheless this refusal to carry out the judgments of the Tribunal had been rather a "surprise decision" and "had been adopted by a small majority in an atmosphere of liquidation" and in the fear of the financial difficulties which might result from these obligations. In 1953 the situation seemed difficult at the U.N., but the reasons invoked were similar.
The International Court of Justice, in its Advisory Opinion of 13 July 1954, expressed its views on the subject and stated that the precedent of 1946 was not conclusive "in view of the complete lack of identity between the two situations and of the conclusions already drawn by the Court from the Charter and the Statute of the Administrative Tribunal of the United Nations and other relevant instruments and records... it is unnecessary to consider the question whether the Assembly, which in very special circumstances was winding up the League, was justified in rejecting these awards. The cases adjudicated upon by the Tribunal of the League and the circumstances in which they arose are different from those which led to the request for this opinion" (*I.C.J. Reports*, Advisory Opinion of 13 July 1954, op. cit., p. 62).

(21) The Ninth Assembly of the World Federation of United Nations Associations, in 1954, said that it considered it "impossible for the Ninth General Assembly of the

United Nations not to implement immediately the decisions of the Tribunal and thus to deprive the officials concerned of their long awaited compensation" *(Cahiers des Nations Unies*, Paris, No. 28, pp. 7/8). Cf. also statement by F.I.C.S.A. of 10 July 1954 (Doc. SCC/182).

(22) "The General Assembly,... considering... that important legal questions have been raised in the course of debate in the Fifth Committee with respect to that appropriation, decides to submit the following legal questions to the International Court of Justice for an advisory opinion:

"(1) Having regard to the Statute of the United Nations Administrative Tribunal and to any other relevant instruments and to the relevant records, has the General Assembly the right on any grounds to refuse to give effect to an award of compensation made by that Tribunal in favour of a staff member of the United Nations whose contract of service has been terminated without his assent?

"(2) If the answer given by the Court to question (1) is in the affirmative, what are the principal grounds upon which the General Assembly could lawfully exercise such a right?"

(23) Cf. the letter of U.S. Assistant Secretary of State Hickerson dated 20 February 1952 to the Acting Director-General of UNESCO stating that without that Organization's co-operation in the investigations undertaken it would be impossible for his Government to give continued support to UNESCO (cf. UNESCO General Conference doc. AXC/7 of 6 June 1953). Cf. also *ibidem*, annexes Xb and Xc and doc. AXc/7 of 9 June 1955 (p. 4).

(24) Cf. also the protest of the Staff Association of UNESCO dated 31 July 1953; the Council of that Association "deplored the fact that such a decision, taken supposedly in the interests of the Organization, might give the impression of obedience to the injunctions of a Member State, regardless of the international character of the officials of the Secretariat, and considered that Mr. Leff's threatened transfer was only aimed at obliging him to obey the summons of the Federal Grand Jury of the United States of America." Cf. also *Bulletin of the Staff Association of UNESCO*, No. 11, doc. St.AC/331.'

(25) The first case (Judgment No. 15 indicated above) referred to the order of the Director-General of UNESCO to appear before the American authorities in New York in connection with investigations concerning internal security. The second case was provoked by the Director-General's decision of 17 August 1954 informing Mr. Leff that in view of his refusal to appear before the Loyalty Board and of the latter's unfavourable opinion regarding him, he would not be granted a further appointment on the expiration of his present one. This decision was annulled by Judgment No. 18 of the I.L.O. Administrative Tribunal dated 26 April 1955.

(26) Cf., for example, UNESCO's written statement: "These considerations [of the I.L.O. Administrative Tribunal] are surprising for they are put forward by a tribunal which is not competent to settle disputes between officials and the Administration with regard to non-observance of their contracts. While... the complainants have invoked certain constitutional provisions in support of the international character of their past functions, they have never thought of asking the Tribunal to pronounce on the Director-General's constitutional obligations, on his duties to the Organization or on his relations with a staff member. Such a request would indeed have been outside the Tribunal's competence...." (pp. 159/160).

"In inferring from the attitude taken up by the Director-General in specific circumstances and in regard to a particular State Member the future attitudes which the Director-General would be obliged to take in virtue of this procedure, and in appraising the consequences which would result from this hypothetical situation, the Tribunal was pronouncing an opinion chiefly on the expediency of such an attitude on the part of the Director-General towards a State Member.... The Tribunal here misunderstands the conditions in which administrative responsibility at the level of relations between the Organization and the States Members is exercised" (pp. 163/164, I.C.J., Pleadings, Oral Arguments, Documents, *Judgment of the I.L.O. Administrative Tribunal upon complaints made against UNESCO*, 1956).

(27) The Special Committee had been set up in virtue of resolution 888 (IX) of the General Assembly of 17 December 1954. The Committee held twelve meetings between 4 and 21 April 1955. Its report was adopted on 31 May 1955 (doc. A/2909, annexes I-IV).

(28) "It will be noted that the Secretary-General of the U.N., who is the person best qualified to know the requirements of good international administration, may express reservations before all the competent organs as to the necessity and desirability of a review of the Administrative Tribunal's judgments." (M. Bedjaoui, op. cit., p. 559, note 35).

(29) The United States representative remarked in particular (doc. A/C.5/SR.498, p. 4) that "the United States had made concession after concession in an endeavour to achieve a compromise acceptable to all, successively abandoning the position that the General Assembly should have the right to review Administrative Tribunal awards and that a Member State or a small group of Member States should be empowered to compel such a review. The proposal for the establishment of a fifteen-Power committee to screen applications for review represented the extreme concession which the United States could make." Nevertheless, it has been pointed out that "the whole issue of amending the Statute of the Tribunal has further exacerbated the problem of relationships between Member States and the Secretariat. On the strengths or weakness of these relationships rests much of the effectiveness of the United Nations." (*International Conciliation* No. 504, 1955, p. 160).

In this connection an important influence was exercised by the Kaeckenbeek Committee (see above, chapter 9, note (18)) set up by Dag Hammarskjöld in connection with the complaints made in the spring of 1953 by the United States Government through its representative, Ambassador Lodge, regarding the loyalty to their country of officials of United States nationality in the UN Secretariat. Owing to the Secretary-General's doubts as to the moral and legal validity of the juridical conclusions of the United States on this subject, the normal requirements of *due process* not always having been fully met, a committee of highly qualified persons was appointed to define the principles which should guide the Secretary-General in his decisions. Despite Ambassador Lodge's strong objections to the Secretary-General's failure to act immediately against the officials complained of, the Committee proceeded to a careful examination of several cases, in full independence and to the general satisfaction. The United States Government was soon convinced of the correctness of this course of action, and consultations took place to establish procedures for the examination of the loyalty of a country's own nationals which should conform to the principles thus laid down by the United Nations.

CHAPTER 10

THE PERIOD OF UNIVERSALITY:
THE MATURING OF THE UNITED NATIONS

The creative dynamism of Dag Hammarskjöld

"As soon as the first difficulties were encountered in the application of the Charter, Mr. Trygve Lie acknowledged the responsibility which fell upon him. His 'peace programme' in particular constituted an attempt to meet this responsibility. But it was undoubtedly Mr. Hammarskjöld, who gave the greatest emphasis to the function of Secretary-General. The early outlines of the doctrine which he was to preach in the following years appear in his first report in 1953. Today the edifice is complete; it bears the mark of Dag Hammarskjöld's highmindedness and of his penetrating and lucid intelligence. He was able to combine a realism, which rid the United Nations of a number of myths which had become commonplaces, with a determination not to betray any of the authentic values consecrated in the Charter."[a]

The eight years during which the direction of the Secretariat was in the hands of Dag Hammarskjöld marked an epoch in the evolution of the international civil service. He took up his duties in the midst of a crisis, having to retrieve a disastrous situation, and his career ended with his death "on active service," in performance of his duty during another serious and testing crisis. Dag Hammarskjöld carried out his heavy tasks with serenity, faith and courage and with an incomparable spirit of initiative. Whatever opinion one may have of the steps he took in any particular case, he always acted from a sense of duty, without attempting to evade his responsibilities and with as much imagination as resolution. Faced with dramatic conflicts and personal attacks, he remained until the last day of his life a man of action, true to his convictions, the personification in the eyes of the world of the international outlook to which he had given a philosophical basis, and applying with remarkable consistency his fundamental thesis:

"Working at the edge of the development of human society is to work on the brink of the unknown. Much of what is done will one day prove to have been of little avail. That is no excuse for the failure to act in accordance with our best understanding, in recognition of its limits but with faith in the ultimate result of the creative evolution in which it is our privilege to co-operate."[b]

(a) M. Virally, "Le rôle politique du Secrétaire général..." (op. cit., p. 382).
(b) Dag Hammarskjöld, Chicago address (*United Nations Review*, June 1960).

To the great adventure of international co-operation Hammarskjöld contributed an independent and constructive mind. His addresses at Baltimore, Stanford, Berkeley, Columbus, Chicago, Harvard, Oxford, Lund, Copenhagen, Philadelphia, Oslo, Cambridge, New Delhi and elsewhere, his famous introductions to his annual reports, his press conferences, are all characterized by a logic based on careful and ingenious interpretation of texts, but also on rich practical experience. His vision of "international service"[a] was paralleled by his political realism and was based on a truly universal humanism. If the "process of organic growth" of the U.N.[b] has reached the stage of maturity, that is largely his personal achievement.

His work necessarily forms a *whole* and cannot be arbitrarily broken up. Nevertheless, in order to describe his achievements and the message he has left as faithfully as possible, we must approach them from three angles:
—that of the *administrator* practicing a "dynamic leadership" and leaving a lasting imprint on international administrative thought;
—that of the *politician*—diplomatist, negotiator, mediator;
—that of the *theorist* of international co-operation and of the international civil service, the philosopher of action, the ideologist, constantly lifting the discussion to the plane of principles.

The administrator

By vocation and inclination Dag Hammarskjöld was first an administrative chief. Like Sir Eric Drummond at the League he devoted enormous personal effort to the solution of properly administrative problems. He has thus left an indelible mark on the whole of the international civil service and not only on the U.N. Through the Administrative Committee on Co-ordination, his personal influence extended throughout the United Nations family.

First, his administration was marked by the final adoption of the staff regulations, the formal determination of the standards of conduct to be observed by international officials, the resolution to enforce these standards and a constant effort to improve geographical distribution although the number of States Members of the U.N. doubled during this period.

Secondly, confronted with the functional and geographical extension of the U.N., he undertook a gradual internal reorganization of the Secretariat in order to provide it with a machinery corresponding to his own administrative conceptions, with effective communications and co-ordination, and an elastic planning system.

As an illustration of the gigantic development of the U.N.'s ad-

(a) Dag Hammarskjöld, statement at Idlewild Airport, 9 April 1953 (doc. SG/287).
(b) Dag Hammarskjöld, interview on German television, 9 May 1959 (doc. SG/819, p. 3).

ministrative action during Hammarskjöld's term of office, a few figures may be of interest.[a]

Budgetary expenditure[b]	Number of staff[c]
1954—48,510	4,029
1955—50,089	3,915
1956—50,508	3,769
1957—53,172	3,940
1958—62,505	3,993
1959— 60,802[d]	4,022

Thus the total strength of the staff was stabilized and somewhat reduced. Adjustments were still necessary to meet the growing needs of the U.N.'s expanding programmes, in particular of the Field Services, whose staff represented in 1958 and the following years about 44% of the total.[e] If we consider that the administrative expenses amounted to about 25.5% of budgetary expenditure, and that staff costs were 63.9% of administrative expenditure,[f] some idea will be gained of the immensity of the Secretary-General's task of administrative organization.

To ensure the smooth and regular operation of the machine, the Secretary-General, with the help of experts and various consultative bodies, undertook a series of reforms which, though individually their merits might be questioned, put an end to the disorder and improvisation of the early days of the Secretariat. The following measures are characteristic:

I. *Codification.* The elaboration and adoption of the staff regulations, and of the detailed staff rules accompanying them,[g] stabilized a situation which had hitherto been fluid. The chief aim was a compromise between the staff's legitimate desire for security of tenure and the need to be able to terminate a particular appointment in cases defined in the regulations (if necessary without resorting to the ordinary disciplinary procedures, but always under the impartial control of the Administrative Tribunal). A series of provisions were also adopted concerning the Joint Staff Pension Fund of the United Nations family. This was good for staff morale and was at the same time a factor of

(a) These figures refer to the U.N. only.
(b) In thousands of U.S. dollars.
(c) Figures relating to permanent posts excluding the International Court of Justice, the Office of the High Commissioner for Refugees, Field Services, and special missions (cf. doc. A/3860, supplement 7, p. 9).
(d) Excluding additonal credits (cf. doc. A/4170, supplement 7, p. 1).
(e) Cf. W. R. Sharp, "Field Administration..." (op. cit., p. 42). The figure for the whole United Nations family was 49%.
(f) Cf. Report of the Advisory Committee on Administrative and Budgetary Questions for 1958.
(g) See above, chapter 8, note (16).

unification in the "family".[1] Further provisions concerned the classification of posts; the fixing of salaries and allowances for all categories
of staff, taking into account differences in the cost of living and the
expatriation factor; and a uniform policy regarding leave, including
home leave, for international staff.

II. *Career stabilization.* Permanent appointments (89% in 1956)[a]
gradually replaced temporary appointments. The period of improvisation being over, it was possible, within the framework of the new
reforms, to organize the careers of staff members. The reform of
1957 was a great step forward in this direction. None the less, in
addition to "permanent" or "regular" appointments,[2b] three kinds
of temporary appointment, were retained: probationary, fixed-term
and indeterminate.[3]

To advise the Secretary-General on appointments, promotions and
regrading, advisory bodies were set up consisting of officials appointed
by the Secretary-General from a list of names proposed by the Staff
Council.[4] As a consequence, the staff were given a greater say in the
conduct of their affairs.

As to promotions, the reform put an end to the practice of notifying
each vacancy separately. Each year a general survey of all posts is
undertaken by one of the advisory committees, and at suitable intervals this committee draws up promotion registers which must be kept
up to date thereafter. These registers give the total number of expected
vacancies in each grade which have to be filled by promotion before the
next general review. If, owing to the nature of the work, a vacancy
cannot be filled from the promotion register, the advisory committee
may, exceptionally, without awaiting the next general review, consider
the qualifications of a number of officials and recommend the promotion of the most suitable candidate. Officials of the Secretariat and
of other international organizations are given preference, other things
being equal, over outside candidates for any vacancy. Lastly, each
official must occupy a post in his category for a minimum period before qualifying for promotion; this period is one year in the professional
category and at the top of the General Service category, and six
months for other posts.

Thus, with the help of the staff themselves, machinery in keeping
with modern ideas as to the management of a career civil service
was set up, and the serious initial errors were gradually put right.
Career stabilization, considered to be the keystone of the international
civil service, was strongly promoted by the 1957 reforms.[c] Further-

(a) See above, chapter 8, p. 190 and chapter 8, note (8), p. 205.
(b) Cf. staff rule 104.13 and doc. ST/SGB/94/Rev. 4/amend. 10 of 17 October 1957.
(c) Cf. Doc. ST/ADM/SER.A/437 of 17 October 1957.

more the staff's confidence was gained and sound human relations were established in the Secretariat.

Nevertheless, as the number of Member States increased, the proportion of temporary appointments again began to grow and reached 20.5% on 31 August 1961 (this proportion varied in different regions).[a] Paradoxically but naturally, a reverse process, endangering the stabilization of the staff which had been so laboriously built up, began towards the end of the Hammarskjöld era. According to the experts consulted and the proposals submitted,[5] the percentage of temporary appointments should be stabilized between 20 and 25%, and the General Assembly adopted the figure of 20% in 1957;[b] proposals were made in 1961 for an increase in this rate, but they were never put to the vote.[6] The eastern European countries even asked that permanent appointments should be abolished altogether.[c]

Thus, once again, and not for the last time, the desire for geographical distribution came into conflict with the need for stability and reintroduced the *provisional* factor. Temporary appointments are so short (two years on the average) that their holders obviously cannot make a really useful contribution to the Secretariat unless their work is equally limited. It has therefore been rightly pointed out once again[d] that "the effectiveness of the Secretariat as an international service depends upon its being predominantly a career service."

III. *Standards of conduct of international civil servants.* In response to a request from the Administrative Committee on Co-ordination in October 1951, the International Civil Service Advisory Board drew up in March 1954, while the Secretariat crisis was at its height, a "Report on Standards of Conduct in the International Civil Service". This report[e] was submitted to the Administrative Committee on Co-ordination at its eighteenth session, in May 1954, and was communicated by the Secretary-General during the IXth session of the General Assembly to all the States Members[f] and to the members of the staff.[g] It was both an ethical code and a detailed guide to behaviour. In the foreword, the principle is laid down that high standards of conduct will be maintained only if all the men and women on the staff understand the relation between their conduct and the success

(a) Cf. S. D. Bailey (op. cit., p. 32).
(b) Resolution 1095 (XI of 27 February 1957 and Doc. A/3558 (pp. 31-33)).
(c) General Assembly, XVIth session, Doc. A/C.5/SR869, 1 November 1961 (para. 51).
(d) Cf. for example, 14 the Report (part V) of the American Association for the United Nations, Commission to Study the Organization of Peace (New York, January 1962, World Federation of U.N. Associations Doc. PA 17/20/3/USA, p. 9).
(e) Doc. COORD/CIVIL SERVICE/5.
(f) Doc. A/C.5/726 (para. 18).
(g) Doc. ST/ADM/SER.A/277 of 8 October 1954.

of the international organization which they serve, and if they are jealous of its reputation and eager to safegaurd it. The obligations arising from the Charter, from the constitutions of the specialized agencies and from the Staff Regulations are then described and explained. There thus emerges a sort of doctrine of the international civil service which "by underlining certain basic principles and by suggesting practical applications of these principles to concrete situations... is aimed at promoting increased understanding and improved practices."

Arising out of Article 101, paragraph 3, of the Charter, the report prescribes four positive duties which it calls "basic considerations"—namely:

integrity, which must be judged on the basis of the total behaviour of the person concerned, taking into account such elementary personal or private qualities as honesty, truthfulness, fidelity, probity and freedom from corrupting influences, and bearing in mind that the international civil servant is a *public* as well as an *international* official;

loyalty to the international organization, combined with an international outlook ("which flows from an understanding of and loyalty to the objectives set forth in the Charter... and involves willingness to try to understand and be tolerant of different points of view, different cultural patterns and different work habits");

independence of any authority outside the international organization;

impartiality, "implying objectivity, lack of bias, tolerance, restraint."

To these fundamental standards must be added others—namely: (*a*) As regards conduct *within the Secretariat:* deliberate efforts to overcome biased attitudes, through better understanding and intellectual discipline and through the cultivation of social relations between members of the staff and between supervisors and subordinates;[a] (*b*) As regards relations *with governments and with the representative bodies of the Organization:* The report stresses the non-representative character of the official in relation to his own government (even if seconded by the latter to the Secretariat) or to his country's policy. Once again the principle of independence is insisted upon, and the idea of "liaison officer" is rejected (unless the Secretary-General expressly asks an official to assume this task).[b]

Lastly, the report deals with various other problems: obligation to refrain from any political activity, relations with the public (particularly the press), conduct of the staff away from headquarters (non-political outside activities and obligations in private life). The international civil servant must set himself "a high standard

(a) Cf. T. Aghnides, "Standards of Conduct of the International Civil Servant," in *Revue internationale des Sciences administratives* (No. 1, 1953, pp. 182/183).
(b) Cf. "The International Secretariat of the Future" (op. cit., pp. 34/35, quoted by the report in this connection, pp. 8/9).

of personal conduct... he must exercise restraint even in the use of rights recognized by the existing legislation if this use is likely to reflect unfavourably on the Organization." In general "the international civil servant must accept special restraints in his public and private life, and it is in so doing that he can make his positive contribution to the work and ideals of the international organizations. Integrity, international loyalty, independence and impartiality and the subordination of private interests to the interests of the organization, are daily requirements. The Board looks forward confidently to the development of a proud tradition which will make clear to all who come into contact with the international organizations that their staff members accept the high responsibility which their status demands."[a]

The importance of these standards derives not only from their content based on the essential conception of the international civil service, but also from the fact that they aim at uniformity and deliberately initiate a tradition based on long experience; they are a point of departure for the personnel policy followed by the Secretary-General.[b]

IV. *Reorganization of structures*. The more stable the framework of the Secretariat and the heavier its workload, the more urgent became its internal reorganization. Previous decisions had therefore to be revised, "the initial importance of which had been reduced by subsequent developments," and "the greatest possible efficiency and a continuing self-criticism as to the way in which various tasks were carried out" had to be ensured.[c]

For lack of its own administrative doctrine, the United Nations sought to guide itself by principles of "administrative orthodoxy"[d] based on "strong reasons of principle and logic."[e] The constant development of new activities, particularly economic and social, the provision of technical assistance to underdeveloped States, and the extension of regional activities made it necessary to re-group cognate tasks and to arrange better communications between the headquarters services and the external organs. Thus the object of the reform of 1954 was to eliminate duplication by putting an end to improvised arrangements and to make justifiable economies, as well as to carry on the mass of new work imposed on the Secretariat for political reasons or owing simply to the confusion of international affairs.

(a) Report of I.C.S.A.B., No. 5 (op. cit., chapter VIII, paragraph 53, and chapter IX, paragraphs 56 and 57).
(b) Cf. doc. A/C.5/726, paragraphs 22 ff. and resolution 1227 (XII) of the General Assembly dated 18 December 1957.
(c) Doc. A/2554 of 12 November 1953 (p. 3).
(d) Doc. A/C.5/SR.642 (p. 12).
(e) Doc. A/C.5/728 (p. 8).

After several preparatory studies,[7] the proposed reorganization was accepted, first by the Economic and Social Council,[a] and then by the General Assembly at its IXth session.[b] It essentially comprised the following reforms:

reorganization of the higher posts of the Secretariat by the creation of sixteen Under-Secretaries of equal rank,[8] independently of their duties and title, two of them being "without portfolio";

emphasis on the properly administrative task of the Under-Secretaries, their former standing as "representatives" having been made obsolete by the presence of permanent national delegations at the United Nations "giving opportunities for a continuous and close contact between the Secretary-General personally and various governments";[c] the Under-Secretaries "without portfolio" were to assure co-ordination between different departments or services;

direct subordination to the Secretary-General of certain services specially excluded from the "departmental" structure of the Secretariat and converted into "Offices of the Secretary-General" (Executive Office, Office of Legal Affairs, Office of the Controller, Office of Personnel). The idea was to give the Secretary-General direct supervision over staff and financial questions, at the same time establishing a clearer distribution of responsiblities. This reform, which strengthened the authority of the head of the Secretariat, was the subject of much discussion at the time and some criticism. The fact that Byron Price was not replaced at the head of the administrative services also placed a heavy load on the Secretary-General, while providing strong evidence of his interest in administrative and especially personnel questions;

reorganization of information services both at headquarters and outside;

merger of the Economic Affairs and Social Affairs Departments. On the other hand, the Department of Conference and General Services was divided into two units: Department of Conference Services and Office of General Services;[9]

creation of "vertical departments" away from headquarters side by side with the "horizontal units" at headquarters (transfer of the Narcotics Division to Geneva);[d]

tendency to greater geographical decentralization, with emphasis on the "regional approach," by the reinforcement of the secretarial services of the regional Economic Commissions, by keeping missions

(a) ECOSOC resolution 557 (XVIII), dated 5 August 1954.
(b) General Assembly resolution 343 (IX) dated 17 December 1954.
(c) Doc. A/2554 (p. 8).
(d) Annual Report of the Secretary-General for 1955/1956 (doc. A/3137, p. 65).

"on the spot" for varying periods, by creating certain mixed "regional units."[a]

V. *Elimination of less necessary work.* In pursuance of several previous resolutions, action was taken to relieve the Secretariat's burden by restricting the number of its tasks and reducing the volume of documentation.[b] The Secretary-General had found it necessary to "farm out" work to competent and impartial persons in order to ease the Secretariat's task and to avoid "a constant danger, where agreement cannot be reached at the intergovernmental level, of the Secretariat being asked for compilations of studies involving effort and funds quite disproportionate to the probable value of the results...."[c]

He therefore recommended that the tendency should continue "towards a shift of emphasis from certain of the existing information services and clearing house activities, a more limited framework for the prosecution of certain work requested of the Secretariat in order to bring it within the proper sphere of the Secretariat's competence, the reconsideration of certain low-priority projects by the organs concerned, the recognition of the full responsibility of specialized tasks clearly within their mandate, the taking over, under the Secretariat's general guidance, of certain research, training and other tasks by universities and other private institutions...."[d]

VI. *Gradual improvement of methods and procedures of recruitment in the Secretariat, with special reference to geographical distribution.* The Secretariat's maturity depended on a new approach to the recruitment problem. Organized in a haphazard manner at first, recruitment was now no longer to be considered as a series of isolated operations but as a continuous process. "The main emphasis [was to] be on the follow-up of the staff member's performance, conduct and progress during the probationary period."[e] Qualified candidates must be effectively sought, while the independence of recruiting offices was ensured; qualifications must be thoroughly examined and competitive examinations held when possible. It was also necessary to review the methods of announcing vacancies (posting on the notice board, announcements in the press, relations with various institutions) and to improve the system of tests and interviews. Lastly, thought had to be given to the preliminary and in-service training of international officials.

(a) Cf. docs. A/3041, A/3160, A/C.5/665, A/C.5/667 (pp. 5/6).
(b) ECOSOC resolution 557 A (XVIII) dated 5 August 1954 and doc. A/C.5/630 (p.9).
(c) Doc. E/2598 of 13 May 1954 (p. 12).
(d) *Ibidem* (p.p 3ff.) and doc. A/2884 of 16 December 1954.
(e) Circular by the Director of Personnel, doc. ST/ADM/SER.A/437 of 17 October 1957 (chapter 11).

Owing to obstacles of all kinds, however, recruitment was only partially and gradually reformed during Hammarskjöld's tenure of office. The great idea, discussed in the early days of the United Nations, of setting up an international civil service commission—an impartial and inter-institutional organ responsible for unified and scientifically organized recruitment, or at least endowed with advisory powers[a]— did not seem practicable at this time. The elements of chance and confusion could not yet be entirely ruled out. Progress could only be fragmentary and aimed at reducing favouritism and unpleasant surprises. Nothing could be done in the important matter of the advance training of cadidates, and very little as regards in-service training. Nevertheless, the Office of Personnel played a greater part in the procedure of recruitment and in the advisory bodies as soon as the 1957 reform came into force. Efforts were made to apply the recommendations of the International Civil Service Advisory Board as to methods and standards of recruitment so as to limit, if not to abolish, the haphazard element. The Secretary-General's personal interest in the improvement of recruitment was an added stimulus.

If the efforts at improvement did not lead to a comprehensive reform, completely eliminating all recruitment defects, the reason is to be found in the old problem of *geographical distribution*, since this criterion was still applied both to recruitment at the most junior level and for higher posts in the Secretariat which had to be filled "from outside." The difficulties of the previous period[b] were even intensified. In spite of continuous efforts to achieve the optimum result, it was materially impossible to attain a real and lasting balance, owing to the constant increase in the number of Member States. There were repeated criticisms, and one session of the General Assembly after another recommended a more equitable distribution, with particular emphasis on the recruitment of nationals of countries not yet "represented" in the Secretariat.[c] Nevertheless, the Secretary-General stated in 1956[d] that real progress had been made at the U.N. and that the "Secretariat staff represented the widest nationality distribution and the nearest approach to balanced representation of nationalities of Member States that has ever been achieved in a major international organization."

The situation in the Secretariat at the end of Hammarskjöld's tenure of office was as follows:

(a) Cf. above, chapter 8, p. 197, and note (12). Cf., for example, C. Purves, *International Establishments, Some Notes based on the Experience of the International Administration of the League of Nations Secretariat* (London, 1945, p. 45): A. Pelt, *Peculiar Characteristics of an International Administration* (op. cit., *passim*).
(b) Cf. above, chapter 8.
(c) Resolutions 1097 (XI), 1226 (XII), 1294 (XIII), 1446 (XIV), 1559 (XV).
(d) General Assembly, 10th session, 5th Committee, 513th meeting (doc. A/C.5/689 and doc. A/3103).

TABLE Iᵃ

Number of Member States	As at 31 August		
	1955	1959	1960
I. *Above* desirable range	24	25	27
II. *Within* desirable range	27	38	40
III. With staff members but *below* desirable range	2	8	5
IV. With staff members—total	53	71	72
V. With no staff members	6	11	10
VI. Total number of the staff members at the time . . .	59	82	82ᵇ

(a) Cf. doc. A/C.5/833 of 17 October 1960 (para. 7).
(b) As at 1 April 1961 (cf. doc. A/4776, annex V) the categories were composed as follows:

I. *Western Europe*: Austria, Belgium, Denmark, Greece, Ireland, Netherlands. Norway.
Eastern Europe: Yugoslavia.
Middle East: Iran, Israel, Jordan, Lebanon.
Africa: Ghana, United Arab Republic (before secession of Syria), Union of South Africa.
Asia and the Far East: Ceylon, India, New Zealand, Pakistan, Philippines, Thailand.
Latin America: Bolivia, Chile, Colombia, Cuba, Ecuador, Haiti, Peru.

II. *Western Europe*: Finland, France, Ireland, Italy, Luxembourg, Portugal, Spain, Sweden, United Kingdom.
Eastern Europe: Bulgaria, Czechoslovakia, Hungary, Poland.
Middle East: Afghanistan, Iraq, Saudi Arabia, Turkey, Yemen.
Africa: Ethiopia, Liberia, Morocco, Senegal, Sudan, Togo.
Asia and the Far East: Australia, Burma, Federation of Malaya, Indonesia, Japan, Nepal.
Latin America: Argentina, Brazil, Costa Rica, Dominican Republic, Guatemala, Mexico, Nicaragua, Panama, Paraguay, Uruguay.
North America: Canada, United States.

III. *Eastern Europe*: Romania, Ukraine, U.S.S.R.
Asia and the Far East: China (Formosa).
Latin America: Venezuela.

IV. *Eastern Europe*: Albania, Byelorussia.
Middle East: Cyprus.
Africa: Cameroun, Central African Republic, Chad, Congo (Brazzaville), Congo (ex Belgian), Dahomey, Gabon, Guinea, Ivory Coast, Libya, Madagascar, Mali, Nigeria, Somalia, Tunisia, Upper Volta.
Asia and the Far East: Cambodia, Laos.
Latin America: El Salvador, Honduras.

TABLE II[a]

Number of posts (by geographical regions)

Geographical region	Number of posts on 31 August 1955	Number of posts on 31 August 1960	Difference in %
I. Western Europe	353	360	+ 2
II. Eastern Europe	55	84	+53
III. Near East	30	41	+37
IV. Africa	26	43	+65
V. Asia and the Far East	155	211	+36
VI. Latin America	96	108	+12
VII. North America	300	294	— 2
Total	1015	1141	+12

TABLE III[b]

Distribution by region in comparison with desirable range

Region	Median of desirable range	Number of staff on 31 August 1959	Number of staff on 31 August 1960	Ratio of staff to median of desirable range 1959:%	Ratio of staff to median of desirable range 1960:%
I. Western Europe	299	355	360	118	120
II. Eastern Europe	216	68	84	31	39
III. Middle East	24	39	41	163	171
IV. Africa	27	35	43	130	159
V. Asia and Far East	177	201	211	114	119
VI. Latin America	77	101	108	131	140
VII. North America	388	291	294	75	76
Total	1208	1090	1141	90	94

(a) Cf. doc. A/C.5/833 of 17 October (para. 15). The figures for 1955 refer to the period immediately preceding the admission of a great number of new Member States. The table refers to professional (P1-P5) and directorial (D1, D2) posts, and those of Under-Secretary.
(b) *Ibidem* (para. 13). This table permits a comparison between the situations in 1959 and 1960 and between the number of staff and the median of the desirable range (see also annex to doc. A/C.5/833).

TABLE IVᵃ

Distribution by regions in comparison with median of desirable range

Region	Number of staff on 1 April 1961	Median of desirable range
I. Western Europe	379	299
II. Eastern Europe	84	219
III. Middle East	41	25
IV. Africa	49	56
V. Asia and Far East	204	178
VI. Latin America	107	76
VII. North America	381	392
Total 1245		1245[11]

An analysis of the figures shows that, in recruiting new staff, due account was taken of the principle of balanced geographical distribution; but the composition of the Secretariat having already reached a high degree of stability, the available margin was insufficient to make it possible to change materially the distribution by nationalities. Thus the achieving of geographical balance was recognized to be a continuous and long-term process, aimed at giving the Secretariat as fully international a character as possible in accordance with the provisions of the Charter and taking every advantage of staff movements. Although it was agreed that the possibilities of change were limited, the *rate* of progress was still a subject of disagreement between certain States Members and the Secretary-General.[b] The latter invoked administrative necessity, while several States, some of whom were already sufficiently represented in the Secretariat, were displeased with the existing system of distribution and wished to tie the Secretariat's hands by transforming the *indications* concerning geographical distribution given by the national quotas into a strict arithmetic rule. It was therefore evident that "in reality a State naturally tends to strive less *against* the predominance of another in the Secretariat than *for* its own influence in the Secretariat. Thus systematic geographical distribution, regarded as a good solution, constantly carries in itself the germs of the same disease."[c]

The Salary Review Committee,[d] commenting on the measures to improve geographical distribution which had been introduced by the Secretary-General, said that "the purpose is not to provide various

(a) Cf. doc. A/4776 of 14 June 1961 (para. 82, Table II). The table covers staff at levels G5 to D1 inclusive (cf. also annexes I-IX of doc. A/4776).
(b) Cf. doc. A/C.5/SR.630 (p. 20).
(c) M. Bedjaoui (op. cit., p. 81).
(d) Cf. above, chapter 8, p. 190. Cf. also doc. A/3209 (paras. 35-37) and doc. A/C. 5/689.

nationals with jobs in international secretariats, but to ensure that the international secretariats contain competent personnel coming from and reflecting various backgrounds, with different problems and different cultures and differing psychological and emotional responses.'' The impossibility of applying rigid formulae was thus confirmed once again.

The Secretary-General took a number of steps to mitigate the numerous drawbacks of the disequilibrium which still existed.

Every two months he undertook a study of the distribution of the staff by nationalities, classifying States into several groups entitled to greater or less priority on the basis of the numbers and ranks of their nationals in the Secretariat and giving highest priority to the recruitment of candidates from countries with no "representative" in the Secretariat or with a "representation" below the desirable range.

He periodically studied the manning table of each service, in order to determine what posts were vacant or would soon have to be filled from outside; every three months, countries in the group with the highest priority received a list of vacancies with general indications as to qualifications and salaries, and were invited to submit candidates fulfilling the requisite conditions. Thus, the desire to improve geographical distribution led Dag Hammarskjöld to revert, to some extent, to his predecessor's dangerous practice of using governments as a medium for recruiting. But his personal prestige was at stake and the final decision lay with him.

He frequently invited the permanent delegates of "under-represented" countries to conferences at the Secretariat in order to ensure the necessary contacts. After these meetings, high officials of the Office of Personnel or other staff members visited the countries concerned in order to discuss recruitment.

The Office of Personnel remained constantly in touch with the international officials stationed away from headquarters, so as to keep them informed of recruitment requirements, with particular reference to geographical distribution.

Other steps for the immediate improvement of geographical distribution included an increase in the number of temporary appointments, particularly for officials seconded by the national administrations[a] and increased semi-local recruitment.[b]

Thus, by accepting certain compromises, the Secretary-General reduced the tension resulting from the attitude of "under-represented" or "unrepresented" States. At the same time, by refusing to apply geographical distribution to promotions, he maintained the necessary balance although the practice of filling the higher posts directly from

(a) Cf. above, chapter 8, p. 191 and note (4).
(b) Cf. above, chapter 4, note (53).

outside blocked the possibilities of normal promotion for career personnel above a certain (not very high) level. He also tried to ensure equitable distribution, not only in the Secretariat as a whole, but also in the individual administrative units. He thus aimed at establishing a *modus vivendi* with the States Members and to prevent national "enclaves" from being formed in certain units.

In pursuance of resolution 1446 (XIV) of the General Assembly, the Secretary-General had appointed a committee of experts to review the activities and organization of the Secretariat, including the problem of geographical distribution. This Committee, whose Chairman was Guillaume Georges-Picot, a former Assistant Secretary-General of the United Nations, proposed[a] that recruitment should no longer be based principally on the budgetary contributions of Member States, but that priority should be given to other criteria: membership of the U.N. (this alone automatically giving each State Member a quota of two officials), the population factor and the desirability of securing over-all balance for the seven main geographical regions of the world (Africa, Asia and the Far East, eastern Europe, western Europe, the Middle East, Latin America and North America).

At about the same time, the problem of geographical distribution was exacerbated by the U.S.S.R.'s claim for a number of posts corresponding to its budgetary contribution. The difficulties of recruitment of Soviet nationals and the long period of marked indifference by the U.S.S.R. in the past, as regards the participation of its nationals in the international civil service had resulted in its "representation" in the Secretariat being well below the "desirable range." The legitimate requirement that the desirable range should be attained could only be met by degrees: the rights of existing permanent staff must be respected, the proper percentage of temporary appointments must not be exceeded, the situation could only be remedied when vacancies occurred—often only at long intervals— and it was therefore impossible for the Secretary-General to take radical steps in the matter. Thus, the progress already achieved by long and patient effort was again seriously threatened. On 1 April 1961, the U.S.S.R. had forty-four posts in the Secretariat,[b] whereas its desirable range was 145 to 193.[c] It was therefore very difficult to satisfy that country's claims and at the same time to give a fair representation to the new African Members, while avoiding serious discontent among the existing staff, and without recruiting all new staff from the same source over a long period, which would be contrary to the principles of sound administration.

(a) Cf. doc. A/4776 op. cit., paras 74 ff.).
(b) Internationally recruited posts including those at G5 level. Cf. doc. A/4776, annex II (p. 6).
(c) *Ibidem.*

Dag Hammarskjöld says in this connection:

> "The wide geographical basis prescribed in Article 101 of the Charter was a continuous and long-term effort, and all that the Secretary-General could rightly be asked to do was to bear the instructions in the Charter on that point constantly in mind and to endeavour in the course of changes in staff to see that the Secretariat was as fully international as possible in character.... I must again recall that we are faced not with the problem of recruiting a Secretariat and building the principle of balanced geographical distribution into that process, but rather with the question of a Secretariat which has reached a high degree of stability and in which, therefore, opportunity for change in the international pattern is strictly limited."[a]

Dag Hammarskjöld was unable to solve this puzzle because it was insoluble; the problem changed continually in different ways and for different reasons, independently of administrative requirements. Nevertheless, in spite of everything, the theory of recruitment was explained to and understood by those who were willing to understand it. The deliberate integration of geographical distribution into the long-term recruitment programme still remains to be undertaken; its success depends on the co-operation of the Member States in carrying out the principles of the Charter, and on their comprehension of the requirements of sound public administration.

We cannot examine here the many examples of Dag Hammarskjöld's initiative and achievement as an administrator. He well understood the importance of the administrative factor in international co-operation and the value of apparently minor but methodical and decisive adjustments. Despite several disappointments, the staff of the Secretariat was aware of this and gave him its confidence.

Hammarskjöld thus expressed this conception of the role of the international administration: "In international organizations, questions of the levels of pay and allowances, personnel management and administration go to... the heart of the general manner in which international secretariats are enabled to exercise their role in achieving the objectives of the organizations."[b]

The political leader

> "A few years ago, the idea that the Secretary-General of the U.N. might perform a political role was only accepted with the greatest reserve and scepticism. Moreover, little notice was taken of him: all attention was focussed on the debates of the General Assembly and the Security Council. The great political question seemed to be that of the veto, on which the whole future of the Organization was thought to hinge. It is beginning to be realized how exaggerated was this view, and at the same time the other aspects of the U.N. have emerged from the shadows in which they had been left by the too-violent flood-lighting of the relations between permanent Members.... The prominent

(a) Doc. A/C.5/689, 7 December 1956 (p. 1).
(b) Report of the Secretary-General on the report of the Salary Review Committee, doc. A/C.5/691 of 14 December 1956 (p. 21).

place occupied today [by 'Mr. H'] in international political life has been described.... The Secretary-General of the U.N. found himself on a footing of equality with the heads of the greatest Powers: and he was thus officially recognized as playing a political role of the first importance."[a]

Both at the League of Nations and at the U.N. it has been recognized that the Secretary-General has a sort of "double personality," playing a dual role in the administrative and in the political and diplomatic spheres. We have seen that in Trygve Lie's day[b] the political role had grown substantially as compared with the days of the League of Nations. But the widening of the Secretary-General's duties in this direction was regarded with suspicion and hostility by some of the Great Powers, such as Britain,[c] and by some of the smaller States, such as Belgium and the Netherlands.[d] Despite this state of mind, Trygve Lie played a part on the international political scene, but "what appeared considerable in 1952 was but a pale reflection of the reality of 1958,"[e] and even more of the years which followed.

Because the U.N. was unable to take a united stand on crucial questions, Dag Hammarskjöld was forced to assume growing responsibilities in the political field. To break deadlocks and to avoid the danger of anarchy when it was unable to reach a clear-cut decision, the Security Council, on a number of occasions, delegated powers to the Secretary-General to act on behalf of the U.N., or left him such latitude of interpretation that he was obliged to assume political responsibility. This was a symptom of the growing ineffectiveness of the Council, and sometimes of the General Assembly in face of the conflicts between the great Powers. These bodies had to leave things to the Secretary-General, since he was the permanent organ enjoying, in theory, the confidence of all the States Members and having a large administrative machine at his disposal. The practice was frequently criticized from the point of view of the constitutional division of tasks between the principal organs and the overlapping of powers and jurisdictions as defined in the Charter. Inevitably, very difficult situations arose in which the Secretary-General was bound to take a stand in disputes between Powers, even if he was only carrying out faithfully the instructions he had received and if he tried to cover himself by asking the advice of committees set up for the purpose.

This development was inherent in the function of the Secretary-General. As Dag Hammarskjöld himself observed, "the character of the mandates has in many cases been such that in carrying out his functions the Secretary-General has found himself forced also to

(a) M. Virally, "Le rôle politique du Secrétaire général..." (op. cit., pp. 360/361).
(b) Cf. above, chapter 8, p. 201 ff.
(c) Cf. above, chapter 4. p. 75, and notes (5) and (6).
(d) Cf. S. M. Schwebel (op. cit., p. 165).
(e) M. Virally, "Le rôle politique du Secrétaire général..." (op. cit., p. 362).

interpret decisions in the light of the Charter, U.N. precedents and the aims and intentions expressed by Members. When that has been the case, the Secretary-General has been under the obligation to seek guidance to all possible extent from the main organs; but when such guidance has not been forthcoming, developments have sometimes led to situations in which he has had to shoulder responsibility for certain limited political functions which may be considered to be in line with the spirit of Article 99, but which legally have been based on decisions of the main organs themselves under Article 98 and thus the exclusive responsibility of Member States acting through these organs."[a] It is sufficient to compare this statement with the Noblemaire Report in the days of the League, which stressed the limited extent to which the Secretariat could interpret the wishes of Member States, to see how different is the new conception of the role of the Secretariat and of its chief.[b]

Moreover, Hammarskjöld was a man with a sound knowledge of international relations, imagination, courage and a sense of responsibility. He stood head and shoulders above his fellows and was regarded by some as a diplomatic genius.[c] In any case, he was not a man of compromise, hastily chosen to fill a gap, but a man of inspiration and character, who could be expected to take strong action whatever the risk. "The Secretary-General himself has an inescapable political leadership role: he is accordingly, as are all political leaders, a *risk-taker* and an expendable, not a career official..."[d]

His task was monumental, apparently too great for human strength. Inevitably, he became a sort of "independent executive." The fact that he had no legal authority vis-à-vis the Member States did not prevent the continual enhancement of his "strategic position" in such a way as to make him "the central personality of the U.N. and its incarnation in the eyes of the world."[e] It has been rightly pointed out that: "in diplomatic relations influence does not depend entirely on the material power which each individual has at his command. Personality, prestige and skill have retained an importance here which they have lost in many other spheres. The place occupied in a negotiation may have a strategic and hence an enhanced value, in the same way as, in a Parliament, a 'splinter' party may play a part quite out of proportion to its numerical weakness."[f]

The result was that despite his characteristic moderation and the

(a) Introduction to the Annual Report of the Secretary-General, 1960-1961.
(b) See above, chapter 4.
(c) Cf., e.g., W. Lippmann (*International Organization*, No. 4, 1961, pp. 547/548) and M. Virally, "Le Testament politique de Dag Hammarskjöld" in *Annuaire français de Droit International* (1961, p. 361).
(d) W. S. Sayre, "Strengthening the Secretariat" (op. cit., p. 139).
(e) M. Virally, "Vers une réforme du Secrétariat..." (op. cit., p. 238).
(f) M. Virally, "Le Rôle politique du Secrétaire général..." (op. cit., p. 363).

discretion which he advocated and observed, Hammarskjöld appeared as a sort of "twelfth member" of the Security Council. Although he had no vote, he conducted a diplomatic service and appeared as a sort of Foreign Minister of the United Nations in relation to the Foreign Offices of the Member States, although he himself was not a Minister and although the United Nations had neither a Government nor a Foreign Office. The press has even spoken of the "Hammarskjöld government" or "régime," thus seeking a label for the political potentialities of his position and for the part which he played in the world. He has himself described his role as follows:

> "If the Secretary-General represents an independent but positive evaluation, free of partisan influences and determined by the purposes of the Charter, this means not only that he reinforces the weight that independent opinion may carry in the negotiations. Step by step, he thereby also builds up a practice which may open the door to a more generally recognized independent influence for the Organization as such in the political evolution."[a]

Thus Hammarskjöld here, too, came down resolutely on the side of "creative dynamism".

> "There are two possible lines of action for the Secretary-General in the political questions following out of the competence of the Organization," he adds. "The Secretary-General may interpret his constitutionally objective position in such a way as to refuse to take a stand in emerging conflicts, in order thus to preserve the neutrality of the office. He may, however, also accord himself the right to take a stand in these conflicts to the extent that such a stand can be firmly based on the Charter and its principles, and thus express what may be called the independent judgment of the Organization."[b]

Much has been said of Dag Hammarskjöld's diplomatic methods and they will certainly be discussed in greater detail by posterity. It should be observed that in undertaking enquiries, negotiations, consultations and missions of "observation" whose aim was to reduce tension or prevent hostilities, he pursued the "diplomacy of reconciliation," which he has himself described as an added instrument providing, within the limits of its competence, a further or ultimate support for the maintenance of peace and security.[c] This new diplomacy was, in his opinion, the U.N.'s first duty, since no other organ, national or international, could perform it better,[d] having neither the position nor the necessary means.

As regards his methods of work, Dag Hammarskjöld advocated and practised, in the first place, a *"public,"* that is to say "parliamentary"

(a) Address by Dag Hammarskjöld at Copenhagen, 11 May 1959: "Do we need the U.N.?" (U.N. Review, June 1959, pp. 22 ff.).
(b) *Ibidem.*
(c) Introduction to the Annual Report of the Secretary-General for 1958/59 (p. 1).
(d) Cf. Introduction to the Annual Report of the Secretary-General for 1956/57 (p. 3) and speech by Mr Selwyn Lloyd at the 14th session of the General Assembly (798th meeting) on 17 September 1957.

diplomacy, the importance of which was directly related to the evolution of the international organization, at a time characterized by a great expansion of the means of mass communication. It has been described as "multilateral diplomacy"[a] and consisted of public negotiations amongst several negotiators. In the second place, simultaneously, owing to the danger of public negotiations degenerating into propaganda, Dag Hammarskjöld practised and advocated—always for purposes of reconciliation—various methods of *"quiet diplomacy."* This was to take the place of the *"secret diplomacy"* of former times. No longer based on positions of strength, it still had a "private" character, although generally multilateral. The Secretary-General appeared both as the centre and as the animator of this diplomacy. "It is as a part of the fabric of conciliation, action tirelessly pursued at all levels, covering all problems and between all the Member States, that diplomatic action finds its place and its full significance."[b]

Thus the Secretary-General was always in touch with the permanent delegates of the Member States at headquarters, whom he sometimes brought together at critical moments as an advisory body.[11] He made use of varied and elastic devices including missions on the spot, the sending out of personal representatives and committees of enquiry and so on. Thus *"diplomatic administration"* was the companion of *"political* diplomacy."[c] It has been said that: "the position of the Secretariat is unique in that, of course, it does not represent any country. Nor has it, as has the representative of a government, the means of putting force behind its words."[d]

This confrontation of opposing views in public debates, and simultaneous resort to good offices and private negotiations, led the United Nations to practise a new form of *"preventive diplomacy."*[e] Its aim was eliminate conflicts and to prevent an *"authority vacuum"* by asserting the presence of the United Nations[f] and promoting conditions conducive to a peaceful solution. This helped to localize disputes, to reduce tension and to prevent open hostilities. Sometimes quasi-military police forces were used.[12] Here was the "expression of institutional inventiveness"[g] which exercised a profound influence on

(a) Cf., for example, I.L. Claude Jr., "Multilateralism—diplomatic and otherwise," in *International Organization* (No. 1, 1958, pp. 43 ff.).
(b) M. Virally, "Le rôle politique du Secrétaire général..."(op. cit., p. 393).
(c) Cf. above, chapter 2,
(d) Address by Dag Hammarskjöld at Oslo, 3 June 1958, "Why the U.N.?—An Answer" in *Today's World and the U.N.*, (p. 25, O.P.I., 1959).
(e) Introduction to the Annual Report of the Secretary-General for 1959/60 and address by Dag Hammarskjöld at Copenhagen (op. cit., p. 26).
(f) Introduction to the Annual Report of the Secretary-General for 1959/60 (op. cit., p. 5).
(g) I. L. Claude Jr., "The U.N. and the Use of Force" in *International Conciliation*, No. 532, 1961, pp. 375 ff.).

international relations in Dag Hammarskjöld's time and inspired a successful series of specific arrangements in explosive situations. Of course these personal interventions in conflicts of interest between Powers brought down on the Secretary-General the censure of the dissatisfied, as well as the praise of those States whose interests had been advanced. In the long run, the praise was perhaps more harmful to "Mr. H" than the criticism.

It is interesting to examine, from the administrative angle, the way in which Hammarskjöld tackled the problems raised in Communist China (imprisonment of the American airmen), Palestine, Suez, Lebanon, Jordan, Hungary and the Congo. It will be seen that he placed the whole machinery of the U.N. in the service of peace, at the same time deliberately enlarging the traditional arsenal of diplomacy. The effectiveness of these actions depended, of course, on contingent factors. While strengthening the Secretary-General's personal position as "common denominator," they were also tests of the Secretariat's administrative efficiency, particularly when the work was urgent and complicated (Suez, Congo). Thus the Secretary-General's administrative talents were used in support of his political and diplomatic talents.

The theoretician and the philosopher

Dag Hammarskjöld is the first of the administrative heads of major international organizations to have been able and willing to draw up a doctrine of international co-operation exercised by institutions. In explaining his mission, the role of the U.N. and the means of attaining the purposes of the Charter—of which he was a tireless and unique interpreter—[a] Dag Hammarskjöld, in a series of commentaries, addresses and introductions to his annual reports, was not content with meeting the needs of the moment and dealing with problems empirically, but tried to build up a "philosophy of the Charter." With rare vision, he always sought to grasp the essence of the problems which arose, in order to provide a suitable theoretical basis for the action of the U.N. and its Secretariat and for his own action. It was not only a question of a legal commentary, which others had already undertaken: on the contrary, his purpose was to form a body of principles, constituting a doctrine dictated by practical experience of international life and based on an interpretation of the Charter. In doing this, his intention was at the same time to explain and even to justify his own policy, based on "a certain number of data which do not vary, because they derive from the peculiar nature

(a) Cf. A. W. Cordier, "The Role of the Secretary-General" in *Annual Review of U.N. Affairs* 1960-61 (R. N. Swift, ed., New York, 1961, p. 6).

and structure of the U.N. It is the Secretary-General's duty to realize them clearly and to draw the consequences."[a]

In all this doctrine which he gradually built up "from scratch," and the elements of which will have to be brought together some day,[b] Dag Hammarskjöld submits axioms, sometimes in the form of alternatives offered for the consideration and choice of those who take decisions on the international plane. These axioms belong either to a general philosophy of human, pacifist and practical action, or to the theory of international collaboration as translated into fact by the United Nations. Always he appears as a philosopher "who compels himself to objectivity as priests do to prayer, and binds himself by simply two laws: the United Nations Charter and the law of possibility...."[c]

This is no place to discuss his doctrine in detail. We shall content ourselves with a brief outline, to illustrate the contribution which these ideas can make to the theory of an international civil service.

Philosophy of action

When he took up his duties in 1953, Hammarskjöld said:

> "The qualities we all need today are perseverence and patience, a firm grip of realities, careful but imaginative planning, a clear awareness of the dangers, but also of the fact that fate is what we make it and that the safest climber is he who never questions his ability to overcome all difficulties...."[d]

Hammarskjöld repeatedly came back to this idea that "fate is what you make it";[13] this was his "creative dynamism" which he wished to instill into the administrative action of the Secretariat. He was a champion of realism, emphasizing its necessity in a series of addresses. He took as his motto courageous action based on calculated risk. It is easy to see how this general conception fits in with the precepts of modern administrative science.

Philosophy of international organization

Hammarskjöld did not regard the U.N. as a "kind of monolithic force capable of imposing its order on a domestic chaos. It is itself an arena and a stake. It is a battlefield of national and bloc forces."[e] He saw it as an ingenious mechanism supplementing the traditional systems and progressively bringing the world community to an organ-

(a) M. Virally, "Le rôle politique du Secrétaire général..." (op. cit., p. 381).
(b) M. Virally, "Le testament politique..." (op. cit., p. 356).
(c) P. O'Donovan, "The Precedent of Congo" in *International Affairs* (No. 2/37, 1961, p. 181 ff.).
(d) Dag Hammarskjöld's statement at Idlewild Airport, 9 April 1953 (press release SG/287).
(e) S. Hoffmann, "In Search of a Thread: The United Nations in the Congo labyrinth" in *International Organization* (No. 2, 1962, p. 355).

ized international co-operation in conformity with the Charter.

But, to point the way which the U.N. must follow, a choice must be made between two conceptions of its character, its powers, its structure and its means of action. Hammarskjöld openly raised the question and made his choice, leaving the ultimate decision to the States.

Deriving from the classic system of conferences, "which is naturally the starting point of all the efforts of the U.N.,"[a] that organization goes further. That is a fact not always understood.

> "Certain Members conceive of the Organization as a *static* conference machinery for resolving conflicts of interests and ideologies with a view to peaceful coexistence within the Charter...; other Members have made it clear that they conceive of the Organization primarily as a *dynamic* instrument of governments through which they, jointly and for the same purpose, should seek reconciliation, but through which they should also try to develop forms of executive action undertaken on behalf of all Members, and aiming at forestalling conflicts and resolving them, once they have arisen, by appropriate diplomatic or political means, in a spirit of objectivity and in implementation of the principles and purposes of the Charter."[b]

While both concepts set out from the idea of conference machinery, the second "is only a starting point envisaging the possibility of continued growth of increasingly effective forms of *active* co-operation adapted to experience.... The first concept can refer to history and to the traditions and national policies of the past. The second can point to the needs of the present and of the future in a world of ever-closer international interdependence, where nations have at their disposal armaments of hitherto unknown destructive strength. The first one is firmly anchored in the time-honoured philosophies of sovereign national States in armed competition, of which the most that may by expected in the international field is that they achieve a peaceful coexistence. The second one envisages possibilities of intergovernmental action overriding such a philosophy, and opens the road towards more developed and increasingly effective forms of constructive international cooperation."[c]

Hammarskjöld considered that it was clearly for the governments to make their choice: "The Organization has now reached a stage in its development where Member Nations may find it timely to clarify their views on the direction in which they wish the Organization to develop."[d]

At the same time he considered that: "the principles of the Charter are by far greater than the Organization in which they are embodied,

(a) Introduction to the Annual Report of the Secretary-General for 1960/61 (p. 1).
(b) *Ibidem.*
(c) *Ibidem.*
(d) *Ibidem* (pp. 1 and 8).

and the aims which they are to safeguard are holier than the policies of any single nation or people."[a]

He also strongly condemned any compromise with the principles and ideals of the Organization, which he considered too high a price to pay for immediate results. He urged States to face their responsibilities. He showed that the U.N. was irreplaceable, since it had "a unique and vital role to play."[b]

Dag Hammarskjöld's doctrine made full use of the potentialities of the Charter and advocated constant resort to the latter, in order to give international action not only a negative, but a positive role. He believed that definite possibilities exist, although they are not fully used, to attenuate tensions and disputes between blocs of Powers by preventing local conflicts from degenerating into wider ones. He energetically defended the rights of small nations for whose future the existence and action of the U.N. seemed to him decisive. Thus he translated into doctrine his practical ideas on technical assistance [14] and action to promote economic and social welfare throughout the world.

"Coherent and audacious,"[c] appealing both to moral conceptions and common sense,[15] the doctrine of international organization outlined by Dag Hammarskjöld did not arouse any direct criticism. When the U.N. "launched into the Congo affair, the unexpected developments of which led to a serious breach among its Members and exposed the Secretary-General to very severe criticism involving not only himself personally but his function,"[d] it was his action and not his philosophy which was attacked.

Philosophy of the "Executive"

Examining the Secretary-General's role and taking as starting point the philosophical doctrine of the U.N., Dag Hammarskjöld elaborated and expressed with conviction a comprehensive philosophy of the international executive, a philosophy of essential dynamism and independence of action.[e]

An international organization, political and multipurpose, cannot undertake dynamic and continuous action without "executive arrangements".

> "While great attention is given to the principles and purposes, and considerable space is devoted to an elaboration of what may be called the parliamentary

(a) Statement by Dag Hammarskjöld in the Security Council, S/PV. 751. 31 October 1956.
(b) Dag Hammarskjöld, "The U.N. and the major problems which face the world community" London address on 2 April 1958 in *Today's World and the U.N.* (p. 3).
(c) M. Virally, "Vers une réforme du Secrétariat..." (op. cit., p. 298).
(d) *Ibidem*.
(e) Cf. above, chapter 10.

aspects of the Organization, little is said about executive arrangements. This does not mean that the Charter in any way closes the door to such arrangements or to executive action, but only that, at the stage of international thinking crystallized in the Charter, the conference approach still was predominant, and that the needs for executive action if the new Organization was to live up to expectations and to its obligations under the Charter, had not yet attracted the attention they were to receive in response to later developments....
In fact, therefore, the executive functions and their form have been left largely to practice, and it is in the field of the practices of the Organization that cases may be found in the light of which it is now possible to evaluate the ways in which the Organization may develop its possibilities for diplomatic, political or military intervention of an executive nature in the field."[a]

Hammarskjöld considered Article 24 of the Charter, which confers on the Security Council the primary responsibility for the maintenance of international peace and security "in order to ensure prompt and effective action by the United Nations," as "the key clause" for any executive action to be undertaken by the Council or under its auspices. In this connection he quoted Articles 29, 40 and 48 in virtue of which the Council establishes subsidiary organs, decides on provisional measures and asks, on behalf of the Council, for governmental action. Moreover, "the forms used for executive action by the Security Council—or, when the Council has not been able to reach decisions, in some cases by the General Assembly—are varied and are to be explained by an effort to adjust the measures to the needs of each single situation.... As these, or many of these, arrangements require centralized administrative measures, which cannot be performed by the Council or by the General Assembly, Members have to a large extent used the possibility to request the Secretary-General to perform special functions by instructing him to take the necessary executive steps for implementation of the action decided upon. This has been done under Article 98 ... and has represented the development in practice of the duties of the Secretary-General under Article 97."[b]

Thus events themselves have filled in the blank left by the Charter. It is the Secretary-General who, by the force of circumstances, has become responsible for all kinds of "executive arrangements". How else can the "prompt and effective action by the United Nations," prescribed in Article 24, paragraph 1, of the Charter, and strictly in keeping with its spirit, be carried out? Executive action is indispensable to translate the *words* of the Charter, considered by some as purely theoretical, into deeds, and it is obviously the Secretary-General who must perform that task, though its risks are evident.

In accordance with the active philosophy of the international organization, the Secretary-General may not remain passive in the

(a) Introduction to the Annual Report of the Secretary-General for 1960/1961, p. 5.
(b) *Ibidem*.

face of an international emergency. He must "live dangerously" rather than allow himself to be overtaken by events or paralysed for lack of explicit guidance. In the absence of clear instructions and of a precise policy, the executive organ has to take the initiative, within the framework of the Charter and bearing in mind the purposes of the Organization. This is reminiscent of the "theory of urgency" well known to comparative international law.

In this connection we find in Hammarskjöld's doctrine two essential factors.

In the first place, there is a presumption of power to act. Though the Secretary-General is not authorized to act of his own accord,[a] (except in purely diplomatic cases[b] or in the exercise of his administrative powers,[c] he is nevertheless obliged—even without a definite mandate to this effect—to ensure the normal and necessary progress of executive operations, provided he obtains the necessary approval *ex post facto* from the representative organs.

> "I think it is in conformity with the spirit of the Charter that the Secretary-General should act without this mandate [of the States Members] if such action should seem to him necessary to supplement the provisions of the Charter or traditional diplomacy, and if peace and security should be in danger."[d]

The Secretary-General must therefore continue to act as long as he is not disavowed by the political organs, and in the last resort it is the latter's judgment as regards his intentions and his actions[e] which will be decisive. The Secretary-General is therefore not obliged to refer continually to the policy-making organs to ascertain their political wishes while his action is in progress.

In his Oxford address Hammarskjöld compared the role of the executive in a national parliamentary system with that of an international executive. While the first is normally obliged to refer to the legislature, the second must act at his own risk when and if the international situation allows him to do so. In particular when a dispute between Powers prevents the policy-making organs from taking up a clear-cut position, the Secretary-General cannot "take refuge" in passivity on the pretext that he has no instructions:

(a) Dag Hammarskjöld, "UNEF—Summary Study of the Experience derived from the Establishment and Operation of the Force, Report of the Secretary-General", doc. A/3943, para. 174.

(b) Dag Hammarskjöld, Copenhagen address, 2 May 1959 (op. cit.).

(c) Statement by the Secretary-General in the Security Council, 13 July 1960, S/PV. 873. Cf. also M. Virally, "Les Nations Unies et l'affaire du Congo en 1960. Aperçus sur le fonctionnement des institutions" in *Annuaire français de Droit international* (1960, p. 577).

(d) Statement by Dag Hammarskjöld in the General Assembly, 26 September 1957 (*Revue des Nations Unies*, No. 9, 1957, pp. 54 ff.).

(e) Cf. in this connection, statement by the Secretary-General in the Security Council, 31 October 1956, S/PV. 751.

"Would such refuge be compatible with the responsibility placed upon the Secretary-General by the Charter? Is he entitled to refuse to carry out the decision properly reached by the organs, on the ground that the specific implementation would be opposed to positions some Member States might wish to take, as indicated, perhaps, by an earlier minority vote?

"Of course the political organs may always instruct him to discontinue the implementation of a resolution, but when they do not so instruct him and the resolution remains in effect, is the Secretary-General legally and morally free to take no action, particularly in a matter considered to affect international peace and security?

" ... The answers seem clear enough in law: the responsibilities of the Secretary-General under the Charter cannot be laid aside merely because the execution of a decision by him is likely to be politically controversial. The Secretary-General remains under the obligation to carry out the policies as adopted by the organs; the essential requirement is that he does this on the basis of his exclusively international responsibility and not in the interest of any particular State or group of States.

"This presents us with this crucial issue: is it possible for the Secretary-General to resolve controversial issues on a truly international basis without obtaining the formal decision of the organs? In my opinion and on the basis of my experience, the answer is affirmative.... "[a]

This was Hammarskjöld's doctrine of the Secretary-General's function. It will be seen to what extent he considered the Secretary-General to be bound to maintain an impartial attitude, ever identifying himself with the organization he represents and expressing its independent judgment:

"Considerations of principle and law, important as they are, do not of course suffice to settle all the questions posed by the political tasks entrusted to the Secretary-General. Problems of political judgment still remain. In regard to these problems, the Secretary-General must find constitutional means and techniques to assist him, in so far as possible, in reducing the element of purely personal judgment."[b]

Hammarskjöld spoke also of the Secretary-General's power to interpret the resolutions of the representative bodies. His executive role obliges him to interpret his instructions objectively, whatever they may be, if this proves necessary and until the body concerned itself supplies an interpretation.

In short Hammarskjöld was "so deeply convinced of the decisive importance of this office that he exposed himself most dangerously."[c] The Secretary-General runs the risk of finding himself in a state of dramatic isolation, "a Pope without a church,"[d] obliged to carry a crushing responsibility alone and to perform thankless but absolutely essential functions (a "suicidal task" says one author).[e] This executive

(a) Dag Hammarskjöld, Oxford address (op. cit., pp. 15/16).
(b) Dag Hammarskjöld, (op. cit., p. 16).
(c) S. Hoffmann (op. cit., p. 353).
(d) H. Nicholas, "United Nations" in *Encounter* (January 1962, p. 8).
(e) S. Hoffmann (op. cit., p. 361).

function is bound to undergo further evolution in spite of obstacles and differences of opinion regarding it.

"This whole development has lately become a matter of controversy, naturally and, indeed, unavoidably in the light of differences of approach to the role of the Organization to which attention has been drawn earlier in this Introduction. While the development is welcomed by Member nations which feel a need of growth as regards the possibilities of the Organization to engage in executive action in protection of the Charter principles, it is rejected by those who maintain the conference concept of the Organization. The different opinions expressed on the development are only superficially related to this or that specific action and the way in which it is considered to have been carried through. They are also superficially related to the choice of means used for translating decisions into action. The discussion regarding the development of executive functions is basically one confronting the same fundamentally different concepts of the Organization and its place in international politics, which could be seen also in the different attitudes towards the legal weight of decisions of the Organization."[a]

It remains to be seen, of course, whether the practical tests to which Dag Hammarskjöld refers in support of his doctrine and those which may occur in future will actually confirm it. It remains to be seen, too, whether this responsibility is really within the scope of human ability; whether it takes sufficient account of the limitations of an average man, however gifted and capable he may be. Be that as it may, this doctrine is a valuable contribution to the theory of the modern international organization, and it will inevitably be referred to in the future—whether to support it, to develop it or to criticize it—whenever the problem of the international executive and of the Secretary-General's power is discussed.

Administrative philosophy

Hammarskjöld's doctrine also contains the elements of an "administrative philosophy" adapted to the specific requirements of an international administration.

Here again, Hammarskjöld was not content with simple pragmatism, even though he was sometimes obliged to resort to makeshifts. Conscious of the importance of the theory of public administration based on universally applicable principles,[b] he endeavoured to build on these postulates a valid system. Thus the fragmentary reforms are linked together by a guiding thread which can be traced in the statements of the Secretary-General or his subordinates. For example, in undertaking the structural reform of the Secretariat in 1954, Dag Hammarskjöld suggested new methods of collective work at the top level—integrated and co-ordinated teamwork "reflecting

(a) Introduction to the Annual Report of the Secretary-General for 1960/1961 (chapter 4, p. 5).
(b) Cf. above, chapter 3.

a different administrative philosophy than is usually found in national administrations."[a] In submitting his report on the administration of the staff to the General Assembly on 2 November 1953, the Secretary-General stressed the idea of "good administration," and said that a body of principles would have to be worked out gradually under the judicial control of the Administrative Tribunal.[b] It would be easy to find other proofs of Hammarskjöld's comprehensive administrative vision and of his efforts gradually to build up a world conception. It it most important for the international civil service that his work along these lines should be pursued.

The doctrine of the Secretariat

Dag Hammarskjöld's doctrine forms a logical whole and, as all its elements are interdependent and mutually complementary, it was natural that the problem of the Secretariat, and consequently that of the international civil service, should be prominent therein.

Hammarskjöld relates the solution of this problem to the choice between two conceptions of the international organization: "The Organization," he says, "if regarded as a standing diplomatic conference, might well be serviced by a fully international secretariat, but it does not need it...."[c] An organization so conceived might equally well be "serviced by a Secretariat which was not fully internationalized but was composed so as to represent... trends and ideologies."[d] But "the other approach to the Organization [the conception of creative dynamism] cannot be satisfied with anything less than a secretariat of an exclusively international character, and thus cannot be reconciled with a secretariat composed on party lines and on the assumption that the interests represented in the main organs in this manner should be represented and advocated also within the Secretariat. Thus, again, the choice between conflicting views on the United Nations Secretariat is basically a choice between conflicting views on the Organization, its functions and its future."[e]

As he had made his basic choice clear as regards the organization as a whole, Hammarskjöld naturally opted for a fully independent international civil service. The international organization must be "served by a secretariat of which it is required that, whatever the background and views of its individual members, their actions be guided solely by the principles of the Charter, the decisions of the main organs and the interests of the Organization itself."[f] An independent

(a) Doc. A/C.5/580 of 11 October 1954 (p. 6).
(b) Doc. A/2533. Cf. above, chapter 9.
(c) Introduction to the Annual Report of the Secretary-General for 1960/1961 (p.6).
(d) *Ibidem.*
(e) *Ibidem.*
(f) *Ibidem*, p. 1.

international civil service in this sense becomes a *sine qua non* of an international organization of the type advocated by Hammarskjöld in accordance with the "philosophy of the Charter" (Article 100).

Such an international civil service is a practical possibility.

In the first place Hammarskjöld rejects the idea that it is incompatible with "geographical distribution."

> "In order to avoid possible misunderstandings, it should be pointed out here that there is no contradiction at all between a demand for a truly international secretariat and a demand found in the Charter itself for as wide a 'geographical' distribution of posts within the Secretariat as possible. It is, indeed, necessary precisely in order to maintain the exclusively international character of the Secretariat that it be so composed as to achieve a balanced distribution of posts on all levels among all regions."[a]

Of course the application of this criterion must be well understood and abuses avoided:

> "This, however, is clearly something entirely different from a balanced representation of trends or ideologies. In fact if a realistic representation of such trends is considered desirable, it can and should be achieved without any assumption of political representation within the ranks of the Secretariat, by a satisfactory distribution of posts based on geographical criteria."[b]

If the Secretariat is to be exclusively international, as required by Article 100 of the Charter, the state of mind of its officials must be free from all nationalist tendencies, from intolerance towards others and from exclusive loyalty to their own government. There must also be a balance among the various nationalities.

> "A passive acceptance of a nationalism rendering it necessary to abandon present efforts in the direction of internationalism *symbolized by the International Civil Service*—somewhat surprisingly regarded as a cause of tension—might, if accepted by the Member Nations, well prove to be the *Munich of international cooperation* as conceived after the First World War and further developed under the impression of the tragedy of the Second World War.
>
> "To abandon or to compromise with principles on which such co-operation is built may be no less dangerous than to compromise with principles regarding the rights of a nation. In both cases the price to be paid may be peace."[c]

Hammarskjöld thus insisted that, though many may doubt the possibility of any man's being neutral, neutrality can and does exist.[d]

> "While it may be true that no man is neutral in the sense that he is without opinion or ideals, it is just as true that in spite of this a neutral Secretariat is possible. Anyone of integrity, not subjected to undue pressures, can, regardless of his own views, readily act in an 'exclusively international' spirit and can be

(a) *Ibidem*, p. 6.
(b) *Ibidem*.
(c) Dag Hammarskjöld, Oxford address, (op. cit., p. 18). Italics added.
(d) Cf. above, chapter 3, note (32).

guided in his actions on behalf of the Organization solely by its interests and
principles, and by the instructions of its organs."[a]

It is therefore a question of neutrality of action rather than "neutrality
as regards facts.... Even a man who in that sense is not neutral can
very well undertake and carry through neutral actions, because that
is an act of integrity."[a] In making this distinction between beliefs,
ideas and philosophy on the one hand and action on the other, and
in deducing therefrom the possibility of *neutral actions* undertaken
by officials who have accepted international duties, Hammarskjöld
went back to the Balfour principles, but gave them a psychological
basis. He compared the legal texts with the doctrine and the experience
of international life and concluded that the international official's independence is a realistic formula, although not easy to apply. That
is why he stressed each official's ideology, his essential "psychic
commitment", his understanding of the aims pursued, the distinction
he must make between the international and the intergovernmental
element, and the *esprit de corps* to be developed in the Secretariat
on the basis of all these factors.

This conception of the international civil service solves the problem
by giving paramount importance to the "service atmosphere" which
results from the state of mind of each member of the Secretariat, and
to the respecting by the States Members of the atmosphere thus
created, in order that no international official "may be under—or
consider himself to be under—two masters in respect of his official
functions."[a]

We have here an important contribution to theory, involving a
psychological systematization and elaboration of the principles of the
international civil service, which are categorically confirmed by this
doctrine.

(a) Introduction to the Annual Report of the Secretary-General for 1960/1961,
(p. 6).
(b) Press Conference of 12 June 1961, O.P.I. Note No. 2347, p. 11.
(c) Dag Hammarskjöld, Oxford address, (op. cit., p. 14). Cf. also address to the
staff on Staff Day (8 September 1961).

NOTES

(1) As regards the joint pensions system, cf. General Assembly resolution 248 (III),
680 (VII), 722 (VIII), 874 (IX), 955 (X). Cf. also doc. JSPB/G.4/Rev. 1.

(2) Staff rule *104.13 (a)(i)*: The Permanent Appointment may be granted to staff
members who are holders of a Probationary Appointment and who, by their
qualifications, performance and conduct, have fully demonstrated their suitability as
international civil servants and have shown that they meet the high standards of
efficiency, competence and integrity established in the Charter.
Staff rule *104.13(b)(i)*: The Regular Appointment may be granted when warranted
by specific circumstances, especially such circumstances of a local nature, to staff

members in the General Service and Manual Worker categories who are holders of Probationary Appointments and have shown that they meet the high standards of efficiency, competence and integrity established in the Charter.

(*ii*): The Regular Appointment shall be for an indefinite period and may last until retirement. It shall be governed by the Staff Regulations and Staff Rules applicable to temporary appointments which are not for a fixed term. Regular Appointments shall be subject to review at the end of the first five years.

The appointments made under each of these two headings are reviewed at the end of the first five years.

(3) Staff rule *104.12*: (*a*) *The Probationary Appointment*. The Probationary Appointment may be granted to persons under the age of 50 years who are recruited for career service. The period of probationary service under such an appointment shall normally be two years. In exceptional circumstances it may be reduced, or extended for not more than one additional year. At the end of the probationary service the holder of a Probationary Appointment shall be granted either a Permanent or a Regular Appointment, or be separated from the service.

The Probationary Appointment shall have no specific expiration date and shall be governed by the Staff Regulations and Staff Rules applicable to temporary appointments which are not for a fixed term.

(*b*) *The Fixed-Term Appointment*. The Fixed-Term Appointment, having an expiration date specified in the letter of appointment, may be granted for a period not exceeding five years to persons recruited for service of a prescribed duration, including persons temporarily seconded by national governments or institutions for service with United Nations. The Fixed-Term Appointment does not carry any expectancy of renewal or of conversion to any other type of appointment.

(*c*) *The Indefinite Appointment*. The Indefinite Appointment may be granted only to (i) Persons specifically recruited for the Field Service or mission service who are not granted a Fixed-Term or a Regular Appointment. (ii) Persons recruited subject to a waiver of medical requirements who are not granted a Fixed-Term Appointment. The Indefinite Appointment does not carry any expectancy of conversion to any other type of appointment. The Indefinite Appointment shall have no specific expiration date and shall be governed by the Staff Regulations and Staff Rules applicable to Temporary Appointments which are not for a fixed-term.

(4) Under staff rule *104.14* the following bodies have been established:

—an Appointment and Promotion Board to advise the Secretary-General on the appointment, promotion and review of staff in the General Service and Professional categories and on the appointment and review of staff at the Principal Officer level (except that of UNICEF and TAB);

—an Appointment and Promotion Committee to assist the Board;

—similar committees may be set up at UNICEF and TAB;

—such subsidiary organs as may prove necessary may be set up.

In filling vacancies, preference should normally be given, other things being equal, to officials of the Secretariat or of other international organizations.

(5) The Salary Review Committee recommended in 1956 an increase in the number of temporary appointments up to 20% as and when vacancies occurred (doc. A/3209 of 18 October 1956, para. 54). This proposal was approved by resolution 1095 (XI) of the General Assembly on 27 February 1957 (doc. A/3558 of 25 February 1957, para. 128). The Committee of Experts on the work and organization of the Secretariat proposed in 1961 a subsequent increase in the number of temporary appointments "up to 25% at the end of 1962" (doc. A/4776 of 14 June 1961, para. 92). A similar proposal is contained in the draft resolution submitted by thirteen Afro-Asian countries at the sixteenth session of the General Assembly (cf. doc. A/C.5/L.689 of 22 November 1961).

(6) Cf. S. D. Bailey (op. cit., pp. 32/33) regarding the need to increase the average

length of temporary appointments to five years (staff rule 104.12 (*b*)). Appointments for two years seem too short, except in the case of special missions, for a worthwhile contribution to the Secretariat's work.

(7) In 1951/1952 the Fifth Committee of the General Assembly and the Advisory Committee on Administrative and Budgetary Questions discussed in detail the question of the internal reorganization of the Secretariat. The General Assembly at its sixth session requested the *first* Secretary-General to study the problem as a whole—which he did by submitting a report on 7 October 1952 (doc. A/2214). By its resolution 681 (VII) of 21 December 1952 the General Assembly, without taking a definite stand on the question, again requested the Secretary-General to submit a report to its next session. On 13 September 1953 the *new* Secretary-General asked for a postponement in order to be able to study the question in detail; he submitted his general observations on 12 November 1953 (doc. A/2554) and the General Assembly in its resolution 784 (VIII) took note of it on 9 December 1953 and recommended that the Secretary-General should, to the extent possible, proceed along the lines he had proposed and prepare his 1955 budget estimates within the broad framework of these proposals (doc. A/2884). A study group consisting of six high officials undertook an enquiry at the Secretary-General's request in order to define methods of implementing the plan. Discussions followed during the eighteenth session of the Economic and Social Council and the ninth session of the General Assembly (docs. E/2598, A/2731, A/2745).

(8) The eight posts of Assistant Secretary-General which had been in existence at the U.N. since 1946 were abolished by the reform of 1954 together with the eleven posts of "Principal Director" (grade D.3). They were replaced by sixteen new posts of equal rank whose holders bore different titles, all of a purely "functional" character. They included seven Under-Secretaries, two of them "without portfolio", five heads of "Offices", three or four Deputy Under-Secretaries and the Director-General of the Technical Assistance Administration (until the abolition of the post when that Administration was amalgamated with the Department of Economic and Social Affairs in 1959).

(9) Cf. doc. A/2554 of 12 November 1953, pp. 6 ff. The Department of Conference Services comprised the following services: language and meetings, publications, typing, library.
The Office of General Services comprised, in addition to the Office of the Director, the following services: communications and documents, purchase and supply, building management, field services (missions away from headquarters), and the U.N. postal administration.

(10) The number of Secretariat officials who were nationals of eastern European countries was seventy-two in 1948 and ninety in 1961. The number of Member States in each geographical region was as follows:

(*a*) Western Europe   16
(*b*) Eastern Europe   10
(*c*) Middle East   10
(*d*) Africa   26
(*e*) Asia and the Far East   13
(*f*) Latin America   20
(*g*) North America   2
                         Total   97

Sixteen new African Members were admitted to the U.N. in 1960. This process continued in 1961/62. In Australasia, there were two Member States with thirty nationals in the Secretariat (including G.5 posts). To the figure of 1,245 officials (with grades from G.5 to D.1) given in table IV should be added twenty-three persons, twenty-two of whom were nationals of West European non-member States (two from the Federal Republic of Germany, twenty from Switzerland) and one was stateless (cf. doc. A/4776, para. 82, table II).

(11) During the Suez crisis the Secretary-General set up—and his action was endorsed by the General Assembly—an advisory committee consisting of the Member States which had supplied contingents to the United Nations Emergency Force. The Secretary-General constantly consulted this Committee and presided over its meetings. The Committee took no formal decisions. The views of its members, though they often reflected those of their respective governments, were sometimes purely personal. In both cases they were extremely valuable (cf. A. W. Cordier, op. cit., p. 9).

The same practice was repeated in 1958 during the Lebanon crisis and in 1960 during the Congo crisis. The role of the Advisory Committee during this last crisis was particularly important (*ibidem*).

(12) Cf. Resolutions 998, 1000, 1001 and 1002 of the first special session of the General Assembly on 2, 4, 5 and 7 November 1956.
Cf. also W. R. Frye, *A United Nations Peace Force* (New York, 1957, pp. 9 ff.) and "UNEF—Summary of the Experience derived..." (op. cit., doc. A/3943).
Cf. also in connection with Suez "The Twelfth General Assembly of the United Nations" (European Centre of the Carnegie Foundation, Geneva, 1957, pp. 56 ff., Chapter: "A Miracle of Logistics").

(13) "Awareness of the fact that fate is what we make it" constitutes one of the axioms of Dag Hammarskjöld's philosophy (cf. *International Service*, address at John Hopkins University, Baltimore, in "Three University Addresses on Service to the Community of Nations", 1955, p. 3). Similarly his idea of the "fight between the human and the sub-human" also deserves attention: "the dividing line goes within ourselves, within our own peoples and also within other nations.... We are on dangerous ground if we believe that any individual, any nations or any ideology has a monopoly of rightness, liberty and human dignity", ("Man's Greatest Challenge", address at Cambridge on 5 June 1958 in *Today's World and the United Nations*, 1958, p. 33). Cf. in this connection H. Virally, Le testament politique... (op. cit., pp. 358 ff.).

(14) An example is the action taken by Dag Hammarskjöld to carry out Lester Pearson's idea of the creation of an auxiliary corps for assistance to governments ("OPEX"). In his address at Mc.Gill University on 30 May 1956, Hammarskjöld recommended placing at the disposal of governments—particuarly those of developing countries—highly qualified technicians to meet their urgent requirements until they were able to set up a modern, competent and complete administration. These were to be not international civil servants or technical assistance experts, but specialized administrators recommended or proposed by the United Nations to serve on a short-term basis in the national administrations under the authority of the Ministers responsible for the national public services. The idea was to set up in this way a pool of capable administrators inspired with a spirit of impartiality and ready to serve nations which needed them. The international organization took the initiative of this movement and centralized it, paying part of the remuneration of these specialists. (Cf. ECOSOC resolutions 661 (XXIV) of 30 July 1957 and 681 (XXVI) of 16 July 1958, as well as General Assembly Resolutions 1256 (XIII), 1385 (XIV) and 1530 (XV)).

(15) Cf. A. W. Cordier (op. cit., p. 2): "Despite the lack of a recognizable and consistent world conscience which would give moral authority substance and meaning, there does exist an elementary decency and a belief in a commonsense approach to great objectives which has sufficient prevalence around the world to give moral authority the significance that should necessarily attach to it. Furthermore, moral authority in the day-to-day framework of the activities of the U.N. coalesces with procedures and practices to create actual power effective enough to

get constructive results. Thus, whether it be persuasion, prestige, or power, or infinite combinations of them, or whether it be moral authority geared through many combinations of strong voting majorities, or active collaboration by Members with the Secretary-General in successfully implementing resolutions—in all these ways a kind of common law is built up in the form of successful precedents of action which provide the background for increasing the effectiveness of the organization as it confronts new situations, new disputes and new tasks.''

CHAPTER II

THE PERIOD OF UNIVERSALITY: THE CONGO CRISIS AND THE LEGACY OF DAG HAMMARSKJÖLD

The Congo crisis and the Secretariat

In July 1960 a crisis broke out in the former Belgian Congo which was to provide a supreme test of the U.N.'s usefulness, of the effectiveness of its administrative machinery, and of its ability to act quickly in an extremely difficult political situation and despite every kind of obstacle. At the same time, it provided a test of Dag Hammarskjöld's doctrine.

In the first place, it called for action on a scale unprecedented in the history of modern international organization. The United Nations had to mobilize an enormous human force in order to meet the emergency without delay. It was hampered by distance, by lack of technical and financial resources, by anarchy on the spot which was growing continually worse and by obstructions deliberately raised on all sides. The Secretary-General was obliged to improvise the machinery required for the emergency while at the same time carrying on the normal activities of the Secretariat.

In the second place, extraordinary difficulties were occasioned by diverse political forces which, by calling in question every basic principle, held up administrative action. In this sense "the Congo proved revealing. Latent tendencies gravely affecting traditional conceptions in numerous sectors of international law and organization were suddenly brought into the open...."[a] The U.N. was faced in the Congo with a veritable conspiracy of adverse forces whose aim was the frustration of the international effort—a genuine and persevering effort to put an end to the chaotic situation, to fill the "authority vacuum" and to preserve unity and internal security in the country. In a retrospective survey of the U.N.'s early activities in the Congo we find the following passage:

> "It is as if a malevolent historical force had thrown into one pot all the separate problems with which the Organization has dealt, *seriatim*, in previous crises, plus some enormous new ones as well. It is as if the U.N. has had to play, at once, the role of three mythological figures. *Sisyphus*, of course; three times the

(a) M. Virally, "Les Nations Unies et l'affaire du Congo..." (op. cit., p. 560).

crisis appeared almost over, and the Secretary-General reported that the circle had been closed, only to discover that it was a vicious one. The Congo has also behaved as a Sphynx to the U.N. *Oedipus*: the questions which the Organization has been asked to answer have become increasingly tougher. Finally, the complications have been so great, and the moves of the World Organization have been so laborious, that one is tempted to compare it to *Theseus* looking for the Minotaur in the labyrinth; but Theseus, here, had no thread of Ariadne.[a]

Police operations using international military forces had to be combined with complicated civilian operations on a large scale in the face of internecine conflicts and extraneous influences. Therefore, an unprecedented effort of coordination had to be made. The situation in the Congo combined two kinds of difficulties which had occurred in the past: foreign intervention had to be coped with, as at Suez in 1956, and at the same time order had to be restored within the country, as in Lebanon in 1958.[b]

Although, unlike in Korea, the Security Council was able to act in the Congo from the outset and took a stand with the concurrence of the great Powers, a very serious crisis ensued, due to the subsequent quarrels between these Powers as the U.N.'s action on the spot developed.

From the administrative point of view, the operation was at first comparatively successful. The Secretary-General referred the Congo question to the Security Council in his letter of 13 July 1960 which reproduced the terms of Article 99 of the Charter; thus this Article was for the first time *formally* applied.[1c] The Council's resolution of 14 July 1960, adopted by 8 votes to 0 (with 8 abstentions) was the basis of the U.N.'s operations in the Congo. The *"United Nations Force"* [2] was conceived as a new international police force with a military structure and of international composition. It consisted of over 18,000 men, forming twenty-two battalions, from twenty-nine countries.[d] Simultaneously, a vast civilian operation was undertaken, mobilizing about 650 officials from twenty-eight countries, sent on mission by U.N. headquarters or its field services, or by the specialized agencies of the United Nations family. This team was assisted by about 1,400 Congolese recruited locally.[e]

To get both these operations going in an extremely short space of time required a very special effort on the part of the Secretariat. The logistics were particularly complicated owing to the distances. Improvisation was unavoidable, but, despite numerous deficiencies and the scarcity of resources available, the work was carried out

(a) S. Hoffmann (op. cit., p. 331).
(b) Cf. M. Virally, "Les Nations Unies et l'affaire du Congo..." (op. cit., p. 558).
(c) Doc. S/4381.
(d) Cf. doc. S/4417/Add.10 and doc. S/4557.
(e) Cf. doc. A/4703, of 1 March 1961.

with great speed and in a satisfactory manner. Among the difficulties were the enormous size of the country, the total lack of administrative cadres in a State which had become independent hardly a week before, the mutiny of its armed forces, the exodus of the Belgians, the economic paralysis, the internal chaos, the lack of transport, the separatist tendencies of the provinces, the tribal structure of the population and the conflicting foreign influences. In consequence the civilian and military missions of the U.N. in the Congo had to face almost insurmountable psychological, political and administrative obstacles, and the worsening of the internal situation helped to create a stalemate by prolonging the duration of international action in an unforeseen and unforeseeable manner.

The "gigantic effort of the United Nations in the Congo"[a] is no overstatement, and it has been said that "in attempting to promote order in a society which is hardly capable of producing a conflict sufficiently well ordered to deserve the name of a civil war, the United Nations has undertaken a formidable task, quite beyond the range of responsibilities it has exercised, through the instrumentality of UNEF, in the Suez situation...."[b]

At Secretariat *headquarters*, the Congo crisis meant extra work in plenty for all the departments and services, without, however, leading to any structural changes. All that was done was to create temporarily two special subdivisions—namely,

(*a*) the Office of the Military Adviser, consisting of three military experts and one expert on military aviation, which was a unit of the Office of the Under-Secretary for Special Political Affairs. This unit dealt with all specifically military aspects of the Congo operation, with questions concerning the military personnel, the maintenance of the forces in the Congo and the recruitment of additional troops;

(*b*) the special unit responsible for civilian operations in the Congo, which co-operated closely with the field services section (in the Office of General Services). This unit arranged for the despatch of personnel and equipment, drew up the necessary directives and maintained contact with the specialized agencies and various other participating organs.

Naturally, the constant need to send urgent directives, to move and to supply troops and to make the most varied political contacts raised problems which had to be solved by the Secretariat units directly engaged in the operation—namely, the Office of the Secretary-General, the Office of the Under-Secretary for Political Affairs, the field services section, the services of public information, of legal affairs, of personnel and of the Controller. A committee of adminis-

(a) "Issues before the Sixteenth General Assembly," *International Conciliation* (No. 534, 1961, p. 56).
(b) I. L. Claude Jr., "The U.N. and the Use of Force" (op. cit., p. 377).

trative chiefs, consisting of the Under-Secretary for Special Political Affairs, the Military Adviser and the Chief of the Field Services Section, regularly assisted the Secretary-General in dealing with problems arising from the day-to-day conduct of operations. The heads of various other departments and other Secretariat officials were invited to attend these meetings whenever necessary.

The Congo Advisory Committee was composed of eighteen members, most of whom represented countries which had supplied military contingents to the Congo. The Office of the Under-Secretary for Special Political Affairs was responsible to the Advisory Committee for secretariat services and was also in contact with the permanent delegations of the Member States in regard to the Congo operation and questions of documentation.

In the Congo itself, operations were in the hands of O.N.U.C. (United Nations Operation in the Congo) which was a branch of the Secretariat directly under the Secretary-General, and which was directed on the spot by the Secretary-General's Special Representative and by a civilian Secretariat official responsible for day-to-day operations. Under the first of these officials was the Commander of the United Nations Force, appointed by the Secretary-General, who, although co-operating closely with his superior on current business, was also directly responsible to the Secretary-General on questions connected with the military forces, and the Chief of Civilian Operations in the Congo, who was responsible for the civilian assistance supplied by the United Nations family to the Congo Government.

The terms of reference given by the Security Council in its majority vote of 14 July and its unanimous vote of 22 July[a] had been couched in such general terms that they left a wide margin of interpretation. Hence, the Secretary-General had to take decisions in matters of detail, and his doctrine as to the Secretary-General's role in interpreting the wishes of the representative bodies thus found its full application. Nevertheless, "in order to clarify the intentions of a resolution, to bring out all the implications of a plan of action and also its limitations, the Secretary-General formed the habit of laying down the general principles which were to guide him in the implementation of that resolution."[b] In August 1960, in particular, the Secretary-General asked for a definition of his terms of reference in connection with Katanga's secession, in view of the fact that the Security Council's initial resolution allowed the U.N. to use force in the Congo in legitimate self-defence but not to take part in internal conflicts.

(a) Cf. doc. S/4405.
(b) M. Virally, "Les Nations Unies et l'affaire du Congo..." (op. cit., p. 571).

"The rule on the non-use of arms shows that the whole operation was conceived on the twofold assumption that Belgium would accept the Security Council's resolution and that the Congo authorities would co-operate with the United Nations Force. One of these assumptions—namely, the co-operation of the Katanga local authorities, having proved false, the whole machinery was paralysed."[a]

The Council then decided on 9 August 1960, by 9 votes to 0, with 2 abstentions,[b] that the entry of the U.N. Force into Katanga was necessary and that Belgium should withdraw its troops from that province.

The Secretary-General's legally justified refusal to put an immediate end to the secessionist movement in the Congo by force led to a torrent of criticism against the U.N.'s intervention and to attacks against the whole conception of the undertaking. The co-operation of the Powers in the Security Council was wearing thin. The internecine struggle in the disintegrating Congo Central Government was transferred at the end of August 1960 to the international plane and was converted into a quarrel between the great Powers. Technical assistance to the Congo was assuming growing importance as other members of the United Nations family responded to the invitation of the Security Council on 22 July 1960: "The Organization has put into the field its largest civilian team to date, in a technical assistance effort of unmatched proportions."[c] Hospitals were set up to check the threat of epidemics following the complete breakdown of medical and social services; means of communication were restored; and technicians of all kinds were sent out.[d] A programme was drawn up by O.N.U.C. for the training of indigenous specialists locally, and was put into action in spite of every obstacle.[4] But even these civilian operations were criticized by the contending Congo authorities and by the Members of the Security Council.

This phase began on 17 September 1960 in the Security Council when the U.S.S.R. vetoed the draft resolution submitted by the United States for the confirmation of the Secretary-General's mandate.[e] The General Assembly, which was then meeting in special session under resolution 377 (V), "Uniting for Peace," decided in resolution 1474 (ES IV), of 20 September, adopted by a large majority, that the Secretary-General should continue to take vigorous action to assist the Central Government of the Congo in the restoration and maintenance of law and order throughout the territory and to safeguard its unity, territorial integrity and political independence. The U.S.S.R. then launched in the Security Council, at the special

(a) *Ibidem* (p. 579).
(b) Cf. doc. S/4426.
(c) *International Conciliation*, No. 534, (op. cit., p. 51).
(d) Cf. doc. SG/935 of 20 July 1960 and S/4531 of 21 September 1960 (paras. 41 ff.)
(e) Cf. doc. S/4526.

session of the General Assembly and at the XVth ordinary session of the Assembly in September 1960, a series of attacks against the Secretary-General personally, "who had been unmasked as a lackey of the colonialists and imperialists."[a] A determined offensive was mounted against the Secretary-General and he was asked to resign "in a chivalrous way" as Mr. Khrushchev put it on 3 October at the XVth session;[b] but he refused to do so. The assassination of Patrice Lumumba was announced on 13 February 1961; thereafter the attack—which now took the form of a proposal to replace the post of Secretary-General by a board of three persons (*troika*)[c]—was stepped up still further. The U.S.S.R. no longer asked for Dag Hammarskjöld's voluntary resignation, but for his dismissal, and announced that "henceforward it would not maintain any relations with Hammarskjöld and.... would not recognize him as an official of the United Nations."[d] The installation at the summit of the Secretariat of a triumvirate reflecting the existence of the three contemporary political blocs was insistently demanded by the U.S.S.R., and Mr. Khrushchev maintained that the existing situation "would open the way to the ruin and death of the international organization."[e]

As had happened at the end of Trygve Lie's term of office, the hostility of purely political origin of a group of States Members, guided by and under the direction of a Power having the right of veto, led to personal attacks against the head of the U.N. Secretariat and to a spectacular breach between that group and the Secretary-General; however, the latter remained in office and continued to enjoy the confidence of the great majority of States Members, as was proved by the reception given by their representatives at the XVth session of the General Assembly to Dag Hammarskjöld's announcement that he was remaining at his post.[5f] The crisis had assumed unexpected and dramatic proportions.

Dag Hammarskjöld carried on the United Nations work in the Congo in pursuance of the Security Council's resolution of 21 February 1961,[g] which called for the taking of immediate steps to prevent

(a) Cf. S/PV.901 (statement by the U.S.S.R. representative Zorin at the Security Council meeting of 14 September 1960); doc. A/PV.858, statement by Mr. Zorin at the special session of the General Assembly on 17 September 1960, and statement by Mr. Khrushchev at the XVth session of the General Assembly, A/PV. 862, A/PV. 882.
(b) Cf. A/PV.882 (paras. 30, 31).
(c) Cf. below, chapter 14.
(d) Cf. doc. S/4704, of 14 February 1961, TASS communiqué of 14 February 1961, *International Conciliation*, No. 534, (op. cit., p. 212).
(e) Cf. Mr. Khrushchev's speech at Moscow at the reception of President Nkrumah (Press communiqué of the U.S.S.R. Mission to the U.N., 44/61, of 12 July 1961, p. 4).
(f) Cf. doc. S/PV. 883 (paras. 9, 11).
(g) Doc. S/4741.

civil war, including the use of force as a last resort. Those in charge of international operations in the Congo were in a particularly difficult situation. Fighting between the U.N. Force and the Congo troops was growing in intensity, and the Secretary-General was now criticized for having allowed an armed struggle to break out between the United Nations and the Katanga secessionists. In spite of temporary lulls, fresh political complications soon arose owing to the fact that several States Members, for various reasons connected with their attitude to the Congo operation in general,[6] refused, notwithstanding the General Assembly's resolutions of 20 December 1960 and 21 April 1961,[a] to contribute to the very heavy extra-budgetary expenses involved. The Secretary-General had repeatedly to take a stand on the financing of the Congo operations and to remind the States Members of their responsibilities:

> "Will this organization face the economic consequences of its own actions and how will it be done? Further, if it is not willing to face the financial consequences of its own decisions, is it then prepared to change its substantive possibilities? There is no third alternative....The Secretariat finds itself in a difficult position. On the one hand it has to pursue 'vigorously' the policies decided upon by the General Assembly and the Security Council. On the other hand it is continuously fighting against the financial difficulties with which these decisions, under certain circumstances, face the organization. Of course the organization cannot have it both ways.[b]
> "But how, from the legal and constitutional point of view, can these factors lead to a conclusion that they are not expenses of the organization? The fact that these expenses have been substantial and unusual—indeed unforeseeable at the time of San Francisco—cannot mean that the Charter provision must now be disregarded."[c]

These suggestions were followed to some extent, as most of the States Members of the U.N. wished to avoid paralysing work in the Congo. But no fundamental decision, settling once and for all the complex problem of the financing of operations of this kind, was taken in Hammarskjöld's lifetime. The financial situation was critical, hinging once again on the question of will or lack of will to build a universal community. It has been pointed out that "the difficulties which plague the financial structure of the organization are only symptoms of the great ideological and political rifts which divide the contemporary international scene. The quest for technical formulae and fiscal remedies will probably not succeed unless it is preceded by more fundamental political accommodation.... There has never been a shortage of Cassandras predicting that the United Nations would end with a bang. There now exists a real possibility that it may end in a

(a) Resolutions 1583 (XV), 1590 (XV), of 20 December 1960; 1619 (XV) and 1620 (XV), of 21 April 1961. Cf. also resolution 1739 (XVI), of 20 December 1961. Cf. also resolution 1732 (XVI), of 20 December 1961 and below, note (7).
(b) Doc. A/C.5/843, of 21 November 1960 (pp. 1 and 8).
(c) Doc. A/C.5/864 (p. 5).

whimper. A fiscal crisis has been in the making over the past few years which has become a threat to the very life of the organization...."[a]

At the request of the General Assembly—which confined itself to settling the immediate expenses of the Congo operation—the International Court of Justice, on 20 July 1962, decided by a majority vote that the States Members were obliged under the Charter to participate in the expenses of the operation—recognized as being part of the "expenses of the organization."[7b]

Despite certain tangible successes achieved in the sphere of assistance, the Congo operation was far from concluded when Dag Hammarskjöld lost his life in an air crash in the Congo on 17 September 1961.

Dag Hammarskjöld's legacy: the problem of his replacement

"There is no man of our time who has left a greater imprint on the organization, to which he entirely devoted himself and his exceptional gifts."[c]

Dag Hammarskjöld's strong personality was so closely identified with the United Nations that his tragic death created profound dismay.

After eight years of tireless work, after bringing the Secretariat out of the great crisis of 1953 and raising the U.N.'s prestige to a high pitch, he was suddenly torn from it in the midst of a fresh crisis which seemed likely to shake the very foundations of the edifice to which he had devoted himself.

The Nobel Peace Prize which was awarded to him posthumously was a testimony to his faithfulness to the ideals of the Charter. Whatever may be the judgment of history on his individual actions and his theories, his contribution to the building up of the United Nations will certainly remain outstanding in the annals of international collaboration. The imprint of his personality was very great; he had brought into his own hands the effective direction of the Secretariat to such an extent that it was a matter of extreme difficulty to replace him. Speed was of course necessary in order to ensure the continuity of the international administration. At all costs steps had to be taken to prevent the situation in the Congo from deteriorating for lack of a real chief,[8] and an immediate attempt had to be made to break the deadlock created by the U.S.S.R. proposal, supported by the eastern European countries, to transform the post of Secretary-

(a) J. G. Stoessinger, "Financing the United Nations" *International Conciliation* (No. 535, 1961, p. 72 and p. 3). Cf. also *International Conciliation* No. 539, 1962, (pp. 184ff.).
(b) Advisory opinion of the I. C. J. of 20 July 1962, "Certain Expenses of the United Nations (Art. 17, para. 2 of the Charter)", *I.C.J. Reports* 1962, p. 151.
(c) R. Maheu, then Acting Director-General of UNESCO, "Tribute to Dag Hammarskjöld", in *UNESCO Chronicle* (No. 10, 1961, p. 348).

General into a three-man committee. The U.N.'s survival depended on finding a compromise.

After long and laborious negotiation, such a compromise was achieved. The U.S.S.R., in a spirit of conciliation, without abandoning in principle Mr. Khrushchev's demand for a *troika*, was willing to accept an "interim compromise solution" until the expiration of the late Secretary-General's term of office (April 1963). Under this interim plan, there would be only one Acting Secretary-General helped by a number of Under-Secretaries of nationalities "representing" the regional groups and political tendencies of the world. At the same time, the U.S.S.R. insisted on close co-operation between the Secretary-General and his deputies, although the latter were to have no right of veto. Thus, unanimity at the summit of the Secretariat hierarchy was not demanded, but only a common effort to solve, on a basis of mutual understanding,[a] the problems of the organization.

The representatives of the United States and the U.S.S.R. agreed that U Thant, representative of Burma, should occupy the position of Acting Secretary-General; the XVIth session of the General Assembly confirmed this choice by a unanimous vote, on the unanimous recommendation of the Security Council. The appointment of the Under-Secretaries, an essential element of the compromise, was the subject of somewhat difficult negotiations between the U.S. and U.S.S.R. representatives in consultation with the selected candidate.

This raised once again the problem which had arisen first at the League of Nations and then at the United Nations during the early years of its existence[b]—namely, the part to be played by the Secretary-General's principal assistants at the summit of the hierarchy. It will be remembered the Preparation Commission in London in 1945 had recommended "that the Secretary-General be authorized to prescribe their responsibilities and duties."[c] The question of weakening or reinforcing the authority of the chief over his deputies constantly reappears in discussions regarding the operation of the Secretariat, and can be regarded as a straw which shows which way the political wind is blowing, for or against a strong Secretary-General.

The reappearance of the old idea that the Under-Secretaries should not only be the Secretary-General's principal advisers, but also should keep the balance between political blocs, created new difficulties. The choice of an Acting Secretary-General who did not belong to either of the opposing political blocs made it easier to choose his deputies; but their number remained a bone of contention. The

(a) Cf. press conference of U.S.S.R. representative Zorin on 13 October 1961 in New York (Press release AFP of 14 October 1961).
(b) Cf. above, chapter 5 and chapter 10.
(c) Report of the Preparatory Commission of the United Nations (pp. 82 and 85).

U.S.S.R. reverted to its theory of the *troika*. The European group, comprising all the western European countries, the Scandinavian countries and Greece and Turkey, then stated in a public communiqué[a] that it opposed any U.S.—Soviet arrangement not including in the higher direction of the Secretariat a national of a western European country; the U.S.S.R. opposed such a claim unless an Under-Secretary from eastern Europe were also appointed. In the end, five Under-Secretaries were appointed, from the United States, the U.S.S.R., India, France and Czechoslovakia; but eventually three others were added to "represent" Africa (Nigeria and the United Arab Republic) and Latin America (Brazil). Thus, the Acting Secretary-General had eight immediate colleagues whom he appointed himself and who were to provide him with guidance on the views of all the principal regions of the world. Politically speaking, these eight Under-Secretaries comprised two "representatives" of the Western bloc, two of the Eastern bloc and four of the uncommitted countries.[9]

This arrangement, which gave the miscellaneous group of uncommitted countries a considerable increase in effective influence, enabled a provisional solution to be reached, Dag Hammarskjöld's successor having undertaken to appoint his immediate subordinates on his own responsibility, and to make a statement on the compromise after his appointment.[b] Accordingly he said, on 13 November 1961, in the General Assembly:

> "The debates in the General Assembly have already shown that the international climate can hardly be described as sunny. The organization is also facing a serious financial problem. In the Congo operation, we continue to encounter serious difficulties which clamour for an urgent solution.
> "If I am to discharge these responsibilities, surmount these difficulties, and resolve these problems, I shall need, in the first instance, the wholehearted support, friendly understanding and unstinting co-operation of all my colleagues. I have enjoyed such friendly co-operation from you all for so long as a delegate that I would fain hope that in my new role I shall receive it in even greater measure. For my part, I shall endeavour to co-operate with you all in every possible way.
> "In addition to your co-operation, I shall also need the loyal support of my colleagues in the Secretariat. I know how hard the Secretariat has had to work during the last sixteen months, especially in connection with the Congo operation. The Secretariat has shown itself capable of meeting all demands on it so far, and I count on the continued assistance and team-spirit of my colleagues in the Secretariat, especially in the difficult days ahead that we shall face together. In particular, it is my intention to invite a limited number of persons who are at present Under-Secretaries, or to be appointed as Under-Secretaries, to act as my principal advisers on important questions pertaining to the performance of functions entrusted to the Secretary-General by the U.N. Charter. In extending this invitation, I am fully conscious of the paramount consideration of securing the highest standards of efficiency, competence and integrity, and with due regard to the importance of as wide a geographical basis as possible

(a) Communiqué AFP of 18 October 1961.
(b) Cf. S. D. Bailey (op. cit., p. 60).

as laid down in Article 101 of the Charter. I intend to include among these advisers Dr. Ralph J. Bunche and Mr. Georgy Petrovitch Arkadev.

"It is also my intention to work together with these colleagues in close collaboration and consultation in a spirit of mutual understanding. I am sure that they will seek to work with me in the same manner. Of course this whole arrangement is without prejudice to such future organizational changes as experience may reveal to be necessary."[a]

In this way he explained his plan for the direction of the Secretariat, the Under-Secretaries from the United States and the U.S.S.R. being the only ones to be mentioned by name. No formal statement was made as to how far the Acting Secretary-General would consult his colleagues, the matter being left to his discretion. The supporters of the Soviet plan for the reorganization of the Secretariat were inclined, however, to interpret the compromise in a limitative sense.

The continuity of the Secretariat's work was thus ensured,[b] the problem of finding a permanent successor for Dag Hammarskjöld as Secretary-General being left to the XVIIth session of the General Assembly.

U Thant in charge of the Secretariat

In taking up his duties on 3 November 1961, the Acting Secretary-General stated in the General Assembly that he intended to continue in his new capacity the policy of "non-commitment" which was pursued by his own country, and that he would continue to seek objectivity and universal friendship.

This statement was interpreted by the world press as indicating U Thant's strict neutralism—that is to say his absolute impartiality in approaching world problems and his constant aim to keep the balance between the Powers.[c] In the affairs of the Disarmament Commission and in the dispute between Indonesia and the Netherlands over New Guinea, for example, the new Secretary-General in fact followed this line of conduct, but he was criticized on the ground that he was attempting an "automatic levelling" of the positions taken up on either side, without trying to determine which was in the wrong or which was the aggressor.

U Thant appointed Under-Secretaries as agreed and consulted them individually on the most important problems. In so doing he faithfully carried out the agreement on the basis of which he had been appointed, at the risk of incurring the criticism that he was abandoning his predecessor's methods and taking a first step towards the gradual transformation of the international Secretariat into an inter-governmental organ.

(a) Doc. SG/1060 of 3 November 1961.
(b) Resolution 1640 (XVI) of 3 November 1961.
(c) Cf. for example "Wer ist U Thant?" (*Neue Zürcher Zeitung* of 10 July 1961) and "Le bilan d'U Thant" (*Journal de Genève* of 5-6 September 1962).

In a series of addresses, U Thant put before the public his views on the U.N.'s role in world politics, on the validity of Dag Hammarskjöld's doctrine and on the economic, political and moral conditions for international co-operation.

Speaking of the U.N. he said *inter alia*, that "on the political plane it cannot be repeated too often that the United Nations can only be what its Members make of it. It cannot help but reflect the political realities of the world today, but it would be unfair to blame the United Nations merely because it mirrors the imperfections of the world around us."[1]

Retracing the enormous changes which had occurred in the world since the San Francisco Conference, U Thant stressed that if the United Nations were to enjoy an international authority with substantial powers, the first requisite was mutual confidence. "The build-up of confidence can be successful only if the United Nations is made to reflect adequately the interests and aspirations of all Members, large and small."[b]

"Therefore the development of the United Nations as a really effective instrument of preventing war is of primary importance to every one of us."[c] But "surely it is unreasonable and unrealistic to expect the United Nations to be the instrument of the national policy of any one country, however enlightened that policy may be and however much it may be conceived in the global interest."[d]

As regards the role of the Secretary-General and the Secretariat in particular, U Thant considered[e] that the Secretary-General had the right and the obligation to act spontaneously and without delay as soon as the peace of the world seemed to him to be threatened. Thus, apart from the administration of the Secretariat and the implementation of the resolutions of the General Assembly and of the Security Council, apart from the great task of co-ordinating the activities of the United Nations family, he is, according to this view, called upon to take action and display initiative in political and diplomatic matters. Although the relevant provisions of the Charter are vague, U Thant declared himself in agreement with his predecessor's view that the Secretary-General should act spontaneously to carry out the constitutional purposes of the Organization. As a practical example of this attitude, he quoted the stand he had taken in the Netherlands- Indonesian dispute.[f]

(a) Address of 17 April 1962 to the United States Committee for the United Nations (*U.N. Review*, May 1962, p. 5).
(b) "The small nations and the future of the United Nations," lecture at Uppsala University on 6 May 1962 (*U.N. Review*, June 1962, p. 21).
(c) *Ibidem* (p. 23).
(d) Helsinki address, 18 July 1962 (AFP communiqué of 19 July 1962).
(e) Stockholm address, 10 May 1962 (*Neue Zürcher Zeitung*, 11 May 1962).
(f) *Ibidem*.

U Thant paid many tributes to Dag Hammarskjöld: "Over the years," he said, "his role as a bridge builder was so successful that it became a common practice when any difficult situation came along for the major organs to say in so many words, 'leave it to Dag.' His 'quiet diplomacy' was one of the most successful ways of bridging the gap between extreme positions.... Even more significant was his role as the authentic voice of the conscience of humanity. Many times he had to speak out when others were inclined to be silent...." In quoting Dag Hammarskjöld's statement of 31 October 1956,[a] and in recalling his doctrine concerning the international community, U Thant, at Uppsala and elsewhere,[b] publicly manifested his complete agreement with the main lines of his predecessor's policy.

As regards world policy, U Thant observed that the "balance of terror" as a means of preventing war might be a concept which would justify the great Powers in intervening to prevent conflicts between others, but as regards conflicts between themselves "the time has come for statesmen to say firmly that they do not believe in an indefinite continuation of that delicate balance. This balance seems... to be purely a theoretical conception when considered in the light of political reality."[c] Consequently, U Thant pleaded the necessity of disarmament within the framework of a complete system embracing the two super-Powers:

> "The aim should be to develop the peace-keeping of the United Nations ...but although its moral authority could be built up by channelling international activities through this instrument, its efficacy will always require, ultimately, the supporting enforcement of both the United States and the Soviet Union. In the last analysis it must be a system in which the two giants must be increasingly involved. Such a development of the United Nations would also serve to add another brake to the danger of war between the two giants themselves and forge a permanent link between them."[d]

To achieve this end, the States Members must accept restrictions on their "absolute sovereignty" without, however, abandoning the principle itself.

> "If the United Nations is to grow into a really effective instrument for maintaining the rule of law, the first step must be the willingness of the Member States to give up the concept of the absolute sovereign State, in the same manner as we individuals give up our absolute right to do just what we please as an essential condition of living in an organized society.... Similarly in the community of nations it is increasingly important to restrict the sovereignty of States, even in a small way to start with.... It seems to me that the United Nations must develop in the same manner as every sovereign State has done. If

(a) Uppsala address (op. cit., pp. 23/24).
(b) Address of 30 April 1962 in New York to the New York Bar Association.
(c) Uppsala address (op. cit., p. 22).
(d) *Ibidem*, p. 21. Cf. also U Thant's press conference at the U.N. on 3 August 1962 (*New York Times* of 4 August 1962).

the United Nations is to have a future, it must assume some of the attributes of a State. It must have the right, the power and the means to keep the peace."[a]

The small nations have a special role to play in this context. Once more following Dag Hammarskjöld's ideas, U Thant regards the U.N. as a meeting-place for the new States and as the best guarantee for their independence. In general he assigns to the small nations the principal responsibility for bringing the Great Powers together. The small nations must make their voices heard, on disarmament and nuclear tests, and speak the truth as they see it. "This attitude was shown repeatedly by many of the small nations and not necessarily the Asian-Africans alone during the XVIth session of the General Assembly."[b]

Lastly, speaking of the "Development Decade" proclaimed by the General Assembly of the United Nations in 1961 (resolution 1710 (XVI))—"a wholly new experiment in human co-operation"[c]— U Thant pointed out that the last few years had seen great advance in the knowledge of development factors and that there existed now a moral competition in the fight against that ignorance which lies at the root of economic and social underdevelopment.[d] He spoke of a "realization among more and more people that the relative abundance achieved by more developed nations is not a gift of destiny but a goal which should be available to all,"[e] and advocated co-ordination of effort[f] which he regarded as "one of the principal purposes of the United Nations Charter."[g] This is part of the Acting Secretary-General's faith in man's future; he speaks of "this philosophy which is increasingly in evidence all over the world... an affirmation of community of interest, a mass declaration that human beings must learn to understand one another even if they cannot agree with one another...."[h] For U Thant the fight for a better future is a problem for the conscience of society today.

The main lines of his thought can be read in these addresses, and they also show his constant effort to analyse and explain the true mission of the U.N. and of its Secretary-General.

Thus, the paralysis threatened by the Congo crisis had been avoided, and a hard-won truce had ensured the continuity of the Secretariat's work. But the United Nations found itself at the XVIIth ordinary

(a) Uppsala address (op. cit., p. 23).
(b) *Ibidem.*
(c) "The Decade of Development," address by U Thant to the Danish Student Association, Copenhagen, 8 May 1962 (*U.N.Review*, June 1962, p. 36).
(d) *Ibidem* (pp. 36-39).
(e) *Ibidem* (p. 36).
(f) *Ibidem* and speech by U Thant at the Economic and Social Council meeting at Geneva on 9 July 1962.
(g) Copenhagen address (op. cit., p. 36).
(h) *Ibidem* (op. cit., p. 39) and Uppsala address (op. cit., p. 22).

session of the General Assembly at the end of 1961 at a crossing of the ways. The election of a Secretary-General for a normal term of office, in accordance with the Charter, was an act of the highest importance, the possibilities open to the head of the U.N. having been dramatically illustrated by recent events.[a] At a time when the role of the international organization, the structure of its Secretariat and the essence of the international civil service were yet again called in question, the choice which was made will determine the future direction and growth of international co-operation.

On 30 November 1962, U Thant, on the Security Council's unanimous recommendation, was elected Secretary-General for a normal period of five years as from the date on which he assumed this function in an acting capacity—i.e., as from 3 November 1961. The crisis was thus solved for the time being, notwithstanding the proposals for a modification in the structure of the Secretariat.[b] The Secretariat may therefore be expected to function on the previously established basis until the end of 1966. The new Secretary-General stated in this connection:"[c]

> "I would hope that these years would be marked by an improvement in the international climate, and by better understanding of the difficult problems which the world faces today. These problems can be solved only by goodwill and mutual understanding, and by a spirit of 'give and take'. When the future of mankind itself is at stake, no country or interest group can afford to take a rigid stand, or claim that its position is the only right one, and that others must take it or leave it. No difficult problem can be solved to the complete satisfaction of all sides. We live in an imperfect world, and have to accept imperfect solutions, which become more acceptable as we learn to live with them and as time passes by. In solving these complex problems, I myself and the Secretariat, of which I am proud to be the chief administrative officer, are at the service not only of all Member Governments, but of 'the peoples of the United Nations".

(a) Cf. S. D. Bailey, "*The Secretariat of the United Nations*" (New York. 1962. Carnegie Endowment, passim).

(b) Cf. *The Seventeenth General Assembly of the U.N.* (October 1962, Carnegie Endowment, pp. 171 ff.)

(c) Cf. Press release SG/1386 of 30 November 1962.

NOTES

(1) Before the initiative taken by the Secretary-General on 13 July 1960 regarding the Congo operation, the military assistance of the United Nations against "Belgian aggression" had been called for by the President of the Congo Republic and his Prime Minister in two telegrams to the Secretary-General (doc. S/4832 and 4837). The ex-Belgian Congo not being at that time a member of the U.N. (it became so by a decision of the XVth session of the General Assembly of 20 September 1960, and was admitted on 22 November 1960), the question was referred to the Council under Article 99 of the Charter (cf. doc. S/PV. 873).

(2) The United Nations Force, an international police force created in connection with the Congo question, henceforward had a separate existence from the United

Nations Emergency Force (UNEF) created in 1956 in connection with the Suez affair. Contrary to the Korean example of 1950 when a Member State was asked by the U.N. to constitute such a force for purposes determined by the Organization (cf. *U.N.Review*, No. 6/3 1956, pp. 32/33), the U.N. in the Suez affair appointed directly a military commander responsible for operations to the General Assembly and/or to the Secretary-General, so that UNEF had greater independence vis-à-vis the various national armed forces. In 1957 UNEF numbered 5977 troops composed of nineteen companies of riflemen, three reconnaissance companies and auxiliary services (ibidem, No. 5/4, 1957, p. 16). Considered as a subsidiary organ with the characteristics of a special kind of military body, UNEF consisted in 1961 of about 5,000 men all stationed in the Middle East (*International Conciliation*, No. 534, 1961, p. 202). Cf. also Report of the Secretary-General dated 22 August 1957 (*U.N.Review*, No. 4/4, 1957, p. 15).

(3) Dag Hammarskjöld intended to transform ONUC into a semi-independent branch of the Secretariat like the Office of the High Commissioner for Refugees or UNRWA. But owing to the extreme political complications of the Congo operation, this proposal was never carried out, since the closest permanent touch with the Secretary-General himself had to be maintained throughout the operation.

(4) As regards the scope and results of the U.N.'s civilian operations in the Congo cf., for example, *International Conciliation* No. 534, 1961 (pp. 51-56). On 8 September 1961 Dag Hammarskjöld said to the staff: "I know what I am talking about if I say that short of the heavy work in which you, all of you, have had his or her part, the Congo would by now have been torn to pieces in a fight which in all likelihood would not have been limited to that territory, but spread far around, involving directly or indirectly many or all of the countries from which you come..."

(5) "A new factor had supervened which upset all prognostications, the proposal... to change the structure of the Secretariat by replacing the Secretary-General by by a triumvirate.... Thus Mr. Hammarskjöld's retirement would not have led to the appointment of a new Secretary-General, but would have opened the way to the reform desired by the Soviet Union. This would have meant transforming a political crisis into an extremely serious constitutional crisis. Thus the fundamentals of the problem were entirely transformed and an equivocal situation was created which was to last until the end of the period under consideration. The purpose of the Secretary-General's reply could not be in doubt. On the same day he declared himself ready to defend the institution which he embodied and to assume this "responsibility towards all the Member States to which the Organization is of decisive importance, a responsibility which overrides every other consideration...." (M. Virally, "Les Nations Unies et l'affaire du Congo en 1960", op. cit., pp. 586/587).

(6) On 24 October 1960 the Secretary-General estimated the cost of the United Nations Force in the Congo for the year 1960 at U.S. $66,625,000. The Advisory Committee on Administrative and Budgetary Questions recommended that the expenses on ONUC in 1960 should not exceed U.S. $60,000,000. The United States of America having decided to contribute one-sixth of the sum, or U.S. $10,000,000, and the U.S.S.R. agreeing to furnish U.S. $1,500,000, it remained to find U.S. $48,500,000. The Fifth Committee of the XVth General Assembly, after an exchange of views during which the eastern European countries refused to contribute to these expenses, "the main burden of which should be borne by the Belgian colonizers" (A/C.5/775, para. 8) recommended by 45 votes to 15 (with 25 abstentions) the creation of an *ad hoc* account to cover these expenses. Contributions were considered as legal obligations under Article 17 of the Charter. This recommendation was endorsed by resolution 1590 (XV) of the General Assembly on 20 December 1960 (46 votes to 17 with 24 abstentions). For 1961 the Secretary-General estimated the cost of ONUC at U.S. $135,000,000. The Advisory Committee

on Administrative and Budgetary Questions expressed the hope that this sum might be reduced to U.S. $120,000,000. The Fifth Committee of the XVIth session of the General Assembly was deeply divided "since the sum under consideration was the largest ever to be assessed by the United Nations for a single operation and since the decision would obviously have far-reaching consequences." (J. G. Stoessinger, op. cit., p. 27). The U.S.S.R. objected to the financing of this expenditure being based on Article 17 of the Charter since it constituted "action" by the Security Council under Article 48 of the Charter and consequently the Council alone was competent to deal with the problem of its financing (Article 11 of the Charter). Several countries of Latin America, headed by Mexico, also asked that this expenditure should be treated as a special expenditure to which the penalties provided for in Article 19 should not apply. The Fifth Committee, followed by the General Assembly (resolution 1619 (XV) of 21 April 1961) decided, without referring to Article 17 of the Charter, to appropriate an amount of U.S. $100 million to cover the costs of the operation for the period 1 January to 31 October 1961. It described these expenses as "extraordinary," made no explicit mention of any legal obligation to contribute to it and emphasized the special responsibility of the permanent members of the Security Council for the financing of peace and security operations. In its resolution 1620 (XV) the General Assembly decided to leave it to the XVIth session to consider the methods for covering the costs of such operations. The Secretary-General having emphasized the danger of "imminent bankruptcy" if the situation did not improve (doc. A/C.5/907, p. 4), the General Assembly decided to refer to the International Court of Justice the question of the obligation to participate in the financing of expenses of this kind and the Court gave its opinion on 20 July 1962. As regards the action taken to procure immediate funds for the U.N., cf. *International Conciliation*, No. 539, 1962 (pp. 186/187). Nevertheless, on 30 June 1962 the U.N.'s deficit amounted to U.S. $149,000,000 (ibidem, p. 187), more than one-third of the States Members being in default on their payments to the Organization.

(7) The Advisory Opinion of the I.C.J. of 20 July 1962 concerning "Certain Expenses of the United Nations (Article 17, para. 2 of the Charter" was voted by 9 votes to 5. Judges Sir Percy Spender, Sir Gerald Fitzmaurice and Morelli submitted separate opinions and Judges Winiarski, Basdevant, Moreno, Koretsky and Bustamente y Rivero submitted dissenting opinions. The Court's Opinion states that "the text of Article 17, paragraph 2 of the Charter could lead to the simple conclusion that 'the expenses of the Organization' are the amounts paid out to defray the costs of carrying out the purposes of the Organization.... The Court has examined the resolutions authorizing the expenditures referred to in the request for the advisory opinion in order to ascertain whether they were incurred with that end in view..., and found that they were so incurred. The Court has also analysed the principal arguments which have been advanced against the conclusion that the expenditures in question should be considered as 'expenses of the Organization within the meaning of Article 17, paragraph 2 of the Charter of the United Nations' and has found that these arguments are unfounded. Consequently the Court arrives at the conclusion that the question submitted to it in General Assembly resolution 1731 (XVI) must be answered in the affirmative" (*I.C.J. Reports*, 1962, p. 151 quoted on page 179). Cf. also U Thant's statement in the Fifth Committee during the seventeenth session of the General Assembly on 3 December 1962 (Press communiqué SG/1388) concerning the financial situation of the United Nations and the necessity of respecting the International Court of Justice's opinion in accordance with a well-established tradition.

(8) It was indeed the Secretary-General himself and not his representative on the spot who in Dag Hammarskjöld's time directed in fact and in law the operations in the Congo. This direct responsibility of the Secretary-General's continued to

grow as events developed. The resignation of the Secretary-General's special representative in the Congo, Rajeshwar Dayal (who had succeeded Ralph Bunche) on 26 May 1961, was ascribed to the fact that "the responsibility for the direction and co-ordination of the Operation [was] falling increasingly on United Nations headquarters in New York" (Press release CO/150, 25 May 1961).

(9) The following is an unofficial tabulation of all United Nations officials of Under-Secretary rank indicating their functions and nationalities (1 June 1962).

I. *Under-Secretaries of the Secretariat at Headquarters*
Principal Advisers

Under-Secretary in charge of U.N. Civilian Operations in the Congo (Nigeria)
Under-Secretary for Political and Security Council Affairs (U.S.S.R.)
Under-Secretaries for Special Political Affairs (United States and United Arab Republic).
Under-Secretary for Economic and Social Affairs (France)
Under-Secretary for General Assembly Affairs and "Chef de Cabinet" (India)
Under-Secretary for Conference Services (Czechoslovakia)
Under-Secretary for Public Information (Brazil)

Other Under-Secretaries

Director of Personnel (United Kingdom)
Commissioner for Technical Assistance (China)
Commissioner for Industrial Development (Venezuela)
Under-Secretary for Trusteeship and Information from Non-Self-Governing Territories (Yugoslavia)
Legal Counsel (Greece)
Controller (New Zealand)
Director of General Services (United States)

II. *Officials of Under-Secretary rank, at established offices overseas, appointed by the Secretary-General and responsible to him*

Executive Secretary of the Economic Commission for Europe (Yugoslavia)
Executive Secretary of the Economic Commission for Asia and the Far East (Burma)
Executive Secretary of the Economic Commission for Latin America (Argentina)
Executive Secretary of the Economic Commission for Africa (Ghana)
Director of the European Office of the United Nations (Italy)

III. *Officials of Under-Secretary rank in charge of regular missions, appointed by the Secretary-General and responsible to him*

Chief of Staff, UNTSO (Sweden)

IV. *Ad hoc officials of Under-Secretary rank in charge of special missions, appointed by the Secretary-General and responsible to him, but financed from a separate account*

Commander, UNEF (India)
Officer-in-Charge, ONUC (Ghana)
Commander, ONUC (Ethiopia)

V. *Officials of Under-Secretary rank formally appointed by the Secretary-General, but after consultation with, and on advice of, another organ, responsible primarily to that organ and financed from a separate account*

Chairman, Technical Assistance Board (United Kingdom)
Managing Director, U.N. Special Fund (United States)
Associate Managing Director, U.N. Special Fund (Panama)
Executive Director, U.N. Children's Fund (United States)

Commisioner-General, U.N. Relief and Works Agency for Palestine Refugees in the Near East (United States)

VI. *Officials of Under-Secretary rank formally appointed by the Secretary-General after election by a principal organ and primarily responsible to that organ*

U.N. High Commissioner for Refugees (Switzerland)
U.N. Representative for India and Pakistan (United States)

VII. *Registrar of the International Court of Justice, elected and appointed by the Court* (France).

Part VI: Final Considerations

CHAPTER 12

ACTIONS AND REACTIONS

The role of the international civil service today

"It was said of the U.N. in 1945 that it merely represented the unanimity of the great Powers. Fifteen years later in 1960 it was principally a body of international officials directed by a chief, the Secretary-General. The idea of an international administration represents, as compared with the past, a much more radical and more revolutionary change than the constitution of inter-governmental organs derived from the old system of international conferences."[a]

The part played today by the international administration (inseparable from the idea of the civil servant),[b] is clearly shown by the lines on which it has evolved, although that evolution took place in the shadow of diplomatic events and almost escaped the attention of the public. It represents a fundamental change in the traditional forms of contact between nations. The elements of stability, order and continuity, a necessary part of any administrative undertaking,[c] are of special importance on ground which is continually shifting. The impartiality of the international civil servant, standing at the centre of international relations and by definition devoid of any "representative" character, is the common sense answer to a fundamental need.

The evolution which has taken place proves to those who are willing to learn that in view of the interdependence of national interests throughout the world and of the present state and probable trend of technical progress, any form of isolationism is doomed from the outset. Peoples, wherever they live, are obliged to live *together* and to maintain close and constant relations. Their problems are interconnected in such a way that it is impossible to dissociate them for any length of time. The peoples are obliged to "coexist" whatever their economic or political conceptions, whatever their innate sympathies or antipathies, whatever their forms of government. Interdependence is a fact of which we have strong evidence every day; to leave international relations in a state of anarchy would mean exposing humanity to mortal danger.

This idea has become a commonplace, but we must draw the logical conclusions. One of them is that without the *impartial third party*

(a) M. Virally, "L'O.N.U. d'hier à demain" (op. cit., p. 117).
(b) *Ibidem* (p. 122).
(c) Cf. above, chapter 3.

represented by the international civil servant, it is now impossible to achieve the peaceful settlement on which the survival of peoples depends. This is true even in "normal" times when crises are dormant; even then the daily round of international work is heavy: co-operation with necessitous peoples, combating epidemics or narcotic drugs, ensuring satisfactory conditions of human labour, providing communications of all kinds and forestalling disputes. It is even truer in times of crisis when the world is threatened with disastrous conflagrations and urgently needs the international civil service as a "fire brigade."

The international organization is an indispensable centre of contacts, negotiations and compromise between conflicting interests, and the international civil servant is its active element, always ready to offer his unbiased services to the States Members. Events have strikingly proved that the international civil service was not "invented" by anyone:

> "It would be foolish to suggest that the principle of a permanent international civil service is traceable exclusively to the fact that the late Lord Perth was a permanent civil servant. That principle was imported, not merely because it was familiar and therefore natural to the chief architects of the Secretariat, but also because it was desired to create a body which would be impartial between nations."[a]

The international civil service has naturally imposed itself as a *sine qua non* of the international progress which is so anxiously sought. It follows the classical conception of the civil service in western Europe, which was intuitively chosen as model. Introduced at first with hesitation and on a modest scale, this conception has gradually acquired rights of citizenship in the international world. What other institution could better provide a "common denominator" or more faithfully point to the right road?

"To a delegate whose government seemed to be following the wrong course, Dag Hammarskjöld once described himself as a compass. He said, 'If you insist that north is east, then all that I can do is simply to tell you that north is north'..."[b]

In spite of catastrophes, of recurring crises, of cruel disappointments, the last half-century has proved the ever-growing importance of the international civil service. For half a century it has been continually developing—even outstripping— the legal texts, which are frequently adjusted to fit an evolution that has already taken place in practice. If relative cohesion exists in the international structure, if forms of action are better organized, if the international organization is able to resist the assaults of adverse forces from all quarters, this is due to the discreet and persevering work of the international civil servant. He embodies the "institutionalization" of international co-operation:

(a) C. Parry (op. cit., p. 521).
(b) A. W. Cordier (op. cit., p. 6).

"The international administration is not only a juxtaposition of national services entrusted with international responsibilities, or even a meeting of administrators belonging to different countries and working together. It is much more than this: it is an instrument in the service of the international institution, devoted exclusively to the achievement of international objectives defined in its Statute and given concrete form in the decisions of the inter-governmental organs which direct it. This idea of an 'international public service' is essential."[a]

But is it possible to speak of *one* international civil service in view of the proliferation of parallel organizations with structural, functional and psychological differences and separate statutory regulations? Legally speaking, this may be doubted, in spite of constant efforts to standardize, if not the practices, the formal rules (salary scales, grading of staff, etc.), to allow occasional transfers from one institution to another, and to achieve "trade-union" unity. Psychologically the differences remain considerable, a sort of "separatism" accompanying the process of stabilization. There are formal agreements between organizations, but in practice the desired co-operation does not go beyond the exchange of information, documentation and re-commendations. The co-ordination which is continually advocated is far from complete. Common administrative arrangements covering the whole United Nations family are rare (combined purchases, common utilization of buildings, joint technical studies, technical assistance) and on the institutional plane are confined to the A.C.C., the I.C.S.A.B. and the Joint Staff Pensions Fund. The unexpected increase in the number of regional organizations, each with a large staff, not belonging to the United Nations family, complicates the general picture. There are also wide functional differences between the staffs of the specialized agencies and those of multipurpose organizations of a general political character.

Nevertheless, the ideological unity of the international civil service is gradually growing and tends to promote *rapprochement* on the administrative plane also. Divided geographically and even intrinsically though it may be, the international civil service—faced everywhere with the same dangers—is building up an *esprit de corps* which is a powerful unifying element, in spite of the varying purposes of the organizations and their structural and constitutional differences. Every international civil servant must possess the qualities and characteristics we have described, otherwise he cannot do his duty. These qualities make him a *public* official; they are the qualities which, as we have seen, were developed in the course of history by national public servants. This was understood by Sir Eric Drummond when, in 1932, addressing the Assembly of the League of Nations, he said:

(a) M. Virally, "L'O.N.U. d'hier à demain" (op. cit., p. 118).

"Secretariat officials are required not only to be fully conversant with the circumstances and views of the several countries, with the object of facilitating agreement between them, but also to act as servants of the general public interest, which may on occasions, at all events in appearance, present itself as at variance with the individual interest of this or that country. This aspect of the activity of members of the Secretariat is perhaps the one which presents most difficulties and which demands more special qualities...."[a]

This combination of qualifications and ideas links all international officials together wherever they may work.

"It requires a daily and repeated effort, combined with great mental adaptability, to stand outside oneself. It is no exaggeration to say that many people who fill public offices in their own countries with complete success, would be incapable of the self-discipline that League work demands."[b]

All international officials must be unrelenting in self-discipline, must struggle to preserve their impartiality, to resist external pressures and the temptations offered by their countries of origin or third parties. For example, even the impartiality of the Universal Postal Union, a highly technical organization, had to be defended against attempts to give it a political colour—which led one delegate at a Postal Union Congress to say, "We are postmen."[c] So emerges the uniform pattern of the international civil servant which is the basis for the unity of institutions.

To quote Dag Hammarskjöld, "the United Nations has increasingly succeeded in affirming the original idea of a dedicated professional service responsible only to the Organization in the performance of its duties and protected in so far as possible from the inevitable pressures of national governments. And this has been done in spite of strong pressures which are easily explained in terms of historic tradition and national interests. However, obviously the problem is ultimately one of the spirit of service shown by the international civil servant and respected by Member Governments. The International Secretariat is not what it is meant to be until the day when it can be recruited on a wide geographical basis without the risk that then some will be under—or consider themselves to be under—two masters in respect of their official functions...."[d]

Throughout the evolution of the international civil service, this legacy of nationalism has incited States to oppose the full realization of this conception. Thus arose the "minimalist" school which tended "to confine the Secretariat to a subordinate function... to reduce it to the elementary function of a scribe writing under dictation..."[e]

(a) XIIIth Assembly (1932). Cf. doc. UN.ICSAB/X/4 of 27 March 1961 (annex, p. 1).
(b) Report of the Supervisory Commission of the League dated 20 September 1932.
(c) *British Yearbook of International Law*, No. 25, 1948 (p. 457).
(d) Dag Hammarskjöld, Oxford address (op. cit., p. 12).
(e) E. Giraud (op. cit., pp. 23/24).

and to consider the international organization as a piece of conference machinery. Thus, too, the real influence of the international administration was overestimated; it was thought to be a political factor of the first importance or a malevolent force sometimes acting against certain countries. A sufficient example is the report of the Minority of the Committee of Thirteen in 1930, which asserted that "the political influence of the Secretariat and especially of its principal officers is in fact enormous," and that "it would be a mistake to close our eyes to this fact." It went on:

> "In practice, the work of the Secretariat today is quite different from what was anticipated in 1921. The division of work between the different capitals and Geneva has developed in such a way that the political character of the Secretariat's work has become much more accentuated than was thought likely. Not only does the execution of decisions taken by the various organs of the League constantly require interpretations and judgments of a political nature, but the preliminary work entrusted to it makes it an adviser in the various spheres of League work."[a]

In seeking a mean between these extreme positions, it must nevertheless be realized that the effective influence of such a specialized and impartial international body, always potentially important, has patently asserted itself as the institution has developed. International life itself has contrived to fill a gap by strengthening the role of the "intermediary"—animator, expert, negotiator and executive. It is in this sense that Sir Eric Drummond considered that the judgment of the Minority of the Committee of Thirteen quoted above was entirely right.[b] Apart from exaggerations dictated by the politics of the moment, it may be regarded as prophetic.

The picture is a complex one of light and shade. Nevertheless, if we stick to facts, rejecting myth and prejudice, refusing to oscillate from one extreme to another, we must admit that "when the Secretariat is created, something with a life of its own comes into being. Through its studies, its responsibility for programme implementation, its contacts with governments and with pressure groups, it can exert a real influence...."[c]

Deriving from a secondary instrument at the disposal of Powers taking part in occasional conferences, the international Secretariat has become a living entity, an organized social group exposed not only to the external dangers peculiar to its situation, but also to the internal dangers which threaten any human institution. Each generation must combat the danger within and without; on its success depends the future of international co-operation.

(a) Report of the Minority of the Committee of Thirteen (op. cit., p. 29).
(b) Cf. S. M. Schwebel (op. cit., p. 10).
(c) "Conference on the Concept of a True International Civil Service" (op. cit., p. 11).

The reality and the fluctuation of ideas: principles or postulates?

As we have seen, there is an undoubted hiatus between principles and achievements, between rules and facts. It is this hiatus which is the cause of doubts and pessimism and even of "dejection and despair leading to defeatism—and defeat...."[a]

In the first place, this is due to illusions based on an exaggerated, naïve and unrealistic idealism. If one expects too much from a human institution which is inevitably imperfect and dependent on unforeseen contingencies, one invites disappointment. The approach to the problem must be fundamentally realistic.

The facts of international history must not be forgotten. From time immemorial States have defended their sovereignty. The persistent search for a balance of power between States—a balance which has become a commonplace of international law—is "a phenomenon which was valued in antiquity as much as it is today—only its dimensions have changed or considerably increased."[b] To prevent one's neighbour from acquiring supremacy thus becomes a question of life and death. From this stem rivalries between States and inequality in fact despite equality in theory. The existence of the international community therefore depends on an established political balance which some wish to maintain and others to upset, and membership of the United Nations does not fundamentally change this state of affairs as the history of the international organizations amply illustrates. It is the reason for the pressure exercised by States Members on organizations. While specialized agencies are comparatively immune, the political multipurpose "general international organizations"[c] are naturally a particularly favourable ground for these pressures. The more integrated these organizations, the more self-sufficient their rules and discipline, the more stable their structure and the more continuous their operation—the more likely they are to encounter the opposition of States as soon as an opportunity arises:

> "The international Organization, if it reaches a very high degree of integration, constitutes in the eyes of certain authors the greatest obstacle to the creation of imperialist hegemonies. In the eyes of other authors, it appears as a compromise between the hegemony of the Great Powers and the equality of States. To tell the truth the compromise is never a very secure one and the obstacle to hegemony is never insurmountable. What the Organization permits is the substitution of a hegemony 'by consent' for an 'imposed' hegemony. Within the Organization the Member States can never enjoy perfect equality among themselves. Their influence and even their rights vary. It is therefore not

(a) Dag Hammarskjöld, address to the staff on Staff Day, 8 September 1961.
(b) M. S. Korowicz, *Organisations internationales et souveraineté des Etats membres*, (Paris, 1961, p. 21).
(c) Cf. Moscow declaration of 30 October 1943.

surprising that these influences also vary in each particular sector of the international administration and civil service."[a]

It would therefore be naïve to believe that the voluntary acceptance of
commitments resulting from membership of an international organization automatically puts and end to century-old practices or even diminishes their importance from the point of view of States. In joining
the international organization they accept certain changes in the
forms and methods employed in furthering their policies; but though
they may wish to strengthen international co-operation, they wish
even more to use it to their advantage. They often expect to utilize
the international organization as a centre for useful contacts, a wider
field for their influence, a source of information, a platform for propaganda. At the root of their motives, apart from the wish to strengthen
their international position or to safeguard their independence,
lies either an appetite for power or the fear of the power of other
States. That is why they cannot look with too much favour on any
reinforcement of the impartial element based on independence
vis-à-vis all States. Some States seem incapable of grasping the fundamental idea of the international civil service, others understand
it perfectly well but fear a "world government" or some form of
"super-nationality" or "super-State"[1] which they believe to be promoted by the development of the U.N. and of international administrations.

Consequently, even if States which have just emerged from a serious
world crisis are ready to give a trial to collective institutions and to
free association based on equality, in which they have little real belief, and even if they accept the existence of the organizational set-up
which results, they do so with mental reservations, which in due course
are reflected in their interpretation of constitutional texts according
to the requirements of their national policy. Hence the abyss which
frequently separates the grandiloquent verbiage of principles from
the prose of reality.

While the international civil servant appears as a precursor and as
the instrument of an authority external to the separate States, while
he personifies opposition to national particularism and the limitation
of state sovereignty, it is not surprising that his high viewpoint should
not be shared by States which are immersed in day-to-day politics.
When they embodied in the Charter the principle of the "exclusive
internationalism" of the Secretariat, the founders bowed to the
psychological necessities of the moment, but they did not intend to
accept any restriction of their own prerogatives and ambitions on
purely ideological grounds. The example of Wilson, the founder
of the League, who was disavowed by the parliament of his own coun-

(a) M. Bedjaoui (op. cit., p. 622).

try, reminds us that ideology is constantly and effectively thwarted by the political considerations of the moment. Some States rely on time to allow them to continue their game of hide-and-seek, of juggling with the principles laid down in the texts and of arranging matters to suit their interests. Others, while ready to give up pure empiricism and to enshrine a basic principle in a constitutional rule, rely on being able to transform it by degrees, and hope that the institution will adjust itself to prevailing circumstances. Both—anticipating events to some extent—look on evolution as a powerful and "natural" corrective to over-perfect solutions.

It should be noted that, on the national plane, too, the civil service did not appear suddenly like a *deus ex machina*, created by a legislative text. When, as in western Europe and countries which followed the same administrative pattern, the civil service evolved in the direction of impartiality, anonymity and political objectivity, there was a long process of gradual transformation of century-old customs, of breaking with the spoils system and plurality of jobs, of sweeping away sinecures, privilege and administrative amateurism. Thus, in Great Britain, the Civil Service grew up during the first half of the nineteenth century, but several old abuses subsisted during this period. It was not until 1853 that the Trevelyan-Northcote Report laid down the lines of future reform, put into practice in 1855 and 1870. Public opinion and government policy have since become accustomed to the new ideas, but their acceptance was slow and difficult. Similarly, in France the civil service grew up by degrees, from the time of the *ancien régime* until the Napoleonic reform of the year VIII, and afterwards throughout the nineteenth century, thanks to the monumental jurisprudence of the Conseil d'État, afterwards embodied in written texts. The adjustment of practice to principles has nowhere taken place easily or without occasional setbacks.

The difficulties encountered by the international civil service are therefore easily understood. It is a young institution unsupported by traditions and planted in alien soil. It is rather a matter for surprise that it should have taken root so quickly, and it is natural that at each successive stage it has had to maintain itself against storms and is the target of attacks reflecting the state of international relations. Although it still suffers from early weaknesses, it has already established "a quite remarkable tradition... remarkable because this is such a difficult world in which to appear non-partisan."[a] Of course it is continually shaken by conflicts of interest and national ambition. In view of the perpetual tension between centripetal forces tending towards the universal and centrifugal forces tending towards the

(a) M. A. Kaplan and N. de B. Katzenbach, *The Political Foundations of International Law* (New York, 1961, p. 310).

individual, it will no doubt continue to feel these repercussions in the future. Nevertheless, at the cost of mutual concessions and of complex and sometimes painful adjustments, the international civil service has taken firm root in the international soil, and the world realizes this fact more and more. Despite the pressures to which it is exposed and the continual crises which it has to go through, the principles which govern it are of genuine validity. Most members of this "new profession" consider these principles, despite the dangers to which they are exposed, as a standard which is respected in practice and is continually being reaffirmed. Paradoxically, the contradictory attitudes of the Member States, blowing hot and cold, contribute to the development of the civil service, despite ups and downs in the morale of the Secretariat, since the international civil servant is made increasingly conscious of the part which he has to play in the world today.

Thus the hiatus between theory and practice diminishes as time goes on, despite all appearances to the contrary. Those who believe themselves to be in danger from the international "authority" consciously or unconsciously use many weapons (the misuse of the geographical distribution rule is only one of them). Nevertheless, when States are obliged by the conditions of present-day international life to understand that the international civil service, if it obeys established principles, not only does not threaten them, but on the contrary guarantees their survival, they eventually tend to accept in practice the obligations which they have already accepted in principle. Several examples prove that a sense of moderation and reality usually wins the day, particularly among the smaller States, who are more inclined than the great Powers to accept and even to support the international civil service. Their interests are indeed indirectly but powerfully served by the action of an "exclusively international" Secretariat. "Fifty years ago it might have been necessary to justify the principle of an international secretariat; today we may take it for granted."[a]

This position being established—already a very important victory—the future depends, to an extent greater than may be supposed, on the intellectual, moral and professional standard of the international officials themselves. The quality of training and recruitment is therefore of the greatest importance to the future of the international civil service. The gap between principle and practice will diminish in proportion as the average quality of the civil service improves.

The wisdom of the principles involved, based on a sufficiently long experience and in keeping with the interests of all the States Members, is not in question. It cannot fail to be acknowledged, despite all the imperfections of the existing system, as soon as the unity of the con-

(a) S. D. Bailey (op. cit., p. 33).

temporary world is understood and the necessary conclusions drawn. The position is well summed up in the following passage:

> "On the one hand it is impossible to deny that an impressive network of organizations has been set up and that the realities of international co-operation are considerable. But on the other ... the ultimate limitations of international organization are seldom realized. No doubt this state of affairs is largely a reflection of the state of international society and of existing techniques for the expression of the social will. The whole of the world is not morally committed to the notion that there is only 'one world.' ... The science of international co-operation must for long remain an imperfect one. In a sense international law must always be a primitive law. The jurisprudence of nations must always be rough. The canvas is too large for delicate brushwork. The critic and the constitution-maker must always bear this in mind. Beyond a conclusion of this general sort it would be impertinent to go, except perhaps for the purpose of advocating the diminution of the diplomatic element in international organizations ... and the placing of more emphasis upon the workaday approach of the commercial cooperation and the departments of government within the State. ... [a]

The confusion of public opinion

In spite of the constant effort of the United Nations to educate the public, popular opinion as regards the work of the international organizations is generally confused. Part of the press may almost be said to specialize in persistent attacks on the U.N.[2] These attacks are supported openly or secretly by the opponents of all present-day international co-operation. The international administration is the target of the same criticisms as are regularly levelled against all public administrations; but journalists are, in addition, on the lookout for occult influences, not visible to the ordinary observer. People who do not come into contact with the international organizations in their daily life are often misinformed about them. The international Secretariat is still judged on the basis of the successes or failures of the organization as a whole, just as the Secretariat of the League of Nations suffered unjustly from the eventual breakdown of the Geneva organization. Owing to the large number of international administrations set up under the United Nations, there has been much criticism of structures and operation without proper appreciation of the results achieved. Some criticisms are justified; other are the result of misunderstanding or misinformation.

The general attitude towards the United Nations changes with the course of events. In France that opinion was generally favourable in the early days of the League of Nations and of the United Nations, but criticisms arose as these organizations grew older. Nevertheless, it is rare to hear anyone propose that the United Nations should be abolished. Criticisms are rather directed against its size, which is considered excessive, and against certain drastic interventions regarded

(a) C. Parry (op. cit., p. 537).

as contrary to the purposes and beyond the means of the Organization.

Certain publicists specialize in attacks against the international civil service; some increase the confusion of public opinion by paradoxically supporting the idea of a world government, but combating the international civil service.[3]

In certain countries, too, the attitude of the authorities is more or less hostile or suspicious towards the U.N. Thus in the United States Congress and certain state legislatures, criticisms based on opposition to the idea of a world government have been expressed.[4] Similar criticisms are to be found elsewhere.[5] The national administrations sometimes show hostility to the international administrations for the most varied reasons. These criticisms of national origin spring not only from political prejudice or inter-administration jealousy, but from hostility to the application of particular decisions to which the country in question is opposed. When the incoherence of the United Nations is criticized, and it is accused of converting a series of small muddles into a world muddle, it is frequently forgotten that the Organization is what the States make it, and that the principal source of the evils complained of lies in those States themselves.

Lastly, the staff itself sometimes contributes to an opinion unfavourable to the international civil service. Working in a sort of psychological vacuum, and often in an atmosphere of crisis, tension and uncertainty, threatened by an excessive bureaucracy—all faults due rather to the Member States which hope in this way to obtain greater control over the international administrations than to those administrations themselves—that staff often finds itself in a difficult moral situation. Its reactions to that situation often affect the way in which the Organization as a whole is judged.

Towards the specialized agencies in the United Nations family, particularly those of a technical character, the public attitude is entirely favourable, although little mention is made of their services, which are taken for granted. The accession of newly independent States Members has given rise to changes in the political international organizations which have aroused fresh criticism, although this does not affect the action of the Secretariat itself.

Prospects for the future

The time seems to have gone by when thousands of qualified candidates sought admission to the international secretariats.

"The international recruitment of individuals of required competence remains difficult. They are scarce in the less-developed countries and if highly qualified are apt to be desperately needed at home. Recruitment in more highly developed countries may also run into great difficulties because of the competition for certain types of experts and administrators on the part of national governments and private enterprise. Furthermore the importance of service within inter-governmental organizations is not always recognized, with the result that an individual returning to his home country may have difficulty in finding a suitable job."[a]

Although the situation of international officials has undoubted advantages, it has also certain drawbacks which discourage candidates. There is therefore a serious risk that the initial high standard may be lowered. The Salary Review Committee in 1956 stated:

> "Experience... shows that it is unrealistic to believe that every single staff member must be the best of his kind in the world: the practical requirement is that all the staff should be of a high level of competence, and that the international organizations, like national administrations, should have their fair share of brilliant staff and be content with that. On that assumption, a more practical guide to appropriate scales than abstract principle is the experience of the last ten years, and the experience of today, in the recruitment and retention of staff."[b]

Moreover, the International Civil Service Advisory Board, reporting in 1961 on the difficulties encountered in recruiting and keeping qualified staff, said:

> "Experience in all the larger organizations since 1956 leaves no doubt that the recruiting position which was 'marginally satisfactory' in 1956 is now quite unsatisfactory. No organization has ever sought to do more than ensure that 'all the staff should be of a high level of competence' while obtaining a 'fair share of brilliant staff,' but the point has been reached where even that cannot be achieved and where, all too often, the choice is between accepting unsatisfactory standards or leaving posts unfilled....[c]

Thus, the danger which threatens the international civil service—at least in the case of medium-grade officials—does not stem only from the sustained and even aggravated misuse of the geographical distribution rule, nor from the increase in the number of temporary appointments relative to permanent appointments, it comes from the lack of qualified candidates.

As we have already emphasized, it is precisely the indisputably high quality of the international administrative staff which, apart from measures of jurisdictional control, constitutes the best guarantee that the principles of the Charter will be carried out. Paradoxical though it may seem, the more important it becomes to secure staff that is impartial and qualified from every point of view, the more difficult it is to obtain it. What is more, the standards required are becoming continually higher:

> "To function efficiently, international secretariats require that a substantial portion of their personnel be highly trained and qualified. A knowledge of more than one language is often necessary and always desirable.

(a) "Five Year Perspective 1960-1964", doc. E/3347/Rev. 1 (Consolidated Report of the Economic and Social Council's Committee on the Appraisal of Programmes, 12 April 1960, para. 372 (iii)).
(b) Report, doc. A/3209 (para. 33).
(c) Report, doc. ICSAB/X/4 of 27 March 1961, introduction (para. 2).

> Most of the international secretariats were built up in the post-war period or earlier when the work of the international organizations was considered to be essentially one of research, the establishment of standards and conventions, the servicing of inter-governmental meetings and clearing house functions. The organization, structure, type and size of staff were generally based on this premise. With the shift to development and operations and the growth of international action programmes, new and different kinds of personnel were required."[a]

Thus it becomes urgent to make the best possible use of the existing personnel, reassigning it where necessary and giving it greater mobility. This means "the employment in increasing numbers of an élite of generalists capable of dealing effectively with governments and government departments, men who will command the respect of both local and international personnel. There is evidence that the problem is recognized and that progress is being made in the gradual integration of the several types of international civil servants within international secretariats which are thus becoming more nearly adjusted to contemporary needs."[b]

Intensive work is therefore needed to fill the gaps; recruitment must be properly organized and the staff offered the security, remuneration and moral conditions without which there can be no hope of attracting and keeping the right men and women. The first condition of success is that external considerations, whether political or otherwise, should not be allowed as valid criteria. Any deterioration in the quality of international officials can only have disastrous results. It should be noted that the idea of preliminary training has again been mooted, with the proposal to set up an International Civil Service Institute.[c] It is recognized that the principles of the Charter can be put into effect only by a properly trained and selected staff. The prestige, competence and integrity of international officials are a more effective barrier than legal formulae against States which try to distort the geographical distribution rule to their own advantage.[d]

(a) "Five Year Perspective" (op. cit., para. 372 (i) and (ii)).
(b) *Ibidem* (p. 130).
(c) Report of the British United Nations Association, doc. PA/16/12/1/UK (16th Plenary Assembly of WFUNA of 1961). Cf. also doc. UNESCO/10/C/13: Report by the expert P. Racine, submitted to the 10th session of the UNESCO General Conference regarding the preliminary training of candidates for the international civil service.
(d) Cf., for example, *International Conciliation*, No. 539, 1962 (p. 176 ff.).

NOTES

(1) For expressions of opinion favourable to the idea of a world government, cf. for example: S. de Madariaga, *The World Design* (London, 1937, p. 122) and the speeches of Ernest Bevin on 21 November 1945 and Mackenzie King on 15 December 1945 (cf. M. S. Korowicz (op. cit., p. 250)). In opposition to this idea, cf. the results

of the enquiry of M. Bourquin, *The Sovereign State and the International Organization* (New York, 1959, p. 31 ff.).

(2) As an illustration, it may be interesting to quote *Die Weltwoche* (Zurich), No. 1418, of 13 January 1961 (p. 3): "The international officials are well paid and enjoy many privileges, but their duties principally consist in performing subsidiary functions. Most of them come from countries which have not played a great part in history. At bottom they realize this perfectly well, but all their working conditions are devised in such a way as to compensate them for this subordinate situation. That is why they tend to consider themselves as beings apart, different from everyone else. They even imagine themselves to be the nucleus of a future world government. When the outcome of this attitude is compared with the hard reality of the Congo, the result is simply laughable. While the Congolese, with the help of a thousand or so Belgian officials who have returned, laboriously try to bring order out of chaos, the well paid U.N. officials, thinking themselves very important, sit there doing nothing, left behind by the course of events...." (article by Douglas Brown). Cf. also *Daily Express* (London) of 18 September 1961: "The United Nations Organization is neither united nor organized. It is a sad and dangerous illusion. Dag Hammarskjöld's tragedy is that he gave his life for a false ideal...."

(3) Young women like Diana d'Este (*Peace and Prosperity*, Neuchâtel, 1959, pp. 54/55), who think they can reform the world with their original ideas, look on the Secretariat of the U.N. as simply a "talking shop." She says, "the U.N. gets useless work done by useless officials at useless expense. It has only succeeded in creating magnificent administrative offices where they administer to the air. In the new world organization we shall begin by liquidating the whole of its useless bureaucracy in New York, as well as in Paris, Rome and Geneva. All these tasks will be resumed and managed more simply and efficiently by the new World Government...." Cf. also, for example, V. Orval Watt, *The U.N. Planned Tyranny. Comments on the Dream and the Reality* (New York, 1955), or Chesly Manly, *The U.N. Record: 10 Fateful Years for America* (New York, 1955).

(4) Several volumes of the Foreign Relations Committee of the U.S. Federal Senate published since 1954 contain the records of hearings of hundreds of citizens from different parts of the country regarding a possible reform of the United Nations Charter. They include numerous criticisms of international organizations (especially UNESCO). Cf., for example, M. S. Korowicz (op. cit., pp. 253-254). Similarly, the Senate of the State of Georgia voted, on 19 February 1957, a resolution asking that "United Nations groups should stop promoting a world government."

(5) Cf. Senator E. Pezet's communication at the meeting of the Foreign Affairs Commission of the French Conseil de la République on 6 June 1956, regarding the "inadequacy in number and importance of the French staff at the U.N. and the resulting consequences for French interests" (*Revue politique et parlementaire*, No 660, July 1956, p. 38 ff.).

CHAPTER 13

THE PERSONALITY OF THE CHIEF AND ITS IMPORTANCE

The role of the chief in a public administration

In any administration, particularly if it is international, the chief plays an essential role; a role which has been much discussed by students of administrative science and the complexity of which is now well understood. The work done by any unit largely depends on the chief's character, his breadth of view, his human qualities and his ability to handle men. It is more a question of exercising an influence than of giving orders. It is the chief's *savoir-faire*, his understanding and tolerance, which, in conjunction with organized team-work, harnesses the human forces, stimulates the whole unit, prevents it from getting into a rut and opens up new horizons. His personal loyalty affects that of his subordinates. His prestige, the manner in which he approaches his task, his ability to assign and then supervise the work of his subordinates, create the atmosphere in which the administration works. It may range from indifference to enthusiasm, from mediocrity to a common ambition to achieve the best,[a] from passive acceptance of the aims of the undertaking to personal involvement in those aims, from blind obedience to creative initiative.

> "Human institutions are like machines in this: they need to be 'run in'. Men who are strangers to each other, who have not rubbed against each other for a period and worn down some rough spots in the process, never work as well together as a team which has had time to make its adjustments. Equally, human institutions need decarbonizing from time to time. There is a deposit of habit, of current practice, which checks efficiency if the cylinders are not cleaned out and the valves ground in. Sometimes, though more rarely, they need re-boring. Unlike machines, they develop a great deal of internal resistance to these necessary processes. Business, owing to the constant index of the trading account, has a stimulus not to neglect them too long. The question of how to overcome that resistance in our great public services, against the tremendous force of professional conservatism, is democracy's greatest unsolved problem..."[b]

The special difficulties of an international administration and the heterogeneous nature of its staff mean that the chief's role as organizer,

(a) Cf., for example, E. P. Learned, D. N. Ulrich & D. R. Booz, *Executive Action* (Boston, 1951, p. 67 ff.).
(b) L. Urwick (op. cit., p. 96).

animator and supervisor is still more important. The "climate" in the Secretariat, the staff member's ambition to do his work well without being content merely to despatch current business, the perception of the inner meaning of the collective mission—all depend to a very large extent on the impulse given by the chief. He must ensure the co-operation of different services, the co-ordination of effort, and the maintenance of *human relations* within the group. In view of language barriers, differences of origin and training, the complexity of the work, the friction which inevitably arises and the pressures from outside, it is the chief's job to harmonize the whole effort, judiciously delegating part of his powers, but constantly retaining control over the service as a whole.

In view of the development of international administrative action, of the number of persons taking part in it and of its inherent difficulties, a strong and vigorous personality is needed at the helm. The confidence of the staff in the courage and community spirit of its chief is essential. These are the conditions, not easily fulfilled, which make an international administration into a positive force.

The dual nature of the Secretary-General's functions

We have already spoken of the "double personality" of the chief of an international secretariat; he plays both an administrative and a political and diplomatic role. Between these two activities there is some contradiction, in the sense that it is difficult for a single human being, however gifted, to perform both these tasks successfully and if he does so it can only be temporarily. Each of them is a crushing burden in itself, and a delegation of authority to deal with one or the other is indispensable now and then. The volume of work and especially the overriding priority of the political side continually prevent the Secretary-General from giving sufficient attention to his administrative task.

Opinions differ, indeed, as to the relative importance of these tasks. Those who emphasize the Secretary-General's specifically administrative function claim that the continuity of "administrative policy" suffers from his continual involvement in diplomatic negotiations. One author says:

> "The Secretary-General has two capacities under the Charter, political and administrative. If the Secretariat is to be strengthened, the problem arises as to which of the two roles, or what combination of them, is to be emphasized. If a choice between the two roles *has* to be made, it is healthier to opt for the administrative role. But a balance should be struck between the two roles, delicate though it may be."[a]

(a) A. Khalidy, "Strengthening the Secretariat," *Annals* (vol. 296, 1954, op. cit., p. 135). Cf. also W. Chamberlin (*ibidem*, p. 131 ff.).

Others give priority to the Secretary-General's essentially political work, considering that it fulfils one of the principal purposes of the Charter and that it is irreplaceable. Another author has said:

> "The Secretariat will be strengthened, then, by a Secretary-General who consciously seeks, not to 'balance' his political and administrative roles in ways which de-emphasize his political leadership, but rather to fashion his administrative organization to strengthen his political performance."[a]

The same opinion was expressed in the Noblemaire Report (1920)— namely, that the Secretary-General and his deputy were too much absorbed by administrative questions, from which they should be relieved by the delegation of authority to the Under-Secretaries-General.

A study of the development of the League of Nations and of the United Nations shows the efforts made to strike a balance between these two parallel aspects of the Secretary-General's task, the problem being of course easier in the specialized agencies which are predominantly technical.

Here the personality of each successive Secretary-General has been decisive. Some of them gave clear proof of their abilities as statesmen and political leaders:

> "In practice, a few outstanding individuals have undertaken imaginatively and adventurously to develop the potentialities of these offices. The list of international officials who have undertaken to push beyond the limits of administrative functions to make creative contributions to world order must certainly include such names as Albert Thomas, Trygve Lie, Dag Hammarskjöld, Brock Chisholm, David Morse and Jean Monnet... [b]

Others proved excellent administrators, among them Sir Eric Drummond, Lord Boyd-Orr and Gunnar Myrdal.

Nevertheless, as the Secretary-General's function developed, particularly in the multi-purpose "general" organizations like the United Nations,[c] it became more and more difficult to organize work at the summit of the Secretariat hierarchy in such a way as to ensure a fair division of labour and adequate co-ordination and supervision.

Brief appraisal of some Secretaries-General

Each of the successive Secretaries-General of the League of Nations and the I.L.O., and later of the U.N., left the imprint of their personality and particular gifts on the position they occupied.

Sir Eric Drummond, as we have seen, remained true to the tradition of the British Civil Service, of which he had been a member, and regarded himself primarily as an administrator. He was discreet in

(a) W. S. Sayre (*ibidem*, p. 139).
(b) I. L. Claude Jr., *Multilateralism—Diplomatic and Otherwise* (p. 51).
(c) Cf. S. D. Bailey (op. cit., p. 40).

his dealings with the representative bodies—to the extent of hardly ever speaking at their meetings—and played, in the eyes of the world, the part of "secretary" in the real sense of the term. He disclaimed any wish to take part in politics or to exercise any initiative in this sphere. His effacement became proverbial. Appearances, however, were deceptive. Although he had been chosen not as a statesman but as an experienced administrator, he soon earned the confidence of the national delegates on political questions. As soon as they arrived at headquarters, they would go to see Sir Eric and consult him on the political problems of the day, and he was able to give them a penetrating and impartial survey of the situation. In return, he enjoyed a confidence of which he never took advantage. Hence, although remaining deliberately in the background, he enjoyed considerable political prestige. The political figures of the time were not looking for a leader to take charge of the world political organization; indeed, they would probably have been unable to find one. But they soon discovered, to their surprise, that the self-effacing Sir Eric played a much greater part than they had anticipated:

> "he did not appear on the stage but he spoke behind the scenes . . . his preferences were not in favour of taking a strong line. . . . He was a man of the 19th century who believed in the stability of many fragile things, in the relative wisdom of man, in slow evolution, in the possibility of reverting to pre-war conditions by practising within the framework of the new institution the methods of traditional diplomacy with a few corrections. He did not look very far into the future. . . . [a]
>
> "Historians of the League have noted the self-restraining role played by the Secretary-General. He never addressed the Assembly of the League and in the Council 'he tended to speak . . . as a secretary of a committee and not more than that.' For him to have entered into political tasks which involved in substantial degree the taking of a position was regarded as compromising the very basis of the impartiality essential for the Secretariat." [b]

For the same reason, after Sir Eric Drummond's resignation, it was again an administrator who was elected to succeed him. The government delegates chose Joseph Avenol, not for his political sense, but as an administrative chief. The choice of the first Secretary-General was afterwards criticized on the ground that he lacked the qualities of a statesman:

> "The purely administrative tasks could well have been entrusted with advantage to a man of Sir Eric's fibre, but the political tasks should have been in the hands of a statesman. . . . Experience proves that it is a statesman who must be chosen as head of a political agency. He must be an international leader. Unless he is that, no international agency can exhaust the possibilities inherent in its mission." [c]

(a) E. Giraud (op. cit., pp. 50/51).
(b) Dag Hammarskjöld, Oxford address (p. 4).
(c) E. F. Ranshofen-Wertheimer (op. cit., p. 49).

This theoretical criticism should be considered in the light of the actual influence exercised *ad personam* by Sir Eric Drummond. Such a comparison will make it easier to understand the influence of the personality of the head of the Secretariat in the context of international relations. It will also make it easier to understand the choice of the successive Secretaries-General of the United Nations after the Second World War, when all the qualifications of the respective candidates were deliberately taken into account.

Sir Eric Drummond was acknowledged to be a very able administrative chief. From the outset he attached primary importance to the establishment of an international civil service and to its internal administrative management. His conception of the international administrative problem, his administrative wisdom and his creative spirit were decisive in laying the foundations of the international administration. His initiative at a crucial stage of the international civil service should be appreciated at its true value. He was given a free hand, but the importance of his persevering creative work was underestimated at the time. It was thanks to him that this "new human category" came into being between 1920 and 1933.

With *Albert Thomas* we have a different type of personality—a politician, a trade-unionist, a social campaigner and reformer. His dynamism and his combination of political and administrative skills earned him a reputation for "electric leadership"[a] at the head of the I.L.O. As a man of action, he found an outlet in the international sphere for his energy.

> "He possessed every endowment for such a (political) career—fierce energy, intellectual power, eloquence and debating skill, and a passionate devotion to the cause of social justice.... In any case it was certain that such a man would not be content with any position which did not leave him wide powers of initiative and leadership."[b]

The head of the Secretariat of the League had been chosen for his conservatism, in order that he should execute a policy of *consolidation* of the Peace of Versailles. It was natural that the head of the I.L.O.—an essentially *progressive* and even *aggressive* organization—should be a representative of the trade-union and socialist world, dedicated to social progress and coming from a country in which the working classes had succeeded in winning a degree of protection for paid work.

It has been said that the universally acknowledged success of the I.L.O. was mainly due to the "incomparable dynamic personality" of its first Director,[c] his inexhaustible energy and initiative and his constant stimulation of the staff which he had so judiciously selected. But the relative success of the I.L.O. was also due to the general

(a) L. M. Goodrich, "The United Nations" (op. cit., p. 142).
(b) F. P. Walters (op. cit., pp. 195/196).
(c) B. W. Schaper (op. cit., p. 232).

atmosphere, political as well as economic and social, in which it worked.

Attempts have been made to compare Sir Eric and Albert Thomas,[a] but the comparison is hardly valid, because the work and purpose of their two organizations was so different. But we can contrast their methods of action, while recognizing in both men the same dedication to the ideal of the international civil service.

It is extremely interesting to compare the personalities of the first two Secretaries-General of the United Nations. Here we are dealing with two men occupying the same post successively in the same organization, in a political environment which did not change substantially between 1946 and 1961. Both Secretaries-General took bold political initiatives, considering themselves to be authorized and even obliged to do so by the text and by the spirit of the Charter. Both interpreted the role of Secretary-General in a wide sense.

Trygve Lie, as we have seen, delegated the greater part of his administrative duties to a deputy. It is possible to blame this delegation for some of the early mistakes, particularly in the important matter of recruitment. The first Secretary-General dealt with administrative problems only at times of crisis. On the other hand, he deliberately emphasized the political aspect of his job and often took diplomatic action, in spite of the difficulties involved. Like Albert Thomas, he appealed to world public opinion. He established his right to intervene actively in negotiations and disputes, and did so on several occasions, particularly in the Korean conflict. It has been said that his motto was *carpe diem* while Sir Eric Drummond's was *festina lente*.[b] Be that as it may, Trygve Lie's theory of the "political neutrality" of the Secretary-General—which meant taking a part in diplomatic activity, since neutrality did not go so far as abstention—left a lasting impression.

But it was *Dag Hammarskjöld* who was the shining example of what could be done by a Secretary-General. He fully exercised "executive leadership," both administrative and political. He showed that an exceptionally gifted personality could overcome every difficulty and could exercise both sides of his "dual function" with equal energy. He also displayed great imagination in devising and realizing new uses for the Secretariat at every level of international action. New methods were thus worked out, with varying success, and a theory afterwards elaborated. Dag Hammarskjöld's actions were often criticized, but his personal prestige was such that his work "*per ambigua ad astra*"[c] remains an example of what can be done by a Secretary-General who displays courage and initiative.[1] Moreover, he has left

(a) E. Giraud (op. cit., pp. 49 ff.).
(b) G. L. Goodwin (op. cit., p. 397).
(c) Cf. C. C. O'Brien, *To Katanga and Back. A.U.N. Case History* (London, 1962, p. 47).

behind a doctrine which is a political testament of lasting value.

Principle of single or corporate management

Since the "heroic" early days of the international administration, there have been many discussions of the problem of the corporate or single direction of the international secretariat. For instance, at the League of Nations in 1930, a corporate executive was insistently demanded, at least as an alternative, in the form of a "governing body" presided over by the Secretary-General and composed of the principal officers of the Secretariat. This idea has cropped up again and again. There are plenty of arguments in its favour. International co-operation, particularly in general political organizations, requires such delicate handling that there seems an obvious advantage, *prima facie*, in its direction by a corporate body, acting perhaps with greater discernment and objectivity than a single man. The chief may need the advice of a body of close collaborators representing varied national cultures and influences. From the purely political point of view such a solution has some advantages.

Nevertheless, it has always been rejected for reasons of "good administration." In order to ensure uniform management and a clear chain of command and to avoid holding up administrative action, one man of sufficient stature must direct the Secretariat. Experience has shown that a single chief, thanks to his personality and impartiality, is better able than a corporate body to ensure prompt and decisive international action. All the cogs of the international machine are collective; but at the controls there must be one man acting on his own responsibility under the supervision of corporate organs and in accordance with their decisions, with the help of a general staff consisting of his immediate subordinates. Thus not only was intuitive respect shown for a principle proved by administrative experience everywhere, but it was deliberately sought to obviate the hesitations, doubts and arguments which characterize administrative action of collective bodies. That is why at every period there has been a difference between the method of appointment of the chief and that of his subordinates, even of his direct assistants. The purpose is to establish the chief's prestige and authority on a solid basis. At most, it has sometimes been proposed or agreed that advisory meetings should take place within the Secretariat in order to give the chief the benefit of regular exchanges of views with his colleagues. Thus, the Secretary-General has the advantage of well-considered advice, but can act quickly and without impediment.

The superiority of single over corporate management in international administration was strongly stressed by the specialists invited by the Carnegie Foundation to discuss the subject at the end of the Second World War, in preparation for the post-war international organization; they were convinced that if administrative action was to be effective, any corporative solution must be rejected. Nevertheless, this solution was once again proposed in another quarter with the Swiss Federal Council as a model, the future Secretary-General to be only *primus inter pares* and responsibility to be collective. But it was again pointed out that "the basic character of the relationship between the head of the international secretariat and the policy-shaping bodies, as well as sound administrative practice, militates against divided responsibility in the shape of a governing body or policy-shaping council of highest officials. The casual character of the past relationship between the head and his principal collaborators should, on the other hand, be replaced by the creation of an advisory body meeting at frequent intervals...."[a]

After full discussion, it was decided to reject the proposal of a body representing the interests of the States Members at the summit of the Secretariat. Comparing the international secretariat with a national ministerial department, the former officials of the League Secretariat who had met to discuss this problem observed that "administrative experience has proved that a national ministry or department cannot be directed by a commission or governing body. In the case of a vast international administration, this would be still more impractical."[b]

The problem was discussed yet again when the United Nations was set up, particularly as the founders of the organization could not fail to realize that the higher direction of the new Secretariat would have increased diplomatic importance. A conflict of ideas arose during the negotiations at Dumbarton Oaks in 1944, when the Big Four prepared "proposals for the creation of a general international organization." As in 1930, China proposed that the Secretary-General and his six deputies should be elected by the Security Council and the General Assembly; the Secretary-General was not to be the national of a great Power, and among his deputies only four should "represent" the latter. But no compromise was reached at Dumbarton Oaks, and the "proposals" finally voted did not contain any clause concerning the Secretary-General's deputies. On the proposal of the U.S.S.R., the Secretary-General was to be elected by the General Assembly on the recommendation of the Security Council. Since the great Powers had a veto in the latter, their unanimity was necessary for the choice of the Secretary-General.

The question was again discussed at the San Francisco Conference, when the U.S.S.R., true to its own conception of the corporative structure of the State from top to bottom, pronounced categorically in favour of a "directorate" composed of the Secretary-General and

(a) E. F. Ranshofen-Wertheimer (op. cit., p. 74).
(b) *Ibidem*, p. 73.

his deputies, all elected for two years. The three great Powers at first accepted this proposal, only stipulating that the [term of office should be increased to three years. This time, the opposition came from the smaller States, who feared that the Secretary-General would lose all authority, and that the need for incessant internal conciliation within the "directorate" would make administrative action ineffectual.[a] Subsequently three of the Big Four—the United States, Great Britain and China—changed their minds and opposed the election of any member of the Secretariat except the Secretary-General; and even his election is described in the Charter as an "appointment." At the same time the U.S.S.R. agreed that the posts of deputies to the Secretary-General and their number should not be specified in the Charter, though continuing to demand that these deputies should be elected. But the majority at the San Francisco Conference opposed any concession aimed at weakening the Secretary-General's authority and at setting up a collective directorate. In the end, the idea of single management of the Secretariat and of increasing the Secretary-General's prestige in relation to his deputies won the day. Later, the same arrangement was accepted for the other members of the United Nations family, on the model of the U.N. and following the examples of the League and the I.L.O. The opinions expressed by competent persons during the interlude of the Second World War no doubt played an important part in these decisions.

As we have seen, the problem of the U.N. Secretary-General's deputies was settled from 1946 to 1954 by an agreement between the great Powers[b] which gave them a "semi-representative" character. In 1954 Dag Hammarskjöld put an end to this state of affairs, but the problem was brought up again by the U.S.S.R. in 1960 at the XVth session of the General Assembly.

So a single directorate was chosen for the secretariats of all the international organizations. In fact, this solution prevailed throughout the history of the international civil service both in the constitutional texts and in practice, and after long reflection and discussion by the founders and executors. There were two main reasons for this.

Firstly, the administrative chief had to be free to perform adequately his complex task. The reasons were as much psychological (a "corporative" solution might submerge the Secretary-General's personality) as political (the Secretariat needed a *single* animator and intermediary, whose essential services would supplement those of the advisory bodies), but the foremost consideration was that of "good administration." It was increasingly realized that in order to give the administrative chief the personal authority which he needed

(a) Cf., for example, N. Acton, "Le rôle du Secrétaire général de l'O.N.U. Les origines d'une fonction" in *Le Monde combattant* (November 1960, p. 15 ff.).
(b) Cf. above, chapter 7.

and to allow him to implement the resolutions of the representative bodies quickly and effectively, it was essential that he alone should be responsible to the representative bodies for his actions. This accumulation of responsibilities rules out "pluralism." Side by side with democratic structures and representative bodies, there had to be an executory and executive instrument capable of ensuring the implementation of programmes and resolutions continuously and on behalf of the Organization. This is a universal administrative principle.[2]

Secondly, and this is closely bound up with the foregoing, it was desired to use advisory groups, not to replace the administrative chief, but to help him by providing for consultations within the Secretariat. Thus, advisory committees composed of his colleagues did not detract from the Secretary-General's prestige in the hierarchy. In the course of the international organization's history, indeed, the Secretary-General has, of his own accord, on several occasions, set up temporary advisory bodies representing those States Members which were most closely concerned in a particular question. Such periodical consultations proved useful to the Secretary-General, whether there was unanimity or disagreement amongst the members of the group. Unanimity was inevitably the result of a compromise, while disagreement served as a barometer of the pressures in the international atmosphere and sometimes made it possible to evade an approaching storm. The first type of advisory body does not seem to have been really satisfactory in practice,[a] but it has nevertheless been tried again from time to time. The second kind, on the contrary, making possible useful contacts and preliminary exchanges of opinion, has proved very valuable in times of crisis.

(a) Cf. above, chapter 8 and S. D. Bailey (op. cit., p. 61).

NOTES

(1) It is interesting to recall Woodrow Wilson's idea that there is "no law to prevent anyone from expanding his work to the extent of his abilities, the limits of each function varying with its successive holders" (cf. P.H. Appleby, "Morality and Administration in Democratic Government" (The Edward Douglass White Lecture on Citizenship, Louisiana University Press, Baton Rouge, 1952, pp. 240-241)).

(2) Specialists in administrative science, on the basis of a comparison of current practices, have come to the conclusion that discussion in a corporate body can lead to a fruitful exchange of views and enable a common decision to be reached, subject to "self-control of egoism" and "skill in integration." The axioms emerging from these studies constitute a sort of "science of comitology," but their postulates do not seem to be realizable on the international plane. Among the weaknesses of collective action are a tendency to evade the issue, the encouragement of irresponsibility, the frequent desire to reach conclusions prematurely. "A corporation has by definition neither a soul to be damned nor a body to be kicked," says L. Urwick (op. cit., p. 72).

Thus it may be concluded that while the corporate system lends itself perfectly to jurisdictional purposes or to parliamentary debate, a committee cannot as a rule effectively undertake any type of "operational action." It has been said that "the best kind of committee is a committee of one" (*ibidem*, p. 71), and that "when Charles Kettering, long Vice-President of Research of General Motors Corporation, itself a sizeable organization, was told that Lindbergh had flown the Atlantic all by himself, he received the news with a singular absence of surprise. 'It would have been remarkable', said Kettering, 'if he had made it with a committee.' (J. K. Galbraith, "Public Administration and the Public Corporation," in *Indian Journal of Public Administration* (No. 4, 1961, pp. 438/439). In the United States of America the Presidential Committee on Administrative Organization (Brownlow Committee) observed in 1937 (new edition of the report in 1947, pp. 32 and 58): "For purposes of management, boards and commissions have turned out to be failures. Their mechanism is inevitably slow, cumbersome, wasteful and ineffective and does not lend itself readily to co-operation with other agencies.... The conspicuously well-managed administrative units in the Government are almost without exception headed by single administrators.... A weak administration can neither advance nor retreat successfully—it can merely muddle.... Strong executive leadership is essential to democratic government today...."

CHAPTER 14

THE FUTURE OF THE INTERNATIONAL CIVIL SERVICE

The reorganization proposed in 1960

At the XVth session of the General Assembly, Premier Khrushchev again raised the question of the higher direction of the Secretariat, in connection with the Congo crisis and the attacks on the Secretary-General—adding, however, that in the Soviet view the United Nations was "useful and necessary."[a] This time, he proposed not only that the Secretary-General should be replaced by a triumvirate, but that recruitment should be organized on the same tripartite basis, contrary to the very essence of the international civil service. According to the Soviet view,

> "the U.N. Secretariat must be adapted...to the conditions which will come into being as disarmament decisions are implemented. An identical point of view has emerged...regarding the necessity of following up an agreement on disarmament with the establishment of armed forces of all countries, under international control, to be used by the U.N. in accordance with the decision of the Security Council.[b]
> "It has been said that, after an agreement on disarmament has been reached, international armed forces should be formed. We are, in principle, in agreement with this. But the question arises, who will command these forces? The United Nations Secretary-General?...Is it really permissible for the fate of millions to be dependent on the action of the one man occupying that post?... There can be no disarmament, there can be no international armed forces, in the absence of guarantees for all three groups (of States) against the misuse of these armed forces.[c]

Thus the general problem of disarmament and of the constitution of international armed forces was used as a major argument in favour of the corporative conception of the Secretariat put forward by the U.S.S.R. Clearly this was a reaction against the intervention of the United Nations Force in the Congo—a force which was directly under the Secretary-General's orders and might serve as a precedent for a future armed "police" force in the case of a general disarmament agreement. The U.S.S.R.'s solution would be "to set up, in the place of a Secretary-General... a collective executive organ of the United

(a) General Assembly, XVth session, A/P.V.869, 23 September 1960 (para. 273).
(b) *Ibidem*, (paras. 278/279).
(c) A/P.V.882, 3 October 1960 (paras. 48/49).

Nations consisting of three persons each of whom would represent a certain group of States belonging to the military bloc of western Powers, socialist States and the neutralist States.... That would provide a definite guarantee that the work of the U.N. executive organ would not be carried on to the detriment of any of these groups of States. The United Nations executive organ would then be a genuinely democratic organ; it would really guard the interests of all States Members of the United Nations...."[a]

Commenting on this proposal, Mr. Khrushchev pointed out that the contemporary world consisted in fact of three groups of countries: the socialist States, the States belonging to the western military bloc and the "neutralist"—i.e., uncommitted States. In his view the executive organ of the U.N. should consist of representatives of each of these three groups of States, so as to reflect the real situation of the present day world, and so as to "provide a definite guarantee that the work of the United Nations executive organ would not be carried on to the detriment of any one of these groups of States."[b] Thus "the last few months of 1960 and the first few months of 1961 sufficed to bring about a dramatic and perhaps decisive turning point in the history of the United Nations.... Soviet diplomacy was the prime mover of this development; the Congo question was the occasion or the lever and the position of the Secretariat and its chief the objective.[c]

The real target of this "offensive"[d] against Dag Hammarskjöld and his conduct of the Congo crisis was the institution personified by the Secretary-General. The purpose of the proposal was to stop any further extension of the Secretary-General's powers on the basis of Dag Hammarskjöld's doctrine and his Congo policy. Permanent control, exercised by joint directors meeting in committee, meant that decisive action would be paralysed by the threat of a veto, since decisions would always have to be collective. Although the U.S.S.R. proposal seemed to be a tacit admission of Dag Hammarskjöld's theory of dynamic international action and of the need for the Secretary-General to exercise imagination and initiative, it sought to dilute his effective power by remodelling the higher directorate of the Secretariat on the lines of the U.N. councils.

While, as we have shown, this proposal for the reorganization of the Secretariat on a corporate basis was by no means new, the motives behind it in 1960/61 were unusual. Instead of a deliberate attempt to restrict the Secretary-General's role, as had long ago been advocated by the "minimalist" school—the new aim was "a broad expansive

(a) A/P.V.862, 22 September 1960 (para. 285).
(b) *Ibidem* (paras. 283-285).
(c) M. Virally, "Vers une réforme du Secrétariat..." (op. cit., p. 236).
(d) *Ibidem* (p. 242).

strategy of maximizing United Nations authority to the largest possible extent,"[a] on condition that it was given a political character by according an equal influence to the three political blocs. This tripartism proposed by the U.S.S.R. was a categorical denial of any possibility of "neutrality" on the part of individuals, if not of countries.

> "While there are neutral countries, there are no neutral men," said Mr. Khrushchev. "There can be no such thing as an impartial civil servant in this deeply divided world, and the kind of political celibacy which the British theory of the civil servant calls for is in international affairs a fiction."[b]
> "Let those who believe in saints hold to their opinion; we do not credit such tales...."[c]
> "We cannot expect any Secretary-General to be the impartial representative of three different groups of States...."[1][d]

Thus, according to Mr. Khrushchev's view, no human being could free himself from the influence of his country's national interests. The national influence was such that it was incompatible with an international civil service based on the British model.[2] The supporters of the plan do not deny the possibility of such an attitude at the national level in a public administration; but impartiality seems to them "un natural" in an international administration. They think it unwise to entrust the direction of the Secretariat to a single man, setting him up as a sort of arbitrator; only a committtee of three "representatives" of blocs of States reflecting the political situation of the moment seems to them to provide the necessary balance.

Moreover, the U.S.S.R., not content with the reorganization of the higher direction of the Secretariat, proposes the extension of the tripartite system to the entire staff, contrary to the practice since 1919.

> "The two parts of this scheme are at any rate consistent, since it is proposed that the geographical distribution of the staff should be such as to ensure equitable and perhaps even equal representation of the three groups of States which are to be represented separately at the head of the Secretariat. This tripartism is accordingly the keystone of the Soviet plan."[e]

We therefore have here a comprehensive plan which would completely upset the conceptions hitherto accepted and applied and which would put an end to the international secretariat, as conceived in the days of the League of Nations, for political and ethical reasons.[3]

The same plan was submitted by the U.S.S.R. at the UNESCO General Conference in 1960, and later in connection with the system

(a) A. Dallin, "The Soviet View of the U.N." in *International Organization* (No. 1, 1962, p. 26).
(b) Interview of Mr. Khrushchev by Walter Lippmann, *New York Herald Tribune* of 17 April 1961 (quoted also by Dag Hammarskjöld in his Oxford address, op. cit., p. 1).
(c) A/P.V.882, 3 October 1960 (para. 22).
(d) *Ibidem* (paras. 30/31).
(e) M. Virally, "Vers une réforme du Secrétariat..." (op. cit., p. 246).

of inspection provided for in the draft treaty to end nuclear tests.[a] The Soviet member of the Committee of Experts on the work and organization of the Secretariat, in his separate opinion annexed to that Committee's report, advocated a twofold reform: the transformation of the post of Secretary-General into a tripartite committee and the reorganization of the whole staff on the same lines.[b] Subsequently several Soviet specialists expressed themselves in favour of the plan. For example J. Korovin stated: "This militarization of the functions of the Secretary-General once again emphasizes the impossibility of further having the Secretary-General play the part of dictator who is in sole command of the U.N. armed forces...."[c] This author admitted that the replacement of the Secretary-General by a committee would cause complications but insisted that it was necessary. Similarly, D. Yefimow[d] asked for a modification of the Secretariat's structure on the lines of the U.S.S.R. proposal in order to ensure the reflection of the contemporary world in the U.N. Various articles by other eastern European writers [5] confirm the intention that in the proposed "directorate" there should be a veto similar to that which exists in the Security Council.[e]

The Soviet plan was, however, widely criticized. Dag Hammarskjöld pointed out that the very existence of the international organization depended on the problems being solved, since any weakening of the Secretariat might have catastrophic consequences. He vigorously upheld the idea that an official could be neutral, on the international as well as on the national plane.[f] He expressed the belief that the plan was in contradiction with the Charter. "A weak or non-existent executive would mean that the United Nations would no longer be able to serve as an effective instrument for active protection of the interests of those many Members who need such protection."[g]

The representatives of several States Members opposed the Soviet plan during the XVth session of the General Assembly, objecting both to the idea of the *troika* and to that of a "political representation of blocs" in the Secretariat. For example, the Irish representative said: "The United Nations..., is the most precious thing we possess in common. Let us maintain it intact and learn to use it with increasing skill and sureness."[h] The Burmese representative said: "The setting

(a) Cf. S. D. Bailey (op. cit., p. 48, note).
(b) Opinion of A. Roschin, doc. A/4776 of 14 June 1961 (appendix, pp. 1 ff.).
(c) J. Korovin, "Ways of Reorganization in the U.N. Executive Organs" in *International Affairs*, (Moscow, December 1960, pp. 7 ff.).
(d) D. Yefimow, "The United Nations and the Contemporary World" (*Ibidem*, pp. 3-6).
(e) E.g. E. Piontek, "Troika i ONZ" (The troika and the United Nations) (*Prawo i Życie*, in Polish, Warsaw, No. 20, 1961, p. 6).
(f) Cf. above, chapter 4, note (20).
(g) General Assembly, XVth session, A/P.V.883, 3 October 1960 (paras. 9, 11).
(h) A/P.V.890, 6 October 1960 (para. 94).

up [of a] new grouping of neutral or unaligned States would mean bloc policy, which in turn would result in a further splitting of an already divided world."[a] The Tunisian representative said:

> 'To embrace one political dogma or another, to subscribe to the establishment of a new permanent coalition of interests or to the strengthening of any of those already existing, would not only mean the abandonment of our freedom but would also upset, to a dangerous degree, the already tenuous balance which allows the United Nations to function."[b]

The Indian representative said:

> "We are not neutral in regard to war or peace. We are not neutral in regard to domination by imperialist or other countries. We are not neutral with regard to ethical values. We are not neutral with regard to the greatest economic and social problems that may arise. Neutrality is a concept that arises only in war.... We are not neutral or neutralist, positive or otherwise. We would take part, we would participate, we would express our views. Even that expression 'positive neutrality' is a contradiction in terms. There can no more be positive neutrality than there can be a vegetarian tiger.[c]

Thus, the medium and smaller nations were definitely against the proposed reorganization. A similar stand was taken by the great Powers other than the U.S.S.R. Not more than a dozen countries favoured the troika plan at the XVIth session of the General Assembly.[6] Accordingly, the plan was not put to the vote. After Dag Hammarskjöld's death, when U Thant had been elected Acting Secretary-General,[d] the only remaining vestige of the "troika" plan was the idea of "advisers" to the Secretary-General with consultative powers, but the Soviet delegation seemed to regard the problem as still a live one which might be brought up again at any moment.

In their separate opinions in 1960, the Uruguayan and United States members of the Committee of Experts mentioned above categorically opposed the U.S.S.R. plan.[7]

Among the opinions in the same sense we may quote the following:

> "No elaborate evidence is required to show that Khrushchev has not been willing to tolerate an analogous *ménage à trois* either within the leadership in the Kremlin, or in Soviet industrial management, or in relations among communist parties. Soviet insistence on tripartite equality and veto in the executive organs conflicts directly with the time-honoured Bolshevik administrative principle of *edinonachalie*—unity of authority—which has been reaffirmed on innumerable occasions as 'the basic method of operating the Soviet economy and the Soviet State.' "[e]
>
> Since the objective of '*edinonachalie*' is above all maximum efficiency, one may

(a) A/P.V.897, 10 October 1960 (para. 104).
(b) *Ibidem* (para. 46).
(c) A/P.V.906, 17 October 1960 (para. 99).
(d) Cf. above, chapter 11.
(e) Extract from *Bol'shaia sovetskaia Entsiklopediia* (2nd editon, Moscow, 1952, Vol. XV pp. 475/476).

conclude that the Soviet purpose in opposing it in the U.N. is its reverse.[a]
If it were possible to consider the idea of a three-man executive apart from the
proposal that members of the Secretariat should 'represent' groups of States,
and with no possibility of the veto being exercised in administrative or executive matters—if, in other words, the three men were to be international officials,
responsible only to the U.N., neither seeking nor receiving instructions from
external authorities, and reaching decisions by majority vote, the *troika* idea
would not raise major questions of principle, although it might raise major
administrative problems. But the plain fact is that the *troika* can be made
tolerable for the U.N. only by emasculating it."[a]

The *troika* proposal cannot be regarded, and has not been presented, as being
merely a matter of administrative adjustment. To replace a single, independent
Secretary-General by a political triumvirate, each armed with a veto on administrative or executive action, would make the U.N. helpless in any situation in
which one of the triumvirs considered that, in order to 'represent' a group of
States, he had to block a particular action, even if in pursuance of a decision
of a policy-making organ, and what situation can be conceived in which this
possibility would not exist? The *troika* system would confine the Organization
to being a forum for conference diplomacy and could bring to a halt a wide
range of operational activities, first in the political field and later in economic
and social fields also. It would be the medium and smaller nations whose
interests would be most adversely affected."[b]

"It is not enough to say that the Soviet proposal risks weakening the Secretariat
and detracting from its efficiency. There is a much greater risk that it will
totally paralyse it, except for the purely material secretarial services of the
representative bodies whose work is of a routine nature and which do not
require any fresh decisions. It is more than likely to destroy it entirely as an
international administration. Corporate direction by the representatives of
national interests cannot fail to have effects from top to bottom of the hierarchy,
which will reflect the tendencies and divisions at the summit. Three parallel
hierarchies will develop, introducing the principle of argument at every level
and confusing structural divisions. No administration could survive such a
split. It would be condemned to immobility as a body and to individual
actions at subordinate levels leading to *faits accomplis*, whatever decisions might
be taken at the summit."[c]

We might quote many more writers and politicians[8] who point out
that the plan would inevitably transform the international Secretariat into an intergovernmental organ, and deprive the United Nations
of the only executive organ which it possesses under the Charter, the
only organ designed for deeds as well as words.

An impartial judge must conclude that a "corporate executive"
would increase the already enormous difficulties of international
administrative action and would create inextricable political complications. Sooner or later, the result would be stagnation, since the
time for immediate action is not the time for discussions of principles.

"There would certainly be distortion:...Loyalty to the group would replace
loyalty to the Organization. The triumvirate would consider its first duty to
be, not to keep itself independent of national interests, but to serve them.

(a) A. Dallin (op. cit., p. 32).
(b) S. D. Bailey (op. cit., p. 64).
(c) M. Virally "L'O.N.U. d'hier à demain" (op. cit., pp. 123/124).

It would only be able to do this by seeking instructions and carrying them out. ...Since unanimity is required, it is likely that this complicated system of negotiations would lead in many cases to inaction or to decisions which would be inapplicable owing to their vagueness and contradictions."[a]

Thus the idea of reorganizing the directorate of the Secretariat on a corporate basis is very dangerous, even without the proposed extension of the tripartite system to the whole international civil service. The acceptance of such an idea would be a drastic retrograde step, and would cause untold damage to the international administrative machinery set up so laboriously in the last half-century.

Prospects for the future

Experience has abundantly shown that the international civil service is a unique instrument for ensuring the continuous and effective co-operation between modern States in every sphere, whether they have common or divergent interests. There can be no doubt that mankind would be threatened with chaos if it ceased to exist. Its economic, social and cultural achievements have been striking; since international action is fast developing on these lines, the essential part played by the international civil service in co-operation between nations must be obvious, even to the most sceptical and pessimistic.

Though there have been mistakes, failures and discouragement, the importance of the international administration's task is self-evident. It has become for all "a centre for harmonizing the actions of nations in the attainment of common ends."[b]

The fact that the administration is effectively international—and not only intergovernmental or multinational—is part of the historic process of the drawing together of mankind. From small beginnings, it has grown unceasingly, despite troubles and dangers. The existence in the international arena of an impartial body dedicated to the general interest, to the persistent search for methods of collective action, to a "neutral" approach to world problems, thus appears indispensable. It is impossible to imagine the world of the future without such a factor; necessary in the past, it will be doubly so in the future.

The permanent existence of administrative organs inspired with an international spirit, ignoring all selfish bias and acting with maximum objectivity, is not only a possibility, it is an established fact. The interdependence of nations, which has far surpassed all anticipations, means that these organs may expect to take up an even heavier load. The conditions of modern life make the process an irreversible one.

(a) *Ibidem* (p. 123).
(b) Statement by Dag Hammarskjöld, *U.N. Review*, (No. 11/IV., May 1958, pp. 10 and 7).

In a divided world in which administrative efficiency has not generally reached a very high standard and in which popular education is still rudimentary, we cannot expect such an enormous and revolutionary undertaking to attain its objectives immediately. It reflects our imperfections; it is a mirror of our time. The international administration is still young; it must fight against confusion, misunderstanding and distortion. The number of units into which it is broken up, defying co-ordination, means that fragmentation is one of its major difficulties.

> "The international organization is still in its infancy, the developments of the last generation are merely the precursors of more effective forms of international organization on a far more ambitious scale and the law now being evolved by the rapid accumulation of precedent must therefore be sufficiently solid to support a more imposing superstructure than we can yet visualize."[a]

It would appear, however, that the progress made in forming an international Administration increasingly engaged in "operational" activities in direct contact with peoples, embracing a vast network of miscellaneous organs all over the world, has outstripped the progress of international political co-operation. Politically, we still live in an era of "concerts of nations" or "alliances," and even of opposing blocs, who use the international organization as a platform; but administratively we are already at a more advanced stage. Tens of thousands of men and women work full-time in an atmosphere of impartiality, for objectives which transcend national policy. Their work is open to criticism, and is in fact criticized—like that of any public administration—but they are daily providing proof that continual and organized co-operation between men and women differing in civilization, training, psychology and political ideas is practicable and indeed essential to progress.

In the light of experience, and trying to keep this phenomenon in perspective, we can look to the future with confidence, although the goal is far distant and the road hazardous. Even if the international organization should be eclipsed for a time, owing to hostility between nations (an ever-present threat), the world will never be able to do without an international civil service, which will have a greater burden of work than ever. We may indeed expect a further expansion, and must take care to avoid a repetition of old mistakes and ensure that the international secretariats will develop sufficiently to be able to cope with their new tasks. Since the U.N. and its "family" were created in the pre-atomic era, and since Trygve Lie's and Dag Hammarskjöld's reforms were introduced before the conquest of space began, it is obvious that, in addition to its present important work, the international administration has before it entirely new fields of

(b) C. W. Jenks, "The Proper Law..." (op. cit., p. XXXVII).

exploration and action, on a scale difficult to visualize. Thus, the survival of the international civil service is assured. Transcending all petty considerations and all out-of-date insularity, despite confusion, misunderstanding, hypocrisy and greed, some form of final balance, relative though it may be, is certain and is adumbrated by international administrative action.

The problems of the international civil service must be approached without any "feudal" preconception. A reasonable and unequivocal balance must be sought. Teams of professional and also of temporary or even voluntary pioneers[9] must be trained for their difficult work, and they must be given a clear and definite scale of values. Steps will have to be taken to attract the élite of the newly independent peoples, which look on the international organizations as the best guarantee of their existence. Lastly, universal principles of good administration must not be forgotten, or there will be a danger of administrative "underdevelopment" on the international plane. The international administration must continue to set an example of sound administrative methods to the uncommitted nations; thus the traditional principles of public service, worked out by the West in the course of centuries, will be understood and perhaps adopted by the new countries.

We may anticipate that the specialized agencies of the United Nations will continue to contribute as effectively as in the past to consolidating the international civil service. Their role in this sphere is particularly important, and the gradual and inevitable advance of standardization will not fail to strengthen them. Further "regionalization" of services and programmes will probably follow, in order to adjust the concentrated volume of work to actual needs and available resources. Improved recruitment and a sound personnel policy, applied with courage and ingenuity by the right man at the head of the international civil service, will remove some of the present defects which we have described. Two factors may be decisive: first, the average international civil servant must be of a high standard, every effort being made to avoid the creation of a "large, unwieldy international bureaucracy filled with office-seekers of all the participating countries."[a] Secondly, modern States must be induced to respect, by persuasion and moral pressure, the moral obligations they have freely accepted and to renounce in their own interest any attempt to transform a basis of co-operation into a battleground. Both these propositions are practical and are the outcome, not of a mystical ideal, but of a conviction—which all must share—that the survival of the world and the independence of the peoples which compose it are at stake.

(a) J. T. Shotwell, "The Great Decison" (op. cit., p. 214).

NOTES

(1) The rigidity of the U.S.S.R. Government's position seems to have been attenuated later, judging by the interview given by N. Khrushchev to C. L. Sulzberger in September 1961. He refers to the application of the *troika* principle, not to disarmament control, if a treaty should be concluded on the subject, but only, if it were created, to an international armed force. In the latter case, the command of that force should be organized on the *troika* principle (*New York Times* of 8 September 1961).

(2) The system of "executive pluralism" used to be applied by several countries, including the United States of America in the early days of independence. The revolutionary Committees of Correspondence not only had a policy-making role, but could initiate action. Nevertheless, since Alexander Hamilton and Thomas Jefferson, the United States has, in the light of experience, followed a unipersonal system. Since this reversal, executive pluralism has no longer been applied, except in organs of co-ordination, planning and political orientation and in the municipal sphere (cf. L. White, *The Federalists* (New York, 1948, pp. 472/473).

(3) N. Khrushchev says: "The capitalist world has its own code of ethics, the Communist world another, and the neutral countries a third" (General Assembly, XVth session, A/P.V.882, 3 October 1960, paras. 48, 12). Cf. the rejoinder of the Indian representative, V. K. Krishna Menon—above, chapter 13.

(4) "In the present state of international affairs it has become a matter of particularly urgent importance that the office of Secretary-General should be reorganized in such a way as to ensure that the executive organ of the U.N. should be headed not by a single person, the Secretary-General, but by three persons representing the present three main groups of States—the socialist States, the neutralist States and the members of western military blocs. In addition, the entire staff of the U.N. Secretariat should be reorganized on the same basis, so that the three main groups of States referred to above are represented in it on an equal footing. All practical measures taken to reorganize the individual departments of the Secretariat should be aimed at the achievement of these objectives." (Opinion of A. Roschin, Soviet expert, doc. A/4776, p. 5.)

(5) Cf., for example, in *Poland*—R. Sonnenfeld, "Sekretarz generalny ONZ, Ewolucja i Tendencje" (The Secretary-General of the U.N., Evolution and Trends) (*Sprawy Miedzynarodowe*, Warsaw, No. 2, February 1962, pp. 25 ff.); in *Eastern Germany*—H. Richter, "Generalsekretär oder kollektives Exekutivorgan der UN" ("Secretary-General or executive pluralism at the United Nations?") (*Deutsche Aussenpolitik*, No. 4, 1961, p. 438 ff.).

(6) Cf., for example, S. D. Bailey (op. cit., p. 59).
Specially worthy of attention are the two successive resolutions of the General Assembly of the United Nations which amount to votes of confidence in Dag Hammarskjöld in reply to the attacks directed against him in connection with the Congo question: firstly, the resolution adopted at the IVth special session on 19 September 1960 asking the Secretary-General to continue his efforts in the Congo (this resolution was carried by 70 votes to 0 with the U.S.S.R., the eastern European countries, France and the Union of South Africa abstaining); and, secondly, the resolution adopted at the XVth session (15 April 1961) concerning the "necessary and effective measures to be taken by the Secretary-General" in the Congo, which was carried by 83 votes to 11, (U.S.S.R., eastern European countries, Cuba and Guinea) with 5 abstentions. The first of these votes took place after the U.S.S.R. Premier's public attack on Dag Hammarskjöld, and the second in response to a proposal that the pursuit of international action in the Congo should not be explicitly entrusted to the "Secretary-General."

(7) In his separate opinion, the United States expert L. M. Goodrich said *inter alia*: "The proposal that the Secretary-General be replaced by three persons representing three basic groups of States ... is not only open to the objection that it would require the amendment of the Charter, but also, and this is much more serious, to the objection that it would permit the complete paralysis of action. It would also introduce into the organization of the Secretariat criteria which are ephemeral in nature and incapable of exact definition, the recognition of which is not in harmony with the basic purposes and principles of the organization" (doc. A/4776, appendix, p. 12).

Cf. also the separate opinion of the Uruguayan expert F. Urrutia (ibidem, p. 6 ff.).

(8) Thus, in Great Britain, Joseph B. Godber, Minister of State at the Foreign Office, said in the House of Commons that the Soviet draft was "reactionary, narrowly nationalistic in outlook, and entirely at variance with the spirit which activates Member States of the U.N." (vol. 645, *Debates of the House of Commons*, Cols. 1098-10, 1 August 1961). Adlai Stevenson, United States representative at the United Nations, expressed the opinion that if the U.S.S.R. plan had been applied in the sixteenth century, the result would have been that "the conduct of international affairs would have been entrusted to a triumvirate consisting of the Pope, the Sultan and Martin Luther" (speech at the Princeton Club, Washington D.C., 17 May 1961).

(9) As regards the use of "voluntary technical staff" who must take the oath, comply with the staff regulations and rules and obey the head of the Secretariat, cf., resolution 849 (XXXII) of ECOSOC and doc. E/TAC/109 of 12 July 1961, E/3548 of 3 August 1961, and the explanatory note of the permanent United States delegation to the U.N. (19 April 1961) ("The Peace Corps and the U.N." in *International Associations* (No. 12, December 1961, p. 797 ff.).

SELECT BIBLIOGRAPHY[a]

ABBOUSCH, W. F., "Secretary-General of the U.N.: Constitutional Powers and Development" (University of Cincinnati, Doctor's thesis, 1959).

ADATCI and DE VISSCHER, "Les privilèges et immunités diplomatiques des agents de la Société des Nations" *Yearbook of the Institute of International Law* (Vol. 31, Basle, 1924).

AGO, Roberto, "L'Organizzazione internazionale della Società delle Nazioni alle Nazioni Unite" (*La Comunita Internazionale*, I, 1946, p. 20).

AHMED, L. N., *Administrative Committee on Coordination: An Inter-Secretariat Coordinating Machinery of the U.N. Family and Agencies* (University of Kansas, Doctor's thesis, 1955).

ANGLIN, D. G., „Lester Pearson and the Office of Secretary-General" (*International Journal*, Toronto, No. 17, 1962, p. 145).

ARONSTEIN, Georges, "Le statut des fonctionnaires internationaux "(Reports to the 8th and 9th Plenary Assemblies of the World Federation of United Nations Associations, 1953 and 1954.)

ARONSTEIN, Georges, "Les tribunaux administratifs et le statut des fonctionnaires internationaux" (*Journal des Tribunaux*, Brussels, No. 4078, 1955, p. 561).

AVERY, Joyce James, "The Birth of International Man" (*Common Cause*, November, 1950).

*BAILEY, Sydney D., "International Civil Service" (*Christian Century*, No. 74, 20 February 1957).

BARANDON, Paul, *Die Vereinten Nationen und der Völkerbund in ihrem rechtsgeschicht-lichen Zusammenhang* (Doctor's thesis, Hamburg, 1948).

BARANDON, Paul, "Die Rechtsstellung der internationalen Funktionäre" (*Zeitschrift für ausländisches und internationales Privatrecht*, 1950, p. 953).

BARTLETT, T. A., *U.N. Secretariat at Work* (Stanford University, Doctor's thesis, 1959).

BARTOS, Milan, "Position and Function of the Secretary-General: Proposals for the Reorganization of the U.N. Secretariat" (*Review of International Affairs*, Belgrade, No. 253/11, 1960, p. 6).

BARTOSCH, Ferdinand, "Das Völkerbundsekretariat" (*Archiv für Sozialwissenschaft und Sozialpolitik*, No. 6/68, 1933, p. 702).

*BASTID, Suzanne, "Statut juridique des fonctionnaires des Nations Unies" (*The United Nations: Ten Years' Legal Progress*, collection of essays. Netherlands Student Association for the United Nations, The Hague, 1956, p. 145).

BASTID, Suzanne, "Les tribunaux administratifs internationaux et leur jurisprudence" (*Recueil des cours A.D.I.*, vol. 92, The Hague, 1957, p. 343).

*BEDJAOUI, Mohammed, "Jurisprudence comparée des tribunaux administratifs internationaux en matière d'excès de pouvoir" (*Annuaire français de droit international*, Paris, 1956, p. 482).

(a) To avoid repetition, the works cited in *footnotes* and *end of chapter notes* are not included in this select bibliography. The reader is therefore asked to consult the two indexes (p.   ) and particularly the name index ; the names of *authors* in the latter are preceded by an asterisk. Moreover this bibliography does not include studies which do not deal directly and specifically with the subject of this book, or general treaties and manuals on public international law.

BEDJAOUI, Mohammed, "Le syndicalisme des fonctionnaires internationaux" (*Annuaire français de droit international*, Paris, 1957, p. 435).

BEDJAOUI, Mohammed, "Application de la loi locale aux fonctionnaires internationaux. Note sur les jugements du Tribunal administratif de l'O.N.U. de 7 Décembre 1956 et 12 Juillet 1957" (*Journal de droit international*, No. 1, 1959, p. 216).

BEDJAOUI, Mohammed, "Les tribunaux administratifs internationaux" (*Jurisclasseur de droit international*, Paris, 1960, fasc. 230, 231).

BEHANAN, K. T., *Realities and Make-believe. Personnel Policy in the United Nations Secretariat* (New York, 1952).

BEHRENS, E. B., *The International Labour Office. A Survey of certain problems of International Administration* (London, 1924).

BENAR, Georges, "Fichier sur la Fonction publique internationale" (*Annales de la Faculté de Droit d'Istanbul*, No. 7, 1957, p. 522).

BENAR, Georges, "Fichier synthétique de jurisprudence administrative internationale" (*ibidem*, No. 8, 1958, p. 568).

BENAR, Georges, "Les recours devant le Tribunal administratif de l'O.I.T." (*ibidem*, No. 8, 1958, p. 453).

BENAR, Georges, & HEMAND, J. F., "Le Comité chargé des demandes de réformation de jugements du Tribunal administratif des Nations Unies "(*ibidem*, No. 7, 1957, p. 511).

BERNADET, P., *L'O.A.C.I., Service public international* (Doctor's thesis, Paris, 1946).

BERNARD, Joël, *De la responsabilité internationale des Etats envers l'O.N.U. pour dommages corporels subis par ses agents ou représentants sur leur territoire* (Doctor's thesis, Paris, 1950).

BIGBEE, Paul W., "Training applied to an International Organization" (*Personnel Administration*, No. 3/8, 1947, p. 123).

BISHOP, William, "Reparation for injuries suffered in the service of the United Nations" (*American Journal of International Law*, Washington Vol. 43, 1949, p. 589).

BJORKLUND, Sven, "Training for International Civil Service" (*Columbia Journal of International Affairs*, vol. 2, 1948, p. 14).

BLELLOCH, D., "On being an International Civil Servant" (*The Listener*, 17 February 1955, p. 287).

BOGDANOW, O. V., "Immunity of Employees of International Organizations and Its Violation and Distortion by Imperialist Reaction" (Thesis, Law Institute of the Soviet Academy of Science; summary: *The Current Digest of the Soviet Press*, No. 34/IV, 18 October 1952).

BOITEL, Michel, "Situation et problème actuels de la fonction publique internationale" (*Politique étrangère*, Paris, No. 1/18, 1953, p. 5).

BOISVIEUX, R., "La fonction publique internationale dans l'évolution des rapports interétatiques et l'élaboration de l'ordre international positif" (*La Revue administrative*, Paris, No. 63, 1958, p. 228).

BOOTH, David A., "The United Nations, the United States and the International Civil Service" (*Revue internationale des sciences administratives*, Brussels, No. 4/21, p. 703).

BORISOW, S. (in Russian) "Refusal of the International Court to grant the Secretary-General of the U.N. the full powers requested by him" (*Sovietskoye Gosudarstvo i Pravo*, Moscow, No. 7, 1951, p. 5).

BORSI, Umberto, "Il Tribunale amministrativo della Società delle Nazioni" (*Rivista di Diritto publico*, Milan, No. 1, 1928, p. 73).

BOUDREAU, Frank G., "International Civil Service: the Secretariat of the League of Nations" (*Pioneers in World Order, An American Appraisal of the League of Nations*, Harriel E. Davis, pub., New York, 1944, p. 76).

BRANDON, M., "The United Nations 'laissez-passer' " (*The British Yearbook of International Law*, London, 1950, p. 448).

BRANDON, M., "Immunity of U.N. Employees" (*International and Comparative Law Quarterly*, London, No. 2, 1953, p. 482).

BREYCHA-VAUTHIER, A. C., "Le fonctionnaire international" (*La Diplomatie contemporaine*, International seminar at Klesheim, Vienna, 1959, p. 265).

BROCAS, Patrice, "Les relations internationales et les fonctionnaires internationaux" (7th International Congress of Administrative Sciences, Berne, 1947, p. 158).

BURNHAUSER, Peter, *Die Entwicklung der Rechtsstellung internationaler Beamter* (Doctor's thesis, Erlangen, 1954).

CABOT-LODGE, H., "Maintaining Charter Standard for International Civil Servants" (*Department of State Bulletin*, Washington, 27 April 1953, p. 620).

CAETANO, Marcello, "Les relations internationales et les fonctionnaires internationaux" (7th International Congress of Administrative Sciences, Berne, 1947, p. 209).

CALDERWOOD, Howard B., "The Higher Direction of the League Secretariat" (Southern Methodist University, Arnold Foundation, *Studies in Public Affairs* No. 3/V, Dallas, Texas, 1937).

CALVEZ, J. Y., "Un triumvirat remplacera-t-il M. H.?" (*Revue de l'action populaire*, Paris, No. 147, 1961, p. 415).

CARMOY (de), G., "Thoughts on some administrative problems of international Organization" (*Revue internationale des sciences administratives*, Brussels, No. 3/VI, 1950, p. 464).

CASTAÑON, G. F., "Cualidades intelectuales y morales del funcionario internacional" (*Escuela de Funcionarios internacionales, Cursos y conferencias*, II, Madrid, 1955-56, p. 249).

CECIL (Viscount) of Chelwood, *A Great Experiment* (London, 1941).

CHATENET, Pierre, "Le rôle des administrations nationales dans la formation des fonctionnaires européens" (*La fonction publique européenne*, Colloque de Sarrebruck, Brussels-Stuttgart, 1956, p. 189).

CHAUMONT, Charles, "Perspective d'une théorie du service public à l'usage du droit international contemporain" (*La technique et les principes du droit public, Mélanges en l'honneur de Georges Scelle*, Paris, vol. 1, 1950, p. 115).

CHEN, W. C., *Personnel System of the U.N., a Study of International Civil Service* (St. Louis University, Doctor's thesis, 1951).

CHIESA, Fernando, "Les jurisdictions administratives internationales" (*Revue internationale des sciences administratives*, Brussels, No. 1/20, 1954, p. 67).

CLAUDE, Inis, Jr., *Swords into Plowshares* (New York, 1956).

COHEN, Benjamin V., *The United Nations: Constitutional Developments, Growth and Possibilities* (Cambridge, Massachusetts, Harvard Univ. Press, 1961).

COHN, M., "Espionage and Immunity. Some Recent Problems and Developments" (*British Yearbook of International Law*, No. 25, 1948, p. 404).

COLLIARD, Claude-Albert, "Los Funcionarios internacionales" (*Escuela de Funcionarios internacionales, Cursos y conferencias*, II, 1955-56, p. 229).

Conference on Human Relations in International Administration (Carnegie Endowment, La Tour-de Peilz, 15-22 February 1957, Washington, 1957).

Conference on the Concept of a True International Civil Service (Carnegie Endowment, Vevey, 7-14 February 1956, Washington, 1957).

Conference on Training for International Administration (proceedings of the Conference held in Washington on 21 and 22 August 1943, Carnegie Endowment, Washington, 1944).

CORBOS, B. (in Greek), *International Protection of United Nations Officials. Theory of Functional Protection* (Athens, 1954).

CROZAT, Charles & BENAR, Georges, "Recueil de la Fonction publique internationale" (*Annales de la Faculté de Droit d'Istanbul*, No. 7, 1957, p. 129).

CUILLE, Georges, *Le statut des fonctionnaires internationaux* (Doctor's thesis, Paris, 1959).

DAUSSIN, Armand, "Perfectionnement des fonctionnaires européens: rôle des organisations européennes" (*La fonction publique européenne*, Colloque de Sarrebruck, Brussels-Stuttgart, 1956, p. 163).

DAUSSIN, Armand, "La fonction publique internationale" (*Technique, Art, Science*, April, 1957).

DAUSSIN, Armand, "Vers une fonction publique européenne" (*Annuaire européen*, vol. VI, 1960, p. 122).

DAVIES, J. G. W., "The Work of the Secretariat" (*Annual Review of U.N. Affairs*, New York, 1952, p. 135).

DAVIS, Kathryn W., "The Soviet Union and the League of Nations, 1919-1933" (*Geneva Special Studies*, No. 1/V. 1934).

DEHAUSSY, Jean, "Procédure de réformation des jugements du Tribunal administratif des Nations Unies" (*Annuaire français de droit international*, Paris, 1956, p.468).

DELISLE BURNS, C., "International Administration" (*The British Yearbook of International Law*, London, vol. 7, 1926, p. 54).

*DENDIAS, Michel, "L'Administration internationale dans son évolution et l'Organisation des Nations Unies" (*Revue hellénique de droit international*, Athens, No. 1-2, 1948, pp. 15 and 119).

DENDIAS, Michel, *Les relations internationales et les fonctionnaires internationaux* (7th International Congress of Administrative Sciences, Berne, 1947, p. 169). Developing an International Civil Service (*Columbia Journal of International Affairs*, spring 1948).

DEVEZE, Albert, "Fonctionnaire international — Statut — Engagement de durée définie — contrôle judiciaire" (*Journal des tribunaux*, Brussels, No. 4078, 16 October 1955, p. 566).

DINH, Nguyen Quoc, "Les privilèges et immunités des organismes internationaux d'après les jurisprudences nationales depuis 1945" (*Annuaire français de droit international*, Paris, 1957, p. 262).

*DRUMMOND, Sir Eric, "The Secretariat of the League of Nations" (*Public Administration*, London, Vol. IX, 1931, p. 228).

EEK, H., "The Secretariat as the principal organ of the United Nations" (*Acta scandinavica iuris gentium*, Copenhagen, 1953, p. 3).

EGGER, Max, *Die Vorrechte und Befreiungen zugunsten internationalen Organisationen und ihrer Funktionäre* (Vienna, 1954).

EIFLER, R. K., "Privileges and Immunities of U.N. Delegates and Officials; the International Organizations Immunities Act" (*Michigan Law Review*, Ann Arbor, Vol. 46, 1948, p. 381).

ELVIN, L., "An International Civil Service? What should be done?" (*Fabian Journal*, July 1957, p. 5).

EVANS, A. A., "The International Secretariat of the Future" (*Public Administration*, London, No. 2/22, 1944, p. 74).

EVANS, Luther H., *Problems of Administration in International Affairs. A memorandum* (Foundation of World Organization, New York — London, 1952, p. 331).

FEUER, G., *Les aspects juridiques de l'assistance technique dans le cadre des Nations Unies et des institutions spécialisées* (preface, Mrs. S. Bastid, Paris, 1957).

FISCHER, Georges, "La compétence du Secrétaire général" (*Annuaire français de droit international*, Paris, 1955, p. 345).

FISCHER, Georges, "O.I.T. Privilèges et immunités (*ibidem*, p. 385).

FISCHER, Georges, "UNESCO. Accord relatif au siège" (*ibidem*, p. 393).

Fonctionnaires internationaux (*Dictionnaire diplomatique*, Académie diplomatique internationale, Vol. I, p. 918).

FOWLER, Donald D. & Bryce, Murray D., "Building Team Spirit in an International Staff" (*Personnel Administration*, Washington, No. 5/16, 1953, p. 22).

FREEMAN, H. A., "International Administrative Law. A Functional Approach to Peace" (*Yale Law Journal*, New Haven, Connecticut, Vol. 57, 1948, p. 976).

FREI, Paul-Henri, *De la situation juridique des représentants des membres de la S. d. N. et de ses agents" (commentaire de l'article 7 du Pacte)* (Paris, 1929).

*FRIEDMANN, W. G., "The United Nations and National Loyalties" (*International Journal*, Toronto, No. 8/53, 1952, p. 17).

FRIEDMANN, W. G., "Loyalty Test and the U.N." (*Canadian Forum*, Toronto, 1953, p. 30).

FRIEDMANN, W. G., FATOUROS, A. A., "The United Nations Administrative Tribunal" (*International Organization*, No. 1/XI, 1957).

GARCIA ARIAS, L., "La distribución nacional de los altos funcionarios de las Naciones Unidas" (*Cuadernos de politica internacional*, Madrid, No. 27, 1956, p. 119).

*GAUDEMET, Paul-Marie, "Le fonctionnaire européen — Notion — Rôle — Condition juridique" (*La fonction publique européenne*, Colloque de Sarrebruck, Brussels-Stuttgart, 1956, p. 19).

GAUDEMET, Paul-Marie, "Statut juridique des fonctionnaires européens" (*Der europäische Beamte*, Munich-Berlin, 1955, p. 37).

GAUDEMET, Paul-Marie, "Le statut des fonctionnaires internationaux en droit interne" (La Revue administrative, Paris, No. 67, 1959, p. 5 and *Revue internationale des sciences administratives*, Brussels, No. 1, 1959).

GESSNER, L. M., "Le droit administratif international. A propos de l'ouvrage de M. de Martens" (*Revue de droit international et de législation comparée*, The Hague-Paris, Vol. 18, 1886, p. 329).

*GIRAUD, Emile, "Función de la Secretaría de una institución internacional y cualidades que se requieren de los funcionarios internacionales" (*Escuela de Funcionarios internacionales, Cursos y conferencias*, II, Madrid, 1955-56, p. 275).

GIRAUD, Émile, "The qualifications of International Civil Servants" (*UN Special*, Geneva, No. 4, 1952, p. 21).

*GOODRICH, L. M., "Geographical Distribution of the Staff of the U.N." (*International Organization*, No. 3/XVI, 1962, p. 465).

GRAWITZ, Madeleine, "Jurisprudence internationale. Tribunal administratif des Nations Unies. Jugements Nos. 55 et 64" (*Annuaire français de droit international*, Paris, 1955, p. 290).

GRAWITZ, Madeleine, "Tribunal administratif des Nations Unies. Jugements des 2 et 3 décembre 1955, 30 août et 1er septembre 1956" (*ibidem*, 1956, p. 453).

GREEN, L. C., "The Status of the International Civil Service" (*Current Legal Problems*, London, No. 7, 1954, p. 192).

GREEN, L. C., "The International Civil Servant: his employer and his state" (*Grotius Society Transactions*, London, No. 40, 1954, p. 147).

GRUNEBAUM-BALLIN, Paul, "De l'utilité d'une juridiction spéciale pour les règlements des litiges intéressant les services de la S. d. N. " (*Revue de droit international et de législation comparée*, Brussels-Paris, 1921, p. 67).

GUETZKOW, Harold, *Multiple Loyalties: Theoretical Approach to a Problem of International Organization* (Woodrow Wilson School of Public International Affairs, Princeton University, publ. No. 4, Princeton, New Jersey, 1955).

GUTTERIDGE, Frank, "Le Comité d'enquête et d'appel de l'O.M.S." (*Annales de la Faculté de droit d'Istanbul*, No. 8, 1958, p. 547).

HALL, Clyde C., "An Experience in Recruitment for the United Nations" (*Personnel Administration*, Washington, No. 4/16, 1953, p. 11).

HAMILTON, T. J., "Can U.N. have a Civil Service?" (*Foreign Policy Bulletin*, New York, 1 March 1953, p. 1).

HAMILTON, T. J., "U.N. — From Expansion to Bankruptcy" (*Freedom and Union*, No. 6, 1961, p. 8).

HAMILTON, T. J., "U.N.'s Most Expensive Coin" (*ibidem*, No. 5, p. 3).

HARRIS, J., *The Development of an International Civil Service for the Administration of Relief and Rehabilitation of War Devastated Areas* (Washington, 1944).

HARTNETT, Robert C., *U.S. Communists in the United Nations* (America, New York, 17 January 1952, p. 421).

HAUPTMANN, Gerhard, *Die Rechtsstellung der internationalen Funktionäre* (Doctor's thesis, Göttingen, 1952).

HESSEL, Stéphane, "Le Secrétariat des Nations Unies et la Fonction publique internationale" (*Les Nations Unies, Chantier de l'Avenir*, Paris, Vol. II, 1960-1961).

HEYMAN, J. F., "Organismes paritaires de recours et tribunaux administratifs" (*Annales de la Faculté de droit d'Istanbul*, No. 8, 1958, p. 497).

HEYMAN, J. F., *Les juridictions administratives internationales* (Doctor's thesis, Dijon, 1958).

HILL, David Jayne, "Immunités diplomatiques et consulaires et immunités à reconnaître aux personnes investies de fonctions d'intérêt international" (*Annuaire de l'Institut de droit international*, vol. 33, 1927, p. 399).

*HILL, Martin, *Immunities and Privileges of International Officials. The Experience of the League of Nations* (Washington, Carnegie Endowment, 1947).

HILL, Norman L., *International Administration* (New York, 1931).

HIRSCK, Carl Georg, *Die rechtliche Stellung der internationalen Beamten unter besonderer Berücksichtigung der Funktionäre des Völkerbundsekretariats in Genf* (Bonn, 1928).

HOGG, R. D., "The Secretariat" (*Annual Review of U.N. Affairs*, New York, 1953, p. 120).

HOLDEN, F. W., "The Secretariat of the U.N." (*Public Administration*, London, Vol. 24, 1946, p. 112).

*HONIG, F., "The International Civil Service. Basic problems and contemporary difficulties" (*International Affairs*, London, No. 30, 1954, p. 175).

HONIG, F., "The independence of the International Civil Service. Charter Requirements and Reality" (*Acta scandinavia iuris gentium*, No. 3-4/24, 1954, p. 35).

HOWELL, F. — FOWLER, D., "Personnel Programmes of International Organizations" (*Publ. Personnel Review*, No. 4/17, 1956, p. 281).

HUET, Pierre, "Les tribunaux administratifs des organisations internationales" (*Journal de droit international*, Paris, No. 44, 1950, p. 336).

Idéologies nationales et fonction publique internationale (*ibidem*, 1954, p. 276).

IVANOV, F. (in Russian) "The juridical authority of international administrative tribunals" (*Sovietskoye Gosudarstwo i Pravo*, Moscow, No. 3, 1957, p. 62).

IVRAKIS, Solon-Cléanthe, "Speculations round the Privileges and Immunities of the U.N." (*Revue hellénique de droit international*, Athens, No. 2-4, 1954, p. 175).

JACKSON, Elmore, "The Developing Role of the Secretary-General" (*International Organization*, No. 3/11, 1957, p. 431).

JAMES, Alan, "The Soviet Troika Proposals" (*The World Today*, No. 9/17, 1961, p. 368).

JAMES, Alan, "Neutral Men and Neutral Action" (*International Relations*, No. 4, 1961, p. 234).

*JENKS, C. Wilfred, *The Headquarters of International Institutions* (London, 1945).

JENKS, C. Wilfred, "University Preparation for International Administration" (*Columbia Jouranl of International Affairs*, No. 5/13, 1948).

JENKS, C. Wilfred, "International Immunities" (London, 1961).

JESSUP, Philip C., "The International Civil Servant and His Loyalties" (*Journal of International Affairs*, New York, No. 2, 1955, p. 55).

JESSUP, Philip C., "Status of International Organization Privileges and Immunities of their Officials" (*American Journal of International Law*, Washington, vol. 38, 1944, p. 638).

JORION, E., "Les droits et les obligations des fonctionnaires internationaux" (*Revue internationale des sciences administratives*, Brussels, No. 1/30, 1954, p. 149).

JULLY, Laurent, "Deux récentes décisions de la Cour internationale de Justice" (*Friedens-Warte*, Bâle, No. 3, 1949).

K. G., "International Officials: a Question of Loyalties" (*The World Today*, November 1954, p. 488).

KAUFMANN, Sigmund, *Die Immunität der Nicht-Diplomaten. Ein Beitrag zur Kodifikation des Völkerrechts* (Leipzig, 1932).

*KAZANSKY, Pierre (in Russian) *The Future of the Major Administrative Unions of States* (1897).

KAZANSKY, Pierre (in Russian), *The major administrative Unions of States* (vol. I, 1897).

KENNEDY, D. S., "A Note on the Salary, Allowance and Leave System of the United Nations" (*Public Administration Review*, Chicago, No. 3/XI, 1951, p. 192).

KERN, Ernst, "Die Rechtsstellung der europäischen Beamten" (*Der europäische Beamte*, Munich-Berlin, 1955, p. 49).

KERN, Ernst, "Europäische Beiträge für ein überstaatliches Beamtenrecht. Probleme des zwischenstaatlichen Dienstes" (*Der öffentliche Dienst*, Dusseldorf, 1952, p. 204, 1953, p. 65).

KERN, Ernst, "Impératifs d'une fonction publique européenne" (*Revue internationale des sciences administratives*, No. 1, 1959).

KING, John Kerry, *International Administrative Jurisdiction* (Brussels, International Institute of Administrative Sciences, 1952).

KORDT, Erich, "Der Funktionär amtlicher internationaler Organisationen. Erörterung des politischen und rechtlichen Standorts" (*Um Recht und Gerechtigkeit*, Festschrift für Erich Kaufmann, Stuttgart-Cologne, 1950, p. 191).

KORDT, Erich, "Auswahl und Ausbildung von Bediensteten bei europäischen zwischenstaatlichen Organisationen" (*Der europäische Beamte*, Munich-Berlin, 1955, p. 9).

KOUZBARI, Walid Y., *Les pouvoirs politiques du Secrétaire général des Nations Unies* (Doctor's thesis, Paris, 1959).

KRABBE, L. T., *Le Secrétariat général de la Société des Nations et son activité* (Copenhagen, 1924).

KRABBE, L. T., *League of Nations Secretariat* (preface by Sir Eric Drummond, Geneva, 1930).

KRISHNA, Rao K., "The Status of Experts of the Expanded Programme of Technical Assistance of the United Nations" (*Revue de droit international pour le Moyen Orient*, Beirut, No. 5/1, 1956, p. 42).

KRYLOW, S. B. (in Russian) *Materials for a history of the United Nations* (Moscow, 1949).

KUNZ, Joseph L., "Experiences and Techniques in International Administration" (*Iowa Law Review*, Iowa City, Vol. 31, 1945-46, p. 40).

KUNZ, Joseph L., "The legal position of the Secretary-General of the United Nations" (*American Journal of International Law*, Washington, No. 4/40, 1946, p. 786).

KUNZ, Joseph L., "Privileges and Immunities of International Organizations" (*ibidem*, Vol. 41, 1947, p. 826).

L. M., "Some Functions and Problems of the International Civil Servant" (*Indian Yearbook of International Affairs*, section II, Madras, VI, 1956, p. 229).

La Fonction publique européenne (Statut futur, formation, perfectionnement).
Colloque de Sarrebruck 7-10 November 1955 (Sarrebruck, editors: R. Bruns & G. Langrod, University of the Sarre, Brussels-Stuttgart, 1956). Separate German version: *Der Europäische öffentliche Dienst*, 1957.

La Fonction publique internationale et l'action internationale d'assistance technique *(Orientation à la fonction internationale*, Paris, 1958).

LAL, S., "The International Civil Servant" (*The Indian Journal of Public Administration*, New Dehli, No. I/II, 1956, p. 12.

LANGROD, Georges, "L'aspect administratif de l'organisation internationale" (*Revue hellénique de droit international*, Athens, No. 2-4, 1949, p. 183).

LANGROD, Georges, "Studies on International Administration: International attempts at Public Administration Training" (*ibidem*, p. 200).

LANGROD, Georges, "Le Tribunal administratif des Nations Unies" (*Revue de droit public et de science politique*, Paris, 1951, p. 71).

LANGROD, Georges, "L'organisation des Nations Unies pour l'Alimentation et l'Agriculture (FAO) et les Sciences sociales" (*Revue internationale d'histoire politique et constitutionnelle*, Paris, No. 3/4, 1951, 2nd series, p. 306).

LANGROD, Georges, "Problèmes fondamentaux de la fonction publique internationale" (*Revue internationale des sciences administratives*, Brussels, No. 1, 1953, p. 9).

LANGROD, Georges, "La jurisprudence du Tribunal administratif des Nations Unies" (*Rivista di diritto internazionale*, Milan, No. 2-3, 1954, p. 243).

LANGROD, Georges, "La crise de la fonction publique internationale (*Annales universitatis saraviensis*, Sarrebruck, 1953, No. 3, p. 146; *ibidem*, No. 4, 1955, p. 248: *ibidem*, No. 4, 1955, p. 331).

LANGROD, Georges, Les réalisations jurisprudentielles du Tribunal administratif international de Genève" (*Revue de droit international et de droit comparé*, Brussels, No. 1-2, 1955, p. 7).

LANGROD, Georges, "Le Secrétariat de l'O.N.U." (*Archiv des Völkerrechts*, Tübingen, No. 1/6, 1956).

LANGROD, Georges, "La réforme du Tribunal administratif des Nations Unies" (*Zeitschrift für ausländisches öffentliches Recht und Völkerrecht*, Stuttgart, No. 2/17, 1956, p. 249).

LANGROD, Georges, "Tendances administratives et réformes internes aux Nations Unies en 1957" (*Annales universitatis saraviensis*, No. 4, 1956-1957, p. 244).

LANGROD, Georges, "Problèmes du Secrétariat international" (*Revue générale de droit international public*, Paris, No. 3, 1957).

LANGROD, Georges, "Les problèmes administratifs du régionalisme international. Histoire et réalisations du Panaméricanisme" (*Revue hellénique de droit international*, Athens, No. 1, 1957, p. 132).

LANGROD, Georges, "Le progrès de l'idée de 'carrière' dans la fonction publique internationale" (*Sentier d'Europe*, Turin, No. 2, 1958, p. 13).

LANGROD, Georges, "Organisation professionnelle et action sociale des fonctionnaires internationaux" (*Stato sociale*, Rome, No. 3, 1958, p. 268).

LANGROD, Georges, "Catégories apparentées aux fonctionnaires publics internationaux" (*ibidem*, No. 3, 1959, p. 268).

LANGROD, Georges, "La fonction publique internationale à la lumière des tendances et des réalisations à l'O.N.U. au cours des années 1957 et 1958 (*Annales universitatis saraviensis*, Sarrebruck, No. 2/3, 1959, p. 141).

LANGROD, Georges, "Les Institutions européennes et leur aspect administratif" (*Stato sociale*, Rome, No. 7, 1959, p. 657).

LANGROD, Georges, "Observations sur le recrutement à la fonction publique internationale" (*Revue hellénique de droit international*, Athens, No. 1, 1960, p. 97).

LARRY, Leonard L., *International Organization* (New York, 1951).

*LASH, Joseph P., "Dag Hammarskjöld's Conception of His Office" (*International Organization*, No. 3/XVI, p. 542).

LASSALLE, Claude, "Contribution à une théorie de la fonction publique supranationale" (*Revue de droit public et de Science politique*, Paris, No. 3, 1957, p. 472).

LEHMAN, William, "International Personnel Administration" (*Personnel Administration*, Washington, No. 10, 1947, p. 5).

LEHMANN, Herbert, "Some Problems of International Administration" (*Public Administration Review*, Chicago, 1945, p. 93).

LEWIS, G. "The Selection and Training of International Civil Servants" (*Cahiers de Bruges*, No. 2/7, 1957, p. 67).

LIANG, Yuen-Li, "The Legal Status, Privileges and Immunities of the Specialized Agencies" (*American Journal of International Law*, Washington, 1948, p. 900).

LIANG, Yuen-Li, "U.N. Headquarters Agreement" (*ibidem*, p. 445).

LIANG, Yuen-Li, "Reparation for Injuries suffered in the Service of the U.N." (*ibidem*, 1949, p. 460).

*LIE, Trygve (in Danish), "Administrative Problems of the United Nations" (*Nordisk Admin., Tidsskrift*, Copenhagen, No. 4/37, 1956, p. 246).

LISSITZYN, Oliver J., "U.N. Administrative Tribunal. Effect of Awards" (*American Journal of International Law*, Washington, No. 4/48, 1954, p. 655).

LOPEZ-RODO, Laureano, "Perfectionnement des fonctionnaires européens: rôle des établissements d'enseignement" (*La fonction publique européenne*, Colloque de Sarrebruck, Brussels-Stuttgart, 1956, p. 235).

*LOVEDAY, A., "Staff Salaries in the U.N. Family" (*International Organization*, No. 4/XI, 1957, p. 635).

MACE, Daniel, *Le fédéralisme administratif et l'O.A.C.I.* (Doctor's thesis, Lille, 1951).

MAKOWSKI, Julian (in Polish) "The international officials and their immunities" (*Rocznik prawa miedzynarodowego*, Warsaw, 1949, p. 177).

MARGOLIS, E., "The Plea of Privilege against Self-incrimination by U.N. Employees" (*Virginia Law Review*, vol. 40, 1954, p. 283).

MARTIN, William, "La condition des fonctionnaires internationaux" (*Nouvelle revue suisse*, 1926, p. 421).

MARTONFFY, Charles, *Les relations internationales et les fonctionnaires internationaux* seventh International Congress of Administrative Sciences, Berne, 1947, p. 172).

MASLAND, John W., "The Secretariat of the United Nations" (*Public Administration Review*, Chicago, 1945, p. 364).

MENZEL, Eberhard, "Die Privilegien und Immunitäten der internationalen Funktionäre" (*Verfassung und Verwaltung in Theorie und Wirklichkeit*, Festgabe für Wilhelm Laforet, University of Mainz, No. 3, Mainz, 1952, p. 325).

MERCIER, Jacques, "L'indépendance des fonctionnaires internationaux dans la jurisprudence du Tribunal de l'O.I.T." (*Le Droit au service de la paix*, nouvelle série, Brussels, No. 4, 1956, p. 23).

MERCIER, Jacques, "Tribunal administratif de l'O.I.T. Jugements des 2 et 6 septembre, 26 avril et 19 octobre 1955" (*Annuaire français de droit international*, Paris, 1955, p. 296).

MERROW, C. E., "Administrative Progress and Problems in the U.N. and its Agencies" (*Department of State Bulletin*, 31 October 1955, p. 715).

MIELE, M., "Privilèges et immunités des fonctionnaires internationaux" (Milan, 1958).

MIGLIAZZA, Alessandro, *Il fenomeno dell' Organizzazione e la comunità internazionale* (Milan, 1958).

MITRANY, David, "Problems of International Administration" (*Public Administration*, London, No. 1/23, 1945, p. 2).

MITRANY, N., "Les mythes de l'énergie nucléaire et la bureaucratie internationale" (*Cahiers internationaux de sociologie*, Paris, No. 21, 1956, p. 138).

MITCHELL, James M., "International Personnel Psychology" (*Public Personnel Review*, Chicago, No. 3/18, 1957, p. 151).

MOATS, Helen M., *The Secretariat of the League of Nations, International Civil Service or Diplomatic Conference* (Thesis, Chicago, 1936).

MODEROW, Wlodzimierz, "Observations sur l'affaire des fonctionnaires américains congédiés par le Secrétaire général à la demande du gouvernement des Etats-Unis" (*Politique étrangère*, Paris, No. 19, 1954, p. 501).

MOLLER, R., "International Civil Service" (*Federal News*, London, 1947, p. 15).

*MOLITOR, André, "Vers une Fonction publique européenne" (*Cahiers de Bruges*, No. II, 1957, p. 84).

MONACO, Ricardo, "La condizione giuridica esterna dei funzionari internazionali" (*Rivista trimestrale di diritto pubblico*, No. 2/1, 1951, p. 390).

MONACO, Ricardo, "L'immunità giurisdizionale delle Istituzioni specializzate delle Nazioni Unite (*Rivista di diritto internazionale*, Milan, 1953, p. 472).

MOORE, Bernard, "The Secretariat: Role and Functions" (*Annual Review of U.N. Affairs*, New York, 1949, p. 20).

MORELLI, Gaetano, "L'Instituto internazionale di Agricoltura e la giurisdizione italiana (*Foro Italiano*, No. 1, 1931, p. 1425).

MOSTAFAVI, R., *Le fonctionnement technique du Secrétariat des Nations Unies* (Doctor's thesis, Paris, 1952).

MOYNIER, G., *Les bureaux internationaux des unions universelles* (Paris, 1892).

MYRDAL, Gunnar, *Realities and Illusions in regard to Intergovernmental Organizations* (Oxford University Press, London, 1955).

MYRDAL, Gunnar, "The Research Work of the Secretariat of the Economic Commission for Europe" (*Economic Essays in Honour of Eric Lindall*, 1956).

NEGULESCO, Paul, "Principes de droit international administratif" (*Recueil des cours de A.D.I.*, 51, I, 1935, p. 583).

NEHLAOUI, Fayez, *Le Secrétaire général des Nations Unies* (Doctors' thesis, Paris, 1949).

NOGMAALS (in Dutch), "The Law on United Nations officials" (*Wordende Wereld*, The Hague, No. 1/7, 1955, p. 10).

OBERN, Alfred Gaylord, *Selected Regional International Organizations. A Comparative Study in International Administration* (thesis, American University, Washington, 1955).

ODDINI, Mario, "Elementi internazionalistici ed elementi interindividuali nella organizzazione internazionale" (*Rivista di diritto internazionale*, vol. 36, 1953, p. 410).

ODDINI, Mario, "Principi strutturali del Segretariato delle Nazioni Unite" (*ibidem*, No. 2-3/38, 1955, p. 297).

ORVE (de), José Ramon, "Extensión de los privilegios diplomaticos en el Pacto de la Liga de las Naciones (*La Rivista de Ciencias juridicas y sociales*, Madrid, No. 18/5, 1922, p. 167).

*PARRY, Clive, "The International Civil Servant" (*The Listener*, London, 18 August 1955, p. 243).

PARRY, Clive, "The Secretariat of the U.N." (*World Affairs*, London, No. 3/IV, 1950, p. 350).

PEJU, Marcel, "Abraham Feller, ou son propre bourreau" (*Temps modernes*, Paris, March 1953, p. 1424).

PEREZ-MONTERO, José, "Privilegios e immunidades de los funcionarios internacionales" (*Actos del I Congreso Hispano-Luso-Americano*, Derecho internacional, Vol. II, Madrid, 1953, p. 217).

PERRENOUD, Georges, *Régime des privilèges et immunités des missions diplomatiques étrangères et des organisations internationales en Suisse* (Doctor's thesis No. 461, Geneva, 1949).

PEUCH, J., "Le contrat de fonction publique internationale" (*Annales de la Faculté de droit de Beyrouth*, 1957, p. 147).

PFUEHL, Eberhardt, *Privilegien und Immunitäten internationaler Funktionäre* (Doctor's thesis, Berlin, 1952).

PILOTTI, Massimo, "Les recours des particuliers devant les juridictions internationales" (*Problèmes fondamentaux du droit international*, Mélanges Jean Spiropoulos, 1957, p. 351).

PLANTEY, Alain, *La formation et le perfectionnement des fonctionnaires nationaux et internationaux* (Brussels, International Institute of Administrative Sciences, 1955).

POELJE (Van), G. A., "Jurisdictions administratives internationales" (*General report*, ninth International Congress on Administrative Sciences, Istanbul, 1953).

POSEGA, Kurt, *Vorrechte und Befreiungen der internationalen Funktionäre* (Doctor's thesis, Göttingen, 1929).

POTTER, Pitman B., "International Administration, Factor for Human Unity or Discord" (*Approach to Group Understanding*, 1947, p. 173).

POWERS, E. W., "U.N. Administrative Tribunals as Adjudicators of Disputes

Arising out of Employment Contracts with International Organizations" (*Michigan Law Review*, Ann Arbor, No. 4/54, 1956, p. 533).

PREUSS, Lawrence, "Diplomatic Privileges and Immunities of Agents Invested with Functions of International Interest" (*American Journal of International Law*, Washington, No. 4/25, 1931, p. 694).

PREUSS, Lawrence, "The International Organizations Immunities Act" (*ibidem*, vol. 40, p. 332).

PRICE, Byron, "The Secretariat" (*Annual Review of United Nations Affairs*, New York, 1951, p. 104).

PUGET, Henry, "Le Tribunal administratif des Nations Unies. Ses décisions récentes en matière de licenciement et leur inexécution" (*Jurisclasseur périodique*, Paris, 10 April 1952, No. 994, 15/26, doctrine 994).

*PURVES, Chester, *The International Secretariat of the Future* (London, Royal Institute of International Affairs, 1944).

PURVES, Chester, *The International Administration of an International Secretariat* (*ibidem*, 1945).

PYMAN, T. A., "The United Nations Secretary-Generalship; a review of its status, functions and role" (*Australian Outlook*, Melbourne, No. 15, 1961, p. 240).

RACINE, Pierre, "La Fonction publique internationale sous l'aspect psychologique et humain" (*Cahiers chrétiens de la fonction publique*, Paris, No. 36, 1958 and "La Fonction publique internationale et l'action internationale d'assistance technique" Paris, International Civil Service Training Organization: O.F.I., 1958, p. 105).

*RANSHOFEN-WERTHEIMER, Egon F., "The International Civil Service of the Future" (*International Conciliation*, No. 418, New York, 1946).

RANSHOFEN-WERTHEIMER, Egon F., Cf. BARTOSCH Ferdinand (pseud.).

RANSHOFEN-WERTHEIMER, Egon F., "International Administration: Lessons from the Experience of the League of Nations" (*American Political Science Review*, Washington, Vol. 37, 1943, p. 872).

RANSHOFEN-WERTHEIMER, Egon F., "The position of the Executive and Administrative Heads of the U.N." (*ibidem*, 1945, p. 323).

RANSHOFEN-WERTHEIMER, Egon F., "Training for International Administration" (*Journal of the National Association of Deans of Women*, No. 21, 1944, p. 792).

RANSHOFEN-WERTHEIMER, Egon F., "Formation des fonctionnaires européens: objet de l'enseignement" (*La fonction publique européenne*, Colloque de Sarrebruck, Brussels-Stuttgart, 1956, p. 127).

RANSHOFEN-WERTHEIMER, Egon F., "Verwaltungs und personalpolitische Fragen der Vereinten Nationen" (*Die Vereinten Nationen und Oesterreich*, VIII, Vienna, 1957, and *La Fonction publique internationale et l'action internationale d'assistance technique* Paris, International Civil Service Training Organization: O.F.I., 1958, p. 145).

REUTER, Paul, "Les organes subsidiaires des organisations internationales" (*Hommage d'une génération de juristes au Président Basdevant*, Paris, 1960).

REY, Francis, "Les immunités des fonctionnaires internationaux" (*Revue de droit international privé*, Paris, vol. 23, 1928, pp. 253 and 432).

RIBEREAU, Gayon (Mrs.), *Le contrôle de l'activité du Tribunal administratif des Nations Unies* (Mémoire, Institut des Hautes études internationales de l'Université de Paris, 1958).

ROGERS, William C., "The international Civil Service" (*Public Personnel Review*, Chicago, No. 3/7, 1946, p. 156).

ROSEN, S. McKee, *The Combined Boards of the Second World War: an Experiment in International Administration* (New York, 1952).

ROSENHEIM, H. "Y a-t-il une fonction publique internationale?" (*Notre opinion*, Association du personnel de l'UNESCO, No. 20, 1957, p. 13).

*SALTER (Lord), "The International Character of the League of Nations Secretariat" (*The United States of Europe*, London, 1930).

SAYRE, James Brown, *Experiments in International Administration* (London — New York, 1919).

SBAROUNIS, A. J., "Taxation of U.N. Officials" (*Revue hellénique de droit international*, Athens, 1954, p. 1).

SCHLOCHAUER, Hans-Jürgen, *Der Rechtsschutz gegenüber der Tätigkeit internationaler und übernationaler Behörden* (Frankfurt, 1952).

SCHMIDT, Fritz, *Die völkerrechtliche Stellung der Mitglieder des ständigen Sekretariats des Völkerbundes, des Internationalen Arbeitsamtes und des ständigen internationalen Gerichtshofes, im Vergliech zu einander* (Doctor's thesis, Cologne, Quakenbrück, 1930).

SCHOKKING, G. J., "Die internationale Bürokratie: theoretische Probleme eines neuen Forschungsgebietes" (*Zeitschrift für Politik*, Berlin, 1955, p. 133).

*SCHWEBEL, Stephen M., "The Origins and Development of Article 99 of the Charter. The Powers of the Secretary-General of the United Nations" (*British Yearbook of International Law*, vol. 28, 1951, p. 371).

SCHWEBEL, Stephen M., "The International Character of the Secretariat of the U.N." (*ibidem*, vol. 30, 1953, p. 71).

SCHWELB, Egon, "The Diplomatic Privileges (Extension) Act of 1944" (*Modern Law Review*, London, Vol. 8, 1945).

SCOTT, Frank R., "The World's Civil Service" (*International Conciliation*, No. 446, New York, 1954).

SECRETAN, Jacques, *Les immunités diplomatiques des représentants des Etats membres et des agents de la S. d. N.* (Thesis, Lausanne, 1928).

SECRETAN, Jacques, "The independence granted to agents of the international community in their relations with national public authorities" (*British Yearbook of International Law*, vol. 16, 1935, p. 56).

SECRETAN, Roger, "Les privilèges et immunités diplomatiques des agents de la S. d. N." (*Revue de droit international privé*, Paris, 1925, p. l).

SEIDL-HOHENVELDERN, Ignaz, "Rechtsbeziehungen zwischen internationalen Organizationen und den einzelnen Staaten" (*Archiv des Völkerrechts*, No. 1/4, 1953, p. 30).

SEIDL-HOHENVELDERN, Ignaz, "Perfectionnement des fonctionnaires européens: rôle des administrations nationales" (*La fonction publique européenne*. Colloque de Sarrebruck, Brussels-Cologne, 1956, p. 215).

SHAFQUAT, C. M., "The U.N. and its agents" (*Pakistan Horizon*, Karachi, No. 3, 1950, p. 45).

SIRAUD, Pierre, *Le Tribunal administratif de la S. d. N.* (Doctor's thesis, Paris, 1942).

SLOAN, F. Blaine, "Reparation for Injury to agents of the U.N." (*Nebraska Law Review*, vol. 28, 1949, p. 401).

SPENCER, M. J., "Jurisdictional Immunity of U.N. Employees — the Gubitchev Case" (*Michigan Law Review*, Ann Arbor, Vol. 49, 1950, p. 101).

*SRIVASTAWA, A. K., "The Problem of Loyalty in International Organizations" (*Indian Quarterly*, 1958, p. 77).

*STONE, Donald C., "Organizing the U.N.: its six Principal Organs" (*Public Administration Review*, Chicago, No. 6, 1946, p. 115).

STONE, Donald C., "An Application of Scientific Management Principles to International Administration" (*American Political Science Review*, Washington, No. 42, 1948, p. 915) *Status and Role of the Secretariat of the United Nations* (United States Senate, Committee on Foreign Relations, Subcommittee on the U.N. Charter, Staff Study No. 12, Washington, 1954).

STREITHAUPT, K., "Grundlagen und Gestaltungsformen des überstaatlichen Dienstes: Wie steht es um das Dienstrecht der Montanunion?" (*Zeitschrift für Beamtenrecht und Beamtenpolitik*, No. 5, 1953, p. 105).

STEIN, E., "Mr. Hammarskjöld, the Charter Law and the future Role of the United Nations Secretary-General" (*American Journal of International Law*, Washington, No. 56, 1962, p. 9).

Subversives in the United Nations (*Stanford Law Review*, No. 5, 1953, p. 769).

SWEETSER, Arthur, "The World's Civil Service" (*Iowa Law Review*, No. 4/30, 1945, p. 478).

TCHEN Ts'iuen-Cheng, *La notion d'intégrité des fonctionnaires internationaux* (Doctor's thesis, Paris, 1958).

TEAD, Ordway, "The Importance of Administration in International Action" (*International Conciliation*, No. 407, 1945).

TOMMASI DI VIGNANO, A., *Immunità e privilegi dei fonzionali delle organizzazioni internazionali* (Milan, 1960).

TOLL (von) Benno, *Die internationalen Bureaus der allgemeinen Verwaltungsvereine* (Tübingen, 1910).

TORRES-BODET, Jaime, "The United Nations and National Loyalties" (*UNESCO Courier*, 6 March 1952).

TSIROPINAS, Dimitri G., *Le Tribunal administratif des Nations Unies* (ninth International Congress of Administrative Sciences, Istanbul, 1953).

ULE, Carl-Hermann, *Les juridictions administratives des organisations supranationales et internationales* (*ibidem*).

"United Nations and the Agencies: I. Staffing Problems, II. Secretariat's Role" (*Planning*, Political and Economic Planning, London, No. 15/298, 1949, p. 303, No. 16/299, 1950, p. 165).

VARIAS, Romeroso S., "Functionarios internacionales: sus immunidades y privilegios" (*Cuadernos de Politica Social*, Madrid, No. 25, 1955, p. 65).

VELLAS, P., *L'évolution récente du statut des fonctionnaires internationaux* (Mélanges en l'honneur de Jacques Maury, Toulouse, 1959).

VINCENT, Claude, "Le Secrétaire général des Nations Unies. Son rôle politique" (*Mémoire*, Grenoble, 1960).

VOLLENHOVEN (van) C., "Diplomatic Prerogatives of Non-Diplomats" (*American Journal of International Law*, Washington, 1925, p. 469).

WACKERNAGEL, Jacob, *Les relations internationales et les fonctionnaires internationaux* (seventh International Congress of Administrative Sciences, Berne, 1947, p. 236).

*WALTERS, F. P., *Administrative Problems of International Organization* (London, Oxford University Press, 1941).

WARNOTTE, Daniel, *Les fonctionnaires internationaux* (seventh International Congress of Administrative Sciences, Berne, 1947, p. 135).

WATTS, A. D., "Recent decisions of the I.L.O. Administrative Tribunal" (*International and Comparative Law Quarterly*, London, Vol. 5, 1956, p. 483).

WEISS, George, "Training an International Civil Service" (*London Quarterly of World Affairs*, No. 10, 1945, p. 112).

WEN, Chou Chao, *The Personnel System of the U.N. A Study of International Civil Service* (Thesis, St. Louis University, 1951).

WENGLER, W., "Recours judiciaire à instituer contre les décisions d'organes internationaux" (*Yearbook of the Institute of International Law*, No. 44/I, 1952, p. 224, No. 45, 1954, p. 265).

*WHITE, Leonard D., *Civil Service in War Time* (Chicago, 1945).

WILCOX, F. O. — MARCY, Carl, *Proposal for Changes in the U.N.* (Washington, Brookings Institution, 1955).

WILCOX, Francis O. & HAVILAND, H. Field, *The United States and the United Nations* (Baltimore, 1961).

WILSON, Joseph V., "Problems of an International Secretariat" (*International Affairs*, London, vol. 20, 1944, p. 542).

WOLF, Francis, *Le droit aux privilèges et immunités des institutions spécialisées des Nations Unies* (Thesis, Montreal, 1948).

WOLF, Francis, "Le Tribunal administratif de l'O.I.T." (*Revue générale de droit international public*, Paris, No. 4, 1954, p. 279).

WOLF, Francis, "Note sur la 4ème session du Tribunal administratif de l'O.I.T." (*ibidem*, 1955, p. 137).

WRIGHT, Quincy, "Responsibility for Injuries to U.N. Officials" (*American Journal of International Law*, Washington, Vol. 43, 1949, p. 95).

WRIGGINS, Howard & Bock, Edwin A., *The Status of the U.N. Secretariat. Role of the Administrative Tribunal* (New York, Woodrow Wilson Foundation, 1954).

YIEN-CHENG, Y., N. Y. University (Doctor's thesis, 1958) — cf. Young, T. C.

INDEX OF NAMES[a]

(a) This index does *not* contain the names appearing in the "Select Bibliography" (p. 329), unless the persons concerned are explicitly mentioned in the text. The names of *authors* (of writings quoted in the text) are preceded by an asterisk. This also applies to politicians whose *writings* deserve quotation.

SUBJECT INDEX

DATE DUE
